THE WORLD'S CLASSICS

583

SIX
CAROLINE PLAYS

Oxford University Press, Amen House, London, E.C.4

GLASGOW NEW YORK TORONTO MELBOURNE WELLINGTON
BOMBAY CALCUTTA MADRAS KARACHI LAHORE DACCA
CAPE TOWN SALISBURY NAIROBI IBADAN ACCRA
KUALA LUMPUR HONG KONG

SIX
CAROLINE PLAYS

Edited with an Introduction

by

A. S. KNOWLAND

LONDON

OXFORD UNIVERSITY PRESS

NEW YORK   TORONTO

1962

This volume of Six Caroline Plays *was first published
in* The World's Classics *in* 1962

Selection, editing, and Introduction
© *Oxford University Press* 1962

9.30.75

62-4796

CONTENTS

CONTENTS

INTRODUCTION

THE reign of Charles I is not an inspiring one for the student of drama. Most of the great writers of the Jacobean period were stale, silent, or dead. Those who were alive and productive can be divided into two groups, gentlemen—the amateurs at court and the two universities—and professionals. Of the latter Massinger is the most considerable; the comparative ease of accessibility to his work is both a measure of his stature and the reason that none of it appears in this volume. The most prolific and most consistent in attainment is James Shirley. Behind these two stretches out a line that reaches to the closing of the theatres and beyond: Richard Brome, Shakerley Marmion, Thomas Nabbes, Thomas Randolph ('the tribe of Ben'), Henry Glapthorne, Davenport, to name only a selection. The gentlemen include Lodowick Carlell, Cartwright, Habington, Jasper Mayne, Strode, Suckling, and Killigrew. Davenant, soldier of fortune and, like Killigrew later, theatre-manager, bridges the division.

A volume such as this cannot cover the whole range of dramatic activity in the period. All the plays chosen are comedies except one, a tragi-comedy. If the selection is thought biased, the defence is that the best work of the period was done in those genres. The plays have been selected not to illustrate a view of the development of drama but for their intrinsic merit as plays acted or written (wholly or in part, since *The Parson's Wedding* was revised after the Restoration) in the reign of Charles I. If the aim of the selection had been to give examples of the work not only of the leading professional dramatists but of all the species of amateur playwright as well—courtier, academic and non-academic—the volume would have been much thicker and but not necessarily weightier.

Thomas Randolph, precocious, brilliant, and shortlived, who belongs as much to Cambridge and the academic drama as to London and the public theatres, is the most appealing of the academics, but his best play, *Hey for Honesty*, is somewhat regretfully omitted on the grounds that it is an adaptation, though a free one, of Aristophanes' *Plutus*. In the case of Cartwright and Strode, both Oxford men, the omission is hardly a matter for regret. Cartwright, whom Anthony à Wood called 'the most noted poet, orator and philosopher of his time', was flattered by his reputation. Clearly it was the Persian costumes of *The Royal Slave* and the scenery of Strode's *The Floating Island* that created the sensation which Wood with some provincial awe describes when both plays were performed before their majesties on the occasion of their visit to Oxford in August 1636. Although *The Royal Slave* made sufficient impact on the queen for her to command another performance at Hampton Court, it is unlikely, as G. E. Bentley points out, to have made a lasting impression upon a court already accustomed to the scenic fancies of Inigo Jones.

But the effect was felt elsewhere. Richard Brome clearly had Suckling's *Aglaura* as the target of his criticism both in the prologue to *The Antipodes*, acted in the same year by the queen's men that the king's men acted *Aglaura*, and again in the prologue and epilogue of *The Court Beggar*. For this play Suckling himself bought the costumes ('no tinsel, all the lace pure gold and silver', says Aubrey); a contemporary estimated that it cost him 'three or four thousand pounds setting out'. But neither *The Royal Slave* nor *The Floating Island* nor *Aglaura* is as interesting as their contemporary reputations suggest. Richard Brome (*c.* 1590–1652 or 1653) is far more deserving of attention than either the amateurs Suckling, Cartwright, and Strode or his fellow professionals and members of the 'tribe of Ben', Marmion and Nabbes. In whatever sense he was Jonson's 'man' or 'servant', there is no doubt of his dramatic discipleship. In this respect Brome is far from being alone. The more one reads of the drama of the period, the more massive Jonson's achievement appears.

Brome was a popular dramatist and his popularity derives from his characteristic qualities: simplicity of characterization, uncomplicated language, plenty of plot-interest, a spice of bawdy, and a combination of romantic elements with realism in the depiction of London life. He is limited in range and derivative in characterization, language, and incident. He cannot draw a gallant. The wind that blows through *The Jovial Crew*, thought by many to be his best play, is a very literary breeze. We need not accept Bonamy Dobrée's claim that *A Mad Couple Well Matched* is the first play in the Restoration manner—it is too much a hotchpotch of earlier styles for this—but it does contain two remarkably prophetic scenes: the conversation between Lady Thrivewell and her husband in Act I scene ii, which for Brome is unusually urbane and sophisticated, and the shop scene with Alicia Saleware and Lady Thrivewell, Act II scene i, which is interesting for the suave malice of the dialogue. The rest of the play is run-of-the-mill stuff, cut to a familiar pattern of intrigue and humours and deftly avoiding all the moral issues.

In *The Antipodes*, however, it is possible that one stumbles upon that refreshing thing in the drama of the time, an original conception. This seventeenth-century *Erewhon*, where the law 'punisheth the robb'd and not the thief', has the merit of possessing a backbone of social satire to which the concerns of Peregrine, his father Joyless, and their respective wives are neatly attached by means of the homoeopathic cure administered by that Caroline psychiatrist Dr. Hughball. But, like all Brome's plays, it is far too long: the satirical episodes are too many and the romantic discovery of the relationship between Diana and the eccentric Lord Letoy superfluous.

In range, technique, productivity, and consistency of attainment, Shirley (1596–1666) was Brome's superior. A professional to his finger-tips, Shirley knew what he could do and what his public wanted. His powers, which were not negligible, were extraordinarily well adapted to satisfying the needs of his audience, and he certainly does not deserve Dryden's contemptuous dismissal. He is imitative, it is true —of Jonson, Fletcher, and Shakespeare—but he sounds at times his own clear silver notes. At its best his verse is mellifluous, at its worst flabby. Too prolific to be fastidious in his versification, too well-bred to rub shoulders with Webster and Tourneur, whose powerful ghosts nevertheless haunt his two best tragedies, *The Cardinal* and *The Traitor*, his well-oiled talent moved most easily and most frequently in the grooves of comedy and tragi-comedy. Literary Shirley is, but it is doubtful if any other contemporary dramatist matches his polished professional veneer. That he could suggest profounder sonorities is shown by the justly famed 'The glories of our blood and state', which is more than the elegy for a doomed society that it has been called: it tolls a bell for the human condition.

To a modern taste his best work in comedy is his earliest, a group of plays (to which *The Lady of Pleasure* belongs) on fashionable London life, which it is now a commonplace of criticism to see as foreshadowing the Restoration manner, with their town and country antagonism, their opposition of gallant and citizen, passion and respectability, individual conduct and social *mores*, their public admission of the pleasures of sex, their women beating against the bars of marriage, their men resolutely setting their faces against it while steadily backing into the very trap they think they want to avoid. But with this manner goes an inconsistency of moral attitude that is typical of the time. Aretina, for example, in *The Lady of Pleasure*, having enjoyed her sin, is 'converted' and left unpunished; but the awakened sense of guilt is just another theatrical trick. Quite without the simplicity of moral conviction that characterizes Dekker, Shirley approaches neither Jonson's detachment nor Shakespeare's compassion. Though on the whole mercifully lacking that witty obscenity which Richard Flecknoe said was the importation of Beaumont and Fletcher into drama, he contrives to exude a whiff of fashionable immorality while satisfying with his 'beneficial and cleanly way of poetry' the demands of Sir Henry Herbert's censorship. If Shirley were alive today one imagines that he would be writing for the glossy magazines.

There is a connexion between the moral ambivalence (which is found in other playwrights besides Shirley) and the manufactured partnership of comic and serious elements in Jacobean and Caroline tragi-comedy. Both spring from a refusal to face issues squarely or to explore a situation thoroughly. That such an attitude is not an essential ingredient to the mixture of tragi-comedy can be shown by

Much Ado About Nothing and *The Playboy of the Western World*, plays in which comic and serious elements are honestly integrated, but it is typical of Fletcher's tragi-comedy. *The Wedding* is a tragi-comedy in the Fletcherian sense, 'in respect it wants deaths, which is enough to make it no tragedy, yet brings some near it, which is enough to make it no comedy . . .'. It is also a 'mongrel tragi-comedy' in the Sidneian sense, in that the comic sub-plot has no connexion whatsoever with the serious business of the play. This derives its strength from the character of the villain, Marwood, who interrupts his friend's wedding with the information that the bride-to-be is not chaste. The situation is contrived, but this much at least can be said for the play, that the consequences of Marwood's action are faced. If knowledge is withheld from the audience, so is it withheld also from the main characters, for Marwood believes with all sincerity in the truth of his information. Apart from the comic sub-plot—simple, derivative, but effective in a slap-stick way—*The Wedding* contains some slick 'theatre' of the kind likely to appeal to those who probably constituted Shirley's audience, the diminishing circle of patrons of the private theatres.

Shirley and Brome, one may suppose, lived their lives in the theatre. Davenant (1605/6–1668) and Killigrew (1611/12–1682/3) were both amateurs but both later in their careers professionally caught up in 'theatre business, management of men'. Davenant's tragi-comedies can be left to those who like to trace lines of development in literary history; his comedies have been butted into undeserved neglect by that heavy but useful animal, historical importance. *The Wits* has something of the full flavour, like that of a nut or an apple, which Synge held to be essential to the language of good drama. Certainly the language of *The Wits*, with its luxuriance and antiseptic callousness, at least as it appears in the 1636 version (the one printed here), commended itself to Charles I. Sir Henry Herbert's view of the play was unlikely to have been so favourable, for it seems clear that the play would not have been licensed but for the intercession with the king of Davenant's patron, Endymion Porter. It was a favourite with Pepys, whose diary shows that he

saw it six times after the Restoration, three times in its
revised form, 'corrected and enlarged'. It was the revised
version that Davenant printed in the 1673 folio of his works.
The enlargement consists in the expansion of the elephantine
humours of Constable Snore and his companions. The
nature of the correction can be seen from a comparison of
the 1636 and 1673 texts; in the latter correction has been
taken to the point of emasculation.

It is the energy and sparkle of *The Wits*' language that
justifies the well-tried comic formula on which the play is
based; similarly, what gives Killigrew's comedy, *The Parson's
Wedding*, its special flavour is its language and its attitudes.
It is written throughout in prose, but a prose that is little
'pointed', a prose truly conversational, a 'naked natural way
of speaking' if not the close way of Sprat's defence of the
Royal Society's stylistic ideals. From time to time the conversational level rises above that of small-talk and smut; is
it too fanciful to suggest that in some speeches of the ex-
perienced and in her way wise, Wanton, the peculiarly
modern note is caught of frustration, of desire for a partnership between men and women that will satisfy those insistent
and often competitive duns, the flesh, the heart, and society?

But if part of the success of some plays of the period lies
in their language, so does their failure. The great leviathans
of Elizabethan and Jacobean comedy, Falstaff, Volpone, Sir
Epicure Mammon, Sir Giles Overreach, show their poetic
backs above the element of social realism they live in. What,
one is compelled to ask, are all these Caroline fish that lie
gasping on the strand?

There are two main reasons why the poetic drama of the
period is unsatisfactory. One is the very simple one that the
dramatists themselves are just not good enough: in their
response to the human condition they lack both range and
depth of awareness. They observe without transfiguring
what they see and without penetrating far enough into the
area of their vision. Hence their verse is derivative and
literary, what Gerard Manley Hopkins called Delphic,
because it is not fed by a considered experience of life. The
second reason is that they use a medium, poetry, which is
not suited to their purpose, and indeed which can only be

used effectively by one who possesses the very equipment of sensitivity that they lack. Their vision rarely extends farther than the surface of a very small area of experience, yet they strive to express this vision in a medium which is in essence profoundly penetrating. It is as if a million-volt generator were being used to supply electricity to one domestic light-bulb. In many plays of the time either there is no justification for the use of verse at all or there is at best only a fitful connexion between the medium employed and the purpose to which it is put. Occasionally, it is true, the latter is the case and a spark leaps the gap: the result is the purple passage, the fine set piece, which has no organic connexion with the rest of the play, which, to adapt Eliot's words, is not dramatically justified but is merely fine poetry shaped into dramatic form. The near-contemporary criticism of Suckling's *Aglaura*, that "'twas full of fine flowers but they seemed rather stuck than growing there' is applicable to much of the drama of the period.

But, of course, there is no such thing as a period of drama between 1625 and 1642 in the sense that it has a flavour of its own. These Caroline dramatists are inheritors of a well-worked literary field. They are share-croppers, anxious to get a quick return with a minimum of effort in a shrinking market. They inherit and continue the Jacobean manner within the conditions peculiar to their age. These conditions include a diminishing audience. The Caroline audience got the drama it deserved—amusement art, in Collingwood's phrase, designed to provide an entertainment for a tired courtier, a jig and a tale of bawdry, it may be, slick 'theatre' and a reassuring moral, an escape from the pressure of the times,

> before the short-hair'd men
> Do crowd and call for justice.

Yet something is worth salvaging from the 'epidemical ruin of the scene' which put a stop to formal drama in 1642. Shirley's grace and lucidity, Brome's popular appeal, Davenant's wit, Killigrew's prose naturalism, all deserve a place in the story. These men help to make the transition to Restoration drama more intelligible.

                                                A. S. KNOWLAND

NOTE ON THE TEXTS

ALL the plays have been edited afresh from the first editions even where later or modern editions are in existence. The treatment of the texts follows the lines customarily taken in the *World's Classics* series. The punctuation and the spelling have been modernized though I have allowed myself some inconsistency in the names of characters (e.g. Meager in *The Wits* and Cameleon in *The Wedding*). Where the copy text is inconsistent in the forms of speech prefixes these have been standardized. Certain other forms have also been standardized: Mr. and Mrs. as Master and Mistress; wo'not &c., as will not; -ed/'d forms in accordance with metrical requirements. There are some passages, mostly in *The Wedding* and *A Mad Couple Well Matched* in which I have printed (not always with complete conviction) copy-text verse as prose and prose as verse. In very few instances the lineation of the copy-text has been altered. Stage directions within inverted commas, including those for a character's entrance, are in the words, modernized and where necessary repunctuated, of the copy-text. Directions for a character's *exit* within a curved bracket indicate that an *exit* is marked in the copy-text though not always in the form printed. All matter within square brackets is editorial.

The Lady of Pleasure, acted in 1635, was entered on the Stationers' Register on 13 April 1637 and printed in the same year. The text is based on a copy of the 1637 edition in the Central Library at Bristol, though, as with all texts, copies other than the copy-text have been consulted. Modern editions consulted: ed. Gifford and Dyce, *The Dramatic Works of James Shirley*, 6 vols., 1833; ed. W. A. Neilson, *The Chief Elizabethan Dramatists* (Boston), 1911; ed. C. R. Baskervill, V. B. Heltzel, A. H. Nethercot, *Elizabethan and Stuart Plays* (New York), 1934.

The Wedding, probably acted in the summer of 1626, was first printed in 1629. It was reprinted in 1633 and again in

1660. The text of the play is based on a copy of the 1629 edition in the Central Library at Bristol. The 1629 edition contains a number of commendatory poems which are not reproduced here. Modern edition consulted: ed. Gifford and Dyce, op. cit.

A Mad Couple Well Matched, acted before 10 August 1639, is the first play in a volume called *Five New Playes* printed in 1653. It was reprinted by R. H. Pearson in *The Dramatic Works of Richard Brome Containing Fifteen Comedies Now First Collected in Three Volumes*, 1873. The text is based on a copy of the play in the 1653 volume, *Five New Playes*, in the Bodleian Library.

The Antipodes, acted 1638, was entered on the Stationers' Register on 19 March 1639/40 and printed in 1640 with commendatory verses which are not reproduced here. The text is based on a copy of the 1640 edition in the Brotherton Collection in the library of the University of Leeds. Modern edition consulted: ed. G. P. Baker in C. M. Gayley, *Representative English Comedies*, vol. iii, 1914.

The Wits, acted 28 January 1633/4, was entered on the Stationers' Register on 4 February 1635/6 and printed in 1636. It appears in another volume, *Two Excellent Plays*, printed in 1665, and again, revised, in the folio of Sir William Davenant's works printed in 1673. The text is based on a copy of the 1636 edition in the Brotherton Collection in the library of the University of Leeds. The play also appears in *The Dramatic Works of Sir William D'Avenant*, ed. J. Maidment and W. H. Logan, 5 vols., 1872–4.

The Parson's Wedding is one of the plays in the folio edition of Killigrew's collected works printed in 1664. It bears a separate title-page dated 1663. It was reprinted in Dodsley's *A Select Collection of Old Plays*, 1744, and in subsequent editions including that by W. C. Hazlitt, 1875. It also appears in Montague Summers' *Restoration Comedies*, 1921. A. Harbage, in *Thomas Killigrew, Cavalier Dramatist*, 1930, and G. E. Bentley, in *The Jacobean and Caroline Stage*, vol. iii, 1956, give the evidence for believing that the play was written *c.* 1642, though it was clearly revised after the Restoration. The text is based on a copy of the play in the 1664 folio in the library of Trinity College, Dublin.

THE
LADY OF
PLEASVRE.

A
COMEDIE,

As it was Acted by her Majesties Servants, at the private
House in *Drury* Lane.

Written by *James Shirly.*

LONDON,
Printed by *Tho. Cotes,* for *Andrew Crooke;*
and *William Cooke.*
1637.

To the Right Honourable Richard, Lord Lovelace, of Hurley

My Lord:

I cannot want encouragement to present a poem to your Lordship, while you possess so noble a breast, in which so many seeds of honour, to the example and glory of your name, obtained before your years a happy maturity. This comedy, fortunate in the scene, and one that may challenge a place in the first form of the author's compositions, most humbly addresseth itself to your honour. If it meet your gracious acceptance, and that you repent not to be a patron, your lordship will only crown the imagination and for ever, by this favour, oblige,

My Lord,

The most humble services of your honourer,

JAMES SHIRLEY

PERSONS OF THE COMEDY

Lord.
Sir Thomas Bornwell.
Sir William Scentlove.
Master Alexander Kickshaw.
Master John Littleworth.
Master Haircut.
Master Frederick, [*nephew to* Aretina.]
Steward *to the* Lady Aretina.
Steward *to the* Lady Celestina.
Secretary.
Servants, &c.

Aretina, Sir Thomas Bornwell's *lady*.
Celestina, *a young widow*.
Isabella.
Mariana.
Madam Decoy.
[Gentlewoman.]

Scene: the Strand.

THE LADY OF PLEASURE

ACT I [SCENE I]

'*Enter* Aretina *and her* Steward.'

Steward. Be patient, madam; you may have your
    pleasure.
Aretina. 'Tis that I came to town for. I would not
Endure again the country conversation
To be the lady of six shires—the men
So near the primitive making they retain
A sense of nothing but the earth, their brains
And barren heads standing as much in want
Of ploughing as their ground; to hear a fellow
Make himself merry, and his horse, with whistling
Sellinger's Round; to observe with what solemnity
They keep their wakes and throw for pewter candlesticks!
How they become the morris, with whose bells
They ring all in to Whitsun ales, and sweat
Through twenty scarfs and napkins till the hobby-horse
Tire, and Maid Marian, dissolv'd to a jelly,
Be kept for spoon meat!
    Steward. These, with your pardon, are no argument
To make the country life appear so hateful,
At least to your particular, who enjoy'd
A blessing in that calm, would you be pleas'd
To think so, and the pleasure of a kingdom.
While your own will commanded what should move
Delights, your husband's love and power join'd
To give your life more harmony. You liv'd there
Secure and innocent, belov'd of all,
Prais'd for your hospitality, and pray'd for.
You might be envied, but malice knew
Not where you dwelt. I would not prophesy,
But leave to your own apprehension
What may succeed your change.

Aretina. You do imagine,
No doubt, you have talk'd wisely, and confuted
London past all defence. Your master should
Do well to send you back into the country
With title of superintendent-bailie.

Steward. How, madam!

Aretina. Even so, sir.

Steward. I am a gentleman, though now your servant.

Aretina. A country gentleman,
By your affection to converse with stubble.
His tenants will advance your wit and plump it so
With beef and bag-pudding.

Steward. You may say your pleasure;
It becomes not me dispute.

Aretina. Complain to the lord of the soil, your master.

Steward. You're a woman of an ungovern'd passion, and
I pity you.

'*Enter* Sir Thomas Bornwell.'

Bornwell. How now? What's the matter?

Steward. Nothing, sir.   (*Exit* Steward.

Bornwell. Angry, sweetheart?

Aretina. I am angry with myself,
To be so miserably restrain'd in things
Wherein it doth concern your love and honour
To see me satisfied.

Bornwell. In what, Aretina,
Dost thou accuse me? Have I not obey'd
All thy desires, against mine own opinion
Quitted the country and remov'd the hope
Of our return by sale of that fair lordship
We liv'd in, chang'd a calm and retir'd life
For this wild town, compos'd of noise and charge?

Aretina. What charge more than is necessary
For a lady of my birth and education?

Bornwell. I am not ignorant how much nobility
Flows in your blood, your kinsmen great and powerful
I' th' state; but with this, lose not your memory
Of being my wife. I shall be studious,
Madam, to give the dignity of your birth

All the best ornaments which become my fortune;
But would not flatter it, to ruin both
And be the fable of the town, to teach
Other men loss of wit by mine, employ'd
To serve your vast expenses.

  Aretina.   Am I then
Brought in the balance? So, sir!

  Bornwell.   Though you weigh
Me in a partial scale, my heart is honest,
And must take liberty to think you have
Obey'd no modest counsel to affect,
Nay, study ways of pride and costly ceremony:
Your change of gaudy furniture, and pictures
Of this Italian master and that Dutchman's;
Your mighty looking-glasses like artillery
Brought home on engines; the superfluous plate,
Antic and novel; vanities of tires;
Fourscore-pound suppers for my lord your kinsman,
Banquets for tother lady, aunt, and cousins;
And perfumes that exceed all; train of servants
To stifle us at home, and show abroad
More motley than the French or the Venetian
About your coach, whose rude postilion
Must pester every narrow lane till passengers
And tradesmen curse your choking up their stalls,
And common cries pursue your ladyship
For hind'ring o' their market.

  Aretina.   Have you done, sir?

  Bornwell. I could accuse the gaiety of your wardrobe
And prodigal embroideries, under which
Rich satins, plushes, cloth of silver dare
Not show their own complexions; your jewels,
Able to burn out the spectator's eyes
And show like bonfires on you by the tapers:
Something might here be spar'd with safety of
Your birth and honour, since the truest wealth
Shines from the soul, and draws up just admirers.
I could urge something more.

  Aretina.   Pray do; I like
Your homily of thrift.

Bornwell.   I could wish, madam,
You would not game so much.

   Aretina.   A gamester too!

   Bornwell. But are not come to that acquaintance yet
Should teach you skill enough to raise your profit.
You look not through the subtlety of cards
And mysteries of dice; nor can you save
Charge with the box, buy petticoats and pearls,
And keep your family by the precious income;
Nor do I wish you should: my poorest servant
Shall not upbraid my tables nor his hire,
Purchas'd beneath my honour. You make play
Not a pastime but a tyranny, and vex
Yourself and my estate by't.

   Aretina.   Good! Proceed.

   Bornwell. Another game you have, which consumes more
Your fame than purse: your revels in the night,
Your meetings call'd the Ball, to which repair,
As to the court of pleasure, all your gallants
And ladies, thither bound by a subpoena
Of Venus and small Cupid's high displeasure;
'Tis but the Family of Love translated
Into more costly sin. There was a play on't,
And had the poet not been brib'd to a modest
Expression of your antic gambols in't,
Some darks had been discover'd, and the deeds too.
In time he may repent and make some blush
To see the second part danc'd on the stage.
My thoughts acquit you for dishonouring me
By any foul act, but the virtuous know
'Tis not enough to clear ourselves, but the
Suspicions of our shame.

   Aretina.   Have you concluded
Your lecture?

   Bornwell. I ha' done; and howsoever
My language may appear to you, it carries
No other than my fair and just intent
To your delights, without curb to their modest
And noble freedom.

   Aretina.   I'll not be so tedious

In my reply, but without art or elegance
Assure you I keep still my first opinion;
And though you veil your avaricious meaning
With handsome names of modesty and thrift,
I find you would entrench and wound the liberty
I was born with. Were my desires unprivileg'd
By example, while my judgement thought 'em fit,
You ought not to oppose; but when the practice
And tract of every honourable lady
Authorize me, I take it great injustice
To have my pleasures circumscrib'd and taught me.
A narrow-minded husband is a thief
To his own fame, and his preferment too;
He shuts his parts and fortunes from the world,
While from the popular vote and knowledge men
Rise to employment in the state.

Bornwell.   I have
No great ambition to buy preferment
At so dear rate.

Aretina.   Nor I to sell my honour
By living poor and sparingly. I was not
Bred in that ebb of fortune, and my fate
Shall not compel me to't.

Bornwell.   I know not, madam,
But you pursue these ways—

Aretina.   What ways?

Bornwell. In the strict sense of honesty; I dare
Make my oath they are innocent.

Aretina.   Do not divert
By busy troubling of your brain those thoughts
That should preserve 'em.

Bornwell.   How was that?

Aretina. 'Tis English.

Bornwell. But carries some unkind sense.

'*Enter* Madam Decoy.'

Decoy. Good morrow, my sweet madam.

Aretina. Decoy, welcome; this visit is a favour.

Decoy. Alas, sweet madam, I cannot stay; I came
But to present my service to your ladyship.

I could not pass by your door but I must take
The boldness to tender my respects.

Aretina. You oblige me, madam, but I must
Not dispense so with your absence.

Decoy. Alas, the coach, madam, stays for me at the door.

Aretina. Thou shalt command mine; prithee, sweet Decoy.

Decoy. I would wait on you, madam, but I have many
Visits to make this morning. I beseech—

Aretina. So you will promise to dine with me.

Decoy.   I shall
Present a guest.

Aretina.   Why then, good morrow, madam.

Decoy. A happy day shine on your ladyship. (*Exit* Decoy.

'*Enter* Steward.'

Aretina. What's your news, sir?

Steward.   Madam, two gentlemen—

Aretina. What gentlemen? Have they no names?

Steward.   They are
The gentleman with his own head of hair,
Whom you commended for his horsemanship
In Hyde Park and becoming the saddle
The tother day.

Aretina.   What circumstance is this
To know him by?

Steward.   His name's at my tongue's end—
He lik'd the fashion of your pearl chain, madam,
And borrow'd it for his jeweller to take
A copy by it—

Bornwell [*Aside*]. What cheating gallant's this?

Steward. That never walks without a lady's busk,
And plays with fans—Master Alexander Kickshaw.
I thought I should remember him.

Aretina.   What's the other?

Steward. What an unlucky memory I have!
The gallant that still danceth in the street,
And wears a gross of ribbon in his hat;
That carries oringado in his pocket,
And sugar-plums to sweeten his discourse;
That studies compliment, defies all wit

On black and censures plays that are not bawdy—
Master John Littleworth.

Aretina.   They are welcome; but
Pray entertain them a small time, lest I
Be unprovided.

Bornwell.   Did they ask for me?

Steward. No, sir.

Bornwell.   It matters not, they must be welcome.

Aretina. Fie! How's this hair disorder'd? Here's a curl
Straddle[s] most impiously. I must to my closet.

                       (*Exit* Aretina.

Bornwell. Wait on 'em; my lady will return again.

                       [*Exit* Steward.]

I have to such a height fulfill'd her humour,
All application's dangerous. These gallants
Must be receiv'd or she will fall into
A tempest and the house be shook with names
Of all her kindred. 'Tis a servitude
I may in time shake off.

     '*Enter* Alexander [Kickshaw] *and* Littleworth.'

Alexander. } Save you, Sir Thomas!
Littleworth. }

Bornwell. Save you, gentlemen!

Alexander.   I kiss your hand.

Bornwell. What day is it abroad?

Littleworth. The morning rises from your lady's eye;
If she look clear, we take the happy omen
Of a fair day.

Bornwell.   She'll instantly appear,
To the discredit of your compliment.
But you express your wit thus.

Alexander.   And you modesty,
Not to affect the praises of your own.

Bornwell. Leaving this subject, what game's now on foot?
What exercise carries the general vote
O' th' town now? Nothing moves without your knowledge.

Alexander. The cocking now has all the noise; I'll have
A hundred pieces of one battle. Oh,
These birds of Mars!

Littleworth.   Venus is Mars his bird too.

Alexander. Why, and the pretty doves are Venus's,
To show that kisses draw the chariot.

Littleworth. I am for that skirmish.

Bornwell.   When shall we have
More booths and bagpipes upon Banstead downs?
No mighty race is expected?—But my lady returns.

'*Enter* Aretina.'

Aretina. Fair morning to you, gentlemen.
You went not late to bed by your early visit.
You do me honour.

Alexander.   It becomes our service.

Aretina. What news abroad? You hold precious intelligence.

Littleworth. All tongues are so much busy with your praise
They have not time to frame other discourse.
Will please you, madam, taste a sugar-plum?

Bornwell. What does the goldsmith think the pearl is worth
You borrow'd of my lady?

Alexander.   'Tis a rich one.

Bornwell. She has many other toys whose fashion you
Will like extremely. You have no intention
To buy any of her jewels?

Alexander.   Understand me—

Bornwell. You had rather sell, perhaps. But, leaving this,
I hope you'll dine with us.

Alexander. I came a purpose.

Aretina. And where were you last night?

Alexander.   I, madam? Where
I slept not; it had been sin, where so much
Delight and beauty was to keep me waking.
There is a lady, madam, will be worth
Your free society; my conversation
Ne'er knew so elegant and brave a soul,
With most incomparable flesh and blood;
So spirited, so courtly speaks the languages;
Sings, dances, plays o' th' lute to admiration;
Is fair and paints not; games too, keeps a table,

And talks most witty satire; has a wit
Of a clean Mercury.

Littleworth. Is she married?

Alexander.   No.

Aretina. A virgin?

Alexander.   Neither.

Littleworth.   What, a widow? Something
Of this wide commendation might have been
Excus'd. This such a prodigy?

Alexander.   Repent
Before I name her. She did never see
Yet full sixteen, an age in the opinion
Of wise men not contemptible; she has
Mourn'd out her year too for the honest knight
That had compassion of her youth and died
So timely. Such a widow is not common;
And now she shines more fresh and tempting
Than any natural virgin.

Aretina. What's her name?

Alexander. She was christen'd Celestina; by her husband,
The Lady Bellamour. This ring was hers.

Bornwell. You borrow'd it to copy out the posy.

Alexander. Are they not pretty rubies? 'Twas a grace
She was pleas'd to show me, that I might have one
Made of the same fashion, for I love
All pretty forms.

Aretina.   And is she glorious?

Alexander. She is full of jewels, madam; but I am
Most taken with the bravery of her mind,
Although her garments have all grace and ornament.

Aretina. You have been high in praises.

Alexander.   I come short;
No flattery can reach her.

Bornwell [*Aside*].   Now my lady
Is troubled, as she fear'd to be eclips'd.
This news will cost me somewhat.

Aretina.   You deserve
Her favour for this noble character.

Alexander. And I possess it by my stars' benevolence.

Aretina. You must bring us acquainted.

Bornwell.   I pray do, sir;
I long to see her too. Madam, I have
Thought upon't and corrected my opinion.
Pursue what ways of pleasure your desires
Incline you to; not only with my state
But with my person I will follow you.
I see the folly of my thrift, and will
Repent in sack and prodigality
To your own heart's content.

Aretina. But do not mock.

Bornwell. Take me to your embraces, gentlemen,
And tutor me.

Littleworth. And will you kiss the ladies?

Bornwell. And sing and dance. I long to see this beauty.
I would fain lose a hundred pounds at dice now.
Thou shalt have another gown and petticoat
Tomorrow. Will you sell me running-horses?
We have no Greek wine in the house, I think;
Pray send one of our footmen to the merchant,
And throw the hogsheads of March beer into
The kennel, to make room for sacks and claret.
What think you to be drunk yet before dinner?
We will have constant music, and maintain
Them and their fiddles in fantastic liveries.
I'll tune my voice to catches. I must have
My dining-room enlarg'd to invite ambassadors;
We'll feast the parish in the fields, and teach
The military men new discipline,
Who shall charge all their great artillery
With oranges and lemons, boy, to play
All dinner upon our capons.

Alexander.   He's exalted.

Bornwell. I will do anything to please my lady;
Let that suffice, and kiss o' th' same condition.
I am converted; do not you dispute,
But patiently allow the miracle.

Aretina. I am glad to hear you, sir, in so good tune.

'*Enter* Servant.'

Servant. Madam, the painter.

Aretina. I am to sit this morning.
Bornwell. Do, while I give new directions to my steward.
Alexander. With your favour we'll wait on you. Sitting's
but
A melancholy exercise without
Some company to discourse.
Aretina. It does conclude
A lady's morning work: we rise, make fine,
Sit for our picture, and 'tis time to dine.
Littleworth. Praying's forgot.
Alexander. 'Tis out of fashion. (*Exeunt.*

[SCENE II]

'*Enter* Celestina *and her* Steward.'

Celestina. Fie, what an air this room has!
Steward. 'Tis perfum'd.
Celestina. With some cheap stuff. Is it your wisdom's
thrift
To infect my nostrils thus? Or is't to favour
The gout in your worship's hand you are afraid
To exercise your pen in your account book?
Or do you doubt my credit to discharge
Your bills?
Steward. Madam, I hope you have not found
My duty with the guilt of sloth or jealousy
Unapt to your command.
Celestina. You can extenuate
Your faults with language, sir, but I expect
To be obey'd. What hangings have we here?
Steward. They are arras, madam.
Celestina. Impudence! I know't.
I will have fresher, and more rich, not wrought
With faces that may scandalize a Christian
With Jewish stories stuff'd with corn and camels.
You had best wrap all my chambers in wild Irish,
And make a nursery of monsters here
To fright the ladies comes to visit me.

Steward. Madam, I hope—
Celestina.   I say I will have other,
Good Master Steward, of a finer loom—
Some silk and silver, if your worship please
To let mine be at so much cost. I'll have
Stories to fit the seasons of the year,
And change as often as I please.
Steward.   You shall, madam.
Celestina. I am bound to your consent, forsooth! And is
My coach brought home?
Steward. This morning I expect it.
Celestina. The inside as I gave direction,
Of crimson plush?
Steward.   Of crimson camel plush.
Celestina. Ten thousand moths consume't! Shall I ride
      through
The streets in penance, wrapp'd up round in haircloth?
Sell't to an alderman: 'twill serve his wife
To go a-feasting to their country house,
Or fetch a merchant's nurse-child and come home
Laden with fruit and cheese-cakes. I despise it.
Steward. The nails adorn it, madam, set in method
And pretty forms.
Celestina.   But single gilt, I warrant.
Steward. No, madam.
Celestina.   Another solecism! Oh, fie!
This fellow will bring me to a consumption
With fretting at his ignorance. Some lady
Had rather never pray than go to church in't.
The nails not double gilt? To market wi't!
'Twill hackney out to Mile End, or convey
Your city tumblers to be drunk with cream
And prunes at Islington.
Steward.   Good madam, hear me.
Celestina. I'll rather be beholding to my aunt
The countess for her mourning coach than be
Disparag'd so. Shall any juggling tradesman
Be at charge to shoe his running-horse with gold,
And shall my coach nails be but single gilt?
How dare these knaves abuse me so?

Celestina.   That all your business?
Haircut. Though it were worth much travel, I have more
In my ambition.
Celestina.   Speak it freely, sir.
Haircut. You are a widow.
Celestina.   So.
Haircut.   And I a bachelor.
Celestina. You come a-wooing, sir, and would perhaps
Show me a way to reconcile these two?
Haircut. And bless my stars for such a happiness.
Celestina. I like you, sir, the better that you do not
Wander about, but shoot home to the meaning;
'Tis a confidence will make a man
Know sooner what to trust to. But I never
Saw you before and I believe you come not
With hope to find me desperate upon marriage.
If maids, out of their ignorance of what
Men are, refuse these offers, widows may,
Out of their knowledge, be allow'd some coyness;
And yet I know not how much happiness
A peremptory answer may deprive me of.
You may be some young lord, and though I see not
Your footmen and your groom, they may not be
Far off, in conference with your horse. Please you
To instruct me with your title, against which
I would not willingly offend.
   Haircut.   I am
A gentleman; my name is Haircut, madam.
   Celestina. Sweet Master Haircut, are you a courtier?
   Haircut. Yes.
   Celestina.   I did think so by your confidence.
Not to detain you, sir, with circumstance,
I was not so unhappy in my husband
But that 'tis possible I may be a wife
Again; but I must tell you, he that wins
My affection shall deserve me.
   Haircut.   I will hope,
If you can love. I shall not present, madam,
An object to displease you in my person;
And, when time and your patience shall possess you

With further knowledge of me and the truth
Of my devotion, you will not repent
The offer of my service.
  Celestina.   You say well.
How long do you imagine you can love, sir?
Is it a quotidian, or will it hold
But every other day?
  Haircut.   You are pleasant, madam.
 Celestina. Does't take you with a burning at the first
Or with a cold fit, for you gentlemen
Have both your summer and your winter service.
 Haircut. I am ignorant what you mean, but I shall never
Be cold in my affection to such beauty.
 Celestina. And 'twill be somewhat long ere I be warm in't.
 Haircut. If you vouchsafe me so much honour, madam,
That I may wait on you sometimes, I shall not
Despair to see a change.
  Celestina.   But now I know
Your mind, you shall not need to tell it when
You come again; I shall remember it.
 Haircut. You make me fortunate.

'*Enter* Steward.'

 Steward. Madam, your kinswomen,
The Lady Novice and her sister, are
New lighted from their coach.
  Celestina.   I did expect 'em:
They partly are my pupils. I'll attend 'em. (*Exit* Steward.
 Haircut. Madam, I have been too great a trespasser
Upon your patience; I'll take my leave.
You have affairs, and I have some employment
Calls me to court. I shall present again
A servant to you.   (*Exit* Haircut.
 Celestina.   Sir, you may present,
But not give fire, I hope. Now to the ladies.
This recreation's past; the next must be
To read to them some court philosophy. (*Exit* Celestina.

ACT II [SCENE I]

'*Enter* Sir Thomas Bornwell.'

Bornwell. 'Tis a strange humour I have undertaken,
To dance and play and spend as fast as she does;
But I am resolv'd—it may do good upon her,
And fright her into thrift. Nay, I'll endeavour
To make her jealous too. If this do not
Allay her gambolling, she's past a woman,
And only a miracle must tame her.

'*Enter* Steward.'

Steward. 'Tis Master Frederick, my lady's nephew—
Bornwell.   What of him?
Steward. Is come from the university.
Bornwell.   By whose directions?
Steward. It seems my lady's.
Bornwell.   Let me speak with him
Before he see his aunt.   [*Exit* Steward.]
                    I do not like it.

'*Enter* [Steward, *with*] Master Frederick.'

Master Frederick, welcome! I expected not
So soon your presence. What's the hasty cause?
Frederick. These letters from my tutor will acquaint you.
Steward. Welcome home, sweet Master Frederick.
Frederick.   Where's my aunt?
Steward. She's busy about her painting in her closet.
The outlandish man of art is copying out
Her countenance.
Frederick.   She is sitting for her picture?
Steward. Yes, sir; and when 'tis drawn she will be hang'd
Next the French cardinal in the dining-room.
But when she hears you're come she will dismiss
The Belgic gentleman, to entertain
Your worship.
Frederick.   Change of air has made you witty.
Bornwell. Your tutor gives you a handsome character,
Frederick, and is sorry your aunt's pleasure

Commands you from your studies. But I hope
You have no quarrel to the liberal arts;
Learning is an addition beyond
Nobility of birth. Honour of blood
Without the ornament of knowledge is
A glorious ignorance.

 Frederick. I never knew more sweet and happy hours
Than I employ'd upon my books. I heard
A part of my philosophy, and was so
Delighted with the harmony of nature
I could have wasted my whole life upon't.

 Bornwell [*Aside*]. 'Tis pity a rash indulgence should corrupt
So fair a genius. She's here. I'll observe.—

  '*Enter* Aretina, Alexander, Littleworth.'

 Frederick. My most lov'd aunt!
 Aretina.   Support me, I shall faint.
 Littleworth. What ails your ladyship?
 Aretina.   Is that Frederick,
In black?
 Alexander. Yes, madam; but the doublet's satin.
 Aretina. The boy's undone.
 Frederick.   Madam, you appear troubled.
 Aretina. Have I not cause? Was not I trusted with
Thy education, boy, and have they sent thee
Home like a very scholar?
 Alexander.   'Twas ill done,
Howe'er they us'd him in the university,
To send him to his friends thus.
 Frederick.   Why, sir, black
(For 'tis the colour that offends your eyesight)
Is not within my reading any blemish;
Sables are no disgrace in heraldry.
 Alexander. 'Tis coming from the college thus that makes it
Dishonourable. While you wore it for
Your father it was commendable; or were
Your aunt dead, you might mourn, and justify.
 Aretina. What luck I did not send him into France!
They would have given him generous education,

Taught him another garb, to wear his lock
And shape as gaudy as the summer; how
To dance and wag his feather *à la mode*;
To compliment and cringe; to talk not modestly,
Like 'Ay, forsooth', and 'No, forsooth', to blush
And look so like a chaplain. There he might
Have learn'd a brazen confidence, and observ'd
So well the custom of the country that
He might by this time have invented fashions
For us, and been a benefit to the kingdom,
Preserv'd our tailors in their wits, and sav'd
The charge of sending into foreign courts
For pride and antic fashions. Observe
In what a posture he does hold his hat now!
 Frederick. Madam, with your pardon, you have practis'd
Another dialect than was taught me when
I was commended to your care and breeding.
I understand not this; Latin or Greek
Are more familiar to my apprehension;
Logic was not so hard in my first lectures
As your strange language.
 Aretina.   Some strong waters! Oh!
 Littleworth [*Offering his box of comfits*]. Comfits will be
  as comfortable to your stomach, madam.
 Aretina. I fear he's spoil'd for ever; he did name
Logic, and may for aught I know be gone
So far to understand it. I did always
Suspect they would corrupt him in the college.
Will your Greek saws and sentences discharge
The mercer, or is Latin a fit language
To court a mistress in? Master Alexander,
If you have any charity, let me
Commend him to your breeding. I suspect
I must employ my doctor first, to purge
The university that lies in's head;
It alters his complexion.
 Alexander.   If you dare
Trust me to serve him.
 Aretina.   Master Littleworth,
Be you join'd in commission.

    Littleworth.   I will teach him
Postures and rudiments.
    Aretina.   I have no patience
To see him in this shape—it turns my stomach.
When he has cast his academic skin,
He shall be yours. I am bound in conscience
To see him bred; his own state shall maintain
The charge while he's my ward. Come hither, sir.
    Frederick. What does my aunt mean to do with me?
    Steward. To make you a fine gentleman and translate you
Out of your learned language, sir, into
The present Goth and Vandal, which is French.
    Bornwell [*Aside*]. Into what mischief will this humour ebb?
She will undo the boy; I see him ruin'd.
My patience is not manly, but I must
Use stratagem to reduce her: open ways
Give me no hope.   (*Exit* Bornwell.
    Steward. You shall be obey'd, madam.
              (*Exeunt all except* Steward *and* Frederick.
    Frederick. Master Steward, are you sure we do not dream?
Was 't not my aunt you talk'd to?
    Steward.   One that loves you
Dear as her life. These clothes do not become you;
You must have better, sir—
    Frederick.   These are not old.
    Steward. More suitable to the town and time. We keep
No Lent here, nor is't my lady's pleasure you
Should fast from anything you have a mind to,
Unless it be your learning, which she would have you
Forget with all convenient speed that may be,
For the credit of your noble family.
The case is alter'd since we liv'd i'th' country.
We do not [now] invite the poor o'th' parish
To dinner, keep a table for the tenants;
Our kitchen does not smell of beef; the cellar
Defies the price of malt and hops; the footmen
And coach-drivers may be drunk like gentlemen
With wine; nor will three fiddlers upon holidays
With aid of bagpipes, that call'd in the country
To dance and plough the hall up with their hobnails,

Now make my lady merry. We do feed
Like princes and feast nothing but princes,
And are these robes fit to be seen amongst 'em?

Frederick. My lady keeps a court then. Is Sir Thomas
Affected with this state and cost?

Steward.   He was not,
But is converted; and I hope you will not
Persist in heresy, but take a course
Of riot, to content your friends. You shall
Want nothing, if you can be proud and spend it
For my lady's honour. Here are a hundred
Pieces will serve you till you have new clothes.
I will present you with a nag of mine,
Poortender of my service—please you accept;
My lady's smile more than rewards me for it.
I must provide fit servants to attend you,
Monsieurs for horse and foot.

Frederick.   I shall submit,
If this be my aunt's pleasure, and be rul'd.
My eyes are open'd with this purse already,
And sack will help to inspire me. I must spend it?

Steward. What else, sir?

Frederick.   I'll begin with you, to encourage
You to have still a special care of me.
There is five pieces—not for your nag.

Steward. No, sir, I hope it is not.

Frederick.   Buy a beaver
For thy own block. I shall be rul'd. Who does
Command the wine-cellar?

Steward.   Who command but you, sir?

Frederick. I'll try to drink a health or two, my aunt's
Or anybody's; and if that foundation
Stagger me not too much, I will commence
In all the arts of London.

Steward.   If you find, sir,
The operation of the wine exalt
Your blood to the desire of any female
Delight, I know your aunt will not deny
Any of her chambermaids to practise on;
She loves you but too well.

Frederick.   I know not how
I may be for that exercise. Farewell, Aristotle!
Prithee commend me to the library
At Westminster; my bones I bequeath thither,
And to the learned worms that mean to visit 'em.
I will compose myself. I begin to think
I have lost time indeed. Come, to the wine-cellar!

                                        (*Exeunt* Frederick *and* Steward.

[SCENE II]

'*Enter* Celestina, Mariana, Isabella.'

Mariana. But shall we not, madam, expose ourselves
To censure for this freedom?
Celestina.   Let them answer
That dare mistake us. Shall we be so much
Cowards to be frighted from our pleasure
Because men have malicious tongues and show
What miserable souls they have? No, cousin,
We hold our life and fortunes upon no
Man's charity. If they dare show so little
Discretion to traduce our fames, we will
Be guilty of so much wit to laugh at 'em.
Isabella. 'Tis a becoming fortitude.
Celestina.   My stars
Are yet kind to me, for, in a happy minute
Be't spoke, I'm not in love, and men shall never
Make my heart lean with sighing, nor with tears
Draw on my eyes the infamy of spectacles.
'Tis the chief principle to keep your heart
Under your own obedience; jest, but love not.
I say my prayers, yet can wear good clothes,
And only satisfy my tailor for 'em.
I will not lose my privilege.
Mariana. And yet they say your entertainments are—
Give me your pardon, madam—to proclaim
Yourself a widow and to get a husband.
Celestina. As if a lady of my years, some beauty,
Left by her husband rich, that had mourn'd for him

A twelvemonth too, could live so obscure i'th' town
That gallants would not know her and invite
Themselves without her chargeable proclamations.
Then we are worse than citizens: no widow
Left wealthy can be throughly warm in mourning,
But some one [of] noble blood or lusty kindred
Claps in, with his gilt coach and Flandrian trotters,
And hurries her away to be a countess.
Courtiers have spies, and great ones with large titles,
Cold in their own estates, would warm themselves
At a rich city bonfire.

   Isabella. Most true, madam.

   Celestina. No matter for corruption of the blood:
Some undone courtier made her husband rich,
And this new lord receives it back again.
Admit it were my policy, and that
My entertainments pointed to acquaint me
With many suitors, that I might be safe,
And make the best election—could you blame me?

   Mariana. Madam, 'tis wisdom.

   Celestina.   But I should be
In my thoughts miserable to be fond
Of leaving the sweet freedom I possess,
And court myself into new marriage fetters.
I now observe men's several wits and windings,
And can laugh at their follies.

   Mariana.   You have given
A most ingenious satisfaction.

   Celestina. One thing I'll tell you more, and this I give you
Worthy your imitation from my practice:
You see me merry, full of song and dancing,
Pleasant in language, apt to all delights
That crown a public meeting, but you cannot
Accuse me of being prodigal of my favours
To any of my guests. I do not summon
By any wink a gentleman to follow me
To my withdrawing chamber; I hear all
Their pleas in court; nor can they boast abroad,
And do me justice, after a salute,
They have much conversation with my lip.

I hold the kissing of my hand a courtesy,
And he that loves me must upon the strength
Of that expect till I renew his favour.
Some ladies are so expensive in their graces
To those that honour 'em, and so prodigal,
That in a little time they have nothing but
The naked sin left to reward their servants;
Whereas a thrift in our rewards will keep
Men long in their devotion, and preserve
Ourselves in stock, to encourage those that honour us.

   Isabella. This is an art worthy a lady's practice.

   Celestina. It takes not from the freedom of our mirth
But seems to advance it, when we can possess
Our pleasures with security of our honour;
And, that preserv'd, I welcome all the joys
My fancy can let in. In this I have given
The copy of my mind, nor do I blush
You understand it.

   Isabella. You have honour'd us.

          '*Enter* Celestina's Gentlewoman.'

   Gentlewoman. Madam, Sir William Scentlove's come to
     wait on you.

   Celestina. There's one would be a client. Make excuse
For a few minutes.   [*Exit* Gentlewoman.]

   Mariana.   One that comes a-wooing?

   Celestina. Such a thing he would seem, but in his guilti-
     ness
Of little land his expectation is not
So valiant as it might be. He wears clothes,
And feeds with noblemen; to some, I hear,
No better than a wanton emissary
Or scout for Venus' wildfowl, which made tame,
He thinks no shame to stand court sentinel
In hope of the reversion.

   Mariana.   I have heard
That some of them are often my lord's tasters:
The first fruits they condition for, and will
Exact as fees for the promotion.

Celestina. Let them agree, there's no account shall lie
For me among their traffic.

'*Enter* Gentlewoman.'

Gentlewoman. Master Haircut, madam,
Is new come in, to tender you his service.
   Celestina. Let him discourse a little with Sir William.
                           (*Exit* Gentlewoman.

   Mariana. What is this gentleman, Master Haircut,
    madam?
I note him very gallant, and much courted
By gentlemen of quality.
   Celestina.   I know not,
More than a trim gay man. He has some great office,
Sure, by his confident behaviour.
He would be entertain'd under the title
Of servant to me, and I must confess
He is the sweetest of all men that visit me.
   Isabella. How mean you, madam?
   Celestina. He is full of powder:
He will save much in perfume for my chamber
Were he but constant here. [*To* Isabella] Give 'em access.

'*Enter* Sir William Scentlove, Master Haircut.'

   Scentlove. Madam, the humblest of your servants is
Exalted to a happiness if you smile
Upon my visit.
   Haircut. I must beg your charity
Upon my rudeness, madam; I shall give
That day up lost to any happiness
When I forget to tender you my service.
   Celestina. You practise courtship, gentlemen.
   Scentlove.   But cannot
Find where with more desert to exercise it.
What lady's this, I pray?
   Celestina.   A kinswoman
Of mine, Sir William.
   Scentlove.   I am more her servant.

Celestina. You came from court now, I presume.

Haircut.   'Tis, madam,
The sphere I move in, and my destiny
Was kind to place me there, where I enjoy
All blessings that a mortal can possess
That lives not in your presence; and I should
Fix my ambition, when you would vouchsafe
Me so much honour, to accept from me
An humble entertainment there.

Celestina.   But by
What name shall I be known? In what degree
Shall I be of kindred to you?

Haircut.   How mean you, madam?

Celestina. Perhaps you'll call me sister: I shall take it
A special preferment; or it may be
I may pass under title of your mistress,
If I seem rich and fair enough to engage
Your confidence to own me.

Haircut.   I would hope—

Celestina. But 'tis not come to that yet. You will, sir,
Excuse my mirth.

Haircut. Sweet madam!

Celestina.   Shall I take
Boldness to ask what place you hold in court?
'Tis an uncivil curiosity,
But you'll have mercy to a woman's question.

Haircut. My present condition, madam, carries
Honour and profit, though not to be nam'd
With that employment I expect i'th' state,
Which shall discharge the first maturity
Upon your knowledge; until then, I beg
You allow a modest silence.

Celestina.   I am charm'd, sir;
And if you 'scape ambassador, you cannot
Reach a preferment wherein I'm against you.
But where's Sir William Scentlove?

Haircut. Give him leave
To follow his nose, madam; while he hunts
In view, he'll soon be at a fault.

Celestina.   You know him?

Haircut. Know Scentlove? Not a page but can decipher
   him;
The waiting-women know him to a scruple;
He's call'd the blister-maker of the town.
   Celestina. What's that?
   Haircut. The laundry ladies can resolve you,
And you may guess: an arrant epicure
As this day lives, born to a pretty wit,
A knight, but no gentleman. I must
Be plain to you: your ladyship may have
Use of this knowledge, but conceal the author.
   Scentlove. I kiss your fairest hand.
   Mariana.   You make a difference;
Pray reconcile 'em to an equal whiteness.
   Scentlove. You wound my meaning, lady.
   Celestina. Nay, Sir William
Has the art of compliment.
   Scentlove.   Madam, you honour me
'Bove my desert of language.
   Celestina.   Will you please
To enrich me with your knowledge of that gentleman?
   Scentlove. Do you not know him, madam?
   Celestina.   What is he?
   Scentlove. A camphire ball. You shall know more here-
   after.
He shall tell you himself and save my character;
Till then, you see he's proud.
   Celestina. One thing, gentlemen,
I observe in your behaviour, which is rare
In two that court one mistress: you preserve
A noble friendship; there's no gum within
Your hearts; you cannot fret, or show an envy
Of one another's hope. Some would not govern
Their passions with that temper.
   Scentlove.   The whole world
Shall not divorce our friendship. Master Haircut—
Would I had lives to serve him! He is lost
To goodness does not honour him.
   Haircut.   My knight!
   Celestina [*Aside*]. This is right playing at court shuttlecock.

'*Enter* Gentlewoman.'

Gentlewoman. Madam, there is a gentleman desires
To speak wi' ye, one Sir Thomas Bornwell.
    Celestina.   Bornwell?
    Gentlewoman. He says he is a stranger to your ladyship.
    Scentlove. I know him.
    Haircut.   Your neighbour, madam.
    Scentlove. Husband to the lady that so revels in the
    Strand.
    Haircut. He has good parts, they say, but cannot help
His lady's bias.
    Celestina.   They have both much fame
I' th' town for several merits. Pray admit him.

                       [*Exit* Gentlewoman.]
    Haircut [*Aside*]. What comes he for?

'*Enter* Sir Thomas.'

Bornwell. Your pardon, noble lady, that I have
Presum'd, a stranger to your knowledge,
    Celestina.   Sir,
Your worth was here before you, and your person
Cannot be here ingrateful.
    Bornwell [*Kissing* Celestina]. 'Tis the bounty
Of your sweet disposition, madam. [*To* Isabella] Make me
Your servant, lady, by her fair example,
To favour me. [*Aside*] I never knew one turn
Her cheek to a gentleman that came to kiss her
But she'd a stinking breath.—Your servant, gentlemen.
Will Scentlove, how is't?
    Celestina.   I am sorry, coz,
To accuse you: we in nothing more betray
Ourselves to censure of ridiculous pride
Than answering a fair salute too rudely.
Oh, it shows ill upon a gentlewoman
Not to return the modest lip, if she
Would have the world believe her breath is not
Offensive.
    Bornwell. Madam, I have business
With you.

Scentlove. His looks are pleasant.

Celestina.   With me, sir?

Bornwell. I hear you have an exc'llent wit, madam;
I see you fair.

Celestina.   The first is but report,
And do not trust your eyesight for the last,
'Cause I presume you're mortal and may err.

Haircut. He is very gamesome.

Bornwell.   You've an exc'llent voice—
They say you catch'd it from a dying swan—
[With] which, join'd to the sweet harmony of your lute,
You ravish all mankind.

Celestina.   Ravish mankind?

Bornwell. With their consent.

Celestina.   It were the stranger rape.
But there's the less indictment lies against it;
And there is hope your little honesties
Cannot be much the worse, for men do rather
Believe they had a maidenhead than put
Themselves to the rack of memory how long
'Tis since they left the burden of their innocence.

Bornwell. Why, you are bitter, madam.

Celestina.   So is physic.
I do not know your constitution.

Bornwell. You shall, if please you, madam.

Celestina.   You're too hasty;
I must examine what certificate
You have first, to prefer you.

Bornwell.   Fine! Certificate?

Celestina. Under your lady's hand and seal.

Bornwell.   Go to,
I see you are a wag.

Celestina.   But take heed how
You trust to't.

Bornwell.   I can love you in my wedlock
As well as that young gallant o' th' first hair,
Or the knight-bachelor, and can return
As amorous delight to your soft bosom.

Celestina. Your person and your language are both
    strangers.

Bornwell. But may be more familiar; I have those
That dare make affidavit for my body.

Celestina. D'ye mean your surgeon?

Bornwell.　　　　　　　　　　My surgeon, madam?
I know not how you value my abilities,
But I dare undertake as much, to express
My service to your ladyship, and with
As fierce ambition fly to your commands,
As the most valiant of these lay siege to you.

Celestina. You dare not, sir.

Bornwell.　　　　　　　　How, madam?

Celestina.　　　　　　　　　　I will justify't.
You dare not marry me—and I imagine
Some here, should I consent, would fetch a priest
Out of the fire.

Bornwell.　　I have a wife indeed.

Celestina. And there's a statute not repeal'd, I take it.

Bornwell. You're in the right; I must confess you've hit
And bled me in a master vein.

Celestina.　　　　　　　You think
I took you on the advantage. Use your best
Skill at defence, I'll come up to your valour
And show another work you dare not do:
You dare not, sir, be virtuous.

Bornwell.　　　　　　　　I dare,
By this fair hand I dare; and ask a pardon
If my rude words offend thy innocence,
Which in a form so beautiful would shine
To force a blush in them suspected it,
And from the rest draw wonder.

Haircut.　　　　　　　I like not
Their secret parley; shall I interrupt 'em?

Isabella. By no means, sir.

Scentlove.　　　　　Sir Thomas was not wont
To show so much a courtier.

Mariana.　　　　　　　He cannot
Be prejudicial to you: suspect not
Your own deserts so much; he's married.

Bornwell. I have other business, madam. You keep music;
I came to try how you can dance.

Celestina. You did? [*Aside*] I'll try his humour out of
    breath.—
Although I boast no cunning, sir, in revels,
If you desire to show your art that way,
I can wait on you.
    Bornwell.   You much honour me.
Nay, all must join to make a harmony.   '*They dance.*'
    Bornwell. I have nothing now, madam, but to beseech,
After a pardon for my boldness, you
Would give occasion to pay my gratitude.
I have a house will be much honour'd
If you vouchsafe your presence, and a wife
Desires to present herself your servant.
I came with the ambition to invite you;
Deny me not; your person you shall trust
On fair security.
    Celestina.   Sir, although I use not
This freedom with a stranger, you shall have
No cause to hold me obstinate.
    Bornwell.   You grace me.
Sir William Scentlove—
    Haircut.   I must take my leave.
You will excuse me, madam; court attendances—
    Celestina. By any means.
    Bornwell.   Ladies, you will vouchsafe
Your company?
    Isabella.   }
    Mariana. }   We wait upon you, sir.   (*Exeunt omnes.*

ACT III [SCENE I]

'*Enter* Lord, *unready,* Haircut *preparing his periwig.*
Table and looking-glass.'

Lord. What hour is't?
Haircut.   'Bout three a-clock, my lord.
Lord. 'Tis time to rise.
Haircut.   Your lordship went but late
To bed last night.

Lord.   'Twas early in the morning.

'*Enter* Secretary.'

Secretary. Expect a while—my lord is busy.
Lord. What's the matter?
Secretary.   Here is a lady
Desires access to you upon some affairs
She says may specially concern your lordship.
Lord. A lady? What her name?
Secretary.   Madam Decoy.
Lord. Decoy? Prithee admit her.

'*Enter* Decoy.'

Have you business, madam,
With me?
Decoy. And such I hope as will not be
Offensive to your lordship.
Lord.   I pray speak it.
Decoy. I would desire your lordship's ear more private.
Lord. Wait i' th' next chamber till I call.
           (*Exeunt* Secretary *and* Haircut.
           Now, madam.
Decoy. Although I am a stranger to your lordship,
I would not lose a fair occasion offer'd
To show how much I honour and would serve you.
Lord. Please you to give me the particular,
That I may know the extent of my engagement.
I am ignorant by what desert you should
Be encourag'd to have care of me.
Decoy.   My lord,
I will take boldness to be plain; beside
Your other excellent parts, you have much fame
For your sweet inclination to our sex.
Lord. How d'ye mean, madam?
Decoy.   I' that way your lordship
Hath honourably practis'd upon some
Not to be nam'd, your noble constancy
To a mistress hath deserv'd our general vote,
And I, a part of womankind, have thought
How to express my duty.

Lord.   In what, madam?
Decoy. Be not so strange, my lord; I know the beauty
And pleasures of your eyes, that handsome creature
With whose fair life all your delight took leave,
And to whose memory you have paid too much
Sad tribute—
Lord.   What's all this?
Decoy.   This: if your lordship
Accept my service, in pure zeal to cure
Your melancholy, I could point where you might
Repair your loss.
Lord.   Your ladyship, I conceive,
Doth traffic in flesh merchandise.
Decoy.   To men
Of honour like yourself. I am well known
To some in court, and come not with ambition
Now to supplant your officer.
Lord.   What is
The lady of pleasure you prefer?
Decoy.   A lady
Of birth and fortune, one upon whose virtue
I may presume, the lady Aretina.
Lord. Wife to Sir Thomas Bornwell?
Decoy.   The same, sir.
Lord. Have you prepar'd her?
Decoy. Not for your lordship till I have found your pulse.
I am acquainted with her disposition;
She has a very appliable nature.
Lord. And, madam, when expect you to be whipp'd
For doing these fine favours?
Decoy.   How, my lord?
Your lordship does but jest, I hope; you make
A difference between a lady that
Does honourable offices and one
They call a bawd. Your lordship was not wont
To have such coarse opinion of our practice.
Lord. The lady Aretina is my kinswoman.
Decoy. What if she be, my lord? The nearer blood
The dearer sympathy.
Lord.   I'll have thee carted.

Decoy. Your lordship will not so much stain your honour
And education to use a woman
Of my quality—
　　Lord.　　　　　'Tis possible you may
Be sent off with an honourable convoy
Of halberdiers.
　　Decoy.　　　Oh, my good lord!
　　Lord. Your ladyship shall be no protection
If thou but stay'st three minutes.
　　Decoy.　　　　　　　I am gone.
When next you find rebellion in your blood,
May all within ten mile o' th' court turn honest.

　　　　　　　　　　　　　(*Exit* Decoy.

　　Lord. I do not find that proneness since the fair
Bella Maria died; my blood is cold;
Nor is there beauty enough surviving
To heighten me to wantonness.

　　　　　　'*Enter* Haircut [*and* Secretary.]'
　　　　　　　　　　Who waits?
And what said my lady?
　　Haircut. The silent language of her face, my lord,
Was not so pleasant as it show'd upon
Her entrance.
　　Lord.　　Would any man that meets
This lady take her for a bawd?
　　Haircut.　　　　　She does
The trade an honour, credit to the profession.
We may in time see baldness, quarter noses
And rotten legs to take the wall of foot-cloths.
　　Lord. I ha' thought better. Call the lady back.
I will not lose this opportunity.
Bid her not fear.　　　　　　[*Exit* Secretary.
　　　　　　The favour is not common
And I'll reward it. I do wonder much
Will Scentlove was not here today.
　　Haircut. I heard him say this morning he would wait
Upon your lordship.

　　　　　　'*Enter* Secretary *and* Decoy.'
　　　　　　　She is return'd, sir.

Secretary. Madam, be confident my lord's not angry.

Lord. You return welcome, madam. You are better
Read in your art, I hope, than to be frighted
With any shape of anger when you bring
Such news to gentlemen. Madam, you shall
Soon understand how I accept the office.

Decoy. You are the first lord since I studied carriage
That show'd such infidelity and fury
Upon so kind a message. Every gentleman
Will show some breeding, but if one right honourable
Should not have noble blood—

Lord.   You shall return
My compliment in a letter to my lady
Aretina. Favour me with a little patience.
[*To Haircut*] Show her that chamber.

Decoy.   I'll attend your lordship.
                                   (*Exeunt* Haircut *and* Decoy.

Lord [*To Secretary*]. Write. *Madam, where your honour is
in danger, my love must not be silent.*—

'*Enter* Scentlove *and* Kickshaw.'

Scentlove and Kickshaw!

Alexander.   Your lordship's busy.

Lord. Writing a letter—nay, it shall not bar
Any discourse.

Secretary.   Silent.

*Lord. Though I be no physician, I may prevent a fever in
your blood.*—
And where have you spent the morning's conversation?

Scentlove. Where you would have given the best Barbary
In your stable to have met on honourable terms.

Lord. What new beauty? You acquaint yourselves
With none but wonders.

Scentlove.   'Tis too low—a miracle.

Lord. 'Twill require a strong faith.

Secretary.   Your blood.

*Lord. If you be innocent, preserve your fame, lest this
Decoy, madam, betray it, to your repentance.*—
By what name is she known?

Scentlove. Ask Alexander; he knows her.

Alexander.   Whom?

Scentlove. The lady Celestina.

Lord. He has a vast knowledge of ladies. 'Las, poor
    Alexander!
When dost thou mean thy body shall lie fallow?

Alexander. When there is mercy in a petticoat.
I must turn pilgrim for some breath.

Lord.   I think
'Twere cooler travel if you examine it
Upon the hoof through Spain.

Scentlove. Through Ethiopia.

Lord. Nay, less laborious to serve a prenticeship
In Peru, and dig gold out of the mine,
Though all the year were dogdays.

Secretary.   To repentance.

Lord. *In brief, this lady, could you fall from virtue, within
my knowledge will not blush to be a bawd.*

Scentlove. But hang't, 'tis honourable journey-work:
Thou art famous by't, and thy name's up.

Alexander.   So, sir.
Let me ask you a question, my dear knight:
Which is less servile—to bring up the pheasant,
And wait, or sit at table uncontroll'd,
And carve to my own appetite?

Scentlove.   No more;
Th'art witty, as I am—

Secretary.   A bawd.

Scentlove.   How's that?

Alexander. Oh, you are famous by't, and your name's up,
    sir.

Lord. *Be wise, and reward my caution with timely care of
yourself, so I shall not repent to be known your loving kinsman
and servant.*
Gentlemen, the lady Celestina,
Is she so rare a thing?

Alexander.   If you'll have my
Opinion, my lord, I never saw
So sweet, so fair, so rich a piece of nature.

Lord. I'll show thee a fairer presently, to shame

Thy eyes and judgement: look o' that. [*To* Secretary] So;
   I'll subscribe.
Seal it; I'll excuse your pen for the direction.
  Alexander. Bella Maria's picture. She was handsome.
  Scentlove. But not to be compar'd—
  Lord. Your patience, gentlemen; I'll return instantly.

                    (*Exit* Lord.

  Alexander. Whither is my lord gone?
  Secretary. To a lady i'th' next chamber.
  Scentlove.   What is she?
  Secretary. You shall pardon me—I am his secretary.
  Scentlove [*Aside*]. I was wont to be of his counsel. A new
    officer,
And I not know't? I am resolv'd to batter
All other with the praise of Celestina.
I must retain him.

           '*Enter* Lord.'

  Lord. Has not that object
Convinc'd your erring judgements?
  Alexander. What, this picture?
  Lord. Were but your thoughts as capable as mine
Of her idea, you would wish no thought
That were not active in her praise above
All worth and memory of her sex.
  Scentlove.   She was fair,
I must confess; but had your lordship look'd
With eyes more narrow and some less affection
Upon her face—
  Alexander.   I do not love the copies
Of any dead—they make me dream of goblins;
Give me a living mistress, with but half
The beauty of Celestina. Come, my lord,
'Tis pity that a lord of so much flesh
Should waste upon a ghost, when they are living
Can give you a more honourable consumption.
  Scentlove. Why, do you mean, my lord, to live an infidel?
Do, and see what will come on't; observe still
And dote upon your vigils; build a chamber
Within a rock, a tomb among the worms,

Not far off, where you may in proof apocryphal
Court 'em not devour the pretty pile
Of flesh your mistress carried to the grave.
There are no women in the world: all eyes,
And tongue[s] and lips are buried in her coffin!

Lord. Why, do you think yourselves competent judges
Of beauty, gentlemen?

Both.   What should hinder us?

Alexander. I have seen and tried as many as another
With a mortal back.

Lord.   Your eyes are brib'd,
And your hearts chain'd to some desires; you cannot
Enjoy the freedom of a sense.

Alexander.   Your lordship
Has a clear eyesight, and can judge and penetrate.

Lord. I can, and give a perfect censure of
Each line and point, distinguish beauty from
A thousand forms which your corrupted optics
Would pass for natural.

Scentlove.   I desire no other
Judge should determine us, and if your lordship
Dare venture but your eyes upon this lady,
I'll stand their justice and be confident
You shall give Celestina victory
And triumph o'er all beauties past and living.

Alexander. I dare, my lord, venture a suit of clothes
You will be o'ercome.

Lord.   You do not know my fortitude—

Scentlove. Nor frailty; you dare not trust yourself to see
      her.

Lord. Think you so, gentlemen? I dare see this creature,
To make you know your errors, and the difference
Of her whose memory is my saint. Not trust
My senses? I dare see, and speak with her.
Which holds the best acquaintance to prepare
My visit to her?

Scentlove. I will do't, my lord.

Alexander. She is a lady free in entertainments.

Lord. I would give this advantage to your cause:
Bid her appear in all the ornaments

Did ever wait on beauty, all the riches
Pride can put on, and teach her face more charm
Then ever poet dress'd up Venus in;
Bid her be all the Graces and the Queen
Of Love in one, I'll see her, Scentlove, and
Bring off my heart, arm'd but [with a] single thought
Of one that is dead, without a wound; and when
I have made your folly prisoner, I'll laugh at you.

    Scentlove. She shall expect you: trust to me for knowledge.

    Lord. I'm for the present somewhere else engag'd;
Let me hear from you.   *[Exit* Lord.]

    Scentlove.   So; I'm glad he's yet
So near conversion.

    Alexander.   I am for Aretina.

    Scentlove. No mention of my lord.

    Alexander.   Prepare his lady;
'Tis time he were reduc'd to the old sport;
One lord like him more would undo the court.

                    (*Exeunt* Alexander *and* Scentlove.

[SCENE II]

'*Enter* Aretina *with a letter,* Decoy.'

    Decoy. He is the ornament of your blood, madam;
I am much bound to his lordship.

    Aretina.   He gives you
A noble character.

    Decoy.   'Tis his goodness, madam.

    Aretina [*Aside*]. I wanted such an engine. My lord has
Done me a courtesy to disclose her nature.
I now know one to trust, and will employ her.—
Touching my lord, for reasons which I shall
Offer your ladyship hereafter, I
Desire you would be silent; but, to show
How much I dare be confident in your secrecy,
I pour my bosom forth: I love a gentleman
On whom there will not need much conjuration
To meet. Your ear.—   [*Whispers to* Decoy.]

Decoy. I apprehend you, and I shall
Be happy to be serviceable. I am sorry
Your ladyship did not know me before now.
I have done offices, and not a few
Of the nobility but have done feats
Within my house, which is convenient
For situation, and artful chambers,
And pretty pictures to provoke the fancy.

'*Enter* Littleworth.'

Littleworth. Madam, all pleasures languish in your
     absence.
Aretina. Your pardon a few minutes, sir.—[*To* Decoy]
     You must
Contrive it thus.
Littleworth. I attend, and shall account it
Honour to wait on your return.
Aretina.   He must not
Have the least knowledge of my name or person.
Decoy. I have practis'd that already for some great ones,
And dare again, to satisfy you, madam.
I have a thousand ways to do sweet offices.
Littleworth. If this lady Aretina should be honest,
I ha' lost time. She's free as air; I must
Have closer conference; and, if I have art,
Make her affect me, in revenge.
Decoy.   This evening?
Leave me to manage things.
Aretina.   You will oblige me.
Decoy. You shall commend my art and thank me after.
                              (*Exit* Decoy.
Aretina. I hope the revels are maintain'd within.
Littleworth. By Sir Thomas and his mistress.
Aretina.   How? His mistress?
Littleworth. The lady Celestina. I ne'er saw
Eyes shoot more amorous interchange.
Aretina.   Is't so?
Littleworth. He wears her favour with mere pride.
Aretina.   Her favour?

Littleworth. A feather that he ravish'd from her fan,
And is so full of courtship, which she smiles on—
 Aretina. 'Tis well.
 Littleworth.   And praises her beyond all poetry.
 Aretina. I'm glad he has so much wit.
 Littleworth [*Aside*].   Not jealous!
 Aretina [*Aside*]. This secures me. What would make other
  ladies pale
With jealousy gives but a licence to my wand'rings.
Let him now tax me if he dare—and yet,
Her beauty's worth my envy, and I wish
Revenge upon it, not because he loves,
But that it shines above my own.

     '*Enter* Alexander.'

 Alexander. Dear madam!
 Aretina [*Aside*]. I have it.—You two gentlemen profess
Much service to me. If I have a way
To employ your wit and secrecy—
 Both.   You'll honour us.
 Aretina. You gave a high and worthy character
Of Celestina.
 Alexander. I remember, madam.
 Aretina. Do either of you love her?
 Alexander.   Not I, madam.
 Littleworth. I would not if I might.
 Aretina.   She's now my guest,
And by a trick invited by my husband,
To disgrace me. You gentlemen are held
Wits of the town, the consuls that do govern
The senate here, whose jeers are all authentic;
The taverns and the ordinaries are
Made academies where you come, and all
Your sins and surfeits made the time's example;
Your very nods can quell a theatre,
No speech or poem good without your seal;
You can protect scurrility, and publish;
By your authority believ'd, no rapture
Ought to have honest meaning.
 Alexander.   Leave our characters—

Littleworth. And name the employment.

Aretina.   You must exercise
The strength of both your wits upon this lady,
And talk her into humbleness or anger,
Both which are equal to my thought. If you
Dare undertake this slight thing for my sake,
My favour shall reward it. But be faithful,
And seem to let all spring from your own freedom.

Alexander. This all? We can defame her; if you please,
My friend shall call her whore or anything,
And never be endanger'd to a duel.

Aretina.   How's that?

Alexander. He can endure a cudgelling, and no man
Will fight after so fair a satisfaction.
But leave us to our art and do not limit us.

Aretina. They are here; begin not till I whisper you.

'*Enter* Sir Thomas, Celestina, Mariana, Isabella.'

Aretina. Je vous prie, madame, d'excuser l'importunité
de mes affaires, qui m'ont fait offenser par mon absence une
dame de laquelle j'ai reçu tant d'obligation.

Celestina. Pardonnez-moi, madame, vous me faites trop
d'honneur.

Aretina. C'est bien de la douceur de votre naturel que
vous tenez ce langage; mais j'espère que mon mari n'a pas
manqué de vous entretenir en mon absence.

Celestina. En vérité, monsieur nous a fort obligées.

Aretina. Il eût trop failli s'il n'eût tâché de tout son
pouvoir à vous rendre toutes sortes de services.

Celestina. C'est de sa bonté qu'il nous a tant favorisées.

Aretina. De la vôtre, plutôt, madame, qui vous fait
donner d'interprétation si bénigne à ses efforts.

Celestina. Je vois bien que la victoire sera toujours à
madame, et du langage et de la courtoisie.

Aretina. Vraiment, madame, que jamais personne [n']a
plus désiré l'honneur de votre compagnie que moi.

Celestina. Laissons-en, je vous supplie, des compliments,
et permettez à votre servante de vous baiser les mains.

Aretina. Vous m'obligez trop.

Bornwell. I have no more patience; let's be merry again

In our own language. Madam, our mirth cools.—
Our nephew!

'*Enter* Frederick [*drunk, and* Steward].'

Aretina. Passion of my brain!

Frederick. Save you, gentlemen! Save you, ladies!

Aretina.   I am undone.

Frederick. I must salute, no matter at which end I begin.
           [*Kisses* Celestina.]

Aretina. There's a compliment.

Celestina. Is this your nephew, madam?

Aretina. Je vous prie, madame, d'excuser les habits et le
rude comportement de mon cousin. Il est tout fraîchement
venu de l'université, où on l'a tout gâté.

Celestina. Excusez-moi, madame, il est bien accompli.

Frederick. This language should be French by the
motions of your heads and the mirth of your faces.

Aretina. I am dishonoured.

Frederick. 'Tis one of the finest tongues for ladies to
show their teeth in. If you'll Latin, I am for you, or Greek
it; my tailor has not put me into French yet. *Mille basia,
basia mille.*

Celestina. Je ne vous entends pas, monsieur;
I understand you not, sir.

Frederick.   Why, so!
You and I, then, shall be in charity:
For though we should be abusive, we ha' the benefit
Not to understand one another. Where's my aunt?
I did hear music somewhere, and my brains,
Tun'd with a bottle of your capering claret,
Made haste to show their dancing.

Littleworth [*Offering his comfit-box to* Aretina]. Please you,
   madam,
They are very comfortable.

Steward.   Alas, madam,
How would you have me help it? I did use
All means I could, after he heard the music,
To make him drunk, in hope so to contain him;
But the wine made him lighter, and his head
Flew hither ere I miss'd his heels.

Alexander. Nay, he spoke Latin to the lady.

Aretina. Oh, most unpardonable! Get him off
Quickly and discreetly, or if I live—

Steward. 'Tis not in my power; he swears I am
An absurd sober fellow, and if you keep
A servant in his house to cross his humour,
When the rich sword and belt comes home, he'll kill him.

Aretina. What shall I do? Try your skill, Master Little-
    worth.

Littleworth. He has ne'er a sword.—Sweet Master
    Frederick.—

Bornwell. 'Tis pity, madam, such a scion should
Be lost. But you are clouded.

Celestina.   Not I, sir,
I never found myself more clear at heart.

Bornwell. I could play with a feather. Your fan, lady.
Gentleman, Aretina, ta-ra-ra-ra! Come, madam.

Frederick. Why, my good tutor in election,
You might have been a scholar.

Littleworth.   But I thank
My friends they brought me up a little better.
Give me the town wits, that deliver jests
Clean from the bow, that whistle in the air
And cleave the pin at twelvescore! Ladies do
But laugh at a gentleman that has any learning.
'Tis sin enough to have your clothes suspected.
Leave us, and I will find a time to instruct you.
Come, here are sugar-plums. 'Tis a good Frederick.

Frederick. Why, is not this my aunt's house in the Strand?
The noble rendezvous? Who laughs at me?
Go, I will root here if I list, and talk
Of rhetoric, logic, Latin, Greek, or anything,
And understand 'em too. Who says the contrary?
Yet in a fair way I condemn all learning,
And will be as ignorant as he, or he,
Or any taffeta, satin, scarlet, plush,
Tissue, or cloth o'bodkin gentleman,
Whose manners are most gloriously infected.
Did you laugh at me, lady?

Celestina.   Not I, sir;

But if I did show mirth upon your question,
I hope you would not beat me, little gentleman.
   Frederick. How? Little gentleman! You dare not say
These words to my new clothes and fighting sword.
   Aretina. Nephew Frederick!
   Frederick.   Little gentleman!
This an affront both to my blood and person.
I am a gentleman of as tall a birth
As any boast nobility. Though my clothes
Smell o' the lamp, my coat is honourable,
Right honourable, full of or and argent.
A little gentleman!
   Bornwell.   Coz, you must be patient;
My lady meant you no dishonour, and
You must remember she's a woman.
   Frederick. Is she a woman? That's another matter.
D'ye hear? My uncle tells me what you are.
   Celestina. So, sir.
   Frederick.   You call'd me little gentleman.
   Celestina.   I did, sir.
   Frederick. A little pink has made a lusty ship
Strike her topsail; the *Crow* may beard the *Elephant*,
A whelp may tame the *Tiger*, spite of all
False decks and murderers; and a little gentleman
Be hard enough to grapple with your ladyship,
Top and top-gallant. Will you go drink, uncle,
Tother enchanted bottle? You and I
Will tipple, and talk philosophy.
   Bornwell. Come, nephew.
You will excuse a minute's absence, madam.
[*To* Steward] Wait you on us.
   Steward.   My duty, sir.
   (*Exeunt all but* Celestina, *and* Alexander *and* Littleworth
   Aretina. Now gentlemen!
   Alexander. Madam, I had rather you accuse my language
For speaking truth than virtue suffer in
My further silence; and it is my wonder
That you, whose noble carriage hath deserv'd
All honour and opinion, should now
Be guilty of ill manners.

Celestina.   What was that
You told me, sir?
  Littleworth.   Do you not blush, madam,
To ask that question?
  Celestina.   You amaze rather
My cheek to paleness. What mean you by this?
I am not troubled with the hiccup, gentlemen,
You should bestow this fright upon me.
  Littleworth.   Then
Pride and ill memory go together.
  Celestina.   How, sir?
  Alexander. The gentleman on whom you exercis'd
Your thin wit was a nephew to the lady
Whose guest you are, and though her modesty
Look calm on the abuse of one so near
Her blood, the affront was impious.
  Littleworth.   I am asham'd on't;
You an ingenious lady, and well manner'd?
I'll teach a bear as much civility.
  Celestina. You may be master of the college, sir,
For aught I know.
  Littleworth.   What college?
  Celestina.   Of the bears.
Have you a plot upon me? D'ye possess
Your wits, or know me, gentlemen?

        '*Enter* Bornwell [*behind*].'

  Bornwell. How's this?
  Alexander. Know you? Yes, we do know you to an atom.
  Littleworth. Madam, we know what stuff your soul is
        made on.
  Celestina. But do not bark so like a mastiff, pray.
[*Aside*] Sure they are mad.—Let your brains stand awhile
And settle, gentlemen. You know not me;
What am I?
  Littleworth. Thou'rt a puppet, a thing made
Of clothes and painting, and not half so handsome
As that which play'd Susanna in the fair.
  Celestina. I heard you visited those canvas tragedies,
One of their constant audience, and so taken

With Susan that you wish'd yourself a rival
With the two wicked elders.

    Alexander.   You think this
Is wit now. Come, you are—

    Celestina.   What, I beseech you?
Your character will be full of salt and satire,
No doubt. What am I?

    Alexander.   Why, you are a woman—

    Celestina. And that's at least a bow wide of your know-
      ledge.

    Alexander. Would be thought handsome, and might pass
i' th' country
Upon a market-day; but [so] miserably
Forfeit to pride and fashions that if heaven
Were a new gown, you'd not stay in't a fortnight.

    Celestina. It must be miserably out of fashion then.
Have I no sin but pride?

    Alexander.   Hast any virtue?
Or but a good face to excuse that want?

    Celestina. You prais'd it yesterday.

    Alexander.   That made you proud.

    Celestina. More pride?

    Alexander.   You need not to close up the praise;
I have seen a better countenance in a sibyl.

    Celestina. When you wore spectacles of sack, mistook
The painted cloth and kiss'd it for your mistress.

    Alexander. Let me ask you a question: how much
Have you consum'd in expectation
That I would love you?

    Celestina.   Why, I think as much
As you have paid away in honest debts
This seven year. 'Tis a pretty impudence,
But cannot make me angry.

    Littleworth.   Is there any
Man that will cast away his limbs upon her?

    Alexander. You do not sing so well as I imagin'd,
Nor dance; you reel in your coranto, and pinch
Your petticoat too hard; you've no good ear
To th' music, and incline too much one shoulder,
As you were dancing on the rope and falling.

You speak abominable French, and make
A curtsy like a dairy-maid. [*Aside*] Not mad?

    Littleworth. Do we not sting her handsomely?

    Bornwell.   A conspiracy!

    Alexander. Your state is not so much as 'tis reported,
When you confer notes, all your husband's debts
And your own reconcil'd—but that's not it
Will so much spoil your marriage—

    Celestina.   As what, sir?
Let me know all my faults.

    Alexander.   Some men do whisper
You are not over-honest.

    Celestina.   All this shall not
Move me to more than laughter, and some pity,
Because you have the shapes of gentlemen;
And though you have been insolent upon me,
I will engage no friend to kick or cudgel you,
To spoil your living and your limbs together;
I leave that to diseases that offend you,
And spare my curse, poor silken vermin, and
Hereafter shall distinguish men from monkeys.

    Bornwell [*Coming forward*]. Brave soul! You brace of
        horse-leeches! I have heard
Their barbarous language, madam; you're too merciful;
They shall be silent to your tongue; pray punish 'em.

    Celestina. They are things not worth my character nor
        mention
Of any clean breath; so lost in honesty
They cannot satisfy for wrongs enough,
Though they should steal out of the world at Tyburn.

    Littleworth. We are hang'd already.

    Celestina. Yet I will talk a little to the pilchards.
You two, that have not 'twixt you both the hundred
Part of a soul, coarse woollen-witted fellows,
Without a nap, with bodies made for burdens;
You that are only stuffings for apparel,
As you were made but engines for your tailors
To frame their clothes upon and get them custom,
Until men see you move; yet, then you dare not,
Out of your guilt of being the ignobler beast,

But give a horse the wall, whom you excel
Only in dancing of the brawls, because
The horse was not taught the French way. Your two faces,
One fat like Christmas, tother lean like Candlemas,
And prologue to a Lent, both bound together
Would figure Janus, and do many cures
On agues and the green disease by frighting;
But neither can, with all the characters
And conjuring circles, charm a woman, though
She'd fourscore years upon her and but one
Tooth in her head, to love or think well of you;
And I were miserable to be at cost
To court such a complexion as your malice
Did impudently insinuate. But I waste time
And stain my breath in talking to such tadpoles.
Go home and wash your tongues in barley-water,
Drink clean tobacco, be not hot i' th' mouth,
And you may 'scape the beadle. So I leave you
To shame and your own garters. [*To* Bornwell] Sir, I must
Entreat you, for my honour, do not penance 'em;
They are not worth your anger. How shall I
Acquit your lady's silence?
    Bornwell [*To* Aretina].   Madam, I
Am sorry to suspect, and dare revenge—
    Celestina. No cause of mine.
    Bornwell [*To* Celestina].   It must become me to attend
    you home.
    Celestina. You are noble. Farewell, mushrooms!
                    [*Exeunt* Bornwell *and* Celestina.]
    Aretina. Is she gone?
    Littleworth.   I think we pepper'd her.
    Alexander. I am glad 'tis over,
But I repent no service for you, madam.

'*Enter* Servant *with a letter*.'

To me? From whence? A jewel! A good preface;
Be happy the conclusion.
    Aretina. Some love letter—   '*He smiles upon't.*'
    Littleworth. He has a hundred mistresses; you may

Be charitable, madam: I ha' none;
He surfeits, and I fall away i' th' kidneys.
 Alexander. I'll meet.   [*Exit* Servant.]
[*Aside*] 'Tis some great lady, questionless, that has
Taken notice and would satisfy her appetite.
 Aretina. Now, Master Alexander, you look bright o' the
  sudden;
Another spirit's in your eye.
 Alexander. Not mine, madam,
Only a summons to meet a friend.
 Aretina. What friend?
 Littleworth.   By this jewel, I know her not.
 Aretina. 'Tis a she-friend. I'll follow, gentlemen.
We may have a game at sant before you go.
 Alexander. I shall attend you, madam.
 Littleworth.   'Tis our duty.
      [*Exeunt* Alexander *and* Littleworth.]
 Aretina. I blush while I converse with my own thoughts.
Some strange fate governs me, but I must on;
The ways are cast already, and we thrive
When our sin fears no eye nor perspective. (*Exit* Aretina.

ACT IV [SCENE I]

'*Enter two men leading* Alexander *blinded, and go off
suddenly.*'

 Alexander. I am not hurt; my patience to obey 'em,
Not without fear to ha' my throat cut else,
Did me a courtesy. Whither ha' they brought me?
     [*He pulls the bandage from his eyes.*]
'Tis devilish dark: the bottom of a well
At midnight, with but two stars on the top,
Were broad day to this darkness. I but think
How like a whirlwind these rogues caught me up
And smothered my eyesight. Let me see:
These may be spirits, and for aught I know
Have brought me hither over twenty steeples.

Pray heaven they were not bailiffs—that's more worth
My fear—and this a prison. All my debts
Reek in my nostril, and my bones begin
To ache with fear to be made dice; and yet
This is too calm and quiet for a prison.
What if the riddle prove I am robb'd? And yet
I did not feel 'em search me. How now! Music!

'*Enter* Decoy *like an old woman, with a light.*'

And a light! What beldam's this? I cannot pray.
What art?
   Decoy.   A friend. Fear not, young man; I am
No spirit.
   Alexander.   Off!
   Decoy.   Despise me not for age
Or this coarse outside, which I wear not out
Of poverty. Thy eyes be witness 'tis
No cave or beggar's cell thou'rt brought to. Let
That gold speak here's no want, which thou mayst spend,
And find a spring to tire even prodigality,
If thou be'st wise.   [*Gives him a purse.*]
   Alexander.   The devil was a coiner
From the beginning, yet the gold looks current.
   Decoy. Thou'rt still in wonder. Know I am mistress of
This house, and of a fortune that shall serve
And feed thee with delights. 'Twas I sent for thee;
The jewel and the letter came from me;
It was my art thus to contrive our meeting,
Because I would not trust thee with my fame
Until I found thee worth a woman's honour.
   Alexander [*Aside*]. Honour and fame? The devil means to
      have
A care on's credit: though she sent for me,
I hope she has another customer
To do the trick withal; I would not turn
Familiar to a witch.
   Decoy.   What say'st? Canst thou
Dwell in my arms tonight? Shall we change kisses,
And entertain the silent hours with pleasure
Such as old Time shall be delighted with,

And blame the too swift motion of his wings
While we embrace?

 Alexander [*Aside*]. Embrace? She has had no teeth
This twenty years, and the next violent cough
Brings up her tongue: it cannot possibly
Be sound at root. I do not think but one
Strong sneeze upon her, and well meant, would make
Her quarters fall away; one kick would blow
Her up like gunpowder and loose all her limbs.
She is so cold, an incubus would not heat her;
Her phlegm would quench a furnace and her breath
Would damp a musket bullet.

 Decoy.   Have you, sir,
Consider'd?

 Alexander. What?

 Decoy.   My proposition:
Canst love?

 Alexander. I could have done. Whom do you mean?
I know you are pleas'd but to make sport.

 Decoy.   Thou art not
So dull of soul as thou appear'st.

 Alexander [*Aside*].   This is
But some device: my grannam has some trick in't.—
Yes, I can love.

 Decoy.   But canst thou affect me?

 Alexander. Although to reverence so grave a matron
Were an ambitious word in me, yet since
You give me boldness, I do love you.

 Decoy.   Then
Thou art my own—

 Alexander [*Aside*]. Has she no cloven foot?

 Decoy. And I am thine, and all that I command
Thy servants. From this minute thou art happy,
And fate in thee will crown all my desires.
I griev'd a proper man should be compell'd
To bring his body to the common market.
My wealth shall make thee glorious, and, the more
To encourage thee, howe'er this form may fright
Thy youthful eyes, yet thou wilt find by light
Of thy own sense—for other light is banish'd

My chamber—when our arms tie lovers' knots,
And kisses seal the welcome of our lips,
I shall not there affright thee, nor seem old,
With rivell'd veins: my skin is smooth and soft
As ermines, with a spirit to meet thine,
Active and equal to the Queen of Love's
When she did court Adonis.

 Alexander [*Aside*].   This does more
Confirm she is a devil and I am
Within his own dominions. I must on,
Or else be torn a-pieces. I have heard
These succubi must not be cross'd.

 Decoy.   We trifle
Too precious time away. I'll show you a prospect
Of the next chamber, and then out the candle.

 Alexander. Have you no sack i' th' house? I would go
  arm'd
Upon this breach.

 Decoy.   It shall not need.

 Alexander.   One word,
Mother: have not you been a cat in your days?

 Decoy. I am glad you are so merry, sir. You observe
That bed?

 Alexander. A very brave one.

 Decoy.   When you are
Disrob'd, you can come thither in the dark.
You shall not stay for me; come, as you wish
For happiness.   (*Exit* Decoy.

 Alexander. I am preferr'd. If I
Be modest and obey, she cannot have
The heart to do me harm an' she were Hecate
Herself. I will have a strong faith and think
I march upon a mistress the less evil.
If I 'scape fire now, I defy the devil. (*Exit* Alexander.

[SCENE II]

'*Enter* Frederick, Littleworth, Steward.'

 Frederick. And how d'ye like me now?

 Steward.   Most excellent.

Frederick. Your opinion, Master Littleworth?
Littleworth.   Your French tailor
Has made you a perfect gentleman. I may
Converse now with you and preserve my credit.
D'ye find no alteration in your body
With these new clothes?
   Frederick.   My body alter'd? No.
   Littleworth. You are not yet in fashion then. That must
Have a new motion, garb, and posture too,
Or all your pride is cast away. It is not
The cut of your apparel makes a gallant,
But the geometrical wearing of your clothes.
   Steward. Master Littleworth tells you right; you wear
your hat
Too like a citizen.
   Littleworth.   'Tis like a midwife;
Place it with best advantage of your hair.
Is half your feather moulted? This does make
No show: it should spread over, like a canopy;
Your hot-rein'd monsieur wears it for a shade
And cooler to his back. Your doublet must
Be more unbutton'd hereabouts: you'll not
Be a sloven else. A foul shirt is no blemish;
You must be confident and outface clean linen.
Your doublet and your breeches must be allow'd
No private meeting here. Your cloak's too long:
It reaches to your buttock, and doth smell
Too much of Spanish gravity; the fashion
Is to wear nothing but a cape. A coat
May be allow'd a covering for one elbow,
And some, to avoid the trouble, choose to walk
In cuerpo, thus.
   Steward [*Aside*]. Your coat and cloak's a-brushing
In Long Lane, Lombard.
   Frederick.   But what if it rain?
   Littleworth. Your belt about your shoulder is sufficient
To keep off any storm; beside, a reed
But wav'd discreetly has so many pores,
It sucks up all the rain that falls about one.
With this defence, when other men have been

Wet to the skin through all their cloaks, I have
Defied a tempest and walk'd by the taverns
Dry as a bone.
    Steward [*Aside*]. Because he had no money
To call for wine.
    Fredrick.   Why, you do walk enchanted.
Have you such pretty charms in town? But stay;
Who must I have to attend me?
    Littleworth.   Is not that
Yet thought upon?
    Steward.   I have laid out for servants.
    Littleworth. They are everywhere.
    Steward.   I cannot yet be furnish'd
With such as I would put into his hands.
    Frederick. Of what condition must they be, and how
Many in number, sir?
    Littleworth.   Beside your fencing,
Your singing, dancing, riding, and French master,
Two may serve domestic, to be constant waiters
Upon a gentleman: a fool, a pimp.
    Steward. For these two officers I have enquir'd,
And I am promis'd a convenient whiskin.
I could save charges and employ the pie-wench
That carries her intelligence in whitepots;
Or 'tis but taking order with the woman
That holds the ballads: she could fit him with
A concubine to any tune; but I
Have a design to place a fellow with him
That has read all Sir Pandarus' works, a Trojan
That lies conceal'd and is acquainted with
Both city and suburban fripperies,
Can fetch 'em with a spell at midnight to him
And warrant which are for his turn, can for
A need supply the surgeon too.
    Frederick.   I like
Thy providence—such a one deserves a livery twice a year.
    Steward. It shall not need: a cast suit of your worship's
Will serve; he'll find a cloak to cover it
Out of his share with those he brings to bed to you.
    Frederick. But must I call this fellow pimp?

Littleworth.   It is
Not necessary: or Jack, or Harry,
Or what he's known abroad by will sound better,
That men may think he is a Christian.

    Frederick. But hear you, Master Littleworth, is there not
A method and degrees of title in
Men of this art?

    Littleworth.   According to the honour
Of men that do employ 'em. An emperor
May give this office to a duke; a king
May have his viceroy to negotiate for him;
A duke may use a lord, the lord a knight;
A knight may trust a gentleman; and when
They are abroad and merry, gentlemen
May pimp to one another.

    Frederick.   Good, good fellowship!
But for the fool, now, that should wait on me,
And break me jests?

    Littleworth.   A fool is necessary.

    Steward. By any means.

    Frederick.   But which of these two servants
Must now take place?

    Littleworth.   That question, Master Frederick,
The School of Heraldry should conclude upon.
But, if my judgement may be heard, the fool
Is your first man; and it is known a point
Of state to have a fool.

    Steward.   But, sir, the other
Is held the finer servant: his employments
Are full of trust, his person clean and nimble,
And none so soon can leap into preferment
Where fools are poor.

    Littleworth.   Not all; there's story for't;
Princes have been no wiser than they should be.
Would any nobleman that were no fool
Spend all in hope of the philosopher's stone
To buy new lordships in another country?
Would knights build colleges, or gentlemen
Of good estates challenge the field and fight,
Because a whore will not be honest? Come,

Fools are a family over all the world;
We do affect one naturally; indeed,
The fool is lieger with us.

    Steward.   Then the pimp
Is extraordinary.

    Frederick.   Do not you fall out
About their places.

'Enter Aretina.'

Here's my noble aunt.

    Littleworth. How do you like your nephew, madam, now
    Aretina. Well! Turn about, Frederick. Very well!
    Frederick. Am I not now a proper gentleman?
The virtue of rich clothes! Now could I take
The wall of Julius Caesar, affront
Great Pompey's upper lip and defy the Senate.
Nay, I can be as proud as your own heart, madam:
You may take that for your comfort. I put on
That virtue with my clothes, and I doubt not
But in a little time I shall be impudent
As any page or player's boy. I am
Beholding to this gentleman's good discipline,
But I shall do him credit in my practice.
Your steward has some pretty notions too
In moral mischief.

    Aretina.   Your desert in this
Exceeds all other service, and shall bind me
Both to acknowledge and reward.

    Littleworth.   Sweet madam!
Think me but worth your favour, I would creep
Upon my knees to honour you, and for every
Minute you lend to my reward I'll pay
A year of serviceable tribute.

    Aretina.   You
Can compliment.

    Littleworth [*Aside*]. Thus still she puts me off.
Unless I speak the downright word, she'll never
Understand me. A man would think that creeping
Upon one's knees were English to a lady.

'Enter Alexander [elaborately dressed].'

Alexander. How is't, Jack? Pleasures attend you, madam.
How does my plant of honour?

Aretina.   Who is this?

Alexander. 'Tis Alexander.

Aretina.   Rich and glorious.

Littleworth. 'Tis Alexander the Great.

Alexander.   And my Bucephalus
Waits at the door.

Aretina.   Your case is alter'd, sir.

Alexander. I cannot help these things; the Fates will
    have it;
'Tis not my land does this.

Littleworth.   But thou hast a plough
That brings it in.

Aretina.   Now he looks brave and lovely.

Frederick. Welcome, my gallant Macedonian.

Alexander. Madam, you gave your nephew for my pupil;
I read but in a tavern; if you'll honour us,
The Bear at the bridge foot shall entertain you;
A drawer is my Ganymede; he shall skink
Brisk nectar to us. We will only have
A dozen partridge in a dish; as many pheasants,
Quails, cocks, and godwits shall come marching up
Like the train'd band; a fort of sturgeon
Shall give most bold defiance to an army,
And triumph o'er the table.

Aretina.   Sir, it will
But dull the appetite to hear more, and mine
Must be excus'd. Another time I may
Be your guest.

Alexander. 'Tis grown in fashion now with ladies;
When you please, I'll attend you. Littleworth—
Come, Frederick.

Frederick.   We'll have music; I love noise;
We will outroar the Thames and shake the bridge, boy.

                         (*Exeunt* Frederick *and* Alexander.

Littleworth. Madam, I kiss your hand. Would you would
    think
Of your poor servant: flesh and blood is frail,
And troublesome to carry without help.

Aretina. A coach will easily convey it, or
You may take water at Strand Bridge.
   Littleworth.   But I
Have taken fire.
   Aretina.   The Thames will cool—
   Littleworth. But never quench my heart; your charity
Can only do that!
   Aretina.   I will keep it cold
Of purpose.
   Littleworth. Now you bless me, and I dare
Be drunk in expectation.   [*Exit* Littleworth.]
   Aretina.   I am confident
He knows me not, and I were worse than mad
To be my own betrayer.

'Enter Bornwell.'

               Here's my husband.
   Bornwell. Why, how now, Aretina? What, alone?
The mystery of this solitude? My house
Turn'd desert o' the sudden, all the gamesters
Blown up? Why, is the music put to silence?
Or ha' their instruments caught a cold since we
Gave 'em the last heat? I must know thy ground
Of melancholy.
   Aretina.   You are merry, as
You came from kissing Celestina.
   Bornwell.   I
Feel her yet warm upon my lip; she is
Most excellent company; I did not think
There was that sweetness in her sex. I must
Acknowledge 'twas thy cure to disenchant me
From a dull husband to an active lover.
With such a lady I could spend more years
Than since my birth my glass hath run soft minutes,
And yet be young; her presence has a spell
To keep off age; she has an eye would strike
Fire through ~~and~~ .... ~~as much~~
Bestow'd upon a dull-fac'd chambermaid
Whom love and wit would thus commend. True beauty

Is mock'd when we compare thus, itself being
Above what can be fetch'd to make it lovely;
Or, could our thoughts reach something to declare
The glories of a face or body's elegance—
That touches but our sense, when beauty spreads
Over the soul and calls up understanding
To look what thence is offer'd, and admire.
In both I must acknowledge Celestina
Most excellently fair—fair above all
The beauties I ha' seen, and one most worthy
Man's love and wonder.

Bornwell.   Do you speak, Aretina,
This with a pure sense to commend? Or is't
The mockery of my praise?

Aretina.   Although it shame
Myself, I must be just and give her all
The excellency of women; and were I
A man—

Bornwell. What then?

Aretina.   I know not with what loss
I should attempt her love. She is a piece
So angelically moving, I should think
Frailty excus'd to dote upon her form,
And almost virtue to be wicked with her.   (*Exit* Aretina.

Bornwell. What should this mean? This is no jealousy,
Or she believes I counterfeit. I feel
Something within me, like a heat, to give
Her cause, would Celestina but consent.
What a frail thing is man! It is not worth
Our glory to be chaste while we deny
Mirth and converse with women. He is good
That dares the tempter yet corrects his blood.

(*Exit* Bornwell.

[SCENE III]

'[*Enter*] Celestina, Mariana, Isabella.'

Celestina. I have told you all my knowledge. Since he is
pleas'd

To invite himself, he shall be entertain'd,
And you shall be my witnesses.

    Mariana.   Who comes with him?

    Celestina. Sir William Scentlove, that prepar'd me for
The honourable encounter. I expect
His lordship every minute.

                   '*Enter* Scentlove.'

    Scentlove. My lord is come.

              '*Enter* Lord, Haircut.'

    Celestina. He has honour'd me.

    Scentlove.   My lord, your periwig is awry.

    Lord [*To* Haircut]. You, sir—'*While* Haircut *is busy about
                his hair*, Scentlove *goes to* Celestina.'

    Scentlove. You may guess at the gentleman that's with
      him:
It is his barber, madam, d'ye observe,
An' your ladyship want a shaver.

    Haircut.   She is here, sir.

[*Aside*] I am betray'd! Scentlove, your plot. I may
Have opportunity to be reveng'd.   (*Exit* Haircut.

    Scentlove. She in the midst.

    Lord.   She's fair, I must confess;
But does she keep this distance out of state?

    Celestina. Though I am poor in language to express
How much your lordship honours me, my heart
Is rich and proud in such a guest. I shall
Be out of love with every air abroad,
And, for this grace done my unworthy house,
Be a fond prisoner, become anchorite
And spend my hours in prayer, to reward
The blessing and the bounty of this presence.

    Lord. Though you could turn each place you move in to
A temple, rather than a wall should hide
So rich a beauty from the world, it were
Less want to lose our piety and your prayer.
A throne were fitter to present you to
Our wonder, whence your eyes, more worth than all
They look on, should chain every heart a prisoner.

    Scentlove. 'Twas pretty well come off.

Lord.   By your example
I shall know how to compliment; in this
You more confirm my welcome.
    Celestina.   I shall love
My lips the better if their silent language
Persuade your lordship but to think so truly.
    Lord. You make me smile, madam.
    Celestina.   I hope you came not
With fear that any sadness here should shake
One blossom from your eye; I should be miserable
To present any object should displease you—
    Lord. You do not, madam.
    Celestina.   As I should account
It no less sorrow if your lordship should
Lay too severe a censure on my freedom.
I will not court a prince against his justice,
Nor bribe him with a smile to think me honest.
Pardon, my lord, this boldness, and the mirth
That may flow from me; I believe my father
Thought of no winding-sheet when he begot me.
    Lord [*Aside*]. She has a merry soul.—It will become
Me ask your pardon, madam, for my rude
Approach, so much a stranger to your knowledge.
    Celestina. Not, my lord, so much stranger to my know-
            ledge:
Though I have but seen your person afar off,
I am acquainted with your character,
Which I have heard so often I can speak it.
    Lord. You shall do me an honour.
    Celestina.   If your lordship will
Be patient.
    Lord.   And glad to hear my faults.
    Celestina. That as your conscience can agree upon 'em.
However, if your lordship give me privilege,
I'll tell you what's the opinion of the world.
    Lord. You cannot please me better.
    Celestina.   You're a Lord,
Born with as much nobility as would,
Divided, serve to make ten noblemen
Without a herald, but with so much spirit

And height of soul as well might furnish twenty.
You are learn'd, a thing not compatible now
With native honour, and are master of
A language that doth chain all ears and charm
All hearts where you persuade; a wit so flowing,
And prudence to correct it, that all men
Believe they only meet in you; which, with
A spacious memory, make up the full wonders;
To these you have known valour, and upon
A noble cause know how to use a sword
To honour's best advantage though you wear none.
You are as bountiful as the showers that fall
Into the spring's green bosom, as you were
Created lord of fortune not her steward;
So constant to the cause in which you make
Yourself an advocate, you dare all dangers,
And men had rather you should be their friend
Than justice or the bench bound up together.

    Lord. But did you hear all this?
    Celestina.   And more, my lord.
    Lord. Pray let me have it, madam.
    Celestina. To all these virtues there is added one
(Your lordship will remember when I name it
I speak but what I gather from the voice
Of others): it is grown to a full fame
That you have lov'd a woman.
    Lord.   But one, madam?
    Celestina. Yes, many. Give me leave to smile, my lord;
I shall not need to interpret in what sense.
But you have show'd yourself right honourable,
And for your love to ladies have deserv'd,
If their vote might prevail, a marble statue.
I make no comment on the people's text—
My lord, I should be sorry to offend.
    Lord. You cannot, madam; these are things we owe
To nature for.
    Celestina.   And honest men will pay
Their debts.
    Lord.   If they be able, or compound.
    Celestina. She had a hard heart would be unmerciful

And not give day to men so promising;
But you owe women nothing.
    Lord.   Yes, I am
Still in their debt, and I must owe them love:
It was part of my character.
    Celestina.   With your lordship's
Pardon, I only said you had a fame
For loving women; but of late men say
You have against the imperial laws of love
Restrain'd the active flowings of your blood,
And with a mistress buried all that is
Hop'd for in love's succession, as all beauty
Had died with her and left the world benighted.
In this you more dishonour all our sex
Than you did grace a part, when everywhere
Love tempts your eye to admire a glorious harvest,
And everywhere as full-blown ears submit
Their golden heads, the laden trees bow down
Their willing fruit, and court your amorous tasting.
    Lord. I see men would dissect me to a fibre.
But do you believe this?
    Celestina.   It is my wonder,
I must confess, a man of nobler earth
Than goes to vulgar composition,
(Born and bred high, so unconfin'd, so rich
In fortunes, and so read in all that sum
Up human knowledge, to feed gloriously,
And live at court, the only sphere wherein
True beauty moves, nature's most wealthy garden,
Where every blossom is more worth than all
The Hesperean fruit by jealous dragon watch'd,
Where all delights do circle appetite,
And pleasures multiply by being tasted)
Should be so lost with thought of one turn'd ashes.
There's nothing left, my lord, that can excuse you
Unless you plead—what I am asham'd to prompt
Your wisdom to.
    Lord.   What['s] that?
    Celestina.   That you have play'd
The surgeon with yourself.

Lord.   And am made eunuch?
Celestina. It were much pity.
Lord.   Trouble not yourself:
I could convince your fears with demonstration
That I am man enough, but knew not where,
Until this meeting, beauty dwelt. The court
You talk'd of must be where the Queen of Love is,
Which moves but with your person; in your eye
Her glory shines, and only at that flame
Her wanton boy doth light his quick'ning torch.
    Celestina. Nay, now you compliment—I would it did,
My lord, for your own sake.
Lord.   You would be kind,
And love me then?
Celestina.   My lord, I should be loving
Where I found worth to invite it, and should cherish
A constant man.
Lord.   Then you should me, madam.
    Celestina. But is the ice about your heart fallen off?
Can you return to do what love commands?
    Lord. Cupid, thou shalt have instant sacrifice,
And I dare be the priest. [*Kissing her*] Your hand, your lip;
Now I am proof 'gainst all temptation.
    Celestina. Your meaning, my good lord?
Lord.   I that have strength
Against thy voice and beauty, after this
May dare the charms of womankind. Thou art,
Bella Maria, unprofaned yet;
This magic has no power upon my blood.
Farewell, madam! If you durst be the example
Of chaste as well as fair, thou wert a brave one.
    Celestina. I hope your lordship means not this for earnest.
Be pleas'd to grace a banquet.
Lord.   Pardon, madam.
Will Scentlove, follow; I must laugh at you.
    Celestina. My lord, I must beseech you stay, for honour,
For her whose memory you love best.
Lord.   Your pleasure.
    Celestina. And by that virtue you have now profess'd
I charge you to believe me too: I can

Now glory that you have been worth my trial,
Which I beseech you pardon. Had not you
So valiantly recover'd in this conflict,
You had been my triumph, without hope of more
Than my just scorn upon your wanton flame;
Nor will I think these noble thoughts grew first
From melancholy for some female loss,
As the fantastic world believes, but from
Truth and your love of innocence, which shine
So bright in the two royal luminaries
At court, you cannot lose your way to chastity.
Proceed, and speak of me as honour guides you.

                            (Exeunt Lord *and* Scentlove.*)*

I am almost tir'd. Come, ladies, we'll beguile
Dull time, and take the air another while.

                                     (Exeunt omnes.

ACT V [SCENE I]

'*Enter* Aretina *and* Servant.'

Aretina. But hath Sir Thomas lost five hundred pounds
Already?

Servant. And five hundred more he borrow'd.
The dice are notable devourers, madam;
They make no more of pieces than of pebbles,
But thrust their heaps together to engender.
'Two hundred more the caster,' cries this gentleman.
'I am wi' ye; I ha' that to nothing, sir,' the caster
Again. 'Tis cover'd, and the table too,
With sums that frighted me. Here one sneaks out
And with a martyr's patience smiles upon
His money's executioner, the dice,
Commands a pipe of good tobacco, and
I' th' smoke on't vanishes. Another makes
The bones vault o'er his head, swears that ill throwing
Has put his shoulder out of joint, calls for
A bone-setter. That looks to the box, to bid

His master send him some more hundred pounds,
Which lost, he takes tobacco and is quiet.
Here a strong arm throws 'in-and-in', with which
He brusheth all the table, pays the rooks
That went their smelts a piece upon his hand,
Yet swears he has not drawn a stake this seven year.
But I was bid make haste; my master may
Lose this five hundred pounds ere I come hither.

(*Exit* Servant.

Aretina. If we both waste so fast, we shall soon find
Our state is not immortal. Something in
His other ways appear[s] not well already.

'*Enter* Sir Thomas [*and* Servants.]'

Bornwell. Ye tortoises, why make you no more haste?
Go pay to th' master of the house that money,
And tell the noble gamesters I have another
Superfluous thousand pound; at night I'll visit 'em.
D'ye hear?
Servant. Yes, an' please you.
Bornwell. Do't, ye drudges.

(*Exeunt* Servants.

Ta-ra-ra! Aretina!
Aretina. You have a pleasant humour, sir.
Bornwell. What should a gentleman be sad?
Aretina. You have lost—
Bornwell. A transitory sum; as good that way
As another.
Aretina. Do you not vex within for't?
Bornwell. I had rather lose a thousand more than one
Sad thought come near my heart for't. Vex for trash!
Although it go from other men like drops
Of their life blood, we lose with the alacrity
We drink a cup of sack or kiss a mistress.
No money is considerable with a gamester:
They have souls more spacious than kings! Did two
Gamesters divide the empire of the world,
They'd make one throw for't all, and he that lost
Be no more melancholy than to have play'd for

A morning's draught. Vex a rich soul for dirt,
The quiet of whose every thought is worth
A province!

    Aretina. But when dice have consum'd all,
Your patience will not pawn for as much more.

    Bornwell. Hang pawning! Sell outright, and the fear's
over.

    Aretina. Say you so? I'll have another coach tomorrow
If there be rich above ground.

    Bornwell.   I forgot
To bid the fellow ask my jeweller
Whether the chain of diamonds be made up;
I will present it to my Lady Bellamour,
Fair Celestina.

    Aretina.   This gown I have worn
Six days already; it looks dull; I'll give it
My waiting-woman and have one of cloth
Of gold embroider'd. Shoes and pantables
Will show well of the same.

    Bornwell.   I have invited
A covey of ladies and as many gentlemen
Tomorrow to the Italian ordinary;
I shall have rarities and regalias
To pay for, madam; music, wanton songs,
And tunes of silken petticoats to dance to.

    Aretina. And tomorrow have I invited half the court
To dine here. What misfortune 'tis your company
And ours should be divided! After dinner
I entertain 'em with a play.

    Bornwell.   By that time
Your play inclines to the epilogue shall we
Quit our Italian host and whirl in coaches
To the Dutch magazine of sauce, the Stillyard,
Where deal and backrag and what strange wine else
They dare but give a name to in the reckoning
Shall flow into our room and drown Westphalias,
Tongues, and anchovies, like some little town
Endanger'd by a sluice, through whose fierce ebb
We wade and wash ourselves into a boat,
And bid our coachmen drive their leather tenements

By land, while we sail home with a fresh tide
To some new rendezvous.
   Aretina.   If you have not
Pointed the place, pray bring your ladies hither;
I mean to have a ball tomorrow night,
And a rich banquet for 'em, where we'll dance
Till morning rise and blush to interrupt us.
   Bornwell. Have you no ladies i' th' next room to advance
A present mirth? What a dull house you govern!
Farewell! A wife's no company.—Aretina,
I've summ'd up my estate and find we may have
A month good yet—
   Aretina.   What mean you?
   Bornwell.   And I'd rather
Be lord one month of pleasures, to the height
And rapture of our senses, than be years
Consuming what we have in foolish temperance,
Live in the dark, and no fame wait upon us.
I will live so, posterity shall stand
At gaze when I am mention'd.
   Aretina.   A month good!
And what shall be done then?
   Bornwell.   I'll over sea
And trail a pike. With watching, marching, lying
In trenches, with enduring cold and hunger,
And taking here and there a musket-shot,
I can earn every week four shillings, madam;
And if the bullets favour me to snatch
Any superfluous limb, when I return,
With good friends, I despair not to be enroll'd
Poor Knight of Windsor. For your course, madam,
No doubt you may do well: your friends are great;
Or, if your poverty and their pride cannot
Agree, you need not trouble much invention
To find a trade to live by—there are customers.
Farewell! Be frolic, madam. If I live,
I will feast all my senses, and not fall
Less than a Phaeton from my throne of pleasure,
Though my estate flame like the world about me.
                            (*Exit* Bornwell.

Aretina. 'Tis very pretty.

'*Enter* Decoy.'

Madam Decoy!
Decoy.   What, melancholy
After so sweet a night's work? Have not I
Show'd myself mistress of my art?
    Aretina.   A lady.
    Decoy. That title makes the credit of the act
A storey higher. You've not seen him yet?
I wonder what he'll say.

'*Enter* Alexander *and* Frederick.'

                He's here.
    Alexander. Bear up,
My little Myrmidon. Does not Jack Littleworth
Follow?
    Frederick. Follow? He fell into the Thames
At landing.
    Alexander. The devil shall dive for him
Ere I endanger my silk stockings for him.
Let the watermen alone; they have drags and engines.
When he has drunk his julep I shall laugh
To see him come in pickled the next tide.
    Frederick. He'll never sink, he has such a cork brain.
    Alexander. Let him be hang'd or drown'd, all's one to me;
Yet he deserves to die by water cannot
Bear his wine credibly.
    Frederick.   Is not this my aunt?
    Alexander. And another handsome lady. I must know her.
                      [*Takes* Decoy *aside.*]
    Frederick. My blood is rampant too. I must court some-
      body;
As good my aunt as any other body.
    Aretina. Where have you been, cousin?
    Frederick.   At the bridge,
At the Bear's foot, where our first health began
To the fair Aretina, whose sweet company
Was wish'd by all. We could not get a lay,
A tumbler, a device, a bona roba

For any money; drawers were grown dull;
We wanted our true firks and our vagaries.
When were you in drink, aunt?

    Aretina. How?

    Frederick. Do not ladies
Play the good fellows too? There's no true mirth
Without 'em. I have now such tickling fancies.
That doctor of the chair of wit has read
A precious lecture how I should behave
Myself to ladies; as now, for example.

    Aretina. Would you practise upon me?

    Frederick. I first salute you.
You have a soft hand, madam; are you so
All over?

    Aretina. Nephew!

    Frederick. Nay, you should but smile,
And then again I kiss you, and thus draw
Off your white glove, and start, to see your hand
More excellently white. I grace my own
Lip with this touch, and turning gently thus,
Prepare you for my skill in palmistry,
Which out of curiosity no lady
But easily applies to. The first line
I look with most ambition to find out
Is Venus' girdle, a fair semi-circle
Encircling both the mount of Sol and Saturn;
If that appear, she's for my turn, a lady
Whom nature has prepar'd for the career;
And, Cupid at my elbow, I put forward.
You have this very line, aunt.

    Aretina. The boy's frantic.

    Frederick. You have a couch or pallet? I can shut
The chamber door. Enrich a stranger when
Your nephew's coming into play!

    Aretina. No more.

    Frederick. Are you so coy to your own flesh and blood?

    Alexander. Here, take your playfellow. I talk of sport,
And she would have me marry her.

'*Enter* Littleworth *wet.*'

Frederick. Here's Littleworth.
Why, how now, tutor?
    Littleworth.   I ha' been fishing.
    Frederick. And what ha' you caught?
    Littleworth.   My belly full of water.
    Alexander. Ha! Ha! Where's thy rapier?
    Littleworth.   My rapier's drown'd;
And I am little better. I was up b'th' heels
And out came a tun of water, beside wine.
    Alexander. 'T has made thee sober.
    Littleworth.   Would you have me drunk
With water?
    Aretina. I hope your fire is quench'd by this time.
    Frederick. It is not now as when your worship walk'd
By all the taverns, Jack, dry as a bone.
    Alexander. You had store of fish under water, Jack.
    Littleworth. It has made a poor John of me.
    Frederick. I do not think but if we cast an angle
Into his belly, we might find some pilchards.
    Littleworth. And boil'd by this time. Dear madam, a bed.
    Alexander. Carry but the water-spaniel to a grass plot
Where he may roll himself; let him but shake
His ears twice in the sun, and you may grind him
Into a posset.
    Frederick. Come, thou shalt to my bed,
Poor pickerel.
    Decoy. Alas, sweet gentleman!
    Littleworth. I have ill luck an I should smell by this time.
I am but new ta'en, I am sure, sweet gentlewoman.
    Decoy. Your servant.
    Littleworth.   Pray do not pluck off my skin;
It is so wet, unless you have good eyes,
You'll hardly know it from a shirt.
    Decoy.   Fear nothing.
    Aretina. He has sack enough an I may find his humour.
                (*Exeunt all but* Aretina *and* Alexander.
    Alexander. And how is't with your ladyship? You look
Without a sunshine in your face.
    Aretina.   You are glorious
In mind and habit.

Alexander.　　　Ends of gold and silver!

Aretina. Your other clothes were not so rich. Who was
Your tailor, sir?

Alexander.　　They were made for me long since;
They have known but two bright days upon my back.
I had a humour, madam, to lay things by;
They will serve two days more. I think I ha' gold enough
To go to th' mercer. I'll now allow myself
A suit a week, as this, with necessary
Dependences: beaver, silk stockings, garters,
And roses, in their due conformity;
Boots are forbid a clean leg but to ride in;
My linen every morning comes in new;
The old goes to great-bellies.

Aretina.　　　　　　You are charitable.

Alexander. I may dine wi' ye sometime, or at the Court,
To meet good company, not for the table.
My clerk o' th' kitchen's here, a witty epicure,
A spirit that to please me with what's rare
Can fly a hundred mile a day to market
And make me lord of fish and fowl. I shall
Forget there is a butcher, and to make
My footman nimble he shall feed on nothing
But wings of wildfowl.

Aretina.　　　　　These ways are costly.

Alexander. Therefore I'll have it so; I ha' sprung a mine.

Aretina. You make me wonder, sir, to see this change
Of fortune; your revenue was not late
So plentiful.

Alexander. Hang dirty land and lordships!
I will not change one lodging I ha' got
For the Chamber of London.

Aretina.　　　　　Strange, of such a sudden
To rise to this estate; no fortunate hand
At dice could lift you up so, for 'tis since
Last night; yesterday you were no such monarch.

Alexander. There be more games than dice,

Aretina.　　　　　　　　　It cannot be
A mistress, though your person is worth love.
None possibly are rich enough to feed

As you have cast the method of your riots;
A princess, after all her jewels, must
Be forc'd to sell her provinces.

  Alexander.   Now you talk
Of jewels, what do you think of this?

  Aretina.   A rich one.

  Alexander. You'll honour me to wear't. This other toy
I had from you; this chain I borrow'd of you;
A friend had it in keeping. [*Gives her the jewel and chain.*]
  If your ladyship
Want any sum, you know your friend, and Alexander.

  Aretina. Dare you trust my security?

  Alexander.   There's gold;
I shall have more tomorrow.

  Aretina. You astonish me; who can supply these?

  Alexander. A dear friend I have.
She promis'd we should meet again i' th' morning.

  Aretina. Not that I wish to know
More of your happiness than I have already
Heart to congratulate, be pleas'd to lay
My wonder.

  Alexander. 'Tis a secret.

  Aretina.   Which I'll die
Ere I'll betray.

  Alexander. You have always wish'd me well,
But you shall swear not to reveal the party—

  Aretina. I'll lose the benefit of my tongue.

  Alexander.   Nor be
Afraid at what I say? What think you first
Of an old witch, a strange ill-favour'd hag,
That for my company last night has wrought
This cure upon my fortune? I do sweat
To think upon her name.

  Aretina.   How, sir! A witch?

  Alexander. I would not fright your ladyship too much
At first, but witches are akin to spirits.
The truth is—nay, if you look pale already
I ha' done.

  Aretina. Sir, I beseech you.

  Alexander.   If you have

But courage then to know the truth, I'll tell you
In one word: my chief friend is the devil.
   Aretina. What devil? How I tremble!
   Alexander.   Have a heart;
'Twas a she-devil too, a most insatiate
Abominable devil, with a tail
Thus long.
   Aretina. Goodness defend me! Did you see her?
   Alexander. No; 'twas i' th' dark. But she appear'd first
     to me
I' th' likeness of a beldam, and was brought,
I know not how nor whither, by two goblins,
More hooded than a hawk.
   Aretina.   But would you venture
Upon a devil?
   Alexander. Ay, for means.
   Aretina [*Aside*].   How black
An impudence is this!—But are you sure
It was the devil you enjoy'd?
   Alexander.   Say nothing;
I did the best to please her; but as sure
As you live, 'twas a hell-cat.
   Aretina.   D'ye not quake?
   Alexander. I found myself the very same i' th' morning,
Where two of her familiars had left me.

            '*Enter* Servant.'

   Servant. My lord is come to visit you.
   Alexander.   No words,
As you respect my safety. I ha' told tales
Out of the devil's school; if it be known,
I lose a friend. 'Tis now about the time
I promis'd her to meet again. At my
Return I'll tell you wonders. Not a word! (*Exit* Alexander.
   Aretina [*Looking in her mirror*]. 'Tis a false glass: sure I
     am more deform'd.
What have I done? My soul is miserable.

            '*Enter* Lord.'

   Lord. I sent you a letter, madam.

Aretina.   **You express'd**
Your noble care of me, my lord.

'*Enter* Bornwell, Celestina.'

Bornwell. Your lordship
Does me an honour.

Lord [*To* Celestina]. Madam, I am glad
To see you here; I meant to have kiss'd your hand
Ere my return to court.

Celestina.   Sir Thomas has
Prevail'd to bring me, to his trouble, hither.

Lord. You do him grace.

Bornwell [*To* Aretina]. Why, what's the matter, madam?
Your eyes are tuning *Lachrimae.*

Aretina.   As you
Do hope for heaven, withdraw, and give me but
The patience of ten minutes.

Bornwell.   Wonderful!
I will not hear you above that proportion.
She talks of heaven. Come, where must we to counsel?

Aretina. You shall conclude me when you please.

Bornwell.   I follow.
                              [*Exit* Aretina.]

Lord [*Aside*]. What alteration is this? I, that so late
Stood the temptation of her eye and voice,
Boasted a heart 'bove all licentious flame,
At second view turn renegade, and think
I was too superstitious and full
Of phlegm not to reward her amorous courtship
With manly freedom.

Celestina.   I obey you, sir.

Bornwell. I'll wait upon your ladyship presently.
                              [*Exit* Bornwell.]

Lord [*Aside*]. She could not want a cunning to seem
honest
When I neglected her. I am resolv'd.—
You still look pleasant, madam.

Celestina.   I have cause,
My lord, the rather for your presence, which
Hath power to charm all trouble in my thoughts.

Lord. I must translate that compliment and owe
All that is cheerful in myself to these
All-quick'ning smiles; and rather than such bright
Eyes should repent their influence upon me,
I would release the aspects and quit the bounty
Of all the other stars. Did you not think me
A strange and melancholy gentleman
To use you so unkindly?

 Celestina.   Me, my lord?

 Lord. I hope you made no loud complaint: I would not
Be tried by a jury of ladies.

 Celestina.   For what, my lord?

 Lord. I did not meet that noble entertainment
You were late pleas'd to show me.

 Celestina.   I observ'd
No such defect in your lordship, but a brave
And noble fortitude.

 Lord.   A noble folly;
I bring repentance for't. I know you have,
Madam, a gentle faith, and will not ruin
What you have built to honour you.

 Celestina.   What's that?

 Lord. If you can love, I'll tell your ladyship.

 Celestina. I have a stubborn soul else.

 Lord.   You are all
Compos'd of harmony.

 Celestina.   What love d'ye mean?

 Lord. That which doth perfect both. Madam, you have
  heard
I can be constant, and if you consent
To grace it so, there is a spacious dwelling
Prepar'd within my heart for such a mistress.

 Celestina. Your mistress, my good lord?

 Lord.   Why, my good lady,
Your sex doth hold it no dishonour
To become mistress to a noble servant
In the now court Platonic way. Consider
Who 'tis that pleads to you; my birth and present
Value can be no stain to your embrace;
But these are shadows when my love appears,

Which shall in his first miracle return
Me in my bloom of youth and thee a virgin,
When I, within some new Elysium
Of purpose made and meant for us, shall be
In everything Adonis but in his
Contempt of love, and court thee from a Daphne
Hid in the cold rind of a bashful tree
With such warm language and delight till thou
Leap from that bays into the Queen of Love,
And pay my conquest with composing garlands
Of thy own myrtle for me.

   Celestina.   What's all this?

   Lord. Consent to be my mistress, Celestina,
And we will have it springtime all the year;
Upon whose invitations, when we walk,
The winds shall play soft descant to our feet,
And breathe rich odours to repure the air;
Green bowers on every side shall tempt our stay,
And violets stoop to have us tread upon 'em;
The red rose shall grow pale, being near thy cheek,
And the white blush, o'ercome with such a forehead.
Here laid, and measuring with ourselves some bank,
A thousand birds shall from the woods repair,
And place themselves so cunningly, behind
The leaves of every tree, that while they pay
Us tribute of their songs, thou shalt imagine
The very trees bear music, and sweet voices
Do grow in every arbour. Here can we
Embrace and kiss, tell tales, and kiss again,
And none but heaven our rival.

   Celestina.   When we are
Weary of these, what if we shift our paradise,
And through a grove of tall and even pine
Descend into a valley, that shall shame
All the delights of Tempe, upon whose
Green plush the Graces shall be call'd to dance,
To please us, and maintain their fairy revels
To the harmonious murmurs of a stream
That gently falls upon a rock of pearl?
Here doth the nymph, forsaken Echo, dwell,

To whom we'll tell the story of our love,
Till at our surfeit and her want of joy,
We break her heart with envy. Not far off,
A grove shall call us to a wanton river,
To see a dying swan give up the ghost,
The fishes shooting up their tears in bubbles
That they must lose the genius of their waves—
And such love linsey-woolsey, to no purpose.
    Lord. You chide me handsomely. Pray tell me how
You like this language.
    Celestina.   Good my lord, forbear.
    Lord. You need not fly out of this circle, madam.—
[*Aside*] These widows are so full of circumstance!—
I'll undertake, in this time I ha' courted
Your ladyship for the toy, to ha' broken ten,
Nay, twenty colts—virgins I mean—and taught 'em
The amble, or what pace I most affected.
    Celestina. You're not, my lord, again the lord I thought you,
And I must tell you now, you do forget
Yourself and me.
    Lord.   You'll not be angry, madam—
    Celestina. Nor rude, though gay men have a privilege.
It shall appear, there is a man, my lord,
Within my acquaintance, rich in worldly fortunes,
But cannot boast any descent of blood,
Would buy a coat of arms.
    Lord.   He may—and legs,
Booted and spurr'd to ride into the country.
    Celestina. But these will want antiquity, my lord,
The seal of honour. What's a coat cut out
But yesterday to make a man a gentleman?
Your family, as old as the first virtue
That merited an escutcheon, doth owe
A glorious coat of arms; if you will sell now
All that your name doth challenge in that ensign,
I'll help you to a chapman that shall pay,
And pour down wealth enough for't.
    Lord.   Sell my arms?
I cannot, madam.
    Celestina.   Give but your consent;

You know not how the state may be inclin'd
To dispensation; we may prevail
Upon the Herald's office afterward.

Lord. I'll sooner give these arms to th' hangman's axe,
My head, my heart, to twenty executions
Than sell one atom from my name.

Celestina.   Change that,
And answer him would buy my honour from me—
Honour that is not worn upon a flag
Or pennon, that without the owner's dangers
An enemy may ravish and bear from me,
But that which grows and withers with my soul.
Beside the body's stain, think, think, my lord,
To what you would unworthily betray me.
If you would not for price of gold or pleasure
(If that be more your idol) lose the glory
And painted honour of your house—I ha' done.

Lord. Enough to rectify a satyr's blood.
Obscure my blushes here.

                    '*Enter* Scentlove *and* Haircut.'

Haircut. Or this, or fight with me.
It shall be no exception that I wait
Upon my lord; I am a gentleman;
You may be less and be a knight. The office
I do my lord is honest, sir; how many
Such you have been guilty of heaven knows.

Scentlove. 'Tis no fear of your sword, but that I would not
Break the good laws establish'd against duels.

Haircut. Off with your periwig and stand bare.

Lord.   From this
Minute I'll be a servant to thy goodness.
A mistress in the wanton sense is common;
I'll honour you with chaste thoughts, and call you so.

Celestina. I'll study to be worth your fair opinion.

Lord. Scentlove, your head was us'd to a covering
Beside a hat; when went the hair away?

Scentlove. I laid a wager, my lord, with Haircut,
Who thinks I shall catch cold, that I'll stand bare
This half hour.

Haircut.   Pardon my ambition,
Madam, I told you truth: I am a gentleman,
And cannot fear that name is drown'd in my
Relation to my lord.

Celestina.   I dare not think so.

Haircut. From henceforth call my service duty, madam.
That pig's head that betray'd me to your mirth
Is doing penance for't.

Scentlove.   Why may not I,
My lord, begin a fashion of no hair?

Celestina. Do you sweat, Sir William?

Scentlove.   Not with store of nightcaps.

'*Enter* Aretina, Bornwell.'

Aretina. Heaven has dissolv'd the clouds that hung upon
My eyes, and if you can with mercy meet
A penitent, I throw my own will off,
And now in all things obey yours. My nephew
Send back again to th' college, and myself
To what place you'll confine me.

Bornwell.   Dearer now
Than ever to my bosom, thou shalt please
Me best to live at thy own choice. I did
But fright thee with a noise of my expenses;
The sums are safe, and we have wealth enough,
If yet we use it nobly.—My lord, madam,
Pray honour [us] tonight.

Aretina.   I beg your presence,
And pardon.

Bornwell. I know not how my Aretina
May be dispos'd tomorrow for the country.

Celestina. You must not go before you both have done
Me honour to accept an entertainment
Where I have power; on those terms I'm your guest.

Bornwell. You grace us, madam.

Aretina [*Aside*].   Already
I feel a cure upon my soul, and promise
My after life to virtue. Pardon, heaven,
My shame yet hid from the world's eye.

'*Enter* Decoy.'

Decoy. Sweet madam.
Aretina. Not for the world be seen here! We are lost.
I'll visit you at home—   [*Exit* Decoy.]
                    but not to practise
What she expects. My counsel may recover her.

'*Enter* Alexander.'

Alexander. Where's madam? Pray lend me a little money;
My spirit has deceiv'd me. Proserpine
Has broke her word.
Aretina.   Do you expect to find
The devil true to you?
Alexander.   Not too loud!
Aretina.   I'll voice it
Louder, to all the world, your horrid sin,
Unless you promise me religiously
To purge your foul blood by repentance, sir.
Alexander. Then I'm undone.
Aretina.   Not while I have power
To encourage you to virtue. I'll endeavour
To find out some nobler way at court
To thrive in.
Alexander. Do't, and I'll forsake the devil
And bring my flesh to obedience. You shall steer me.
My lord, your servant.
Lord.   You are brave again.
Alexander. Madam, your pardon.
Bornwell.   Your offence requires
Humility.
Alexander. Low as my heart. Sir Thomas,
I'll sup with you, a part of satisfaction.
Bornwell. Our pleasures cool. Music! And when our
        ladies
Are tir'd with active motion, to give
Them rest, in some new rapture to advance
Full mirth, our souls shall leap into a dance.
                              (*Exeunt omnes.*

FINIS.

THE
WEDDING.

AS IT VVAS LATELY

Acted by her Maiesties Seruants,
at the PHENIX in *Drury-*
Lane.

WRITTEN
By IAMES SHIRLEY, *Gent.*

Horat.——*Multaq; pars mei*
Vitabit Libitinam ——

LONDON;
Printed for *Iohn Groue*, and are to be sold at his Shop in
Chancery-Lane, neere the Rowles, ouer against the
Sappeny-Office. 1633.

To the Right Worshipful William Gowre, Esq.

Sir, I know you and in that your worth, which I honour more than greatness in a patron; this comedy, coming forth to take the air in summer, desireth to walk under your shadow. The world oweth a perpetual remembrance to your name, for excellency in the musical art of poesy, and your singular judgement and affection to it have encouraged me to this dedication, in which I cannot transgress beyond your candour. It hath passed the stage, and I doubt not but from you it shall receive a kind welcome, since you have been pleased to acknowledge the author

Yours,

JAMES SHIRLEY

THE ACTORS' NAMES

Sir John Belfare,	RICHARD PERKINS
Beauford, *a passionate lover of* Gratiana,	MICHAEL BOWYER
Marwood, *friend to* Beauford,	JOHN SUMPNER
Rawbone, *a thin citizen*,	WILLIAM ROBINS
Lodam, *a fat gentleman*,	WILLIAM SHERLOCK
Justice Landby,	ANTHONY TURNER
Captain Landby,	WILLIAM ALLIN
Isaac, Sir John's *man*,	WILLIAM WILBRAHAM
Haver, *a young gentleman, lover of* Mistress Jane, [*disguised as* Jasper],	JOHN YOUNG
Cameleon, Rawbone's *man*,	JOHN DOBSON
Physician.	
Surgeon.	
Keeper.	
Servants.	
Gratiana, Sir John's *daughter*,	HUGH CLARKE
Jane, Justice Landby's *daughter*,	JOHN PAGE
Milliscent, Cardona's *daughter* [Lucibel, *disguised as a young man*],	EDWARD ROGERS
Cardona.	TIMOTHY READ

THE WEDDING

ACT I · SCENE I

'*Enter* Sir John Belfare, *and* Isaac *his man, servants bringing in provision.*'

Belfare. Well done, my masters. Ye bestir yourselves; I see we shall feast tomorrow.

Servant. Your worship shall want no woodcocks at the wedding.

Isaac. Thou hast as many as thou canst carry, and thirteen to the last dozen.

Belfare. Isaac.

Isaac. Sir.

Belfare. Have you been careful to invite those friends you had direction for?

Isaac. Yes, sir; I have been a continual motion ever since I rose. I have not said my prayers today.

Belfare. We shall want no guests then.

Isaac. I have commanded most on 'em.

Belfare. How, sir?

Isaac. I ha' bid 'em, sir. There's two in my list will not fail to dine wi' ye.

Belfare. Who are they?

Isaac. Master Rawbone, the young usurer.

Belfare. Oh, he's reported a good trencherman. He has a tall stomach; he shall be welcome.

Isaac. They say he has made an obligation to the devil, if ever he eat a good meal at his own charge, his soul is forfeit.

Belfare. How does he live?

Isaac. Upon his money, sir.

Belfare. He does not eat it?

Isaac. No, the devil choke him! It were a golden age if all the usurers in London should ha' no other diet. He has a thin-gut waits upon him—I think one of his bastards, begot upon a spider. I hope to live to see 'em both drawn through a ring.

Belfare. Who is the other?

Isaac. The other may be known, too. The barrel at Heidelberg was the pattern of his belly—Master Lodam, sir.

Belfare. He's a great man indeed.

Isaac. Something given to the waste, for he lives within no reasonable compass, I'm sure.

Belfare. They will be well met.

Isaac. But very ill matched to draw a coach. Yet at provender there will be scarce an oat between the lean jade and the fat gelding.

Belfare. How lives he?

Isaac. Religiously, sir; for he that feeds well must by consequence live well. He holds none can be damned but lean men, for fat men he says must needs be saved by the faith of their body.

'*Enter* Master Beauford *and* Captain Landby.'

Belfare. Master Beauford and Captain Landby. Isaac, call forth my daughter.   [*Exit* Isaac.]

Beauford. Sir John, I hope you make no stranger of me; Tomorrow I shall change my title for
Your son, soon as the holy rites shall make me
The happy husband to your daughter. In the meantime
It will become me wait on her.

Belfare. I possess nothing but in trust for thee;
Gratiana makes all thine.   [*Exit* Beauford.]

Captain. I shall presume to follow.

Belfare. Your friendship, noble Captain, to Master Beauford
Makes your person most welcome,
Had you no other merit. Pray enter.   (*Exit* Captain.
Heaven hath already crown'd my grey hairs!
I live to see my daughter married
To a noble husband, the envy of our time,
And exact pattern of a gentleman,
As hopeful as the spring. I am grown proud,
Even in my age.   (*Exit* Belfare.

[SCENE II]

'Enter Marwood [*and* Isaac].'

Marwood. Dost hear, sirrah?

Isaac. Ay, sirrah.

Marwood. Is Master Beauford within?

Isaac. No, sir.

Marwood. I was informed he came hither. Is he not here?

Isaac. Yes, sir.

Marwood. Thou say'st he's not within.

Isaac. No, sir; but 'tis very like he will be tomorrow night, sir.

Marwood. How is this?

Isaac. Would you have him be within before he is married?

Marwood. Witty groom, prithee invite him forth. Say here's a friend.

Isaac. Now you talk of inviting, I have two or three guests to invite yet. Let me see.

Marwood. Why dost not move?

Isaac. An you make much ado, I'll invite you. Pray come to the wedding tomorrow. (*Exit* Isaac.

'Enter Sir John Belfare, Beauford, *and* Captain.'

Belfare. 'Tis he.

Beauford. You were my happy prospect from the window, coz; you are a most welcome guest.

Belfare. Master Marwood, you have been a great stranger to the city, or my house, for the coarse entertainment you received, hath been unworthy of your visit.

Marwood. 'Twas much above my desert, sir. Captain.

Captain. I congratulate your return.

Belfare. Beauford, gentlemen, enter my house, and perfect your embraces there. I lead the way. (*Exit* Belfare.

Beauford. Pray follow.

Marwood. Your pardon.

Captain. We know you have other habit;
You were not wont to affect ceremony.

'Marwood *and* Beauford *whisper.*'

Beauford. How?

Captain. I do not like his present countenance;
It does threaten somewhat. I would not prophesy.
Beauford. Good Captain,
Excuse my absence to our friends within.
I have affairs concerns me with my kinsman;
Which done, we both return to wait on 'em.
Captain. I shall, sir.   [*Exit* Captain.]
Beauford. Now proceed.
Marwood. We are kinsmen.
Beauford. More, we are friends.
Marwood. And shall I doubt to speak to Beauford anything
My love directs me to?
Beauford. What needs this circumstance?
We were not wont to talk at such a distance.
You appear wild.
Marwood. I have been wild indeed
In my ungovern'd youth, but ha' reclaim'd it,
And am so laden with the memory of former errors
That I desire to be confess'd.
Beauford. Confess'd? I am no ghostly father.
Marwood. But you must hear; you may absolve me too.
Beauford. If thou hast any discontentments,
Prithee take other time for their discourse.
I am in expectation of marriage;
I would not interrupt my joys.
Marwood. I must require your present hearing;
It concerns us both, as near as fame, or life.
Beauford. Ha! What is it?
Marwood. We shall have opportunity at your lodging;
The streets are populous and full [of] noise.
So please you, walk. I'll wait on you.
Beauford. I'm your servant.

                    (*Exeunt* Beauford *and* Marwood.

[SCENE III]
'*Enter* Justice Landby *and* Milliscent.'

Justice. Milliscent, where's my daughter?
Milliscent. In compliment with Master Rawbone,
Who is newly enter'd, sir.

Justice. Oh, there's a piece of folly!
A thing made up of parchment; and his bonds
Are of more value than his soul and body,
Were any man the purchaser; only wise
In his hereditary trade of usury;
Understands nothing but a scrivener,
As if he were created for no use
But to grow rich with interest. To his ignorance,
He has the gift of being impudent.
What will he grow to, if he live, that is
So young a monster?

Milliscent. With your favour, sir,
If you hold no better opinion of this citizen,
It puzzles me why you invite him to
Your house and entertainment, he pretending
Affection to your daughter. Pardon me, sir,
If I seem bold.

Justice. As some men, Milliscent,
Do suffer spiders in their chamber, while
They count them profitable vermin.

Milliscent. But he's most like to scatter poison, sir.
Your fame is precious, and your family,
Not mingling with corrupted streams, hath like
An entire river still maintain'd his current
Chaste and delightful.

Justice. Shalt receive my bosom.
I'll sooner match her with an Ethiop
Than give consent she should disgrace our blood.
And herein I but try her strength of judgement
In giving him access. If she have lost
Remembrance of her birth and generous thoughts
She suck'd from her dead mother, with my care
I'll strive to reinforce her native goodness,
Or quite divorce her from my blood. And, Milliscent,
I'll use your vigilance.

Milliscent. Sir, command.

Justice. I will
Not urge how I receiv'd you first a stranger,
Nor the condition of your life with me,

Above the nature of a servant, to
Oblige your faith. I have observ'd thee honest.

Milliscent. You are full of noble thoughts.

Justice. Though I suspect not
The obedience of my daughter, yet her youth
Is apt to err. Let me employ your eye
Upon her still, and receive knowledge from you
How she dispenseth favours. You shall bind
My love the stronger to you.

Milliscent. Sir, I shall be ambitious to deserve your
favour
With all the duties of a servant, and
I doubt not but your daughter is so full
Of conscience and care in the conformity
Of her desires to your will, I shall
Enrich my sight with observation,
And make my intelligence happy.

'*Enter* Cameleon.'

Justice. How now, what's he?

Milliscent. 'Tis Master Rawbone's squire.

Cameleon. Pray, is not my master's worship here?

Justice. Your master's worship? What's that, his spaniel?

Cameleon. No, sir, but a thing that does follow him.

Justice. In what likeness? I hope he does not converse
with spirits.

Cameleon. He'll not entertain an angel but he will weigh
him first. Indeed, I am all the spirits that belong to him.

Milliscent. So I think, but none of his familiar.

Justice. What's thy name?

Cameleon. Cameleon.

Justice. Good; didst ever eat?

Cameleon. Yes, once.

Justice. And then thou caught'st a surfeit, thou could'st
ne'er endure meat since. Wert ever christened?

Cameleon. Yes, twice: first in my infancy, and the last
time about a year ago, when I should have been prentice to
an Anabaptist.

Justice. Does thy master love thee?

Cameleon. Yes, for an I would gold, I might have it; but

my stomach would better digest beef or mutton, if there be any such things in nature.

Milliscent. Here is his master, sir, and Mistress Jane.

'*Enter* Rawbone *and* Jane.'

Rawbone. How now, Cameleon, hast dined?

Cameleon. Yes, sir; I had a delicate fresh air to dinner.

Rawbone. And yet thou look'st as thou hadst eat nothing this sennight. Here, provide me a capon and half a dozen of pigeons to supper.—And when will your worship come home and taste my hospitality?

Jane. When you please, sir.

Rawbone. Yet now I think on't, I must feed more sparingly.

Jane. More liberally, in my opinion.

Rawbone. Would not anybody in the world think so? Did you ever see two such earwigs as my man and I? Do we not look like?

Jane. I think the picture of either o' your faces in a ring, with a *memento mori*, would be as sufficient a mortification as lying with an anatomy.

Rawbone. The reason why we are so lean and consumed is nothing but eating too much. Cameleon, now I think on't, let the pigeons alone, the capon will be enough for thee and I.

Cameleon [*Aside*]. The rump would last us a sennight.

Rawbone. I tell you, forsooth, I ha' brought myself so low with a great diet, that I must be temperate, or the doctor says there's no way but one wi' me.

Cameleon [*Aside*]. That's not the way of all flesh, I'm sure.

Rawbone. It is a shame to say what we eat every day.

Jane. I think so.

Cameleon [*Aside*]. By this hand—if it would bear an oath—we have had nothing this two days but half a lark, which by a mischance the cat had killed too, the cage being open. I will provide my belly another master.

Justice [*Aside*]. Now I'll interrupt 'em.—Master Rawbone.

Rawbone. I hope your worship will reprieve my boldness; 'tis out of love to your daughter.

Justice. Sir, I have a business to you: a friend of mine upon some necessity would take up a hundred pounds.

Rawbone. I'll pawn some ounces to pleasure him.

Justice. It is more friendly said than I expected.

Rawbone. So he bring me good security, some three or four or five sufficient and able citizens for mortality's sake, I'll lend it him.

Justice. Will you not take an honest man's word?

Rawbone. Few words to the wise: I will take any man's word to owe me a hundred pound, but not a lord's to pay me fifty.

Justice. Well, 'tis a courtesy.

Rawbone. He shall pay nothing to me but lawful consideration from time to time, beside the charges of th' ensealing, because he is your friend.

Justice. This is extremity; can you require more?

Rawbone. More? What's eight in the hundred to me? My scrivener knows I have taken forty and fifty in the hundred, *viis* and *modis*, of my own kinsmen when they were in necessity.

Justice. I apprehend the favour.

'*Enter* Isaac.'

How now, Isaac.

Isaac. My master commends his love to you, sir, and does desire your presence together with your daughter and nephew, at the arraignment of my young mistress tomorrow.

Justice. How, knave?

Isaac. She is to be married, or arraigned, i' th' morning, and at night to suffer execution and lose her head.

Justice. Return our thanks, and say we'll wait upon the bride. Jane.   (*Exeunt* Justice *and* Jane.

Isaac. Dear Master Rawbone, I do beseech you be at these sessions.

Rawbone. Thou didst invite me before.

Isaac. I know it, but our cook has a great mind that sentence should likewise pass upon the roast, the boiled, and the baked, and he fears unless you be a commissioner the meat will hardly be condemned tomorrow, so that I can

never often enough desire your stomach to remember you
will come.

Rawbone. Dost think I will not keep my word?

Isaac. Alas, we have nothing but good cheer to entertain
you. I beseech you, sir, howsoever, to feast with us, though
you go away after dinner.

Rawbone. There's my hand.

Isaac. I thank you.

Rawbone. Is Master Justice gone, and Mistress Jane too?
Follow me, Cameleon; I'll take my leave when I come again.

[*Exeunt* Rawbone *and* Isaac.]

Milliscent. Isaac.

Isaac. My little wit, thou wilt come with thy master
tomorrow? I'll reserve a bottle of wine to warm thy sconce.

Milliscent. I cannot promise.

Isaac. If I durst stay three minutes, I would venture a
cup with thee i' th' buttery; but 'tis a busy time at home.
Farewell, Milliscent.   (*Exit* Isaac.

Milliscent. Marriage! As much joy wait upon the bride
As the remembrance of it brings me sorrow.
A woman has undone me; when I die
A coffin will enclose this misery.   (*Exit* Milliscent.

[SCENE IV]

'*Enter* Beauford *and* Marwood.'

Beauford. You prepare me for some wonder.

Marwood. I do;
And ere I come to the period of my story,
Your understanding will admire.

Beauford. Teach my soul the way.

Marwood. I am not, coz, i' th' number of those friends
Come to congratulate your present marriage.

Beauford. Ha!

Marwood. I am no flatterer: the blood you carry
Doth warm my veins, yet could nature be
Forgetful and remove itself, the love
I owe your merit doth oblige me to
Relation of a truth which else would fire

My bosom with concealment. I am come
To divide your soul, ravish all your pleasures,
Poison the very air maintains your breathing:
You must not marry.

    Beauford. Must not? Though as I
Am mortal I may be compell'd within
A pair of minutes to turn ashes, yet
My soul, already bridegroom to her virtue,
Shall laugh at death that would unmarry us,
And call her mine eternally.

    Marwood. Death is
A mockery to that divorce I bring.
Come, you must not love her.

    Beauford. Did I hope thou could'st
Give me a reason, I would ask one.

    Marwood. Do not;
It will too soon arrive, and make you curse
Your knowledge. Could'st exchange thy temper for
An angel's, at the hearing of this reason
'Twould make you passionate and turn man again.

    Beauford. Can there be reason for a sin so great
As changing my affection from Gratiana?
Name it, and teach me how to be a monster,
For I must lose humanity. O Marwood,
Thou lead'st me into a wilderness. She is—

    Marwood. False, sinful. A black soul she has.

    Beauford. Thou hast a hell about thee, and thy language
Speaks thee a devil, that to blast her innocence
Dost belch these vapours. To say thou liest
Were to admit thou hast but made in this
A human error, when thy sin hath aim'd
The fall of goodness. Gratiana false?
The snow shall turn a salamander first,
And dwell in fire; the air retreat, and leave
An emptiness in nature; angels be
Corrupt, and, brib'd by mortals, sell their charity.
Her innocence is such, that wert thou, Marwood,
For this offence condemn'd to lodge in flames,
It would for ever cure thy burning fever
If with thy sorrow thou procure her shed

One tear upon thee. Now, thou art lost for ever,
And arm'd thus, though with thousand furies guarded,
I reach thy heart.   '*Draws*.'

    Marwood. Stay, Beauford!
Since you dare be so confident of her chastity,
Hear me conclude. I bring no idle fable
Patch'd up between suspicion and report
Of scandalous tongues; my ears were no assurance
To convince me without my eyes.

    Beauford. What horror!
Be more particular.

    Marwood. I did prophesy
That it would come to this, for I have had
A tedious struggling with my nature, but
The name of friend o'er-balanc'd the exception.
Forgive me, ladies, that my love to man
Hath power to make me guilty of such language
As with it must betray a woman's honour.

    Beauford. You torture me; be brief.

    Marwood. Then though it carry shame to the reporter,
Forgive me, heaven, and witness an unwelcome truth.

    Beauford. Stay; I am too hasty for the knowledge
Of something thou prepar'st for my destruction.
May I not think what 'tis, and kill myself?
Or at least by degrees, with apprehending
Some strange thing done, infect my fancy with
Opinion first, and so dispose myself
To death? I cannot; when I think of Gratiana,
I entertain a heaven. The worst, I'll hear it.

    Marwood. It will enlarge itself too soon; receive it:
I have enjoy'd her.

    Beauford. Whom?

    Marwood. Gratiana, sinfully, before your love
Made she and you acquainted.

    Beauford. Ha! Thou'st kept thy word thou cam'st to
poison all
My comfort.

    Marwood. Your friendship I ha' preferr'd
To my own fame; and, but to save you from
A lasting shipwreck, noble Beauford, think

It should have rotted here. She that will part
With virgin honour ne'er should wed the heart.

    Beauford. Was ever woman good and Gratiana
Vicious? Lost to honour? At the instant
When I expected all my harvest ripe,
The golden summer tempting me to reap
The well-grown ears, comes an impetuous storm
Destroys an age's hope in a short minute,
And lets me live, the copy of man's frailty.
Surely some one of all the female sex
Engross'd the virtues, and, fled hence to heaven,
Left womankind dissemblers.

    Marwood. Sir, make use
Of reason; 'tis a knowledge should rejoice you,
Since it does teach you to preserve yourself.

    Beauford. Enjoy'd Gratiana sinfully! 'Tis a sound
Able to kill with horror. It infects
The very air; I see it like a mist
Dwell round about, that I could uncreate
Myself, be forgotten, no remembrance
That ever I lov'd woman. I have no
Genius left to instruct me.—It grows late.—

Within.   [*Enter* Servant]
Wait o' my kinsman to his chamber.—
[*To* Marwood] I shall desire your rest; pray give me leave
To think a little.

    Marwood. Cousin, I repent
I have been so open-breasted, since you make
This severe use on't, and afflict your mind
With womanish sorrow. I have but caution'd you
Against a danger, out of my true friendship.
Prosper me, goodness, as my ends are noble.
Goodnight; collect yourself, and be a man.

                    (*Exeunt* Marwood *and* Servant.

    Beauford. And why may not a kinsman be a villain?
Perhaps he loves Gratiana, and envying
My happiness, doth now traduce her chastity.
To find this out time will allow but narrow
Limits. His last words bade me be a man.
A man! Yes, I have my soul; 't does not become

A manly resolution to be tame thus,
And give up the opinion of his mistress
For one man's accusation.—Ha! I' th' morning?
Proper. Yes, Marwood, I will be a man.
His sword shall either make [me] past the sense
Of this affliction, or mine enforce
A truth from him. If thou be'st wrong'd, Gratiana,
I'll die thy martyr; but if false, in this
I gain to die, not live a sacrifice.   (*Exit* Beauford.

ACT II · SCENE I

'*Enter* Cardona *and* Isaac.'

Cardona. To the tailor's man, run!

Isaac. To the tailor's man? Why not to his master?

Cardona. The wedding clothes not brought home yet! Fie, fie!

Isaac. Who would trust a woman's tailor: take measure so long before of a gentlewoman, and not bring home his commodity? There's no conscience in't.

Cardona. The arrant shoe-maker, too.

Isaac. Master Hide, is he not come yet? I called upon him yesterday, to make haste of my mistress' shoes, and he told me he was about the upper-leather—he would be at her heels presently. I left his foot in the stirrup; I thought he would have rid post after me.

Cardona. Prithee, Isaac, make haste. How tedious thou'rt. Hast not thou been there yet?

Isaac. Oh yes, and here again. D'ye not see me? You are so light yourself.

Cardona. As thou goest, call upon Cod the perfumer. Tell him he uses us sweetly, h'as not brought home the gloves yet. And, dost hear, when thou'rt at the Peacock, remember to call for the sprig. By the same token, I left my fan to be mended. And, dost hear, when thou'rt there, 'tis but a little out of the way to run to the Devil and bid the vintner make haste with the runlets of claret; we shall ha' no time to burn it.

Isaac. You need not if it comes from the Devil. Methinks that wine should burn itself.

Cardona. Run, I prithee.

Isaac. Tailors, shoemakers, perfumers, feather-makers, and the devil and all—what a many occupations does a woman run through before she is married.   (*Exit* Isaac.

Cardona. Fie upon't, what a perplexity is about a wedding! I might have been thus troubled for a child of my own, if good luck had served.

[*Gratiana*] ('*Within*'). Cardona.

Cardona. I come, lady bird.   (*Exit* Cardona.

[SCENE II]

'*Enter* Beauford *and* Marwood.'

Marwood. Was this your purpose?

Beauford. This place of all the park affords most privacy. Nature has plac'd the trees to imitate
A Roman amphitheatre.

Marwood. We must be the sword-players.

Beauford. Draw! Imagine all
These trees were cypress, the companions of
Our funeral, for one or both must go
To a dark habitation. Methinks
We two are like to some unguided men,
That having wander'd all the day in a
Wild unknown path, at night walk down into
A hollow grot, a cave which never star
Durst look into, made in contempt of light
By nature, which the moon did never yet
Befriend with any melancholy beam.
O cousin, thou hast led me where I never
Shall see day more.

Marwood. This is the way to make it
A night indeed. But if you recollect
Yourself, I brought you beams to let you see
The horror of that darkness you are going to
By marrying with Gratiana.

Beauford. That name
Awakes my resolution. Consume not

Thy breath too idly; thou'st but a small time
For th'use on't. Either employ it in the unsaying
Thy wrong to Gratiana, or thou hastens
Thy last minute.

    Marwood. I must tell Beauford then
He is ungrateful to return so ill
My friendship. Have I undervalued
My shame in the relation of a truth,
To make the man I would preserve my enemy?
Why dost thou tempt thy destiny with so
Much sin? Dost think I wear a sword I dare
Not manage, or that I can be enforc'd
To a revolt? I am no rebel, Beauford.
Again I must confirm Gratiana's honour
Stain'd, the treasures of her chastity
Rifled and lost. 'Twas my unhappiness
To have added that unto my other sins
I' th' wildness of my blood, which thou may'st punish.

    Beauford. Thou hast repeated but the same in
Substance touching Gratiana.

    Marwood. Truth is ever constant,
Remains upon her square, firm and unshaken.

    Beauford. If what thou hast affirm'd be true, why should
We fight, be cruel to ourselves, endanger
Our eternity, for the error of
One frail woman? Let our swords expect
A nobler cause. What man hath such assurance
In any woman's faith that he should run
A desperate hazard of his soul? I know
Women are not born angels, but created
With passion and temper like to us;
And men are apt to err, and lose themselves,
Caught with the smile of wanton beauty, fetter'd
Even with their mistresses' hair.

    Marwood. I like this well.

    Beauford ('*Aside*'). He has a handsome presence and discourse,
Two subtle charms to tempt a woman's frailty,
Who must be govern'd by their eye or ear
To love. Beside, my kinsman hath been tax'd

For being too prompt in wantonness. This confirms it.—
Then farewell, womankind.

   Marwood. This does become you.

   Beauford. Why should we fight? Our letting blood will not
Cure her, and make her honour white again.
We are friends. Repent thy sin, and marry her.

   Marwood. Whom?

   Beauford. Gratiana.

   Marwood. How, sir, marry her?

   Beauford. Why, canst thou add to it another crime,
By a refusing to repair the ruins
Of that chaste temple thou hadst violated?
Her virgin tapers are by thee extinct,
No odour of her chastity, which once
Gave a perfume to heaven and did refresh
Her innocent soul. They that have spoil'd virginity
Do half restore the treasures they took thence
By sacred marriage.

   Marwood. Marriage? With whom?

   Beauford. Gratiana.

   Marwood. Should I marry a whore?

   Beauford. Thou liest; and with a guilt upon thy soul
Able to sink thee to damnation,   *'Draws again.'*
I'll send thee hence. A whore? What woman
Was ever bad enough to deserve that name?
Salute some native fury, or a wretch
Condemn'd already to hell's torture by it,
Not Gratiana. Thou'st awaken'd justice,
And given it eyes to see thy treachery,
The depth of thy malicious heart. That word hath
Disenchanted me.

   Marwood. Are you serious?

   Beauford. How have I sinn'd in my credulity
'Gainst virtue all this while! What charm bound up
My understanding part, I should admit
A possibility for her to carry
So black a soul, though all her sex beside
Had fallen from their creation? Thou hast
Not life enough to forfeit—what an advantage
To fame and goodness had been lost!

Marwood. Will you fight?

Beauford. Wert thou defenc'd with circular fire, more
Subtle than the lightning, that I knew would ravish
My heart and marrow from me, yet I should
Neglect the danger, and, but singly arm'd,
Fly to revenge thy calumny. A whore! Come on, sir! '*Fight.*'
Thou'rt wounded, ha?

Marwood. Mortally. Fly, Beauford, save thyself. I hasten
   to the dead.

Beauford. Oh, stay a while, or thou wilt lose us both.
Thy wound I cannot call back. Now there is
No dallying with heaven, but thou pull'st on thee
Double confusion. Leave a truth behind thee,
As thou would'st hope rest to thy parting soul:
Hast thou not wrong'd Gratiana?

Marwood. Yes, in my lust, but not in my report.
Take my last breath: I sinfully enjoy'd her.

'*One hollas within.*'

Gratiana is a blotted piece of alabaster.
Farewell, lest some betray thee. Heaven forgive
My offence, as I do freely pardon thine.

Beauford. I cannot long survive;
Is there no hope thou may'st recover?

Marwood. Oh!

Beauford. Farewell for ever then. With thy short breath
May all thy ills conclude; mine but begin
To muster. Life and I shall quickly part;
I feel a sorrow will break Beauford's heart.

(*Exit* Beauford.

'*Enter* Keeper *and* Servant.'

Servant. There are coney-catchers abroad, sir.

Keeper. These whoreson rabbit-suckers will ne'er leave
the ground.

Servant. In my walk last night I frighted some on 'em.
Pox a' these vermin! Would they were all destroyed.

Keeper. So we may chance to keep no deer.

Servant. Why so?

Keeper. An old coney stops a knave's mouth sometimes
that else would be gaping for venison.

Marwood. Oh!

Keeper. Who's that?

Servant. Here's a gentleman wounded.

Keeper. Ha!

Servant. He has bled much.

Keeper. How came you hurt, sir? No, not speak? If he be not past hope, let us carry him to my lodge. My wife is a piece of a surgeon has been fortunate in some cures. Tear a piece of thy shirt, Ralph, to bind his wound quickly. So, so. Alas, poor gentleman, he may live to be dressed, and tell who has done this misfortune. Gently, honest Ralph. He has some breath yet. Would I had my bloodhound here.

('*Exeunt, carry him in.*'

[SCENE III]

'*Enter* Sir John Belfare, Justice Landby, *and his
daughter* Jane, Isaac *waiting.*'

Belfare. You're welcome, Master Landby, and Mistress Jane.

Where's the young captain, sir, your nephew?

Justice. He went betimes to wait upon the bridegroom.

Belfare. They are inseparable friends, as they had divided hearts; they both are glad when either meet a good fortune.

Jane. I'll be bold to see your daughter.

Belfare. Do, Mistress Jane. She has her maid's blush yet; she'll make you amends for this, and ere't be long, I hope, dance at your wedding.   (*Exit* Jane.

Justice. I wish you many joys, sir, by this marriage. Your daughter has made discreet election; she'll have a hopeful gentleman.

Belfare. Master Landby, it would refresh my age to see her fruitful to him; I should find a blessing for a young Beauford and glad to dandle him. The first news of a boy borne by my daughter would set me back seven years. Oh, Master Landby, old men do never truly dote until their children bring 'em babies.

'*Enter* Master Rawbone, *and* Haver [*dressed*] *as his servant.*'

Isaac. Master Rawbone, I'll be bold to present you with a piece of rosemary; we ha' such cheer.

Rawbone. Honest Isaac.

Isaac. Pray do you belong to Master Rawbone?

Haver. Yes, sir.

Isaac. You have eat something in your days?

Haver. Why, prithee?

Isaac. Nothing, nothing, d'ye understand, nothing. You shall eat nothing, unless some benefactors like my master, in pity of your belly, once a year do warm it with a dinner, you must never hope to see roast or sod. He has within this twelvemonth to my knowledge made seven men immortal.

Haver. How!

Isaac. Yes, he has made spirits on 'em, and they haunt such men's houses as my master's, spirits o' th' buttery. Let me counsel ye to cram your corpse today, for by his almanac there's a long Lent a-coming.

Belfare. Never see me but when you are invited.

Rawbone. 'Las, I had rather eat a piece of cold capon at home than be troublesome abroad. I hope, forsooth, Mistress Jane is as she should be.

Justice. She is in health.

Belfare. You've a fresh servant. Master Rawbone, a proper fellow, and maintains himself handsomely.

Rawbone. An he would not ha' maintained himself, I had never entertained him.

Isaac. Where's Cameleon?

Rawbone. I ha' preferred him, Isaac.

Isaac. How?

Rawbone. Turned him away last night, and took this stripling.

'Enter Captain [Landby].'

Captain. 'Morrow, Sir John, where is the early bridegroom?

Justice. Came not you from him?

Belfare. We expect him, sir, every minute.

Captain. Not yet come? His servants told me he went abroad before the morning blushed.

Belfare. We ha' not seen him. Pray heaven he be in health.

Captain. I wonder at his absence.

Rawbone. Captain Landby, young man of war, I do salute thee with a broadside.

Captain. D'ye hear: they say you come a-wooing to my cousin; that day you marry her, I'll cut your throat. Keep 't to yourself.

Haver [*Aside*]. Thou art a noble fellow; things may prosper.

Captain. You come hither to wish God give 'em joy now?

Rawbone. Yes, marry, do I.

Captain. You do lie; you come to scour your dirty maw with the good cheer, which will be damned in your lean barathrum, that kitchen-stuff devourer.

Rawbone. Why should you say so, Captain? My belly did ne'er think you any harm.

Captain. When it does vomit up thy heart, I'll praise it. In the meantime would every bit thou eat'st today were steeped in *aqua fortis*.

Rawbone. What is that, Jasper?

Haver. It is strong water.

Rawbone. Noble Captain, thanks i' faith, heartily. I was afraid you had been angry.

Captain. I'll ha' thee sewed up in a money-bag, and boiled to jelly.

Rawbone. You shall ha' me at your service, and my bags too, upon good security. Is not this better than quarrelling, Jasper?

'*Enter* Cardona.'

Cardona. Is not the bridegroom come yet? Sure he has overslept himself. There is nothing but wondering within. All the maids are in uproar: one says he is a slow thing, another says she knows not what to say; but they all conclude, if ever they marry, they'll make it in their bargain to be sure of all things before matrimony. Fie upon him! If I were to be his wife, I'd show him a trick for 't ere a year came about, or it should cost me a fall, I warrant him. (*Exit* Cardona.

Justice. Sir John, you're troubled.

Belfare. Can you blame me, sir?
I would not have our morning's expectation
Frustrate. I know not what to think.
　Justice. Sir, fear not.
　Belfare. The morn grows old.
　Justice. Hymen has long tapers.
　Belfare. What should procure his absence? He departed
But oddly yesterday.
　Captain. Marwood had engag'd him;
They promis'd to return.
　Belfare. But we see neither.
　Justice. They'll come together; make it not your fear.
Beauford's a gentleman, and cannot be
Guilty of doing such affront, unless
Some misfortune—
　Belfare. That's another jealousy.

'*Enter* Lodam, Cameleon *waiting upon him.*'

　Lodam. Where is Sir John Belfare?
　Belfare. Ha! Master Lodam,
Welcome.
　Lodam. I congratulate—
　Belfare. Saw you Master Beauford, sir?
　Lodam. Yes, I saw him, but—
　Justice. But what?
　Lodam. I know not how he does.
Where is the lady that must be undone tonight,
Your daughter?
　Belfare. My daughter undone? Name what unhappiness—
My heart already doth begin to prophesy
Her unkind fate. Name what disaster, give it
Expression, pray; what is the news?
　Lodam. The news?
Why, would ye know the news? 'Tis none o' th' best.
　Justice. Be temperate, then, in your relation.
　Belfare. What is't?
　Lodam. They say for certain, there were four and twenty
colliers cast away, coming from Newcastle. 'Tis cold news
i' th' city, but there is worse news abroad.
　Belfare. Doth it concern my knowledge? Trifle not.

Lodam. They say that Canary sack must dance again to the apothecaries, and be sold for physic, in hum-glasses and thimbles; that the Spa-water must be transported hither and be drunk instead of French wines. For my part, I am one—

Haver [*Aside*]. Big enough for two.

Lodam. This citadel may endure as long a siege as another. If the pride of my flesh must be pulled down, farewell it. 'T has done me service this forty year. Let it go.

Belfare. Saw you Master Beauford?

Lodam. Yes, Sir John, I saw him, but —'twas three days ago.

Captain. He is ridiculous.

Justice. Do not afflict yourself;
He will give a fair account at his return.

Belfare. Pray heaven he may.

'*Enter* Gratiana, Jane, *and* Cardona.'

My daughter.

Rawbone. Sir, I desire to be acquainted with you.

Lodam. I have no stomach, sir, to your acquaintance; you are a thought too lean.

Rawbone. And you a bit too fat.

Belfare. Dost not wonder, girl, at Beauford's absence?

Gratiana. Not at all, sir; I am not now to learn
Opinion of his nobleness; and I hope
Your judgements will not permit you sin so much
To censure him for this stay.
Fair morning to Master Landby, noble Captain, Master Lodam and the rest.

Rawbone. I am so little
She cannot see me. Give you joy, forsooth;
I hope it is your destiny to be married.

Captain. And yours to be hang'd.

Rawbone. How, sir?

Haver. No harm,
He wishes you long life.

Rawbone. A long halter he does.
What, to be hang'd?

Haver. 'Las, sir, he knows you ha' no flesh to burden you;
Light as a feather, hanging will ne'er kill you.
If he had wish'd, sir, Master Lodam hang'd—

Rawbone. Then I'll to him and thank him.
But here's Mistress Jane.

Captain. You shall command me as your servant. [*To*
Rawbone] Sirrah!

'*Exit. As he goes out he sees* Rawbone *court* Jane.'

Rawbone. I did but ask her how she did. I said never a
word to her. Pox upon his bouncing! I am as fearful of him
as of a gun, he does so powder me.

Gratiana. We have not seen you, sir, this great while.
You fall away, methinks.

Lodam. Losing Lodam, I.

Gratiana. You are not the least welcome, sir.

Lodam. I do give you great thanks, and do mean to dance
at your wedding for't. I do marvel Master Beauford is not
earlier. I should ha' been here with music, lady, and have
fiddled you, too, before you were up. These lean lovers ha'
nothing in 'em, slow men of London.

Belfare. Gratiana.   '*Lodam spies* Jane.'

Lodam. Who's this? She has a mortal eye.

Isaac. Cameleon! How now, turn'd away your master?

Cameleon. No, I sold my place. As I was thinking to run
away, comes this fellow and offered me a breakfast for my
goodwill to speak to my master for him. I took him at his
word and resigned my office, and turned over my hunger to
him immediately. Now I serve a man, Isaac.

Belfare. Isaac.   '*Exit* Isaac *as sent off.*'

Lodam. I do foresee a fall of this tower already; love
begins to undermine it.—Mistress, a word in private.

Rawbone. Jasper, hast a sword?

Haver. Yes, sir.

Rawbone. That's well, let it alone. Did'st see this paunch
affront me?

Haver. He did it in love to the gentlewoman.

Rawbone. In love? Let me see the sword again.

'[Haver] *draws*'.

Would 'twere in his belly. Put it up; thou deserv'st a good
blade, 'tis so well kept.

'*Enter* Isaac.'

Isaac. Master Beauford, Master Beauford!
Belfare. Where?
Isaac. Hard by, within a stone's cast a' my mistress.
Here, sir, here.

'*Enter* Beauford.'

Gratiana. My dearest Beauford, where hast been so long?
Beauford. Oh, Gratiana!
Gratiana. Are you not in health?
Belfare. Not well? 'Tis then no time to chide.
How fare you, sir?
Beauford. I have a trouble at my heart. Pardon
The trespass o' your patience, gentlemen,
I'll publish the occasion of my absence,
So first you give me leave to unlade it here.
But, with your favour, I desire I may
Exempt all ears but Gratiana's, till
A short time ripen it for your knowledge.
Belfare. Ha!
Justice. Let's leave 'em then a while.
Belfare. Into the garden, gentlemen.
Rawbone. With all my heart. In my conscience they'll be
honest together.
Belfare. This begets my wonder. Master Lodam.
Lodam. Good Sir John, I'll wait upon you; it is dinner-
time.

(*Exeunt all except* Beauford *and* Gratiana.
Beauford. I have not time to dwell on circumstance.
I come to take my last leave. You and I
Must never meet again.
Gratiana. What language do I hear?
If Beauford's, it should strike me dead.
Beauford. This day I had design'd for marriage, but I
must
Pronounce we are eternally divorc'd.
O Gratiana, thou hast made a wound
Beyond the cure of surgery. Why did nature
Empty her treasure in thy face and leave thee
A black prodigious soul?

Gratiana. Defend me, goodness!

Beauford. Call upon darkness to obscure thee rather,
That never more thou may'st be seen by mortal.
Get thee some dwelling in a mist, or in
A wild forsaken earth, a wilderness,
Where thou may'st hide thyself and die forgotten.

Gratiana. Where was I lost? Name what offence provok'd
This heavy doom. Dear Beauford, be not so
Injust to sentence me before I know
What is my crime; or, if you will not tell
What sin it is I have committed, great
And horrid as your anger, let me study:
I'll count 'em all before you. Never did
Penitent in confession strip the soul
More naked. I'll unclasp my book of conscience;
You shall read o'er my heart, and if you find
In that great volume but one single thought
Which concern'd you and did not end with some
Good prayer for you, O be just, and kill me.

Beauford. Be just, and tell thy conscience thou'st abus'd it,
False woman. Why dost thou increase thy horror
By the obscuring a misdeed, which would,
Were all thy other sins forgiven, undo thee.
O Gratiana, thou art—

Gratiana. What am I?

Beauford. A thing I would not name; it sounds so fearfully,
'Twould make a devil blush to be saluted
By that which thou must answer to.

Gratiana. I fear—

Beauford. That fear betrays thy guilt. Tell me, Gratiana,
What didst thou see in me to make thee think
I was not worthy of thee at thy best
And richest value, when thou wert as white
In soul as beauty? For sure, once thou wert so.
Hadst thou so cheap opinion of my birth,
My breeding, or my fortunes, that none else
Could serve for property of your lust but I?

Gratiana. Dear Beauford, hear me!

Beauford. A common father to thy sin-got issue,

A patron of thy rifled, unchaste womb?
Oh, thou wert cruel, to reward so ill
The heart that truly honour'd thee. Thy name,
Which sweeten'd once the breath of him that spake it,
And musically charm'd the gentle ear,
Shall sound hereafter like a screech-owl's note,
And fright the hearer. Virgins shall lament
That thou hast sham'd their chaste society,
And oft as Hymen lights his tapers up,
At the remembrance of thy name, shed tears,
And blush for thy dishonour. From this minute
Thy friends shall count thee desperately sick,
And whensoe'er thou goest abroad, that day
The maids and matrons, thinking thou art dead
And going to the grave, shall all come forth
And wait like mourners on thee.
   Gratiana. Ha' ye done?
Then hear me a few syllables. You have
Suspicion that I am dishonour'd.
   Beauford. No,
By heaven I have not; I have too much knowledge
To suspect thee sinful; but in the assurance
Of it I must disclaim thy heart for ever.
Gratiana, my opinion of thy whiteness
Hath made my soul as black as thine already.
Weep till thou wash away thy stain, and then,
I' th' other world, we two may meet again. (*Exit* Beauford.
   Gratiana. Weep inward, eyes, hither your streams impart,
For sure, I have tears enough to drown my heart.
                           (*Exit* Gratiana.

ACT III · SCENE I

'*Enter* Beauford *and* Captain.'

   Captain. You amaze me, Beauford, Gratiana false?
I shall suspect the truth of my conception,
And think all women monsters. Though I never
Lov'd with that nearness of affection

To marry any, yet I mourn they should
Fall from their virtue. Why may not Marwood
Injure her goodness?
    Beauford. What, and damn his soul?
Shall I think any with his dying breath
Would shipwrack his last hope? He mix'd it with
His prayers, when in the stream of his own blood
His soul was launching forth.
    Captain. That circumstance takes away all suspicion again.
Where left you Marwood?
    Beauford. I' the park.
    Captain. Quite dead?
    Beauford. Hopeless. His weapon might have prov'd so
    happy
To have releas'd me of a burden too;
And but that manhood, and the care of my
Eternity forbids, I would force out
That which but wearies me to carry it,
Unwelcome life.
    Captain. Would he were buried.
My fears perplex me for you. Though none see
You fight, the circumstance must needs
Betray you.

'Enter a Surgeon.'

        What's he?
    Surgeon. I would borrow your ear in private.
    Beauford. We are but one to hear; his love hath
Made him too great a part of my affliction.
Speak it.
    Surgeon. The body is taken thence.
    Beauford. Ha!
    Surgeon. I cannot be deceiv'd, sir; I beheld
Too plain a demonstration of the place.
But he that suffer'd such a loss of blood
Had not enough to maintain life till this time,
Which way so e'er his body was convey'd.
I must conclude it short-liv'd. I am sorry
I could not serve you.
    Beauford. Sir, I thank you.

You deserve I should be grateful;   '*Gives him money.*'
It must be so.   (*Exit* Surgeon.

    Captain. What fellow's this?

    Beauford. A surgeon.

    Captain. Dare you trust him?

    Beauford. Yes, with my life.

    Captain. You have done that already in your discovery;
Pray heaven he prove your friend.
You must resolve for flight. You shall take ship—

    Beauford. Never.

    Captain. Will you ruin yourself? There's no security—

    Beauford. There is not, Captain;
Therefore I'll not change my air—

    Captain. How!

    Beauford. Unless thou canst instruct me how to fly from
Myself; for wheresoever else I wander,
I shall but carry my accuser with me.

    Captain. Are you mad?

    Beauford. I have heard in Afric is a tree, which tasted
By travellers, it breeds forgetfulness
Of their country. Canst direct me thither?
Yet 'twere in vain, unless it can extinguish
And drown the remembrance I am Beauford.
No, I'll not move. Let those poor things that dare not
Die obey their fears; I will expect my fate here.

    Captain. This is wildness,
A desperate folly. Pray be sensible.—
Who's this? 'Tis Gratiana.

        '*Enter* Gratiana *with a cabinet of jewels.*'

    Beauford. Ha! Farewell!

    Captain. You shall stay now a little.

    Beauford. I will not hear an accent; I shall lose
My memory, be charm'd into belief
That she is honest, with her voice. I dare not
Trust my frailty with her.

    Captain. She speaks nothing,
Is all a weeping Niobe, a statue,
Or, in this posture, doth she not present
A water-nymph plac'd in the midst of some

Fair garden, like a fountain, to dispense
Her crystal streams upon the flowers, which cannot
But, so refresh'd, look up and seem to smile
Upon the eyes that feed 'em?
Will she speak?

   Gratiana. Though by the effusion of my tears you may
Conclude I bring nothing but sorrow with me,
Yet hear me speak. I come not to disturb
Your thoughts, or with one bold and daring language
Say how unjust you make my suff'rings.
I know not what
Hath rais'd this mighty storm to my destruction,
But I obey your doom, and after this
Will never see you more. First, I release
And give you back your vows; with them, your heart,
Which I had lock'd up in my own, and cherish'd
Better. Mine I'm sure does bleed to part with't.
All that is left of yours this cabinet
Delivers back to your possession;
There's every jewel you bestow'd upon me,
The pledges once of love.

   Beauford. Pray keep 'em.

   Gratiana. They are not mine, since I have lost the opinion
Of what I was. Indeed I have nothing else;
I would not keep the kisses once you gave me,
If you would let me pay them back again.

   Beauford. All women is a labyrinth. We can
Measure the height of any star, point out
All the dimensions of the earth, examine
The sea's large womb and sound its subtle depth,
But art will ne'er be able to find out
A demonstration of a woman's heart.
Thou hast enough undone me; make me not
More miserable, to believe thou canst be virtuous.
Farewell. Enjoy you this; I shall find out
Another room to weep in.   (*Exit* Beauford.

   Captain. Lady, I would ask you a rude question:
Are you a maid?

   Gratiana. Do I appear so monstrous, no man will
Believe my injury? Has heaven forgot

To protect innocence, that all this while
It hath vouchsaf'd no miracle to confirm
A virgin's honour?

   Captain. I am answer'd.
I do believe she's honest. O that I could
But speak with Marwood's ghost now! An thou beest
In hell, I'd meet thee half way, to converse
One quarter of an hour with thee, to know
The truth of all [these] things. Thy devil-jailor
May trust thee without a waiter; he has security
For thy damnation in this sin alone.
I'm full of pity now, and spite of manhood
Cannot forbear. Come, lady, I am so confident—
I know not which way—that you're virtuous—
Pray walk with me. I'll tell you the whole story,
For yet you know not your accuser.

   Gratiana. I am an exile hence, and cannot walk
Out of my way. Beauford, farewell! May angels
Dwell round about thee. Live until thou find,
When I am dead, thou hast been too unkind.

              (*Exeunt* Gratiana *and* Captain.

[SCENE II]

'*Enter* Milliscent *and* Mistress Jane.'

   Jane. May I believe thee, Milliscent, that my father,
Though he give such respect to him I hate,
Intends no marriage? Thou hast releas'd
My heart of many fears that I was destin'd
To be a sacrifice.

   Milliscent. It had been sin
That Milliscent should suffer you perplex
Your noble soul, when it did consist in
His discovery to give a freedom
To your labouring thoughts. 'Tis now no more a secret:
Your father makes a trial of your nature,
By giving him such countenance.

   Jane. What thanks shall I give?

Milliscent. Your virtue hath both unseal'd
My bosom and rewarded me.
    Jane. O Milliscent.
Thou hast deserv'd my gratitude; and I cannot
But in exchange of thy discovery
Give to thy knowledge what I should tremble
To let another hear, for I dare trust thee with it.
    Milliscent. If I have any skill
In my own nature, [I] shall ne'er deceive
Your confidence, and think myself much honour'd
So to be made your treasurer.
    Jane. 'Tis a treasure,
And all the wealth I have, my life, the sum
Of all my joys on earth, and the expectation
Of future blessings too, depend upon it.
    Milliscent. Can I be worthy of so great a trust?
    Jane. Thou art, and shalt receive it, for my heart
Is willing to discharge itself into thee.
O Milliscent, though my father would ha' been
So cruel to his own to have wish'd me marry
Him, 'twas not in the power of my obedience
To give consent to't, for my love already
Is dedicate to one whose worth hath made
Me but his steward of it; and although
His present fortune doth eclipse his lustre
With seeming condition of a servant,
He has a mind deriv'd from honour, and
May boast himself a gentleman. Is not
Thy understanding guilty of the person
I point at? Sure, thou canst not choose but know him.
    Milliscent. Not I.

'*Enter* Haver.'

    Jane. Then look upon him, Milliscent.
    Milliscent. Ha!
    Haver. My master, Mistress Jane, sent me before
To say he comes to visit you.
    Jane. But thou art before him in acceptance. Nay,
You stand discover'd here; in Milliscent you may
Repose safe trust.

Haver. Her language makes me confident
You are a friend.

Milliscent. To both, a servant.

Haver. I shall desire your love.

Jane. But where's this man of mortgages?
We shall be troubled now.

Haver. I left him chewing the cud, ruminating
Some speech or other, with which he means to
Arrest you.

Milliscent. He is enter'd.

'*Enter* Rawbone [*with a scroll in his hand*].'

Haver. I have prepar'd her.

Rawbone. Fortune be my guide then.

Haver. And she's a blind one.

Rawbone. Mistress Jane, I would talk with you in private.
I have fancied a business—and I know you are witty and
love invention—'tis my own, and nobody else must hear it.
[*Reads*] *Be it known to all men by these presents*—

Jane [*Aside*]. This is like to be a secret.

Rawbone. *That I, Jasper Rawbone, citizen, and house-keeper of London*—

Haver [*Aside*]. A very poor one, I'm sure.

Rawbone. *Do owe to Mistress Jane, lady of my thoughts,
late of London, gentlewoman*—

Haver. Is she not still a gentlewoman?

Rawbone. Still a gentlewoman, goodman coxcomb? Did
I not say she was lady of my thoughts? Where was I, now?

Haver. At goodman coxcomb, sir.

Rawbone. *Do owe to Mistress Jane, lady of my thoughts, late
of London, gentlewoman, my true and lawful heart, of England,
to be paid to his said mistress, her executors, or assigns*—

Haver. To her executors? What, will you pay your heart
when she is dead?

Rawbone. 'Tis none of my fault an she will die. Who can
help it? Thou dost nothing but interrupt me. I say, *to be
paid to his said mistress, her executors, or assigns, whensoever
she demand it, at the font-stone of the Temple*—

Haver [*Aside*]. Put it the top of Paul's, an please you;
your conceit will be the higher.

Rawbone. *Which payment to be truly made and performed,*
I bind not my heirs but my body and soul for ever.

Haver. How, your soul, sir?

Rawbone. Peace, fool! My soul will shift for itself; when
I am dead, that will be sure enough. *In witness whereof, I*
have hereunto put my hand and seal—which is a handsome
spiny youth, with a bag of money in one hand, a bond in the
tother, an indenture between his legs—*the last day of the*
first merry month, and in the second year of the reign of King
Cupid.

Haver. Excellent! But in my opinion you had better give
her possession of your heart; I do not like this owing.
Faith, pluck it out and deliver it in the presence of us.

Rawbone. Thou talk'st like a puisne. I can give her
possession of it by delivery of twopence wrapped up in
the wax. 'Twill hold in law, man.—And how, and how d'ye
like it? I could have come over you with verse, but hang
ballads—give me poetical prose. Every mountebank can
rhyme and make his lines cry twang, though there be no
reason in 'em.

Jane. What music have I heard?

Rawbone. Music? Oh, rare!

Jane. He has Medusa's noble countenance;
His hairs do curl like soft and gentle snakes.
Did ever puppy smile so, or the ass
Better become his ears? O generous beast,
Of sober carriage! Sure, he's valiant too:
Those bloodshot eyes betray him, but his nose
Fishes for commendation.

Rawbone. What does she mean, Jasper?

Haver. D'ye not see her love, sir? Why, she does dote
upon you, which makes her talk so madly.

Rawbone. Forsooth, I know you are taken with me. Alas,
these things are natural with me. When shall we be married,
forsooth?

Jane. With your licence, sir.

Haver. D'ye not observe her? You must first procure a
licence.

Rawbone. You shall hear more from me when I come
again. Jasper.   ('*Exit* Rawbone *hastily.*'

Haver. My heart doth breathe itself upon your hand.

(*Exit* Haver.

Milliscent. Your father and Master Lodam.

'*Enter* Lodam, Justice, Cameleon.'

Lodam. Sir, I do love your daughter. I thought it necessary to acquaint you first, because I would go about the business judicially.

Justice. You oblige us both.

Lodam. I'll promise you one thing.

Justice. What's that?

Lodam. I'll bring your daughter no wealth.

Justice. Say you so? What, then you promise her nothing?

Lodam. But I will bring her that which is greater than wealth.

Justice. What's that?

Lodam. Myself.

Justice. A fair jointure.

Lodam. Nay, I'll bring her more.

Justice. It shall not need; no woman can desire more of a man.

Lodam. I can bring her good qualities, if she want any. I ha' travelled for 'em.

Justice. What are they?

Lodam. The languages.

Justice. You suspect she will want tongue? Let me see. Parlez français, monsieur?

Lodam. Diggon a camrag.

Justice. That's Welsh.

Lodam. Pocas palabras.

Justice. That's Spanish.

Lodam. Troth, I have such a confusion of languages in my head, you must e'en take 'em as they come.

Justice. You may speak that more exactly. Hablar spagnuol, signior?

Lodam. Serge . . . dubois . . . Callimancho et perpetuana.

Justice. There's stuff indeed! Since you are so perfect, I'll trust you for the rest. I must refer you, sir, unto my daughter. If you can win her fair opinion, my consent may happily follow. So. She is in presence.

Lodam. Mercie, madame.   '*Salutes* Jane.'

Justice. This fellow looks like the principal in usury, and this rat follows him like a pitiful eight in the hundred. Come hither, sirrah. Your name is Cameleon?

Cameleon. It is too true, sir.

Justice. You did live with Master Rawbone?

Cameleon. No, sir, I did starve with him, an please you. I could not live with him.

Justice. How do you like your change?

Cameleon. Never worse.

Justice. Master Lodam wants no flesh.

Cameleon. But I do. I ha' no justice, sir: my lean master would eat no meat, and my fat master eats up all. Is your worship's house troubled with vermin?

Justice. Something at this time.

Cameleon. Peace, and I'll catch a mouse then.

'*Lies down.*'

'*Enter* Captain *and* Gratiana.'

Justice. My nephew turned gentleman-usher?

Captain. Sir John Belfare's daughter.

Justice. 'Las, poor gentlewoman, I compassionate her unkind destiny.

Captain. Let us entreat a word in private, sir.—

[Captain, Gratiana *and* Justice *retire*.]

Lodam. I cannot tell how you stand affected, but if you can love a man, I know not what is wanting: greatness is a thing that your wisest ladies have an itch after. For my own part, I was never in love before, and if you have me not, never will be again. Think on't between this and after dinner; I will stay o' purpose for your answer.

Jane. You're very short.

Lodam. I would not be kept in expectation above an hour, for love is worse than a Lent to me, and fasting is a thing my flesh abhors. If my doublet be not filled, I know who fares the worse for't. I would keep my flesh to swear by, and if you and I cannot agree upon the matter, I would lose nothing by you.

Jane. You're very resolute.

Lodam. Ever while you live a fat man and a man of

resolution go together. I do not commend myself, but there
are no such fiery things in nature.

Jane. Fiery?

Lodam. 'Tis proved: put 'em to any action and see if they
do not smoke it. They are men of mettle and the greatest
melters in the world: one hot service makes 'em roast, and
they have enough in 'em to baste a hundred. You may take
a lean man, marry yourself to famine, and beg for a great
belly—you see what became of Sir John's daughter. Come,
I would wish you be well advised: there are more commodities in me than you are aware of. If you and I couple,
you shall fare like an empress.

Jane. That will be somewhat costly.

Lodam. Not a token. I have a privilege: I was at the
tavern tother day; i' the next room I smelt hot venison;
I sent but a drawer to tell the company one in the house,
with a great belly, long'd for a corner, and I had half a pasty
sent me immediately. I will hold intelligence with all the
cooks i' the town, and what dainty but I have greatness
enough to command?

Justice [*Coming forward, with* Gratiana, Captain *and*
Milliscent]. I like it well. Be as welcome here as at your
father's. Milliscent, make it your care to wait upon this
gentlewoman, but conceal she is our guest. I should rejoice
to see this storm blown over. Nephew, attend her to her
chamber.   (*Exeunt* Gratiana, Captain *and* Milliscent.

'*Enter* Rawbone *and* Haver *hastily.*'

Rawbone. I ha' been about it.

'*Jostles* Lodam, *and falls down.*'

Lodam. Next time you ride post, wind your horn, that
one may get out a' the way.

Justice. What's the matter, Jane?

Rawbone. 'Tis guts. If I durst, my teeth waters to strike
him.

Justice. What ha' you done?

Lodam. Let him take heed another time.

Haver. Take such an affront before your mistress!

Rawbone. I have a good stomach—

Haver. That's well said.

Rawbone. I could eat him.

Haver. Oh, is it that?

Lodam. Let me alone; nobody hold me.

Rawbone. I'll have an action of battery.

Lodam. Whoreson mole-catcher! Come not near me, weasel.

Rawbone [*Aside, to* Haver]. Prithee, Jasper, do not thrust me upon him.—I do not fear you, sir.

Lodam. Again shall I kick thee to pieces?

Haver [*Aside to* Rawbone]. Let him baffle thee!—To him!

'Haver *thrusts him upon him.*'

Rawbone. I do not fear you.

Justice. Jane, remove yourself.

Jane. Master Rawbone, I am sorry for your hurt.

(*Exit* Jane.

Haver. She jeers you.

Lodam. For this time, I am content with kicking of thee.

'*As* Lodam *offers to go out,* Haver *pulls him back.*'

Haver. My master desires another word wi' ye, sir—. ('*To* Rawbone') You must fight with him.—

Rawbone. Who? I fight?

Lodam. You spider-catcher, ha' you not enough? You see I do not draw.

Justice. Very well.

Haver [*Aside to* Rawbone]. By this hand, you shall challenge him then, if he dare accept it. I'll meet him in your clothes.

Rawbone. Will ye? Hum.—[*To* Lodam] I do not fear you—satisfaction—

Haver. That's the word.

Rawbone. That's the word. You'll meet me, guts—

Lodam. Meet thee? By this flesh, if thou dost but provoke me—you do not challenge me—do not! D'ye long to be minced?

Haver [*Aside to* Rawbone]. At Finsbury.

Rawbone. At Finsbury—

Haver [*Aside to* Rawbone]. Tomorrow morning.

Rawbone. Tomorrow morning. You shall find I dare fight.

Lodam. Say but such another word.

Rawbone. Finsbury, tomorrow morning—there 'tis again.

Justice. I cannot contain my laughter. Ha, ha, ha!

(*Exit* Justice.

Rawbone [*Aside to* Haver]. So, let's be gone quickly, before he threaten me. You made me challenge him; look to't.

Haver. Fear not, I warrant you.

(*Exeunt* Haver *and* Rawbone.

Lodam. Sirrah Noverint, if I can but prove thou dost come within three furlongs of a windmill, I'll set one atop of Paul's to watch thee. Shalt forfeit thy soul, and I'll cancel thy body worse than any debtor of thine did his obligation.—He's gone. And now I think upon the matter, I have somewhat the worst on't: for if I should kill him, I shall never be able to fly—and he has left a piece of his skull, I think, in my shoulder.—Whether am I bound to meet him or no? I will consult some o' the sword-men, and know whether it be a competent challenge. Cameleon.

Cameleon. Sir.

Lodam. Has the rat, your master that was, any spirit in him?

Cameleon. Spirit? The last time he was in the field a boy of seven years old beat him with a trap-stick.

Lodam. Say'st thou so? I will meet him then, and hew him to pieces.

Cameleon. I have an humble suit. If it be so, that you kill him, let me beg his body for an anatomy; I have a great mind to eat a piece on him.

Lodam. 'Tis granted. Follow me. I'll cut him up, I warrant thee.

(*Exeunt* Lodam *and* Cameleon.

[SCENE III]

'*Enter* Beauford *and* Captain [*with a letter*].'

Captain. I have a letter.

Beauford. From whom?

Captain. Gratiana.

Beauford. I would forget that name; speak it no more.

Captain. She is abus'd; and if you had not been Transported from us with your passion,

You would ha' chang'd opinion to have heard
How well she pleaded.

 Beauford. For herself.

 Captain. You might
With little trouble gather from her tears
How clear she was, which, more transparent than
The morning dew, or crystal, fell neglected
Upon the ground. Some cunning jeweller,
To ha' seen 'em scatter'd, would ha' thought some princess
Dropp'd 'em, and covetous to enrich himself,
Gather'd them up for diamonds.

 Beauford. You are then converted.

 Captain. Oh, you were too credulous!
Marwood has played the villain, and is damn'd for 't.
Could but his soul be brought to hear her answer
The accusation, she would make that blush,
And force it to confess a treason to
Her honour, and your love.

 Beauford. You did believe her.

 Captain. I did, and promis'd her to do this service:
She begg'd of me at parting, if she sent
A letter, to convey it to your hand.
Pray read; you know not what this paper carries.

 Beauford. Has she acquainted you?

 Captain. Not me; I guess
It is some secret was not fit for my
Relation; it may be worth your knowledge.
Do her that justice, since you would not hear
What she could say in person, to peruse
Her paper.

 Beauford. It can bring nothing to take off
Th' offence committed.

 Captain. Sir, you know not
What satisfaction it contains,
Or what she may confess in 't. For my sake—

 Beauford ('*Reads*'). *To him that was*—what?—*confident
of her virtue, once an admirer, now a mourner for her absent
goodness.*
She has made the change:
From her that was would ha' become this paper.

Had she conserv'd her first immaculate whiteness,
It had been half profane not to salute
Her letter with a kiss, and touch it with
More veneration than a sybil's leaf;
But now, all ceremony must be held
A superstition to the blotted scroll
Of a more stained writer. I'll not read.
If unprepar'd she win with her discourse,
What must she do when she has time and study
To apparel her defence?
    Captain. Deny her this?
    Beauford. Well, I will read it.

                '*Enter* Servant.'

    Servant. Here's Sir John Belfare.
    Beauford. Say anything t' excuse me. Be 't your care
That none approach the chamber.   [*Exit* Servant.]
    Captain. So, so. Now unrip the seal.

       '*Enter* Sir John Belfare, Isaac.'

    Belfare. Not speak with him? He must have stronger
      guard
To keep me out. Where's Beauford?
    Beauford. Here.
    Belfare. Then there's a villain.
    Beauford. That's coarse language.
    Belfare. I must not spin it finer till you make me
Understand better why my daughter, and
In her, my family, is abus'd.
    Beauford. She has not then accus'd herself. I'll tell you:
I did expect your daughter would have been
My virgin bride; but she reserv'd for me
The ruins of her honour. I would not speak
I' the rude dialect; you may sooner collect
In English.
    Belfare. Is she not honest? Will you
Make her then a whore?
    Beauford. Not I; her own sin made her.
    Belfare. Thou liest; nor can my age make me appear
Unworthy a satisfaction from thy sword.
    Isaac. Does not he call my young mistress whore?

Belfare. Keep me not from him, Captain; he has in this
Given a fresh wound. I came t' expostulate
The reason of a former suffering,
Which unto this was charity. As thou art
A gentleman, I dare thee to the combat.
Contemn not, Beauford, my grey hairs. If thou'st
A noble soul, keep not this distance. Meet me;
Thou art a soldier. For heaven's sake permit me
Chastise the most uncharitable slander
Of this bad man.

Beauford. I never injur'd you.

Belfare. Not injur'd me? What is there then in nature
Left to be call'd an injury? Didst not mock
Me, and my poor fond girl, with marriage,
Till all things were design'd, the very day
When Hymen should have worn his saffron robe,
My friends invited, and prepar'd to call
Her bride? And yet, as if all this could not,
Summ'd up together, make an injury,
Does thy corrupted soul at last conspire
To take her white name from her? Give me leave
To express a father in a tear, or two,
For my wrong'd child. O Beauford, thou hast robb'd
A father and a daughter. But I will not
Usurp heaven's justice, which shall punish thee
'Bove my weak arm. May'st thou live to have
Thy heart as ill rewarded, to be father
At my years, have one daughter and no more,
Belov'd as mine, so mock'd, and then call'd whore.

(*Exeunt* Belfare *and* Isaac,

Captain. 'Las, good old man!

Beauford. My afflictions
Are not yet number'd in my fate, nor I
Held ripe for death.

Captain. Now read the letter.

Beauford. Yes, it cannot make me know more misery.
('*Reads*') *Beauford—I dare not call thee mine—though I could
not hope, while I was living, thou wouldst believe my innocence,
deny me not this favour after death, to say I once loved thee—*
Ha, death! Captain, is she dead?

Captain. I hope she employ'd not me to bring this news.

Beauford. Yes, death! Ha!
Prithee read the rest. There's something
In my eyes; I cannot well distinguish
Her small characters.

Captain: My accuser by this time knows the reward of my injury. Farewell. I am carrying my prayers for thee to another world. Her own martyr, drowned Gratiana.

Beauford. Read all.

Captain. I have.

Beauford. It cannot be; for when thou mak'st an end,
My heart should give a tragic period,
And with a loud sigh break. Drown'd!
'Twas no sin above heaven's pardon,
Though thou hadst been false
To thy first vow and me; I would not had
Thee died so soon; or, if thou hadst affected
That death, I could ha' drown'd thee with my tears.
Now they shall never find thee, but be lost
Within thy watery sepulchre.

Captain. Take comfort.

Beauford. Art dead?
Then here I'll coffin up myself until
The law unbury me for Marwood's death.
I will not hope for life; mercy shall not save
Him, that hath now a patent for his grave.

> (*Exeunt* Beauford *and* Captain.

ACT IV · SCENE I

'*Enter* Milliscent *and* Gratiana.'

Milliscent. 'Tis his command, to whom I owe all service,
I should attend you.

Gratiana. Thou'rt too diligent.
I prithee, leave me.

Milliscent. I should be unhappy
To be offensive in my duty; yet
Had I no charge upon me, I should much
Desire to wait.

Gratiana. On me?

Milliscent. I know not why
Your sorrow does invite me.

Gratiana. Thou'rt too young
To be acquainted wi't.

Milliscent. I know it would not
Become my distance to dispute with you
At what age we are fittest to receive
Our grief's impression.

Gratiana. Leave me to myself.

Milliscent. I must, if you will have it so.

'*Offers to go out.*'

Gratiana. Methought
I saw him drop a tear.—Come back again.
What should he mean by this unwillingness
To part? He looks as he would make me leave
My own misfortune to pity his.—
Thy name?

Milliscent. I am called Milliscent.

Gratiana. Dost thou put on that countenance to imitate
Mine, or hast a sorrow of thy own thou
Wouldst express by't?

Milliscent. Mine does become my fortune;
Yet yours does so exactly paint out misery,
That he that wanted of his own would mourn
To see your picture.

Gratiana. Mine is above
The common level of affliction.

Milliscent. Mine had no example to be drawn by.
I would they were akin, so I might make
Your burden less by mine own suffering.

Gratiana. I thank thy love.

Milliscent. And yet I prophesy
There's something would make mine a part of yours
Were they examin'd.

Gratiana. Passion makes thee wild now.

Milliscent. You have encourag'd me to boldness; pardon
My ruder language.

Gratiana. Didst thou ever love?

Milliscent. Too soon; from thence sprung my unhappiness.

Gratiana. And mine.

Milliscent. My affliction, riper than my years,
Hath brought me so much sorrow, I do not think
That I shall live, to be a man.

Gratiana. I like thy sad expression. We'll converse,
And mingle stories.

Milliscent. I shall be too bold.

Gratiana. We lay aside distinctions if our fates
Make us alike in our misfortunes; yet
Mine will admit no parallel. Ha! We are interrupted.

    '*Enter* Justice, *reading a letter.*'

Let's withdraw, and I'll begin.

Milliscent. You may command, and when
Your story's done, mine shall maintain the scene.

       (*Exeunt* Gratiana *and* Milliscent.

Justice. To maintain such bliss, I will   '*Reads*'
    Wish to be transformed still.
    Nor will't be a shame in love,
    Since I imitate but Jove,
    Who from heaven hath stray'd, and in
    A thousand figures worse than mine
    Wooed a virgin. May not I
    Then for thee a servant try?
    Yes, for such a maid as thee
    Vary as many shapes as he.
    Rawbone clothes my outward part,
    But thy livery my heart.   Haver.

Ha! Young Haver! This letter I found in my daughter's
prayer-book. Is this your saint? How long ha' they con-
spired thus? Report gave out he was gone to travel; it seems
he stays here for a wind, and in the meantime would rig up
my daughter. He is a gentleman, well educated, but his
fortune was consumed by a prodigal father ere he was ripe,
which makes him, I suspect, borrow this shape to court my
daughter. Little does Rawbone think his servant is his rival.
I find the juggling, and will take order they shall not steal a
marriage.

    '*Enter* Captain.'

Nephew, I ha' news for you.

Captain. For me, sir?

Justice. You are a soldier; there's a duel to
Be fought this morning; will you see 't?

Captain. It does not, sir, become a gentleman
To be spectator of a fight in which
He's not engag'd.

Justice. You may behold it, cousin,
Without disparagement to your honour. Rawbone
Has challeng'd Master Lodam, the place Finsbury.

Captain. They fight? A doublet stuff'd with straw, ad-
vancing
A bullrush, were able to fright 'em both
Out a' their senses. They ha' not soul enough
To skirmish with a fieldmouse. They point a duel?
At Hogsdon, to shew fencing upon cream
And cake-bread, murder a quaking custard,
Or some such daring enemy.

Justice. Did not
Affairs of weight compel me to be absent,
I would not miss the sight on't, for the usurer
Hath got his man Jasper t' appear for him
In his apparel.

Captain. Jasper?

Justice. For mirth's sake
You may behold it; and let me entreat,
At your return, perfect relation
Of both their valours.

Captain. You shall, sir.

Justice. And, coz,
If it be possible, procure 'em hither
Before they shift; I much desire to see 'em.

Captain. Promise yourself they shall. I will defer
My conference with Gratiana and
Entertain this recreation.

Justice. So. I have a fancy;
This opportunity will give it birth.
If all hit right, it may occasion mirth.

(*Exeunt* Justice *and* Captain.

'*Enter* Milliscent *and* Gratiana.'

Gratiana. Which part of my discourse compels thee to
This suffering?

Milliscent. Your pardon, lady, I
Did prophesy what now I find: our stories
Have dependence.

Gratiana. How, prithee?

Milliscent. That Marwood,
Whom you report thus wounded, had a near
Relation to me, and 'twas my fortune
To come to close his eyes up and receive
His last breath.

Gratiana. Ha!

Milliscent. I know more than Beauford,
And dying, he oblig'd my love to tell't him
Whene'er we met.

Gratiana. You beget wonder in me.
Did he survive his slander? There is hope
He did recant the injury he did me.

Milliscent. He did confirm he had enjoy'd your person,
And bade me tell Beauford he left behind
A living witness of the truth he died for,
Naming a gentlewoman, Cardona,
That bred you in your father's house, whom he
Affirm'd betrayed your body to his lust.

Gratiana. Cardona?
Piety has forsaken earth!
Was ever woman thus betrayed to sin
Without her knowledge?

Milliscent. Would he had not been
My kinsman. I begin to fear him.

Gratiana. Wherein had I offended Marwood,
He should alive, and dead, so persecute
My fame? Cardona too i' the conspiracy?
'Tis time to die then.

Milliscent. My heart mourns for you
In the assurance of your innocence,
And were I worthy to direct you—

Gratiana. Has malice
Found out another murderer?

Milliscent. Would you be pleas'd to hear me, I could point

You out a path would bring you no repentance
To walk in, if, as I am confident,
Your goodness fears not what Cardona can
Accuse your honour with. Let her be
Examin'd; then her knowledge will quit you,
Or make your suffering appear just. This is
An easy trial; and since Marwood had
A stubborn soul (for though he were my kinsman,
I prefer justice), and held shame to check
His own report, women have softer natures,
And things may be so manag'd, if there be
A treason, to enforce confession from her.
Would you please t' employ me in this service,
And, though unworthy, be directed by me
(I beg it from you), I'll engage my being
You shall find comfort in 't.

    Gratiana. Do anything;
But I am lost already.

    Milliscent. You much honour me.

                    (*Exeunt* Gratiana *and* Milliscent.

[SCENE II]

'*Enter* Lodam *and* Cameleon.'

    Lodam. Cam, see an if he be come yet. Bring me word
hither.

    Cameleon. I see one lying o' the ground.

    Lodam. Is there so? Let's steal away before we be dis-
covered. I do not like when men lie perdu. Beside, there may
be three or four of a heap for aught we know. Let's back,
I say.

    Cameleon. 'Tis a horse.

    Lodam. Hang him, jade! I knew it could be nothing else.
Is the coast clear, Cameleon?

    Cameleon. I see nothing but five or six—

    Lodam. Five or six! Treachery! An ambush! 'Tis valour
to run.

    Cameleon. They be windmills.

    Lodam. And yet thou would'st persuade me 'twas an
ambush for me.

Cameleon. I?

Lodam. Come, thou wert afraid, an the truth were known. But be valiant. I have a sword, and if I do draw, it shall— be against my will. Is he not come yet?

Cameleon. An he were between this and Moorgate, you might scent him.

Lodam. If he come, somebody shall smell ill-favouredly ere he and I part.—Ha! By this flesh, 'tis he. Cam, go tell him I am sick.

'*Enter* Haver, Rawbone (*having changed clothes*),
Captain [*behind*].'

Haver. Master Lodam.

Lodam [*Aside*]. A brace of bullets to my heart.

Captain. Here can I stand and behold the champions.

Lodam. I have expected you this two hours, which is more than I ha' done to all the men I fought withal since I slew the high German in Tothill.

Captain. Whoreson mole-catcher!

Lodam. Draw, spider!

Captain. Well said, toad.

Haver. Let us confer a little.

Lodam. Confer me no conferings! I will have no more mercy on thee than an infidel. An thou'dst been wise, thou mightest ha' kept thee at home with thy melancholy cat that keeps thy study, with whom thou art in commons, and dost feed on rats a' Sundays. Then, perhaps, a leg or an arm, with thy Jew's ears, had satisfied me, when I met thee next. Draw, I say! Why dost not draw?

Haver. I come to give you satisfaction.

Lodam. What, with words? Sirrah Tartar, my fox shall scratch thy guts out, which I will send to the Bear Garden. Dost hear, usuring dog, I'll tell thee my resolution. I do mean to give thee as many wounds before I kill thee as a surgeon's sign has, and when I am weary of scarifying thy flesh, I'll bore thy heart. Which done—mark what I say— I will divide thy quarters. Observe and tremble! Then will I ha' thee put into a tub or barrel, and powder thee, and after three days in pickle, this thing that was thy servant, this cacodemon, whom thou didst starve once, Cameleon, shall in revenge of his pitiful famine eat thee up, devour thee, and grow fat i' the ribs again with thy flesh, Mammon.

Cameleon. I hungrily thank your worship.

Rawbone ('*Aside*'). What have I 'scaped!

Lodam. Which is more, after thou art dead, I will not leave thy soul quiet. I'll torment thy ghost, for I will straight to thy house where I will break open thy chests, lined with white and yellow metal, which I will cast away on pious uses; then summon all thy debtors by a drum, and give 'em in all their bills, bonds, evidences, indentures, defeasances, mortgages, statutes—

Rawbone [*Aside*]. I shall be undone.

Lodam. An there were a million on 'em.

Rawbone [*Aside*]. I'll home and shut up my doors for fear he kill Jasper and use me so indeed.

Captain. If thou dost offer to look home again till they ha' done, I'll cut thee off at thigh.

Rawbone. Ah!

Lodam. Draw, I say!

Haver. Since there is no remedy.

Lodam. His sword appears, Cam.

Cameleon. If he were a coward, you were able to conjure a spirit into him with those threatenings.

Lodam. Pox a' my dullness! Dost hear, scoundrel, if I should incline to mercy, what submission? Ha! Let me see. Ay, ay, live! Thou shalt upon thy knees confess thy rascality and ask me forgiveness in private, in the presence of Mistress Jane, and the twelve companies which at thy charge shall be feasted that day in Moorfields.

Haver. That must not be.

Lodam. Then say, when thou art dead, thou wert offered conditions for thy life. Cam, thou shalt feed, and feed high, Cameleon. Let me see. Come, 'tis my foolish nature to ha' compassion o' thee. I know thou'rt sorry; shalt only confess thyself a rascal under thy hand, then, and stay my intended revenge, which else would ha' been immortal.

Haver. Let me consider.

Lodam. Oho, Cam!

Captain. Both cowards! We shall have no skirmish.

Rawbone [*Aside*]. Now I think on't, what if my man

Jasper should be valiant and kill Lodam, umh? What pickle were I in. Worse—worse—he'll run away, I shall be taken and hanged for the conspiracy. '*Pulls* Haver *by the sleeve.*' Ah, Jasper, rogue that I was, where were my brains to challenge him?—He will not hear. A stubborn knave, he looks as if he meant to kill. Ah, Jasper!

Captain. I ha' seen a dog look like him, that has drawn a wicker bottle rattling about the streets, and leering on both sides where to get a quiet corner to bite his tail off.

Rawbone [*Aside*]. I do imagine myself apprehended already. Now the constable is carrying me to Newgate— now, now I'm at the sessions house, i' the dock—now I'm called—not guilty, my lord—the jury has found the indictment, *billa vera*—now, now comes my sentence.

Haver. I am resolved, sir.

Rawbone [*Aside*]. Ha!

Haver. You shall have what acknowledgement this pen of steel will draw out in your flesh, with red ink, and no other, dear Master Lodam.

Lodam. How?

Captain. So, so.

Rawbone [*Aside*]. Now I'm i' the cart, riding up Holborn in a two-wheeled chariot, with a guard of halberdiers. There goes a proper fellow, says one. Good people, pray for me! Now I am at the three wooden stilts—

Lodam [*Aside*]. Is this Rawbone the coward?—Dost hear, thing, consider what thou dost. Come, among friends thy word shall be as good as a note under thy hand. Tempt not my fury. [*Aside*] Would I were off with asking him forgiveness.

Rawbone [*Aside*]. Hey! Now I feel my toes hang i' the cart—now 'tis drawn away—now, now, now—I am gone.

'*Turns about.*'

Haver. You must show your fencing.

Lodam. Hold! I demand a parley.

Haver. How!

Lodam. 'Tis not for your reputation to deal with a gentleman upon unequal terms.

Haver. Where lie the odds?

Captain. How's this?

Lodam. Examine our bodies: I take it I am the fairer mark. 'Tis a disadvantage. Feed till you be as fat as I, and I'll fight wi' ye, as I am a gentleman.

Haver. It shall not serve your turn.   '*Fight.*'

Lodam. Hold! Murder, murder!

Rawbone. I'm dead, I'm dead.

Captain. Whoreson puff-paste, how he winks and barks. How now, gentlemen, Master Lodam.

Lodam. Captain, [you] should a' come but a little sooner and ha' seen good sport. By this flesh, he came up handsomely to me. A pretty spark, faith, Captain.

Haver. How, sir!

Lodam. But if you be his friend, run for a surgeon for him: I have hurt him under the short ribs, beside a cut or two i'th' shoulder. [*Aside*] Would I were in a miller's sack yonder, though I were ground for't, to be quit on 'em.

Haver. You will not use me thus?

Lodam [*Aside*]. I were best deliver my sword ere I be compelled to 't.—A pretty fellow, and one that will make a soldier. Because I see thou'st a spirit and canst use thy weapon, I'll bestow a dull blade upon thee, squirrel.

Captain. Deliver up your weapon?

Lodam. In love, in love, Captain. He's a spark, a' my reputation, and worthy your acquaintance.

Haver. Thou molly-puff, were it not justice to kick thy guts out?

Lodam. When I am disarmed?

Haver. Take't again, you sponge.

Lodam. What, when I have given 't thee? 'Tis at thy service, an it were a whole cutler's shop: be confident.

Rawbone [*Aside*]. My ague has not left me yet: there's a grudging a' the halter still.

Captain. Master Rawbone, I repent my opinion of your cowardice. I see you dare fight, and shall report it to my cousin. You shall walk home—she'll take 't as an honour—and present your prisoner.

Rawbone. Jasper, let's go home and shift. Do not go, honest Jasper.

Haver. You will be prattling, sirrah. I'll wait upon you, Captain. Master Lodam.

Lodam. I will accompany thee. Thou'rt noble, and fit for my conversation, honest Master Rawbone—a pox upon you!

Captain. Nay, you shall wait a' your master with his leave, good Jasper.

Haver. How now, Jasper?   (*Exeunt omnes.*

[SCENE III]

'*Cornets. A table set forth with two tapers,*
servants placing yew, bays, and rosemary etc.'
Enter Beauford.'

Beauford. Are these the herbs you strew at funerals?
Servant. Yes, sir.
Beauford. 'Tis well. I commend your care
And thank ye. Ye have express'd more duty
In not enquiring wherefore I command
This strange employment than in the very
Act of your obedience. My chamber
Looks like the spring now. Ha' ye not art enough
To make this yew-tree grow here, or this bays,
The emblem of our victory in death?
But they present that best when they are wither'd.
Have you been careful that no day break in
At any window? I would dwell in night
And have no other starlight but these tapers.
Servant. If any ask to speak with you,
Shall I say you are abroad?
Beauford. No; to all do enquire with busy faces,
Pale or disturb'd, give free access.   (*Exeunt* Servants.
What do I differ from the dead? Would not
Some fearful man or woman, seeing me,
Call this a churchyard, and imagine me
Some wakeful apparition 'mong the graves,
That for some treasures buried in my life
Walk up and down thus? Buried? No, 'twas drown'd.
I cannot therefore say, it was a chest.
Gratiana had ne'er a coffin; I have one
Spacious enough for both on's. But the waves
Will never yield to't, for it may be they,

Soon as the northern wind blows cold upon 'em,
Will freeze themselves to marble over her,
Lest she should want a tomb.

      '*Enter* Keeper.'

Thy business?
 Keeper. He died this morning.
A friend of his and yours did practise on him
A little surgery, but in vain. His last
Breath did forgive you. But you must expect
No safety from the law. My service, sir.
 Beauford. I have left direction, that it cannot miss me;
And, hadst thou come to apprehend me for't,
With as much ease thou might'st. I am no statesman:
Officious servants makes no suitors wait;
My door's unguarded; 'tis no labyrinth
I dwell in. But I thank thy love—there's something
To reward it. Justice cannot put on
A shape to fright me.
 Keeper. I am sorry, sir,
Your resolution carries so much danger.   (*Exit* Keeper.
 Beauford. What can life bring to me that I should court it?
There is a period in nature: is't not
Better to die and not be sick, worn in
Our bodies, which, in imitation
Of ghosts, grow lean, as if they would at last
Be immaterial too; our blood turn jelly
And freeze in their cold channel? Let me expire
While I have heat and strength to tug with death
For victory.

'*Enter* Milliscent, [*behind, and servants carrying a chest.*]'

 Milliscent. You may disburden there;
But gently, 'tis a chest of value. Mistress,
I'll give him notice.—Where is Beauford?
 Beauford. Here.
 Milliscent. What place d'ye call this?
 Beauford. 'Tis a bridal chamber.
 Milliscent. It presents horror.
 Beauford. Ha' you anything
To say to me?

Milliscent. Yes.

Beauford. Proceed.

Milliscent. I come to visit you.

Beauford. You are not welcome then.

Milliscent. I did suspect it, and have therefore brought
My assurance wi' me. I must require
Satisfaction for a kinsman's death,
One Marwood.

Beauford. Ha!

Milliscent. Your valour was not noble;
It was a coarse reward to kill him for
His friendship. I come not with a guard of
Officers to attach your person—it
Were too poor and formal. The instrument
That sluic'd his soul out I had rather should
Sacrifice to his ashes; and my sword
Shall do 't, or yours be guilty of another,
To wait upon his ghost.

Beauford. Young man, be not
Too rash, without the knowledge how our quarrel
Rose, to procure thyself a danger.

Milliscent. Make it
Not your fear. I have heard the perfect story,
And ere I fight with thee, shalt see thy error,
Acknowledge thou hast kill'd a friend. I bring
A perspective to make those things that lie
Remote from sense familiar unto thee. Nay,
Thou shalt confess thou know'st the truth of what
Concerns him, or Gratiana.

Beauford. When my soul
Throws off this upper garment, I shall know all.

Milliscent. Thou shalt not number many minutes. Know,
'Twas my misfortune to close up the eyes
Of Marwood, whose body I vow'd never
Should to the earth without revenge, or me,
Companion to his grave. I ha' therefore brought it
Hither. 'Tis in this house.

Beauford. Ha!

Milliscent. His pale corpse
Shall witness my affection.

Beauford. Thou didst promise
To inform me of Gratiana.

Milliscent. And thus briefly:
Marwood reveal'd at death another witness
Of his truth, for Cardona he corrupted
To betray Gratiana to him.

Beauford. Ha! Cardona!
Heaven continue her among the living
But half an hour.

Milliscent. I ha' sav'd ye trouble.
She waits without. In your name I procur'd
Her presence, as you had affairs with her.
She's unprepar'd. A little terror will
Enforce her to confess the truth of all things.

Beauford. Thou dost direct well.

Milliscent. Still remember, Beauford,
I am thy enemy, and in this do but
Prepare thy conscience of misdeed to
Meet my just anger.

Beauford. I am all wonder.

'Milliscent *brings in* Cardona.'

Milliscent. He's now at opportunity.

Cardona. Sir, you sent
To speak with me?

Beauford. Come nearer. I hear say
You are a bawd. Tell me how go virgins
I' th' sinful market? Nay, I must know, hell-cat,
What was the price you took for Gratiana.
Did Marwood come off roundly with his wages?
Tell me the truth, or, by my father's soul,
I'll dig thy heart out.

Cardona. Help!

Beauford. Let me not hear
A syllable that has not reference
To my question, or—

Cardona. I'll tell you, sir.
Marwood—

Beauford. So.

Cardona. Did viciously affect her.
Won with his gifts and flatteries I promis'd

F

My assistance, but I knew her virtue was not
To be corrupted in a thought.

   Beauford. Ha!

   Cardona. Therefore—

   Beauford. What, d'ye study?

   Cardona. Hold! I would deliver
The rest into your ear. It is too shameful
To express it louder than a whisper. [*Whispers to* Beauford.]

   Milliscent. With what unwillingness we discover things
We are asham'd to own. Cardona, [thou] should'st
Ha' us'd but half this fear in thy consent.
And thou had'st ne'er been guilty of a sin
Thou art so loth to part with, though it be
A burden to thy soul. How boldly would
Our innocence plead for us.—But she's done.

   Beauford. Then was Gratiana's honour sav'd?

   Cardona. Untouch'd.

   Beauford. Where am I lost? This story is more killing
Than all my jealousies. O Cardona,
Go safe from hence, but when thou com'st at home,
Lock thyself up and languish till thou die.
Thou shalt meet Marwood in a gloomy shade;
Give back his salary.   (*Exit* Cardona.

   Milliscent. Have I made good
My promise? Do you find your error?

   Beauford. No, I ha' found my horror. Has the chaste
And innocent Gratiana drown'd herself?
What satisfaction can I pay thy ghost?

   Milliscent. Now do me right, sir.

   Beauford. She's gone for ever;
And can the earth still dwell a quiet neighbour
To the rough sea, and not itself be thaw'd
Into a river? Let it melt to waves
From henceforth, that beside th' inhabitants
The very genius of the world may drown,
And not accuse me for her. Oh, Gratiana!

   Milliscent. Reserve your passion and remember what I
come for.

   Beauford. How shall I punish my unjust suspicion?
Death is too poor a thing to suffer for her.

Some spirit guide me where her body lies
Within her watery urn. Although seal'd up
With frost, my tears are warm and can dissolve it,
To let in me and my repentance to her.
I would kiss her cold face into life again,
Renew her breath with mine on her pale lip.
I do not think but if some artery
Of mine were open'd, and the crimson flood
Convey'd into her veins, it would agree,
And with a gentle gliding steal itself
Into her heart, enliven her dead faculties,
And with a flattery 'tice her soul again
To dwell in her fair tenement.
    Milliscent. You lose
Yourself in these wild fancies. Recollect,
And do me justice.
    Beauford. I am lost indeed,
With fruitless passion. I remember thee
And thy design again. I must account
For Marwood's death, is't not? Alas, thou art
Too young and canst not fight. I wish thou wert
A man of tough and active sinews, for
Thy own revenge sake: I would praise thee for
My death, so I might fall but nobly by thee,
For I am burden'd with a weight of life.
Stay, didst not tell me thou hadst brought hither
The body of young Marwood?
    Milliscent. Yes.
    Beauford. Since a mistake, not malice did procure
His ill fate, I will but drop one funeral
Tear upon his wound, and soon finish,
To do thee right.
    Milliscent. Ye shall.   *'A coffin brought in.'*
    Beauford. Does this enclose his corpse? How little room
Do we take up in death that living know
No bounds! Here, without murmuring we can
Be circumscrib'd. It is the soul that makes us
Affect such wanton and irregular paths.
When that's gone, we are quiet as the earth
And think no more of wandering. O Marwood,

Forgive my anger. Thy confession did
Invite thy ruin from me, yet upon—— '*Opens* [*the coffin*].'
My memory forsake me, 'tis Gratiana's
Spirit! Hast thou lost thy heavenly dwelling
To call me hence? I was now coming to thee:
Or, but command more haste and I will count it
No sin to strike myself, and in the stream
Of my own blood to imitate how thou
Didst drown thyself.

    Gratiana. I am living, Beauford—
    Beauford. I know thou art immortal.
    Gratiana. Living as thou art—
    Beauford. Good angels, do not mock mortality!
    Gratiana. And came—
    Beauford. To call me to my answer how I durst
Suspect thy chastity. I'll accuse myself,
And to thy injur'd innocence give me up
A willing sacrifice.

    Gratiana. O my Beauford, now
I am over-blest for my late sufferings.
I have solicited my death with prayers;
Now I would live, to see my Beauford love me.
It was thy friend induc'd me to that letter,
To find if thy suspicion had destroy'd
All seeds of love.

    Beauford. Art thou not dead indeed?
May I believe? Her hand is warm—she breathes
Again—and kisses as she wont to do
Her Beauford. Art Gratiana? Heaven,
Let me dwell here until my soul exhale.

    Milliscent. One sorrow's cur'd. Milliscent, be gone.
Thou hast been too long absent from thy own.

                          (*Exit* Milliscent.

    Beauford. O my joy-ravish'd soul! But where's the youth
Brought me this blessing? Vanish'd! Gratiana,
Where is he? I would hang about his neck
And kiss his cheek. He will not leave me so.
Gone? Sure, it was some angel, was he not,
Or do I dream this happiness? Will not thou
Forsake me too?

Gratiana. Oh, never!

Beauford. Within there—

Bid the young man return, and quickly, lest
My joy, above the strength of nature's sufferance,
Kill me before I can express my gratitude.
Ha' ye brought him?

'*Enter* Officers.'

Officer. Master Beauford, I am sorry we are
Commanded to apprehend your person.

Gratiana. Officers, ha!

Officer. You are suspected to have slain a
Gentleman, one Marwood.

Beauford. Have I still my essence, ha?
I had a joy was able to make man
Forget he could be miserable.

Officer. Come, sir.

Beauford. If e'er extremities did kill, we both
Shall die this very minute.

Gratiana. You shall not go.

Officers. Our authority will force him.

Gratiana. You're villains, murderers.
Oh, my Beauford!

Beauford. Leave me, Gratiana.

Gratiana. Never; I'll die with thee.

Beauford. What can we say unto our misery?
Sav'd in a tempest that did threaten most,
Arriv'd the harbour, ship and all are lost.

Officer. To the next justice.   (*Exeunt omnes.*

ACT V · SCENE I

'*Enter* Sir John Belfare.'

Belfare. Whither art thou fled, Gratiana, that I can
Converse with none to tell me thou art still
A mortal? Taken hence by miracle?
Though angels should entice her hence to heaven,

She was so full of piety to her father,
She would first take her leave.

'*Enter* Isaac *and a* Physician.'

Isaac. There he is, sir. He cannot choose but talk idly,
for he has not slept since the last great mist.

Physician. Mist?

Isaac. Ay, sir; his daughter, my young mistress, went
away in 't, and we can hear no tale or tidings of her. To tell
you true, I would not disgrace my old master, but he is little
better than mad.

Physician. Unhappy gentleman!

Belfare. 'Tis so: he murder'd her;
For he that first would rob her of her honour
Would not fear afterward to kill Gratiana.
He shall be arraign'd for it. But where shall we
Get honest men enough to make a jury,
That dare be conscionable when the judge
Looks on and frowns upon the verdict, men
That will not be corrupted to favour
A great man's evidence, but prefer justice
To ready money? Oh, this age is barren.

Isaac. You hear how he talks.

Belfare. But I ha' found the way: 'tis but procuring
Acquaintance with the foreman of the jury;
The sessions bell-wether, he leads the rest
Like sheep. When he makes a gap, they follow
In huddle to his sentence.

Isaac. Speak to him, sir.

Physician. God save you, Sir John Belfare!

Belfare. I am a little serious; do not trouble me.

Physician. D'ye not know me?

Belfare. I neither know nor care for you, unless
You can be silent.

Physician. I'm your neighbour—

Isaac. Master Doctor.

Belfare. Away, fool!

Isaac. No, sir, a physician.

Belfare. A physician? Can you cure my daughter?

Physician. Ay, sir. Where is she?

Belfare. Cannot you find her out by art? A good
Physician should be acquainted with the stars.
Prithee, erect a figure, grave astronomer;
Shalt have the minute she departed. Turn
Thy ephemerides a little. I'll lend
Thee Ptolemy and a nest of learned Rabbis
To judge by. Tell me whether she be alive
Or dead and thou shalt be my doctor. I'll
Give thee a round *per annum* pension,
And thou shalt kill me for it.

Physician. He has a strange delirium.

Isaac. Ay, sir.

Physician. A vertigo in's head.

Isaac. In his head?

Belfare. What says the raven?

Isaac. He says you have two hard words in your head, sir.

Physician. Have you forgot me, sir? I was but late
Familiar to your knowledge.

Belfare. Ha! Your pardon, gentle sir. I know you now.
Impute it to my grief; 't hath almost made me
Forget myself.

Physician. I come to visit you,
And cannot but be sorry to behold
You thus afflicted.

Belfare. Doctor, I am sick,
I'm very sick at heart; loss of my daughter,
I fear, will make me mad. How long d'ye think
Man's nature able to resist it? Can
Your love or art prescribe your friend a cordial?
No, no, you cannot.

Physician. Sir, be comforted.
We have our manly virtue given us
To exercise in such extremes as these.

Belfare. As these? Why, do you know what 'tis to
Lose a daughter? You converse with men that
Are diseas'd in body, punish'd with a gout
Or fever, yet some of these are held
The shames of physic; but to th' mind you can
Apply no salutary medicine.
My daughter, sir, my daughter—

Physician. Was to blame
To leave you so. Lose not your wisdom for
Your daughter's want of piety.
 Belfare. Speak well
A' th' dead, for living she would not be absent
Thus from me. She was ever dutiful,
Took pleasure in obedience. Oh, my child!
But I have strong suspicion by whom
She's made away. Beauford—
 Physician. How?
 Belfare. He that pretended marriage—he gave her
A wound before.
 Physician. Master Beauford's newly
Apprehended for some fact and carried
'Fore Justice Landby. In my passage hither
I met him guarded.
 Belfare. Guarded for what?
 Physician. Some did whisper he had kill'd—
 Belfare. Gratiana!
Oh, my girl, my Gratiana! Isaac, Beauford is taken. 'Tis
apparent he hath slain my daughter, and shall not I revenge
her death? I'll prosecute the law with violence against him,
not leave the judge till he pronounce his sentence. Then I'll
die, and carry Gratiana the news before him. Follow me.
            (Exeunt omnes.

[SCENE II]

'*Enter* Justice Landby *and* Jane.'

Justice. I expect, Jane, thou wilt reward my care
With thy obedience. He's young and wealthy,
No matter for those idle ceremonies
Of love and courtship.
 Jane. Do I hear my father?
 Justice. He will maintain thee gallant. City wives
Are fortune's darlings, govern all—their husbands,
Variety of pleasure and apparel—
When some of higher title are oft fain
To pawn a ladyship. Thou shalt have Rawbone.

Jane. Virtue forbid it! You are my father, sir,
And lower than the earth I have a heart
Prostrates itself. I had my being from you,
But I beseech you take it not away
Again by your severity.

Justice. How's this? ('*Aside*') I like it well.

Jane. You have read many lectures to me, which
My duty hath receiv'd and practis'd as
Precepts from heaven, but never did I hear
You preach so ill. You heretofore directed
My study to be careful of my fame,
Cherish desert, plant my affection on
Nobleness, which can only be sufficient
To make it fruitful; and d'ye counsel now
To marry a disease?

Justice [*Aside*]. Good! My own girl!—
What is't you said, ha?

Jane. For the man himself
Is such a poor and miserable thing—

Justice. But such another word and I take off
My blessing. How, now, Jane!

Jane [*Aside*]. Alas, I fear
He is in earnest.—Marry me to my grave,
To that you shall have my consent. Oh, do not
Enforce me to be guilty of a false
Vow, both to heaven and angels! On my knees—

Justice. Humble your heart, rise, and correct your
sullenness.
I am resolv'd. Would you be sacrific'd
To an unthrift, that will dice away his skin
Rather than want to stake at ordinaries,
Consume what I have gather'd at a breakfast,
Or morning's draught? And when you ha' teem'd for him,
Turn sempstress to find milk and clouts for babies,
Foot stockings to maintain him in the counter?
Or, if this fail, erect a bawdy citadel,
Well mann'd, which, fortified with demi-cannon
Tobacco pipes, may raise you to a fortune,
Together with the trade?

Jane. O my cruel stars!

Justice. Star me no stars, I'll have my will.

Jane [*Aside*]. One minute
Hath ruin'd all my hopes. Milliscent
Was cruel thus to mock me.

'*Enter* Captain, Haver, Lodam, Rawbone, *and* Cameleon,
    [Haver *and* Rawbone *still in each other's clothes.*]'

Captain. Uncle.   '*Captain and* Justice *whisper.*

Rawbone. Jasper, what case am I in?

Haver. Be wise and keep your counsel. Is not all for your
honour?

Lodam. Lady, I hope by this time you are able to distinguish a difference between Rawbone and myself.

Cameleon [*Aside*]. I find little.

Captain [*To* Justice]. You shall do, noble sir.

Justice. Master Rawbone, the only man in my wishes,
My nephew gives you valiant. Your merit
O'erjoys me, and to show how much I value
Your worth, my daughter['s] yours. I'll see you
Married this morning, ere we part. Receive him
Into your bosom, Jane, or lose me ever.

Jane. I obey, sir. [*Aside*] Will my father cozen himself?

Haver. Ha! Do I dream?

Rawbone. Dream, quotha? This is a pretty dream.

Justice. Master Lodam, I hope you'll not repine at his
fortune.

Rawbone. But Rawbone will pine, and repine, if this be
not a dream.

Lodam. I allow it, and will dine with you.

Cameleon. And I.

Rawbone. Jasper. No, will nobody know me?

Justice. Let 's lose no time. I have no quiet till I call him
son.

Rawbone. Master Justice, do me right. You do not know
who I am. I am—

Justice. An ass, sir, are you not? What make you prattling?

Rawbone. Sir, noble captain, a word. I am—

Captain. A coxcomb. [*To* Haver] Your man is saucy, sir.

Rawbone. Then I am a—sleep.

Captain. I forget Gratiana.

Justice. Cousin, you shall supply my place at church, while I prepare for your return. Some guests we must have. Nay, nay, haste, the morn grows old. We'll ha' a wedding day.

Haver. Here's a blessing beyond hope.

[*Exeunt* Captain, Haver, Jane, *and* Cameleon.]

Rawbone. Sure, I am asleep. I will e'en walk with 'em till my dream be out. [*Exit* Rawbone.]

'*Enter* Beauford, Officers, Marwood *disguised*, Keeper, Gratiana.'

Justice. Master Beauford, welcome—and Gratiana!

Beauford. You will repent your courtesy; I am presented an offender to you.

Officer. Yes, an please your worship, he is accus'd.

Justice. How?

Gratiana. Sir, you have charity; believe 'em not; They do conspire to take away his life.

Keeper. May it please you understand, he has kill'd A gentleman, one Marwood, in our park. I found him wounded mortally, though before He died, he did confess—

Beauford. Urge it no farther; I'll save the trouble of examination And yield myself up guilty.

Gratiana. For heaven's sake Believe him not; he is an enemy To his own life. Dear Beauford, what d'ye mean To cast yourself away? You're more unmerciful Than those that do accuse you, than the law Itself, for at the worst, that can but find You guilty at the last, too soon for me To be divided from you.

Beauford. O Gratiana, I call heaven to witness, Though my misfortune made me think before My life a tedious and painful trouble. My very soul a luggage, and too heavy For me to carry, now I wish to live,

To live for thy sake, till my hair were silver'd
With age; to live till thou wouldst ha' me die,
And wert aweary of me. For I never
Could by the service of one life reward
Enough thy love, nor by the suffering
The punishment of age and time do penance
Sufficient for my injury. But my fate
Hurries me from thee. Then accept my death
A satisfaction for that sin I could not
Redeem alive. I cannot but confess
The accusation.

       '*Enter* Sir John Belfare *and* Isaac.'

    Belfare. Justice, justice! I will have justice!
Ha! Gratiana!
    Gratiana. O my dear father—
    Belfare. Art alive? Oh, my joy! It grows
Too mighty for me; I must weep a little
To save my heart.
    Isaac. My young mistress alive?   (*Exit* Isaac.
    Gratiana. If ever you lov'd Gratiana, plead for Beauford;
He's been abus'd, by a villain. All's discover'd.
We've renewed hearts, and now, I fear, I shall
Lose him again, accused here for the death
Of Marwood, that was the cause of all our suffering.
    Belfare. I ha' not wept enough for joy, Gratiana,
That thou'rt alive yet. I understand nothing
Beside this comfort.
    Gratiana. Dear sir, recollect,
And second me.
    Justice. The fact confess'd, all hope
Will be a pardon, sir, may be procur'd.
Sir John, you're come in a sad time.
    Gratiana. What is the worst you charge him with?
    Keeper. He has slain a gentleman.
    Justice. No common trespass.
    Gratiana. He has done justice.
    Justice. How?
    Gratiana. A public benefit to his country in't.

Justice. Killing a man? Her sorrow overthrows
Her reason.

Gratiana. Hear me! Marwood was a villain,
A rebel unto nature, a profaner
Of friendship's sacred laws, a murderer
Of virgin chastity, against whose malice
Not innocence could hope protection,
But, like a bird gripp'd by an eagle's talon,
It groaning dies.
What punishment can you inflict on him
That in contempt of nature and religion
Enforces breach of love, of holy vows,
Sets them at war whose hearts were married
In a full congregation of angels?
I know you will not say but such deserve
To die. Yet, Marwood being dead, you reach
Your fury to his heart that did this benefit.

Beauford. O Gratiana, if I may not live
To enjoy thee here, I would thou hadst been dead
Indeed, for in a little time we should
Ha' met each other in a better world.
But since I go before thee, I will carry
Thy praise along; and if my soul forget not
What it hath lov'd when it convers'd with men,
I will so talk of thee among the blest
That they shall be in love with thee, and descend
In holy shapes to woo thee to come thither
And be of their society. Do not veil thy beauty
With such a shower; keep this soft rain
To water some more lost and barren garden,
Lest thou destroy the spring which nature made
To be a wonder in thy cheek.

Justice. Where is Marwood's body?

Marwood. Here, sir.

Omnes. Alive!

Milliscent. Ha! Marwood!

Marwood. Alive, as glad to see thee as thou art
To know thyself acquitted for my death,
Which I of purpose by this honest friend,
To whose cure I owe my life, made you believe,

T'increase our joy at meeting. For you, lady,
You are a woman, yet you might ha' been
Less violent in your pleading. Do not
Engage me past respects of mine, or your own honour.

Gratiana. Mine is above thy malice. I have a breast
Impenetrable, 'gainst which, thou fondly aiming,
Thy arrows but recoil into thy bosom
And leave a wound.

Beauford. Friend, we have found thy error.

Marwood. Let it be mine; we have had storms already.

Gratiana. Tell me, injurious man—for in this presence
You must acquit the honour you accus'd—
Discharge thy poison here, inhuman traitor.

Beauford. Thou wilt ask her now forgiveness; she's all
chastity.

Marwood. Why d'ye tempt me thus?

Belfare. It was ill done, sir.

Justice. Accuse her to her face.

Marwood. So, so. You see, I am silent still.

Gratiana. You are too full of guilt to excuse your
treachery.

Marwood. Then farewell all respects, and hear me tell
This bold and insolent woman that so late
Made triumph in my death.

Milliscent. O sir, proceed not;
You do not declare yourself of generous birth
Thus openly to accuse a gentlewoman,
Were it a truth.

Gratiana. He may throw soil at heaven
And as soon stain it.

Marwood. Sirrah boy, who made you so peremptory?
He would be whipp'd.

Milliscent. With what? I am not arm'd,
You see, but your big language would not fright
My youth, were it befriended with a sword;
You should find then I would dare to prove it
A falsehood, on your person.

Justice. How now, Milliscent.

Marwood. Hath my love made me thus ridiculous,
Beauford, that you will suffer such a boy

To affront me? Then, against all the world
I rise an enemy, and defy his valour
Dares justify Gratiana virtuous.

'*Enter* Isaac *and* Cardona.'

Isaac. Believe your eyes.
Cardona. My daughter alive?
Oh, my dear heart.
Marwood. You are come opportunely,
Cardona. Speak the truth, as thou wouldst not
Eat my poniard. Is not Gratiana
A sinful woman?
Cardona. What means Marwood, ha?
Belfare. I am in a labyrinth.
Cardona. Hold! I confess.
You never did enjoy Gratiana.
Marwood. Ha!
Cardona. Let not our shame be public, sir; you shall
Have the whole truth. Oh, that my tears were able
To wash my sin away! Won with your promises,
I did, in hope to make myself a fortune
And get a husband for my child, with much
Black oratory, woo my daughter to
Supply Gratiana's bed, whom with that
Circumstance you enjoy'd, that you believ'd
It was the virgin you desir'd.
Belfare. Is't possible?
Marwood. I am at a confusion. Where's this daughter?
Cardona. She with the fear (as I conceive) of her
Dishonour, taking a few jewels with her,
Went from me, I know not whither; by this time
Dead, if not more unhappy in her fortune.
Marwood. Into how many sins hath lust engag'd me!
Is there a hope you can forgive, and you,
And she whom I have most dishonour'd?
I never had a conscience till now,
To be griev'd for her. I will hide myself
From all the world.
Milliscent. Stay, sir. [*Whispers to* Marwood.]

Gratiana. You hear this, Beauford, father?

Beauford. This she confess'd to me, though I conceal'd
From thee the error. Marwood dead, their shame
Would not ha' given my life advantage. Now
We have o'ercome the malice of our fate,
I hope you'll call me son.

Belfare. Both my lov'd children.

Justice. I congratulate your joy.

Marwood. Beauford, gentlemen,
This is a woman, Lucibel, your daughter,
The too much injur'd maid. Oh, pardon me!
Welcome both to my knowledge and my heart.

Cardona. Oh, my child!

Justice. My servant prove a woman?

Belfare. You'll marry her.

Marwood. It shall begin my recompence.
Lead you to church; we'll find the priest more work.

Justice. He has done some already, for by this time
I have a daughter married to young Haver,
That walk'd in Rawbone's livery. They're return'd.

'*Enter* Captain, Haver, Jane, Lodam, *and* Cameleon.'

Haver. Father, your pardon. Though you meant me not
Your son, yet I must call your daughter wife.
Here I resign my citizen.   [*Removes his disguise.*]

Belfare. Young Haver!

Justice. My blessing on you both.
I meant it so. A letter took off this
Disguise before. Nay, here are more couples,
Enough to play at barley-break.

Rawbone. Master Lodam, you and I are in hell.

Lodam. How?

Rawbone. You and I are friends.

Lodam. I knew by instinct I had no quarrel to thee.
Art thou Rawbone?

Rawbone. I am not drunk.

Lodam. No, but thou art disguised shrewdly.

Rawbone. I will not believe I am awake.

Captain. This is not possible.

Beauford. Leave off to wonder, Captain.

Captain. Sure, this is a dream.

Rawbone. As sure as you are there, Captain. 'Las, we do but walk and talk in our sleep all this while.

Belfare. Away, away!

Lodam. Ay, to dinner, bullies.

Rawbone. D'ye hear, gentlemen, before you go, does nobody know me? Who am I? Who am I?

Justice. You are Master Rawbone, sir, that would have married my daughter, that is now wife, I take it, to this gentleman, your seeming servant.

Rawbone. Dream on, dream on. Jasper, make much a' the wench now thou 'st got her. Am not I finely gulled?

Haver. I think so.

Rawbone. Dream on together. A good jest, i' faith! He thinks all this is true now.

Captain. Are not you then awake, sir?

Rawbone. No, marry am I not, sir.

Captain. What d'ye think a' that, sir?   '*Kicks him.*'

Rawbone. That, sir? Now do I dream that I am kicked.

Captain. You do not feel it then?

Rawbone. Kick, kick your hearts out.

Lodam. Say you so? Let my foot be in too then.

Rawbone. Sure, I shall cry out in my sleep. What a long night 'tis.

Belfare. Set on.

Lodam. Ay, ay, we may come back and take him napping.

Beauford. Come, Gratiana,
My soul's best half, let's tie the sacred knot,
So long deferr'd. Never did two lovers
Meet in so little time so many changes.
Our wedding day is come; the sorrows past
Shall give our present joy more heavenly taste.

(Exeunt all except Rawbone.

Epilogue.

Rawbone. Gentlemen, pray be favourable to wake a fool dormant amongst ye. I ha' been kicked, and kicked to that

purpose. Maybe they knocked at the wrong door—my brains
are asleep in the garret. I must appeal from their feet to your
hands. There is no way but one: you must clap me, and clap
me soundly, d'ye hear. I shall hardly come to myself else.
Oh, since my case without ye desperate stands,
Wake me with the loud music of your hands.

(Exit Rawbone.

FIVE NEW
PLAYES,
(*Viz.*)

THE {
Madd Couple well matcht:
Novella.
Court Begger.
City Witt.
Damoiselle:

By *Richard Brome.*

LONDON, May. 20.

Printed for *Humphrey Moseley. Richard Marriot*, and *Thomas Dring*, and are to be
sold at their Shops, 1653.

FIVE NEW
PLAYES

Prologue

Here you're all met and look for a set speech,
Put into rhyme, to court you and beseech
Your worships but to hear and like the play;
But I, I vow, have no such part to say.
I'm sent a-wooing to you, but how to do't
I ha'nt the skill. 'Tis true I've a new suit,
And ribbons fashionable, yclipt fancies,
But for the compliments, the trips and dances,
Our poet can't abide 'em, and he swears
They're all but cheats, and sugar'd words but jeers.
He's hearkening there, and if I go about
To make a speech, he vows he'll put me out.
Nor dare I write t' you. Therefore, in this condition,
I'll turn my courtship into admonition:
When a good thing is proffer'd, don't be nice;
Our poet vows you shan't be proffer'd twice.

THE PERSONS OF THE COMEDY

Careless, *a young wild heir.*
Sir [Oliver] Thrivewell, *his uncle that adopted him heir.*
Saleware, *a citizen and a cuckold.*
Saveall, Sir [Oliver's] *demure steward.*
Lord Lovely, *a wencher.*
Bellamy, *a woman disguised, and his steward.*
Wat, *a blunt fellow,* Careless's *serving-man.*
Old Bellamy.
[Fitzgerrard, *brother to* 'Bellamy.']
Lady Thrivewell.
Mistress Alicia, Saleware's *light wife.*
Mistress Crosstill, *a rich vintner's widow, and humorous.*
Phoebe, Careless *his whore.*
Closet, *an old crone, nurse-keeper to* Lady Thrivewell.
Apprentices.
Serving-men and attendants.
[Page.]

The Scene: London.

A MAD COUPLE WELL MATCHED

ACT I · SCENE I

'Careless, Wat.'

Careless. Thou hast delivered my letter?

Wat. Yes, sir, to Master Saveall, your uncle's friend. But he has stood your friend so long and so often, to so little purpose in moving your uncle for you, that he holds it utterly in vain to urge him any further, he told me.

Careless. Thou should'st ha' told him I would not be so answered.

Wat. Yes, and then he would have told me, let your master take his course.

Careless. Then you should ha' told him again I have taken all the courses I could, or as any gentleman can, to maintain myself like one. But all my courses are run out, and I have not breath, nor know any ground whereon to begin a new one, unless that thing, my uncle, sets me up again. Nor have I any means to attain to that but by his mediation.

Wat. Then would he ha' told me again what all your courses have been: namely, running into debt by all the ways can be imagined, and cheating by all could be invented; then that the said thing (as you call it), your uncle, before he cast you quite off, had redeemed you out of prison and several holds within the space of fifteen months fourteen times.

Careless. That was not once a month then, or if it had, what had that been to him? 'Twas I that suffered, thou should'st ha' told him, not he.

Wat. He would ha' told me then again that several redemptions cost your uncle at least 2000l, and that upon your last revolt, when he quite gave you over for a castaway, two years since, he cast the third thousand with you upon condition never to afflict him more. And then he married in hope to get an heir—

Careless. Ay, that marrying spoiled all.

Wat. Because you should not after his death cast away all the rest of the thousands, and ten thousands, which you might have lived to inherit, if your uncle's love or Master Saveall's counsel could have prevailed with you against the devil and debauchedness.

Careless. Pox on 't, let it all go! Let that wretched uncle go, and let Saveall go for a punctual ass as he is. I confess he has by his saving help peaced me with my uncle a score of times at least. What had once more been to him?

Wat. Sir, it were better for you to think upon some course by yourself, and me your creature (that have stuck to you or followed you through all fortunes), to maintain rich lace and bravery upon you. And think in time, too, before this be worn out, upon some new ways for your supplies.

Careless. I cannot, nor will I trouble my brains to think of any. I will rather die here in Ram Alley, or walk down to the Temple and lay myself down alive in the old Synagogue, cross-legged among the monumental knights there, till I turn marble with 'em. Think, quotha! What should I think on?

Wat. On your poor whore, sir, as you have brought her. She 's in worse case than yourself. Your clothes are good enough—

Careless. Ay, there 's the devil. I would do something for her if I knew how. But what have I not done that can be done by a forlorn heir?

Wat. Why, though the dice and all other household games and all the cheats belonging unto them have failed you by your and their discoveries, till none dare venture so near you as a man hurls a die or skirrs a card; though all your hidden ways in Hyde Park races are trod out, and all your bowling booties beaten bare off o' the grounds and alleys, and the sweet honeycombs of all your cockpit cosenages cut off; though all your arts of borrowing are crossed out of all men's books before you offer at 'em, while your old debts stand fairly written, and all your marts miscarry of putting out for credit, venison to citizens, or early cherries, codlings and apricots to their wives avail you nothing, cannot something yet be found?

Careless. Nothing, nothing. All projects are confounded.

Wat. Did your father leave you nothing but wit to live upon for this? And did he leave you that but for years, and not for life? And is the term expired?

Careless. Hold thy peace. I am casting for something to be done by me, that shall be worth, an't cost my life, to shame my uncle.

Wat. There's a plot! Think of your poor whore, sir. How shall she live if you cast away yourself?

Careless. I must leave her once, thou know'st.

Wat. If you could leave her now, and betake yourself handsomely to other women, I have thought on a course.

Careless. What? Quickly, what is't?

Wat. To set up a male bawdy-house.

Careless. Fie upon 't!

Wat. You are handsome, lovely, and I think able to do one man's work. Two or three such gentlemen more, which I know and can describe to you, with the ways I'll find to bring in custom, shall fill your purses—

Careless. And empt our bones. I ever had enough of one mistress; variety would destroy me. No gentlemen can be able to hold it out; they are too weak to make common he-whores.

Wat. For a little while, sir, till we have got a stock of rich clothes; and then we will put draymen and wine-porters, Cornish wrestlers and suchlike into those clothes and make them country cavaliers. Have you not seen coarse-snout fair drudges, clapped into bravery, that would do more bodily service in a brothel than twenty ladies' daughters? They are the game-bears of a bawdy-house, can play ten single courses for a clean-bred gentlewoman's one. We will hire fellows for groats a-piece a day, that shall (without the additaments of clary, caudle or cockbroth) get us forty pieces a man before night, or perhaps a hundred by next morning, out of such she-customers as an aunt of mine shall find out for us.

Careless. O base villain! No, I'll never fall so deep below a gentleman as to be master of a bawdy-house.

Wat. Very good decayed gentlemen have done as much; though I urge this but for your pastime, sir.

Careless. No, my first plot shall stand. I will do some notorious death-deserving thing—though these clothes go

to th' hangman for 't, what care I?—in defiance of him that
was my uncle, and his methodical, grave, and orthographical-
speaking friend, Master Saveall, that calls people pe-o-ple.

'*Enter* Saveall.'

O Master Saveall, how have you honoured me! How am
I bound to you for this visit! Sir, hearing that my uncle was
come to town, and you with him, I did presume to write to
you.

   Saveall. Send forth your man.

   Careless. Go forth.   (*Exit* Wat.

   Saveall. One servant is not fit for all offices, although you
keep no more. You presumed indeed; I can no less than call
it a presumption, although it were but unto me you write.
I speak not this in the behalf of any dignity in me, but that
you should overween that I had ability to wrestle any more
with your overgrateful uncle in your behalf. Therein was
your outrecuidance.

   Careless. The miserablest man on earth, in having wearied
out my worthiest friend, on whom the sum of all my hopes
was cast!

   Saveall. No, I am not wearied, but still in the same full
strength. Yet my modesty dissuadeth me from using strength
above reason, and my reason prevaileth with me not to
strive against a torrent.

   Careless. He is then inexorable, and I must perish. But
did you try him for me this last time?

   Saveall. I have both tried and tempted him to his vexation.

   Careless. But did you urge that pious act of mine
Which he once vow'd should never be forgot,
Or unrewarded by him?

   Saveall. Your standing upon merit in that act
Perplexeth nature in him and confounds
Both your desert and his benevolence.
And now, since you have urg'd it, I'll tell you:
Your act was undeniable, most noble
And glorious in a nephew—greater piety
Could not have been expected in a son—

When from the swords of thieves and murderers
Your valour rescued him, but—

Careless. I and my man, I'm sure, made four of the
stoutest purses fly for 't that ever set our country o' the
score. After they had him down, and their points at his
breast and throat, he crying out for help, when I came on by
chance, at a time, too, when I was in his displeasure—nay,
he hated me a whole year together before that—and yet
I did it, and more than so—

Saveall. Fare you well, sir. I thought to have said all this
for you, and more than so too, but—

Careless. Nay, sweet Master Saveall—

Saveall. Good Master Careless, as I can hear, I would be
heard sometimes.

Careless. Indeed I cry you mercy. Pray, sir, speak.

Saveall. I was commending of your act, and do so still.
You did express yourself in blood and nature
A perfect kinsman, and your piety
Drew blessings on you: for, whereas before,
Your uncle left you off to reprobation,
He then receives you a son (being his sister's),
Adopted you, intended you his heir,
And out of his estate then presently
Allowed you two hundred pounds *per annum*,
And gave your man for what he suffered
In the conflict an hundred marks.

Careless. Poor rogue! And he deserved it, I'll be sworn,
for a thieve's mark that he received—a cut o' the coxcomb
that cracked his skull so that he could never bear his drink
since as he could ha' done before. For, sir, as we came in,
I having put by the thrusts of three of 'em, the fourth man
with a full blow—

Saveall. Fare you well, sir, the second time—

Careless. Nay, courteous Master Saveall.

Saveall. I came to speak not with you altogether, but
unto you for to be heard.

Careless. Sir, I will hear you with all due respect.

Saveall. Your uncle having done so gratefully and so
plentifully for you,
You building still on merit for that service

Did hold him so fast bound that you presum'd
To run upon more extravagancies
In all the outways of debauchery,
Till for the one good deed you did for him
He did you forty, in restoring you
From surfeits, wants, wounds and imprisonments;
Till, overborne with charge, and more with anguish
At your outrageous, unexampled riots,
He gave you an irrevocable farewell.
Yet then at your departure—

Careless. Yet then I lived, and could have done till now, merely by being his nephew and supposed his heir, had not he married. But his marriage turned the hearts of all believing citizens from me, where before, a tailor could ha' made me run through all the credit i' the town, when in a suit clinquant and à-la-mode they could inform themselves whose heir I was. But to say truth, I vexed him into wedlock, for before, he valued not a wife at a bachelor's button.

Saveall. Farewell to you the third time.

Careless. Sir, you shall see me die first, and that instantly, that you may tell my uncle I'll be no more his trouble or charge, unless in charity he'll send to bury me.

Saveall. You will not desperately work a violent end upon yourself?

Careless. No, sir; the devil's not so great with me. But my heart—I feel it ready to break. My uncle is no more my uncle, nor you my friend, all by my own fault. And what should I do here but in to my bed and out o' the world presently. Wat! Wat!

'*Enter* Wat.'

[*Wat.*] Ay, here, sir.

Saveall. I have dallied too long and tempted him too far, I fear.

Careless. Lay down my bed.

Wat. Your wench is come indeed, but I hope you will not to bed before he be gone.

Careless. Lay down my bed I say. But first unbutton me.

Wat. Lord, how his heart beats! Pangs of death, I fear.

Saveall. Not so, I hope. I will now come to the point, sir. Master Careless, be comforted.

Careless. I am, and well resolved, I thank my better angel.

Saveall. Your uncle's friends with you.

Careless. Alas, how can that be?

Saveall. I thought your spirit had been higher.

Careless. It will be, sir, anon, I hope.

Saveall. I have but dallied with you to search your temper.

Wat. But you have searched too deep, I fear, sir.

Careless. Ah!

Saveall. Your uncle is friends with you, I say, so far as to make a further trial of your nature. You may be yet his heir, for your aunt despaireth of any child by him, having fruitlessly been married now these two years.

Careless. Ah! But, good sir, can this be?

Saveall. It is, and I will bring you to him and see that all be well.

Careless. Your noble friendship hath revived me, sir. O run and fetch my cloak. Tell Phoebe I cannot stay to give her any satisfaction now; I must go see my uncle first.

(*Exit* Wat.

Saveall. Poor gentleman, how weakly he standeth! The sight of his uncle will recover him. Come, Master Careless, let us go.

'*Enter* Wat *with his cloak.*'

Careless. Sir, what do you think if I should first, according to the reformation of my mind, cut off my undecent hair, and change this garish apparel for a civil, well-worn student's suit? I can be fitted presently hard by.

Saveall. No, the mind reformed is enough; your habit well becometh you.   (*Exeunt* Saveall *and* Careless.

Wat. Now, wit, an't be thy will, go with him. And I hope this will be his last hot fit of the uncle.

'*Enter* Phoebe.'

Phoebe. Your master's gone forth, it seems.

Wat. Called by his fortune, he is so.

Phoebe. Shuns he the sight of me? I'll overtake him.

Wat. Oh, your patience, sweet Mistress Phoebe, a little patience. He's gone to be happy and to make you happy. I dare promise you a satin gown within this sennight.
For let me tell thee, Mistress Phoebe bright,
He's reconciled to his uncle knight.

[*Phoebe.*] Away, pimp, flamster! I came to be serious with him, to let him know the miseries I suffer by the wrongs he has done me, and that I can nor will no longer bear 'em.

Wat. Nor him neither, will you? Take heed what you say, madam Marion.

Phoebe. No, nor him neither, you pandarly parasite, till he make his vows good and me an honest woman.

Wat. By'r lady, a shrewd task, and I fear an impossible work.

Phoebe. Sirrah, I will claw your ugly face till thou undertak'st it with him to make it easy.

Wat. Hold, hold! I'll do you all the good I can.

Phoebe. Oh, will you so?

Wat. How desperately valiant a whore grows when she is so poor that her clothes fear no tearing.—But by what means can you hope to bring this work about?

Phoebe. You know I have a wealthy kinsman in the city.

Wat. Oh, Master Saleware, and he has a wife too that bears it up bravely.

Phoebe. Pimp impudent, shall I claw your face into blushes at my injuries? To be mocked out of my maidenhead when I was upon a good match in the country; then with a promise of marriage to be enticed from my friends into fool's Paradise—that was a new title for the city—and here to be used and abused from lodging to lodging by him that now flies me for the decays he hath brought me to? But my kinsman has money though I have none, and for money there is law to be found, and in a just cause he will not let me sink, he says, for I have told him all.

Wat. But not the how many times, the whens, the wheres, and the wherewithals, I hope, have you?

Phoebe. Sirrah, I shall show you and your master too a way to more civility, since I am thus abused and slighted.

Wat. You have schooled me handsomely, and brought me into sense of your injuries. You have been overwronged, but not overwrought nor overworn. You do excel in beauty, strength, and spirit, which makes you in your very anger now appear so lovely that I profess myself your creature. What would a kiss of this fair hand now make me do, and of those lips what not?   '*She strikes him.*'

Phoebe. Away, you creature'!

Wat. Leave these temptations; do not strike me too deeply in love with you.

Phoebe. Away, you creature!

Wat. 'Tis true I am your creature, as I am my master's; and sometimes the serving creature breaks his fast with a bit off the spit before the same meat is served up to his master's table, but is never denied to dine upon his master's leavings. You cannot think what an appetite that frown gives me.

Phoebe. You are a saucy rascal.

Wat. Good wit, too! My appetite needs no sauce, nor shall you need to make use of law or friend against my master but myself.

Phoebe. You!

Wat. Be ruled by me. If I do not lay you down and join with you presently in a course that shall content you, then— hang me, lady, at your door.

Phoebe. What do you mean?

Wat. In the next room we shall find pen, ink and paper. You shall write him such a letter (as I will dictate to you) that shall so nettle him.

Phoebe. Nay, I did intend to leave him part of my mind in writing before I went.

'*Enter* Saleware.'

O cousin, I want you—

Wat [*Aside*]. A pox of this interrupting cuckold, he hinders all trading but his wive's. Zounds, I was going with full speed a-tilt, as the learned say. Had not this horn-head come, we had writ lines together should have put down *Hero and Leander*.—Hark you, Mistress Phoebe, is this your kinsman that you told me you had told all the business to?

Saleware. Yes, sir, I am the gentleman; and she has told me so much, sir, that I must tell you to tell your master from me, and as I would tell him myself if he were here personally present, he is a most dishonest gentleman if he do her not lawful right by marrying her; and that right I came to demand, and obtain of him, or to denounce the law against him.

Wat. How happy are you that you came short to tell him so; else he would ha' so beaten you as never was citizen beaten since the great battle of Finsbury Field.

Saleware. Your great words cannot make me fear his blows (I am not dashed nor 'bashed) nor cross him out of my book for fear of any such payment. I have him there for four score pound, as you know, though you are pleased to forget me. But *sapientia mea mihi, stultitia tua tibi.*

Wat. Cry mercy, Master Saleware, is it you? I hope Mistress Saleware is well, your most exquisite and most courtly wife, the flower-de-luce of the city.

Saleware. Well, wag, well; you must not now put me off with my wife. She's well and much respected. I come to speak of and for my distressed kinswoman, her whom your wicked master has most wickedly dealt withal. He has deflowered and deluced her and led her from her friends, and out of her country into fool's paradise by making her believe he would marry her. And here he has put her on and put her off with hopes and delays till she is come to both woe and want; and (which may prove her most affliction if he be suffered to forsake her) she is with child by him.

Wat. Say you so, Mistress Phoebe? Here's small show of it yet.

Phoebe. Sirrah, I shall show you and your master too a way to more civility, if I be thus abused and slighted.

Wat. By the way, Master Saleware, how many children have you by your most amiable wife?

Saleware. Sir, that needs not to fall by the way of our discourse.

Wat. But by the way I speak, of getting children. Or, I pray tell me, did not you correct one of her children once, for which your wife reprehended you and bade you correct your own? And how then shall my master be sure that this, if it be one, is his?

Saleware. What an asinego's this! I shall find a time, sir, to talk with your master. In the meantime I tell you that my

kinswoman is a gentlewoman of as good blood as himself,
and of the best in Herefordshire—.

Wat. Yes, Welsh blood.

Saleware. And shall find friends that shall not see her
abused by you nor him. There is law to be found for money,
and money to be found for friends, and friends to be found
in the Arches; and so tell your master. Come away, cousin.

Wat. But one word before you go, sir. Is this gentlewoman, (who was but a country chambermaid when my
master took her to his mercy), of such boasted blood, your
cousin by your own, or by your wive's side, I pray?

Saleware. Sirrah, like a saucy companion as you are,
though you meddle with me, that am a common-council
man, I charge you meddle not with my wife. You have had
two or three jerks at her.

Wat. I was warn'd before, sir, in my own understanding;
for she is for great persons.

Saleware. Then know your distance, sir.

Wat. Yet give me leave to wait you down, sir. [*To*
Phoebe] Cudso! Did it tell it kinsman that it is got with
champkin?

Phoebe. You are a pandarly rascal, and I'll be a terror both
to you and your patron.   (*Exeunt omnes.*

[SCENE II]

'*Enter* Thrivewell, Lady [Thrivewell].'

Thrivewell. How can you think so?

Lady. Think! I see 't apparently upon your face, and hear
it in your sighs. Your broken sleeps tonight, when your own
groans waked you, declared no less. But had I had the
power of some wifes with their husbands, I could have
fetched it out of you. Waking once (I thank you), you took
me in your arm, but when you found 'twas I, you turned
away as in a dream.

Thrivewell. Sure you dream now; whence can this talk
proceed else?

Lady. I must not give it over till I know the cause of your
melancholy fit. Do you doubt my duty or my loyalty?
Perhaps you do, and so make me the cause of your affliction.

Thrivewell. May such a thought within me stick me to the endless torments.

Lady. 'Tis lately entertained, whate'er it be; you came heart-whole to town, and jovial. Ha' you been drawn for security into bonds by any of my friends for great sums, and forced to pay 'em?

Thrivewell. Fie, fie!

Lady. Are any great friends of yours in question, attainted, imprisoned, or run away?

Thrivewell. Psewh.

Lady. Or are you further grieved about your nephew Careless? I thought that your friend Saveall and myself had made his peace with you, and that you had sent for him. Do you repent that?

Thrivewell. No, no, sweetheart, he shall be welcome. And pray let me entreat you make no further inquisition. If, as you suppose, there be a trouble in my thoughts, I shall soon pass it over.

Lady. Tell me, or I shall prove the greater trouble. I would those few examples of women that could not keep their husbands' counsels had been burnt, and the women too, rather than I should be distrusted thus and slighted by a husband.

Thrivewell. Nay thee, you'll grieve me indeed.

Lady. There has been many examples of discreet women that have not only kept their husbands' counsels, but advise and help 'em in extremities, and delivered 'em out of dangers.

Thrivewell. I pray content yourself.

Lady. Be you content to tell me then what troubles you. And I pray you tell me speedily, now presently, or—excuse me in my vow—it is the last request that ever I will make to you, and the last question I'll ever ask you; and (the easier to get it from you), I promise you by the continuance of my faith to you (which by this kiss I seal), be it a deadly injury to myself, I will forgive it freely, not be troubled at it.

Thrivewell [*Aside*]. I shall do that now which few wise men would.
But she's discreet, and has a fortitude
Above the boast of women. Should that fail,

And this too weighty knowledge for a wife
Should prove a torment to her, I'm excus'd:
She pulls it on herself. And for revenge
Should she against her protestation move it,
I am enough above her.

   Lady. You are resolv'd, it seems, to keep your secret
Unto yourself. Much good, sir, may it do you.

   Thrivewell. No, you shall know it, sir, and if unshaken
Now in your love to me, the wonder of all wives.
You're bound by a fair pledge, the kiss you gave me,
To be unmov'd, and to forgive it though
It be a deadly injury to yourself.
It is, and 'tis a great one; and so great,
But that you have seal'd my pardon, the hid knowledge
Of it should feed upon my heart and liver
Till life were banish'd thence, rather than pull
Your just revenge upon me. Yet you frown not!
But before I declare it to your justice,
Let me renew my mercy,   *'Kiss.'*
And on this altar, which I have profan'd
While it breath'd sacred incense, now with penitence
Offer religious vows never to violate
My faith or love to you again. One more,   *'Kiss.'*
Before you hear it; for if then you stand not
Firm to your mercy, it must be my last.

   Lady. What do you but violate your love to me
Now in your most unjust suspicion?

   Thrivewell. I'll trespass so no more. Yet many husbands
(I wish they had my sorrow, and no less
Purpos'd to reformation), wrong their wives.

   Lady. Leave these perambulations; to the point.
You have unlawfully lain with some woman!

   Thrivewell. 'Tis said; and now your doom.

   Lady. Ha, ha, ha! Here's a business!
Would somebody heard you, faith! Nay, of five hundred
That now might overhear us (I mean not only
Gallants but grave substantial gentlemen)
Could be pick'd out a twelve good men and true
To find you guilty, I would then condemn you.
But such a jury must be panell'd first.

Thrivewell. And can you be so mild? Then farewell
thought.

Lady. Thought of your mistress, sir, and then farewell
My jealousy! For let me tell you, sir,
That I have had an ache upon these brows
Since your last being in town. And since you have dealt
So faithfully as to tell me it is one—
There's no more, is there?—

Thrivewell. No, upon my vow.

Lady. Name me the woman. If it be the same
That I suspect, I'll never suspect more.

Thrivewell. As faithfully as to my confessor: Light-weight
Saleware my silkman's wife.

Lady. The same I meant—
You're a fair-dealing husband. On what condition?
Come, this is merry talk. Prithee, on what condition?
Only to bring good custom to her shop
And send her husband venison, flesh for flesh?
I did observe you bought there all last term,
And wish'd me to her shop, and Master Saveall
With divers others, to bestow our moneys.
Troth, she's a handsome one. Prithee, on what
Conditions?

Thrivewell. Thou shalt know all, to purge me of my folly.

Lady. Well said.

Thrivewell. After a costly and a tedious suit,
With many an answer 'No', and 'No such woman',
At length she yields for a hundred pieces;
Had 'em, and I enjoy'd her once.

Lady. That was when you last term sat up all night and
said you sat up with the three lady gamesters.

Thrivewell. It is confessed.

Lady. Fair dealing still.

Thrivewell. But here was the foul dealing, and for which
I hate her now: I having paid so great a fine, and ta'en
possession, thought after to deal rent-free.

Lady. A pepper-corn a quarter if she be pepper-proof.

Thrivewell. But she at my very next approach, which was
but yesterday, denies me egress except I make it a new purchase at the same former rate, and so for all times after.

Lady. Troth, 'tis unreasonable, a hundred pound a time! How rich would citizens be if their wives were all so paid, and how poor the court and country! But husht, here comes Master Saveall with your nephew, I take it. A handsome gentleman! Could he be so debauched?

'*Enter* Saveall, Careless.'

Saveall. Sir, I have brought you home a reformado, and do entreat (for what I have said unto him and he hath fairly answered unto me) that words may not by you be multiplied.

Thrivewell. Not a word of unkindness, nephew; you are welcome. Give me your hand, George; thou art welcome.

Careless [*Aside*]. I shall be George o' horseback once more, I see.— In all humility I thank you, sir.

Thrivewell. Nay, now thou speakest and look'st too tamely, George. I would have thee keep and use the lively spirit that thou hadst, but not to let it fly at random as it has done, George.

Careless. Sir, I have learnt now, by the inconveniences I have met with in those extravagant outflights, the better to contain it within the limits of your leave and fair allowance hereafter.

Thrivewell. Well said, and again welcome, George. But— and this you shall give me leave to say, Master Saveall— I remit your thanks for any inclination I had towards this reconcilement, till I do you some further kindness; only you had good advocates, who pleaded friendly for you, Master Saveall and your aunt there, before she ever saw you, whom you may thank.

Careless [*Aside*]. A man must be so tied now.

Thrivewell. Pray take notice of her.

Careless. I cannot use respect enough, sir.

Thrivewell. I like that modesty.

Saveall. Doubt him in nothing, for he is come home.

Careless. Madam, as you are my generous patroness, and myself so all unworthy, my duty checks me in my approach to you.

Lady. You are the more entirely welcome, cousin. '*Kiss.*'

Careless [*Aside*]. She kisses like an old man's wife: that is, as a child late starved at nurse sucks a fresh flowing breast.

Lady. You must not, sir, be bashful.

Careless. 'Twill less become me to presume, good madam.

Thrivewell. George, here's a lodging for you in this house, and my table has a place for you. Send for your man to wait upon you. Ha' you Wat still?

Careless. Yes, sir; an honest, true-hearted civil fellow he is, as I have managed him. He can say grace now.

Thrivewell. The world's well mended. Tomorrow you shall give me a note of your debts, George, which I'll take order for, if I may presume you have any.

Careless. Some driblets, sir. My credit has not lately wronged me much.

Saveall. You speak sententiously: for credit sought
With tradesmen, then their wares are dearer bought.
So gentlemen are wronged.

Thrivewell. Then not to wrong ourselves, let's in to dance.
                                                (*Exeunt omnes.*

ACT II · SCENE I

'Alicia, Lady [Thrivewell], Servingman, Prentice.'

Alicia. All Cheapside and Lombard Street, madam, could not have furnished you with a more complete bargain. You will find it in the wearing, and thank me both for the goodness of the stuff and of the manufacture.

Lady. But now the price, Mistress Saleware. I grant your commodity is good: the gold and silver laces and fringes are rich and I hope well wrought. Has your man made a note of the particulars and their prices, at the rate of ready money (for I buy so), and not as you would book 'em to an under-aged heir or a court cavalier, to expect payment two or three years hence and find it perhaps never? I come with, 'Here is one for tother.'

Alicia. I know your ladyship's payment[s] such, and they are prized so, madam, to a farthing.

Lady. Let me see: broad plate silver and gold lace, 206

ounces half, and a dram, at five and tenpence the ounce,
60l, 5s—3d, ob. 4. Five and tenpence an ounce is dear.

Alicia. I protest unto you, madam, that parcel of lace, for
a bed as you intend it, was bespoken and agreed for at six
shillings the ounce by a very great person; but because
ready money came not to fetch it off, fortune reserved it here
for you. You could not have been so fitted on the sudden else
within London walls, and I am glad the same fortune was so
favourable to me as by my hands to design it for your ladyship's use and pleasure. I hope, madam, we shall hear of a
young heir a-coming shortly, and that will make it a rich and
fortunate bed indeed. And then Sir Oliver would thank me
too.

Lady [*Aside*]. What a bold slut it is.— Well then, the rest
of the particulars here, of laces and fringes, loops and
buttons, makes the sum of all an hundred pound eight
shillings, fourpence halfpenny. I am no good arithmetician,
but if any be overcast and overpaid, you must allow restitu-
tion.

Alicia. Yes, good madam.

Lady. Is all put up into this box?

Alicia. All, madam.

Lady. Give me my purse. [*To* Servant] Take you home
that while I make payment for it. Your gold-weights,
Mistress Saleware.   (*Exit* Servant.

Alicia. Here, madam, all in readiness.

Lady. You take no gold but what is weight, I presume.

Alicia. 'Tis but light pains to weight it, madam. But let
me save your ladyship that labour.

Lady. Nor shall it be your trouble. Command your
servant, I pray, for a glass of your beer—

Alicia. Some beer for my lady presently.

                                        (*Exit* Prentice.

Lady. That I may tell you in more privacy what perhaps
you would not have him hear. For prentices, though they
are bound to keep their masters' secrets, are not all privy to
their mistresses'. That's more a journeyman's office.

Alicia. Your ladyship is pleased.

Lady. Not very well with myself, for I have gone beyond
my commission in this bargain and exceeded my husband's

allowance. Here's one hundred pounds, eight shillings, four-pence ob. in the bill, and he allows me but the bare hundred pounds.

Alicia. The odd money is but a small matter, madam.

Lady. A great matter in an honest poor country lady's purse, may serve her a whole Christmas at Post and Pair or Farthing Gleek, when the gay gamesters' wives o' the city may command the hundreds out the purses of such poor ladies' husbands. But here is the odd money, eight shillings fourpence halfpenny, and so all's paid.

Alicia. What means your ladyship?

Lady. Do you not understand me? Then I'll tell you that which I thought fit to conceal from your servant, and from your husband too, had he been here. Perhaps he knows not on't. My husband left with you, or lent you the last term, a hundred pound, which he assigned to me, and now I have it in commodity. Had you forgot it, when it was to do you a good turn, when your absent husband failed you, and you wanted it?

Alicia. A good turn, madam?

Lady. Yes, was it not, to have the free use of a hundred pound ready money a whole quarter of a year, through a dead vacation, and at last to take it out in wares? A good turn, I think, for a tradeswoman. Take heed you do not by your sullenness make me suspect another kind of good turn, or that you did my husband any to my injury, nor deny the receipt of his money, lest I take up a violence that will not become me nor you be able to bear. Be therefore well advised both in what you say and who hears me. Somebody comes.

'*Enter* Prentice *with beer.*'

Alicia. Madam, your beer.

Lady. I'll pledge you, Mistress Saleware.

Alicia. I shall presume then, madam.   '*Drinks.*'

Lady. This was right cast, was it not, friend?

Prentice. Your ladyship will find it so.   '*Lady drinks.*'

Alicia. And I hope you will find your money so well bestowed, madam, that you will vouchsafe always to know the shop.

Lady. Ever upon the like occasion, Mistress Saleware. So, most kindly farewell, sweet Mistress Saleware.

Alicia. The humblest of your servants, madam. Open the boot for my lady.

Lady. 'Tis done; my coachman does it.   (*Exit* Lady.

Alicia. I would the devil were in your coachman's coat to take his carriage for his pains.   '*Lady returns.*'

Lady. One more word, Mistress Saleware. [*Aside*] Can it be he?

Alicia. Lay your commands on me, good madam.

'*Curtsy.*'

Lady. Not to your trouble, I perceive a young gentleman attends for conference with you. Is not his name Fitz-gerrard?

Alicia. No, madam, his name is Bellamy, much depend-ing on the young Lord Lovely.

Lady. I thought I had known him. He is a handsome youth. I cannot blame you now with him, but beware of old knights that have young ladies of their own. Once more adieu, sweet Mistress Saleware.   (*Exit* Lady.

Alicia. Most courteous madam—and once more to the devil. But on my life, her chaste ladyship is taken with this beardless Bellamy. How she shot eyes at him!

[*Enter* Bellamy.]

Bellamy. Now may your servant obtain a hearing, lady?

Alicia. My ears are open, sir.

Bellamy. But you are sad or angry. Why seems that brow to threaten a subjection over him that is your vanquished captive? Or has Cupid placed his bow there bent at me, whose heart already lodges all his arrows, never to be restored but by your pity?

Alicia. Fie, fie upon't! What talk is this? I am vexed, and you would mad me,

Bellamy. What has displeased you?

Alicia. A cross business that has happened in my shop today. I being none of the wisest chapwoman have under-sold a parcel of the best commodities my husband had. And should he know't, we should have such a squabble.

Bellamy. Husbands should be so served that do impose those mercenary offices on their wives.

Alicia. Talk so and I will hear you; your amorous notes sound like play speeches.

Bellamy. Servile, nay, slavish offices, ranking their wives with their prentices.

Alicia. They pretend only that we should overlook our servants, when they but set us there for show to draw in custom. But in making us such overseers they are overseen themselves. Shopkeepers' wives will be meddling and dealing in their kind and as they are able, as well as their husbands, some much better and more profitable. But I was over-reached, I confess.

Bellamy. For no great matter, I hope?

Alicia. No, the matter was not much—that never fretted me—but the manner has e'en killed a she-shopkeeper. I cannot be long lived, here under a penthouse, as my lord, you know, told me when he said he would shut me out of this servitude, and that I should change my coat (though my husband could not before he were an alderman) and be ranked with ladies.

Bellamy. My lord has still the same regard of you.

Alicia. So it appears, by the tailor and the mercer whom he sent four days since to measure me out and suit me to his honour and no return of them found yet. His land might ha' been measured all and sold while a poor suit is dreamt on, had he borne the mind of some lord.

Bellamy. I doubt not but this paper will clear that jealousy. And while you read, I'll speak that which I dare not utter through sighs and blushes to an entire attention.
I am of noble blood myself, freeborn,
And not without good education;
But since I am engag'd in this employment
And made an instrument of others' lust,
I find myself a scandal to my name,
To honour and to virtue, the base blot
Of pandar sticking on me. But not this
Alone is my affliction. Here's my torment,
That while I do true service to my lord
(Whom I must ever honour), in my agency

Unto yourself (whom I cannot but love),
I find myself a traitor to his trust
In my negotiation for myself.
Nor can I find it possible to desist
Mine own attempts to you, or forbear to urge
Your constancy to him.

 Alicia. How easy a work
'Twere for one woman to supply 'em both,
And hold her husband play to level acoil:
A wooden two-leav'd book, a pair of tables,
Would do't.

 Bellamy. How wretched is that suppliant who must make
Suit to obtain that which he fears to take!

 Alicia. At the Bear, at the bridge foot, six o'clock; good.
Sir, I find my lord's honourable appointment's here, and
have heard you all this while.

 Bellamy. How I could wish, and was in hope, you had not.

 Alicia. I will not blame you on your lord's behalf,
Because you have enough rebuk'd yourself.
But, sir, if you presume upon the favour
I give your lord, and therefore to obtain me
'Cause I am his, you undervalue me
To think that I can stoop unto his servant,
Though almost his companion, you may think,
After that degradation by degrees,
I may in time descend unto his footman.
I'm no cast garment of his lordship's yet.

 Bellamy. You have schooled me fairly. I am humbled,
lady—   '*Going.*'

 Alicia. D'ye hear, d'ye hear, sir, Master Bellamine, one
word before you go.

 Prentice. What would he buy, mistress? Can you take his
money?

 [*Alicia.*] Sir, d'ye hear? [*To* Prentice] Pray attend you
the tother end o' th' shop. If I cannot handle a customer,
why does your master trust me? [*To* Bellamy] Could a frown
fright you? Let a smile then cheer you.

 Bellamy. And that's a heavenly one,
As that of Cynthia at Endymion.

 Alicia. Pray leave your player-like passionate expressions,

and if you love me, like a man speak to me, as I am a woman.
Are you silent? If you doubt the length of my man's ears at
that distance, you may whisper. What, so? But that is a
right shop-whisper indeed with tradeswomen that are handsome. Is that the most you will give, sir? Could I afford it so,
do you think I'd make two words wi'ye? Yet this before you
go. ('*Kiss.*') Now match it for the price. I'll give it you for
nothing.

Bellamy. I shall forget I have a lord. I must forget him
here.

Alicia. Do so, and if, I say, you love me, speak plainly
what you would have me do, or what you would do with me.
[*Aside*] (I love to daunt these young things that love before
they can love to the purpose or speak to't handsomely, like
a boy that would fain be shooting at wildfowl before he
knows how to discharge a birding-piece.)—I would hear you
speak. You have often muttered and fribbled some intentions towards me, but I would hear you speak. Come, if you
love me, lay by the fear of the lord that sent you, and tell me
roundly now what you would have me do.

Bellamy. I would entreat you—

Alicia. Well, what?

Bellamy. That you would be pleased—

Alicia. With what? Or to do what?

Bellamy. To wear this pair of silk stockings for me.

Alicia. Is that all your suit? 'Tis granted, with my thanks
to you. Have you no more to say?

Bellamy. Yes; I say you are the beautifullest of women
and that my lord in your enjoyment is the happiest—

Alicia. Nay, think not of your lord, but ask me . . . something.

Bellamy. I would, but dare not hope for such a favour;
you'll never grant it my unworthiness.

Alicia. How can you tell?

Bellamy. You will not wrong my lord so as to do it.

Alicia. Not in his sight perhaps. What is it? Come.

Bellamy. It is—

Alicia. It is then; let it be so. Go to school, child.

Bellamy. It is—that you would—let me—give you this
ring, and grace it with your finger.

Alicia. Will that be a wrong to your lord?

Bellamy. Yes, to wear any favours but his own.

Alicia. Does he know this?

Bellamy. No, nor I would not that he should (and given by me) for all the rubies in Cheapside, where I bought this but now, over the way.

Alicia. Come, sir, I'll dally wi'ye no longer. I know what you would have with me.

Bellamy. And now you will betray me. I am shamed then, and undone.

Alicia. No, but I have you o' the hip. 'Tis plain you would lie with me. Deny it if you can.

Bellamy. Oh, dear, did I say so now?

Alicia. What need you when I know it? You would lie with me and you shall. Take courage, man.

Bellamy. But, in good earnest, shall I? Shall I?

Alicia. Yes, in good earnest; you'll find it no trifling business when you come to't once. But, sir, upon condition.

Bellamy. Any condition, lady.

Alicia. All purpose on't is lost, and all comes out else.

Bellamy. Name your condition; I'll perform it if it be in the power of my life.

Alicia. You saw here at your coming a fair lady.

Bellamy. I took no notice of her.

Alicia. But she did of you. She is called the Lady Thrivewell.

Bellamy. Sir Oliver Thrivewell's lady?

Alicia. The same. You have known her, it seems?

Bellamy. Seen her before she was married.

Alicia. I will be brief with you. As you love me, she loves you as eagerly, but with much more boldness. You saw her whisper me, and how loth she was to depart when her eye was upon you.

Bellamy. I did observe it.

Alicia. She is my noble friend and the sweetest lady— I need not set her out. But though you think you suffer in your honour in being an instrument 'twixt your lord and me, with the base blot of pandar sticking on you—these were your words—I have engaged myself for her to be your pandaress. Be so; I shall be even with you in business if you account it so.

Bellamy. What d'ye mean, lady?

Alicia. To urge against myself for that sweet lady, which no woman else I think would do that loves you so unfeignedly as I. But 'tis my fate, and the injunction I must lay upon you, to make me yours, that first you give yourself to her embraces. I'll give you means for your access to her, and your success with her. Which done, and on your faith affirmed to me 'tis so, I will perpetually be yours more freely than your lord's.

Bellamy. You urge this but to try my constancy.

Alicia. For that I'll satisfy you soon. My husband['s] coming—we must tonight at the Bear—my lord writes so.

'*Enter* Saleware.'

Saleware. And there I will direct you in your progress. Ally, how dost? Master Bellamy, how is't? How does my noble lord? You are sad, methinks. Ha' you overbought anything here and so repent your bargain? Or cannot my wife and you agree upon't? You must use Master Bellamy kindly, my sweet Ally: he is our noblest lord's most special favourite, and must find all fair dealing here, as well when I am abroad as at home, sweetheart.

Bellamy. You hear not me complain, sir. Fare you well.

(*Exit* Bellamy.

Saleware. What an asinego's this! He might ha' thanked me for my good words, though I meant him no good will. I hope thou hast over-reached him indeed.

Alicia. Thomas, your hopes are vain, Thomas, in seating me here to over-reach or under-reach anybody. I am weary of this mechanic course, Thomas, and of this coarser habit, as I have told you divers and sundry times, Thomas, and indeed, of you, Thomas, that confine me to 't. But the bound must obey.

Saleware. Never the sooner for a hasty word, I hope, sweet Ally—not of me, nor of my shop, I prithee, at season-able times, love. But for thy habit—though this be decent on a citizen's wife—use thine own fancy. Let it be as courtly or as lady-like as thou pleasest, or my lord desires.

Alicia. Then I am friends again.

Saleware. Troth, and I'll call thee friend. And, I prithee, let that be our familiar and common compellation. Friend—it will sound daintily, especially when thou shalt appear too gallant to be my wife.

Alicia. Then let it be so, friend.

Saleware. In truth it shall, and I am very much taken with it. Friend, I have found a customer today that will take off my rich parcel of broad bed-lace that my Lord Paylate bespoke and left on my hands for lack of money.

Alicia. I have sold it already, friend, with other laces, at a good rate.

Saleware. And all for ready money, friend?

Alicia. Yes, friend, a hundred pounds, and somewhat moe.

Saleware. Who would be, or who could live without such a friend in such a shop? This money comes so pat for a present occasion, to stop a gap. It has stopped a gap already, friend.

Alicia. I have disposed of the money, the odd hundred pound, for apparel, friend, and other accommodations for myself.

Saleware. Never the sooner for a hasty word, I hope, friend.

Alicia. I have done it, friend, whereby to appear more courtly and lady-like, as you say, to gain you more custom to your shop.

Saleware. Ouch, friend, is it so?

Alicia. And, friend, you must not be angry or think much of it, if you respect your profit, friend.

Saleware. I were no friend but a wretch if I would. No, let it go, friend, and—*sapientia mea mihi* is my word—I must not grudge at my friend in anything.

Alicia. Then, friend, let your shop be your own care for the rest of this day; I have some business abroad.

Saleware. Whither, sweet friend?

Alicia. Is that a friendly question?

Saleware. I am corrected, friend. But will you not take a man to wait upon you?

Alicia. To watch me, shall I, and give you account of my actions? Was that spoke like a friend?

Saleware. I am again corrected, friend. Do your own pleasure. You'll return to supper?

Alicia. Yet again?

Saleware. And again I am corrected, friend.

Alicia. Neither to supper nor to bed perhaps.

Saleware. Never the sooner for a hasty word, I hope.

Alicia. But if I chance to stay, you cannot be a faithful friend and ask me where or in what company: friendship, you know, allows all liberty.   (*Exit* Alicia.

Saleware: *Sapientia mea mihi*. A witty wife, with an imperious will,

Being cross'd, finds means to cross her husband still;

And tradesmen that so match must not with gall

Temper their wives, but sweetly by wit-all.

(*Exit* Saleware.

[SCENE II]

'*Enter* Careless, *with two letters in his hand, and* Wat *with a candle and wax*.'

Careless. Does not the world come finely on, Wat, ha? And have not we convenient comings-in already, ha?

'*Show gold*.'

Wat. Better than we know how to have paid for; that's the glory on't.

Careless. I need no more ensconcing now in Ram Alley nor the sanctuary of Whitefriars, the forts of Fuller's Rents and Milford Lane, whose walls are daily battered with the curses of bawling creditors. My debts are paid, and here's a stock remaining of gold, pure gold. Hark, how sweetly it chinks.   '*Careless seals his letters*.'

Wat. Yes, and 'twill ring the changes shortly.

Careless. For necessaries, Wat, for necessaries it shall change and ring all out; and 'twill, so long as I have an uncle and know how to manage him.

Let money fly,

I can no faster spend than he supply.

Wat. For necessaries, sir; but you must not now count sack and tobacco, whores and fiddlers in abundance necessaries.

Careless. Why, pray?

Wat. Because you'll have but little then for extraordinaries, that is to say, in a gentleman, for charitable and pious works and uses.

Careless. The fellow's spoiled.

Wat. Not spoiled neither, for I would but waive your purpose of flying at all new game, and neglect[ing] your poor whore, who now begins to be so violent for wrongs she can no longer bear, that she intends to pursue you with her complaints hither to your uncle's house.

Careless. My uncle's house? My house. Is not the first morning's draught mine?

Wat. With great reason, for you are first dry in the morning.

Careless. Is not the question first asked me, what will you have to breakfast, What will please you for dinner, and what for supper? Has not my uncle let out moneys and taken bonds and mortgages in my name? Do not his tenants crouch to me, and his servants all call me young master? And does not my uncle take care to marry me to ten thousand pound, and a thing like a wife?

Wat. You have got a brave possession here, I must needs say, and I applaud your fortune most in this, that your young aunt, the noble lady here, who you feared would prove a cruel stepdame to you, appears to be more friend to you than your uncle. 'Tis a most gracious sunshine in her.

Careless. She shall lose nothing by't. I have thought a way to requite her.

Wat. But sir, for Mistress Phoebe, will you take no order for the poor soul?

Careless. I do not like your zealous solicitation, but here's an order for her, in answer of her malapert letter you brought me last night. Give it to her, and these five pieces, upon condition that she never come, write, or send to me again, till I send to her.

Wat. That's somewhat hard, sir.

Careless. Nay, look you, Wat, you are a little mistaken in me. I must give over whoring, for special causes thereunto me moving.

Wat. Oh, now I find you. And 'twere richly worth your

patience if you could win the widow by 't, for whom you
stood in fair election once, until your last debauchment.

Careless. I shall stand fairer for her, sir, when I leave
working but a week or two, shall I not?

Wat. Yes, if you leave it quite. But to forsake her whom
you have brought low, to fall to others, were such a thing—

Careless. Well, sir, it may be I will, it may be I won't—
what's that to you? Carry you the letter and the money, and
try how that will work with her.

Wat. I'll do my best, but if she should exclaim and bring
on her cousin, Master Saleware, to be clamorous—

Careless. Her cousin's a cuckold. Exclaim and clamorous!
Give me my money again.

Wat. Nay, I am gone, sir.   (*Exit* Wat.

'*Enter* Saveall.'

Careless. The rogue's in faction with 'em. O noble Master
Saveall, you have most fairly kept your minute with me.
I have written my letter, sealed it and all, here, to the widow.

Saveall. So early? That is well.

Careless. I have written no less than six large epistles this
morning, and sent 'em now by my man to be conveyed into
the country to lords and knights, with all the news, spiritual
and temporal, foreign and domestic, that could possibly fall
into a private gentleman's collection.

Saveall. Is it possible?

Careless. With such dexterity, that if I would make a trade
on 't, I could undo all the newsmongers in town that live
by 't.

Saveall. It is a most commendable practice in a gentleman,
and it will mature your judgement in both the commonwealth and state affairs, and in short time invite you unto
the chair or helm.

Careless. When I am once married and settled, you shall
see. [*Aside*] What an ass 'tis—he believes me.

Saveall. How am I comforted in my mediation for you,
and how overjoyed will your uncle be at the use you make of
your retirements.

Careless. I confess it is (by reason of my unwontedness to
it) some difficulty for me to write to women; wherefore,

since you have so nobly undertaken the conveyance of this, let me beseech you to apologize for the rudeness of my style.

[*Gives him a letter.*]

Saveall. *To the fair hands of the most accomplished in virtue, Mistress Anne Crosstill, present, I pray, with my service.* The outside hath no rudeness on it, and (I doubt it not) she shall find within all sweetness and urbanity.

Careless. As you may interpret it to her, sir.

Saveall. Sir, what I have already said, and do intend to say unto her from her uncle and myself on your behalf, together with what you have here written, shall (I doubt it not) prepare so fair a way of proceeding for you that at your visit of her you may say, *Veni, vidi, vici,* she is your own.

Careless. And then—aha! Master Saveall!

Saveall. Expect your fortune modestly, and when it comes, embrace it with discretion.

Careless. Sir, I am edified.

Saveall. It is well if you be so. I will put my undertaking in action presently. Pray for my good success.

[*Exit* Saveall.]

Careless. I dare not tell him now I cannot, but I wish [him] well for the money's sake. And let the vintners pray, and all the decayed sparks about the town, whom I will raise out of ashes into flame again. Let them pray for my good works. [*Sees* Nurse *coming.*] Oh, my young lady-aunt's grave waiting-woman! If she were not hers, and out of this house, I should take her for a bawd now. But being hers, and here, how much may I mistake? All flesh is frail.

'*Enter* Nurse [Closet] *with caudle cup.*'

Closet. Not to disturb your morning meditations, my lady has sent you—

Careless. And you have brought me—what, sweet Mistress Closet?

Closet. A part of her ladyship's own breakfast. It is very cordial and comfortable to the spirits, I assure you, and delectable to the younger sort, and profitable to the old.

Careless. One of Robert Greene's works, or the mad doctor that preaches boiled in 't, I think.

Closet. 'Tis a composition of mine own, sir, of many

excellent decoctions, of most wholesome, restorative and costly ingredients.

Careless. That it was sent by her makes it more excellent, whose bounteous care of me I must acknowledge exceeds all cost in carving to me and countenancing me at her table, in gracing me in presence of the ladies that come to visit her, in giving charge for decency in all things for my chamber, my fires shining, my odours burning, my livery served in, my soft and costly bed prepared and spread with perfumed linen.—Here's ambergris in this now.

Closet. Oh, is it so? Do you find that?

Careless. But though she is my own uncle's wife, I could e'en say 'tis pity a young man had her not.

Closet. What a wag's this!

Careless. She is a most sweet lady.

Closet. She is a sweet lady indeed; I can best speak it that have known her from the womb hitherto. A sweet infant she was born, and a sweet babe I swaddled it, and a sweet child I nursed it; I trained it up a sweet child. It was in manners a sweet child, at her book and sampler a sweet child. I never whipped it but once, and then it was sweet too, and sprawled but a little, and whimpered but a little, it was so sweet a child. And so she grew upwards and upwards towards woman, and a sweet youngling she was; and so grew upwards and upwards towards man, and then a sweet bride she was; and now a most sweet lady she is, as you say (and I commend you for it). And so she stands at a stay. For now she grows no more upwards than upon her wedding-day, not upwards as I would have her upwards: here I mean, young gentleman, could I but see a sweet babe of hers once by my master, I could be then content to sleep with my ancestors.

Careless. I had rather see your gibship hanged up with polecats in a warren, and your sweet lady with you, though I confess that were some pity. I hope her barrenness, or his, will preserve her from my curse.

Closet. I hope still, and she hopes still. And I make him of this broth for every morning, and many other good strengthening things (I cannot say for the same purpose), for I shall never see him have an heir by her.

Careless. Excellent! That's best of all.

Closet. Because you then are heir, say you so? Is that your love to your aunt?

Careless. No, I protest, Nurse, I meant by the broth—the bottom was the best of all.

Closet. Then I cry mercy.

Careless. Cannot all thy art and her cost find help for my uncle, think'st thou, to get a child?

Closet. Help? What d'ye mean? He might have help and helps enough were she not too virtuous.

Careless. Still thou mistak'st me, nurse.

Closet. Away, wag, away! Your aunt loves you too well to think so of her.

Careless. Nurse, as I hope to inherit anything here-after—

Closet. I should but serve you well to tell her your good thought of her.

Careless. Nurse, by this good . . . piece, I think no harm.

Closet. Nay, nay.

Careless. Take it, I say, and tell her, if thou wilt, that I love her so well that were she not mine uncle's wife, I would get her an heir myself rather than be his.

Closet. Kind young master, now I am heartily sorry that I moved you.

Careless. And for my uncle, were I his heir apparent, I rather wish he might live till all this world were weary of him and the next afraid to take him than I survive him. (Tongue, a pox punish you for lying!) Now I live well, and merrily, good nurse. Wealth and estates bring cares and troubles with 'em. Were all young heirs of my contented mind, parents and patrons would be better prayed for.

Closet. Good gentleman.

Lady ('*Within*'). Nurse Closet! Closet!

Closet. Oh, my lady calls.

Careless. Present my thanks and best respects unto her.

Closet. I should ha' told you first—I ha' forgot. My head is naught.

Careless. What member hast thou good then?

Closet. My lady desires you—this talk has put me out—oh, this head!—my lady desires you—

Careless. Desires she me, nurse?

Closet. Yes, sir, she desires you.

Careless. Refuse me if I desire not her as much, for all she is my uncle's leavings.

Closet. My lady desires you—

Careless. And she shall have me, nurse,—an she were ten uncles' wives and she ten of mine aunts.

Closet. Oh, this head! Nay, now you will not hear me. She desires you to go abroad in the coach with her.

Careless. Any whither: to Islington, Newington, Paddington, Kensington, or any of the city outleaps (I know 'em all) for a spurt and back again. Tell her I am up and ready for her, and could ha' been, without her stirrup-porridge, though I thank her for her care. A man can not be too well prepared or provided for so sweet a lady in so much distress —a very Andromeda, chained to a rock.

'*Takes up his cloak and sword.*'

Closet. What's this you say? I understand no word of it. I would take your answer right, though I faltered in my lady's message.

Careless. The devil's in this overrunning tongue of mine! I could find in my heart to worm him out with my teeth.

Closet. What must I tell my lady, sir?

Careless. That I am more obliged to her ladyship than I was to my mother: she has brought me a new man into the world, and that my being and my life is hers.

'*Enter* Lady.'

Lady. I hope he's a true convertite.— Did I send you to hold discourse here, Closet?

Closet. Nor did I, madam; but I could hear this gentleman a whole day, methinks—he speaks so acknowledgingly of your ladyship's virtue and goodness towards him.

Lady. I am beholding to him. Will you go with me, nephew, to the Exchange? I am to buy some toys there for the country. You may get a fancy by 't.

Careless [*Aside*]. Good, I must wear her favours.

Lady. Or cannot you forbear your study so long?

Careless. To do you service, madam, under whose commands I build my happiness—

Lady. Be not at the distance of compliment with me, good nephew.

Careless. I would not be thought insolent, dear madam.

Lady. Come, the coachman grumbles at my stay, and 'twill be dinner time presently, so the cook will be angry too.

Careless. You are all tenderness to your servants, madam.

(*Exeunt* Lady *and* Careless.

Closet. A sweet gentleman, and bountiful. If my lady had been blest with such a husband, what a place had I had!

(*Exit* Nurse.

ACT III · SCENE I

'*Enter* Crosstill *reading a letter*, Saveall.'

Crosstill. Do you know the contents, Master Saveall, of the familiar epistle you have brought me here?

Saveall. No, lady, but I guess it a fair expression of the writer's affection to you, although he desired me to crave your pardon for the rudeness of his style, it being the first that he hath composed of that consequence.

Crosstill. Ha, ha, ha! I'll trust you, sir, with the full knowledge of it. Pray read it yourself.

Saveall [*Aside*]. I find she is pleased and my endeavour prosperous for the young gentleman. I am sorry that I delayed a day in the delivering of it.

Crosstill. Pray read it out, sir, for I find it so pleasant that I could hear it a whole day together.

Saveall ('*Reads*'). *In the first place you shall give me leave to wonder at your impudence* (*though it be but in your dreams*) *to have a thought that I ever intended, or can be drawn by persuasion, force, or the power of witchcraft, to marry you*— Bless me! Sure if he writ this, the devil dictated to him.

Crosstill. On, sir; that's but his first charge.

Saveall. *Secondly, I am to tell you that I am warm in mine uncle's favour; and 'tis not a piece a time, or five pieces for a piece of pleasure, can undo me; and so I can have change and 'scape the captivity of wedlock.* This could no otherwise be done but by the devil, that ought him the shame.

Crosstill. What follows, I pray? There's the first and second point past. Mark his method.

Saveall. *Thirdly and lastly, let me advise you, since you are so hot upon marriage, though I assure myself you love none but me (and I thank you for 't), that you frame or dissemble an affection to some one of the city who is but comparative to yourself in blood and fortune. And so you may make by-use of me as your friend, and have children like me.*

George Careless

Crosstill. Have you ever heard so quaint a love-letter?

Saveall. Lady, the injury done in it to yourself is unanswerable, but my wrong in being his messenger I will make him answer.

Crosstill. Excuse me, sir, he has done me a favour. I pray inform him so with my great thanks. But for what you conceive a wrong to yourself, use your discretion. You have no more to say to me for him at this present, have you, sir?

Saveall. Not for him but against him; I will unsay all that I said before intended for his good.

Crosstill. But I'll not hear you wrong your former love
And judgement of him so, which made so deep
Impression here that I had lock'd his love
Up as a jewel in my breast; and you
In striving now to wrest it thence may break
The cabinet. I rather wish you'll be
A friendly means to draw his presence hither,
That I myself may mildly question him.

Saveall. Are you serious, lady?

Crosstill. I fear I shall not rest before I see him.
But do not tell him that, lest in this sullen
Humour he force his absence, to afflict
Me more. I'll hold you, sir, no longer.
Deal for me as you can; I know you have
A guess at my desire.

Saveall. I'll do you service in 't.   (*Exit* Crosstill.
I guess that her desire is to do some act of revenge upon him,
and (so it be not mortal) it were but justice in her for so gross
a scorn by him cast upon a well-reputed gentlewoman. Yet
is it observed in her that she has a violent humour to do and
not to do things oftentimes wilfully against all good counsel

or persuasion. She has the spirit of contradiction in her, and
an unalterable resolution upon sudden intentions; a most
incorrigible will she has, that will not bow nor break. This
cross abusive letter, therefore, may do good upon her, however mischievous he might intend it. If she meant well to
him before, it may the faster bring her on. But it amazes me
that he should write so, bearing his uncle and myself in hand
that he so fairly loved her and besought us to negotiate with
her for him. Should she forgive it, yet the wrong to us in his
vile manners is unpardonable. And so, sir, I come to you.

'*Enter* Careless.'

Careless. Oh, Master Saveall—
Saveall. What mischief or despite have I e'er done you
That could provoke your desperate spleen against me,
To wound mine honour?
Careless. What do you mean, good sir?
Saveall. You have employ'd me basely, made me your
Carrier of scandal and scurrility to the hands
Of nobleness and virtue. Could the fiend
Lust that is in you suffer you to write
No other sense or language to a person
Of her fair name and worth than such as ruffians
Would send to strumpets? Or, it being such,

'*Enter* Wat.'

Could not a porter, or your pandar there
Serve for the lewd conveyance?
[*Wat*]. What a welcome's that!
Saveall. You might safer
Ha' sent it so, and your own right hand with it,
Than to have drawn my just revenge upon you.   '*Draws.*'
Careless. Hold, I beseech you; and, sir, though I lose
The widow by my error (which was indeed
But a mere accident), let me not be
So miserable made as to lose you
Before you hear a short examination.
[*To* Wat] Deliver'd you the letter which I sent
Yesterday to the damsel that you wot of?
Wat. Yes, sir; she read it, kiss'd it a hundred times,
Then made a bosom idol on't,

And says you are the noblest gentleman
Under a saint that e'er took care for sinner.
   Careless. Hell take her for a mistaking whore!
She has the widow's letter and the widow hers.
I found it, sir, when you judiciously
Said it was ruffian-like and strumpet-language.
   Wat. How could you err so strangely?
   Careless. Oh, slightly, slightly. Curse o' my heedless
    brain!
And then to be trapp'd with carelessness
When I was so religiously resolv'd
T' incline to virtue and a marriage life,
Thinking with one hand to cast off my follies
And to take hold of virtue with the other.
For, sir (I will confess myself to you),
The letter you convey'd was in defiance
Intended to a whore, a loose-liv'd wanton,
That impudently hopes an interest in me.
   Saveall. It was not so directed.
   Careless. Ay, there was
(The hell confound it on't) my giddiness.
I seal'd both letters ere I superscrib'd 'em,
And so gave each the contrary direction.
   Saveall. 'Twas a gross carelessness, and if you lose
A fortune by 't, do not blame your friends.
   Careless. That fortune should favour a whore before
An honest woman! 'Twas the sweetest letter,
The daintiest winning things—the devil's in 't—
She must not carry't from the widow so.
Fetch me the letter again.
   Wat. Do you think she'll part with 't, sir?
   Careless. Cannot you beat it out of her, sir?
   Wat. I cannot tell how to do that.
   Careless. Thus, sir—I'll give you demonstration, you
malicious rogue, you that conspir'st with her to betray me,
so good a master I have been to thee and so good a friend to
her. I'll recompense you both.
   Wat. You have undone us both, and will discard me now
you are warm in your uncle's bosom again, but—
   Careless. But what, you traitor, you?

Wat. You put me in good mind—and if I do not some-what—

Careless. I owe you somewhat for your last night's absence too, pernicious villain, that kept'st thyself out of the way o' purpose that I should be drunk and abuse myself and the house here. All lay o' your absence. There's somewhat more for that.   '*Beats him.*'

Wat. 'Tis all upon account, sir.

Careless. Who knows an honest serving-man that wants a good master?

[*Wat*]. If I be not revenged, etc.   (*Exit* Wat

Saveall. Was it your man's fault, Master Careless?

Careless. No, faith, to speak truth, he was as much abused in it as you, in doing a thing as contrary to his vile conditions as you did to your noble name. But I crave only your pardon. I know not what I do besides. This cross blow of chance staggers my reason so—

Saveall. Well, sir, since I have found the error, my reason reconciles me to you, and since it grew out of your equal intent to cast off the evil as to embrace the good, I will re-mediate for you to the widow.

Careless. But yet she'll know I have had a whore. Yet then you say 'tis such a running disease among young gentlemen, that not one of a hundred has 'scaped it that have proved staid men afterwards and very sober husbands —as, look you, yonder's one may prove, whom now I have in good sooth a great desire to beat.

'*Enter* Lady *and* Bellamy, *talking.*'

Saveall. In your aunt's presence and in your uncle's house? Though I were not his friend, could you be so outrageous? I muse I see him here though.

Careless. Cry you mercy, sir, are you his friend?

Saveall. I make myself so, he being dependent to my noblest lord, whom I am bound to honour.

Careless. What lord, I pray, that I may honour him too?

Saveall. The Lord Lovely.

Careless. That loves women above wine, wine above wealth, wealth above friend[s], and friends above himself? There's no scandal in all that, sir.

Saveall. It goes so of him indeed, but he loves honour above all those.

Lady. Master Saveall, a word.

Saveall. Your servant, madam.

Careless. In the name of flesh, for what does his lordship employ that angle-worm to my aunt? He has had her this hour in private conference, close chambered up together, not so much as matron Nurse in the room with 'em. 'Tis a fine sleek thing, and almost pity to hunt it, but sure I must beat it, as place and time convenient may serve.

Lady. Pray, Master Saveall, move you my husband for it; I would not meddle in his money matters willingly.

Saveall. Five hundred pound for my lord upon the mentioned security; I will break it to Sir Oliver.

Careless. Is that the business, after so much privacy? Very pretty! My aunt's a woman too, and my uncle may have as forked a fortune as any of the city that lend out money to hedge in lordships.

Lady. I am his lordship's servant.

Bellamy. And I your ladyship's, good madam. And yours, Master Saveall.

Saveall. I am for your way, Master Bellamy.

Careless. And I, sir, an't please you.

(*Exeunt* Bellamy *and* Saveall.

Lady. George Careless, I would speak with you.

Careless. May I not wait upon your gentleman to the gate, madam?

Lady. No, good George. Though I commend your courtesy, yet would I not you should neglect your own dignity.

Careless [*Aside*]. Umh—I am under government.

Lady. The young man, if you have modesty, will think you mock him; if not, you'll make him become arrogant. Know you not whose man he is?

Careless [*Aside*]. No, 'tis apparent this over-slighting of him proclaims she loves him.— Whose follower, madam? And I know lords' followers knights' fellows.

Lady. Not all lords' followers to all knights, George.

Careless. To as many as their fair ladies will give way to, that are not faint-hearted.

Lady. I understand you not, George. Something troubles you. You are not right today.

Careless. I am only as I am in your favour, madam.

Lady. Come, I know what perplexes you, and 'tis therefore that I desire to talk with you. I am not angry with you, but let me tell you, George, although not openly, I took notice of the pickle you came home in last night, after your uncle was in bed; to whom, marvelling at your absence, I excused you, as gone at my request to visit some ladies, with whom you stayed supper, I told him, when you were with your rousers.

Careless. But did you [even so]?

Lady. Indeed I did, and he was satisfied.

Careless. O my sweet lady aunt! I was indeed amongst 'em, and deeply merry.

Lady. And drunk as deeply.

Careless. I will abuse your goodness so no more.

Lady. Stay and hold, George, for your own good.

Careless [*Aside*]. What's now become of me? I am under correction.

Lady. I would you could have seen yourself and how your disguise became you, as I was told. I do but friendly tell you of some passages, as they were to me related by those whom I have charmed to speak no more on 't. Be secure, therefore, in your uncle.

Careless. O my dear heavenly aunt!

Lady. First, at the door you bounced like a giant at the gate of an enchanted castle; before which could be opened, offence was taken by you at your sedan-man, for asking money (as appeared afterwards) more than you brought from the tavern, and leaving their office fouler by a distempered stomachful than you found it. In the strife for these sad causes, your sword being seized on, you, being unable to use it, were found by my servants at lugs with your brace of corpse-bearers in the dirt, and their poor hovel chair turned on his ridge in the kennel.

Careless. I'll never be drunk again.

Lady. I hope you will say so when you have heard all, George. But, by the way, your late stock being spent, here are ten pieces towards a supply.

Careless. O sweet golden aunt!

[*Lady*]. Well, sir, the strife appeased, you were ta'en in. Then, Hey, is there no sack i' the house?—'Tis for you in your chamber, is replied. Up you are had.— Where is the rogue, my man? —Not seen since yesterday.— Fetch me a wench.— Bless us, cries old Sim the butler, we have none i' th' house, nor cannot send for any out o' doors.— Dost tell me that? Is not my lady's woman, my lady's chambermaid, the laundry maid, the wench under the cook, my lady's nurse, old Winterplum, nor my lady herself within? I know, or will know all the she-things in the house.— But why me up in your bed-roll, George?

Careless. Pseigh.   'Beats his head.'

Lady. You remember none o' this?

Careless. It is not worth it, madam.

Lady. Nor how you scared chambermaid, whom I sent in love to see care taken for you, not dreaming of any ill thought in you? Do you remember how you told her, and what you would give her when your uncle died for a small present courtesy? She was fain to satisfy you with a false promise to steal to bed to you, before four men could force or humour you into it.

Careless. What an unhallowed rascal was I!

Lady. 'Tis well you consider it now. And still consider, George, how ill excess of wine, roaring and whoring becomes a gentleman, and how well sobriety, courtesy and noble action; and [what] dangers wait upon the one sort, and what safety accompanies the other!

Careless. Wine, roaring and whoring—I will lay that saying of yours, madam, to my heart. But wine is the great wheel that sets the rest a-whirling.

Lady. True, George; for had you not first been sullied with wine, you would not have abused yourself to ha' tumbled in the dirt with your litter-mules, nor offered to seduce my chambermaid. Suppose you had overcome her, how could you have come off but with shame to yourself and the utter ruin of the poor wench?

Careless [*Aside*]. Still she corrects me for my meddling with base matters and people. She is not angry, she says, though I called for her last night i' my drink. She gives me money. I will now understand her, and whereunto all her former favours and her later admonitions are directed, and presently appear a grateful nephew.

Lady. Nay, be not sad upon it, George. As I would win you from your faults, I would have you still be cheerful. If any thought troubles you, you may be free with me, George.

Careless. O madam, you have made me, and now take me to you.

Lady. How mean you?

Careless. Freely and wholly, the truest, faithfull'st servant, and I think the ablest that any lady of your lacks and longings ever bestowed a favour on, though I say 't myself. You'll swear 't when you have tried me, an't be but hourly for a month together.

Lady. Is the man sound, trow?

Careless. I defy surgeon or the 'pothecary can come against me.

Lady. Sound i' your senses, sir, I mean.

Careless. Oh, for blabbing, madam, never fear me now I am resolved to live soberly and be only yours. And with such pleasure, with such safety, secrecy and fullness, I will so constantly supply you that you shall not have time to dream of the defects of your old man.

Lady. Do you mean your uncle, and not know whose wrong you unnaturally and sinfully pursue?

Careless. No man living, madam, can do it for him more naturally and less sinfully. I am of the same flesh and blood, and bring his youth to your pleasure. How can you think old uncles' children are got? Or how came up the proverb, *She is one of mine aunts*, do you think? You would have a child by him. All your caudles and cockbroths will never do it. An old man's generative spirit runs all into brain, and that runs after covetousness too, get[s] wealth not children. Believe it, much nephew's help belongs to it, and then the children are not degenerate. I cannot think but many uncles know it, and give way to it, because stranger bloods shall not inherit their lands. And so, sweet aunt, if I live not to inherit his, my son may in your first born. There will be a sweet comfort to you.

Lady. But is all this in earnest?

Careless. In earnest? Yes, and I pray so take it and let it be a bargain; and now presently in the chamber I will make you my first payment for the purchase.

Lady. Fie, fie, you do but say so!

Careless. That shall be tried presently. Come, sweet madam, I find you are willing, and I swear I am resolute, and will be as secret as your own woman. If you will not go, I protest I'll carry you.

Lady. Nay, prithee, George, set me down a little.

Careless. Psewgh! I need none o' these wheezings, I.

Lady. But prithee tell me, dost thou not all this only to try me, or am I a rogue, think you, or would'st thou seriously that thine own natural uncle, thy bountiful patron, nay, thy father on the matter, should suffer such a wrong, and done by us?

Careless. Hark there again, madam: have I not proved, sufficiently and plainly, that I shall in doing the feat for him do him the greatest right in the world, in getting him and you an indubitable heir, and to give him both the comfort and the glory of it?

Lady [*Aside*]. Was ever such a reprobate?

Careless. And you can do him no wrong (though you had not a lady's privilege) to cuckold him, for assure yourself he cuckqueans you. Now come, madam.

Lady. You speak not on your knowledge.

Careless. I never was his pimp, but what I have heard I have heard. Now come, madam.

Lady. I have heard Master Saveall protest within these three days that he has thought my husband the chastest man (of a gentleman) that he knows.

Careless. Oh, did he so, madam. Believe it, they two have whored together, and that Saveall has pimped for him oftener than you ever lay with my uncle.

Lady. What, since he married me?

Careless. What else? Saveall is not only his grave parasite but his pimp, and has spent my uncle more in these civil punctual ways than I in all my whole debauches. What did you think he kept him for? Oh, they are a brace of subtle dry tweaks. Come now, madam.

Lady [*Aside*]. What an inhuman villain 's this!

Careless. I'll tell you all now upon our inward acquaintance.

Lady. You have told too much already to have any acquaintance with me at all; nor shall you, unless you presently recant all that you have or would have said upon this subject.

Careless. Madam—

Lady. Stand further and reply not, lest I call in those that shall sadly silence you. Have you abused your uncle, and the next best friend you have i' the world in hope thereby to abuse me most, that was no enemy of yours till now you justly have provoked me?

Careless [*Aside*]. I took not a right course.

Lady. Was this the best construction you could make of my love to you, or a fit requital, to make me an incestuous whore?

Careless [*Aside*]. Yes, yes, a pox! My course was right enough, but I undertook her at an ill season: her spruce springal left her but now. I'll tell her so.— Madam—

Lady. Come, I perceive you are sorry; and that's a part of satisfaction. Therefore, for once I'll wink at your transgression, especially before others. Here's one, you see.

'*Enter* Closet.'

Careless. I do; the devil blind her!

Closet. Madam—

Lady. But tempt me so again and I'll undo you.

Careless ('*Aside*'). I know how you'll undo me, witty madam.— Ah!

Lady. Nay, be not sad, George; discover not yourself and you are safe for once, I tell you.

Careless [*Aside*]. She'll come about, I see.

Lady. But will you, cousin, go and do that for me?

Careless. Most readily, good madam; I have your full directions.

Lady. All, cousin, if you forget not.

Careless. I cannot be so negligent in your service, madam. [*Aside*] I find by this feigned errand she dares not trust her trollop there. I love her wit now too.   (*Exit* Careless.

Lady. He is both schooled and cooled, I hope.— Now, Closet, what's your news?

Closet. Of a citizen, madam, that entreats to speak with your ladyship.

Lady. Do you not know his name or trade?

Closet. Yes, I had both e'en now, but I have such a head.

Lady. If you have lost 'em by the way, pray go back and seek 'em, or bring you his business.

Closet. I asked his business, madam, and told him he might trust me with it without a hand to his book, but he said it could not be delivered but by his own word o' mouth to your ladyship.

Lady. What strange matter is it, trow, or what citizen? Is not his name Saleware?

Closet. Yes, madam, and he is a (oh, this head!)—a—

Lady. A silkman, is he not?

Closet. Yes, madam, the same.

Lady [*Aside*]. I hope his impudent wife has not told him all. If she has, where's his remedy in this woman's law-case?

Closet. There's a gentlewoman with him too, madam.

Lady [*Aside*]. Then we shall have it. 'Tis his wife, sure. Well, I am prepared for the encounter.— Bid 'em come up.

[*Exit* Closet.]

If they grow violent or too bold with me, I'll set my nephew George upon 'em. [*Sees them coming*] 'Tis not his wife; what creature is it, trow?— With me, Master Saleware?

'*Enter* Saleware, Phoebe.'

Saleware. Craving your pardon, madam, a few words in the behalf of this poor kinswoman of mine touching a gentleman who I hear lives in your house, Master George Careless, madam, by whom she has received much injury.

Lady. How, sir, I pray?

Saleware. Pray, madam, read this letter. [*To* Phoebe] Weep not, but hold up thy head, coz. We will not be dashed nor 'bashed in a good cause. Pray read you, madam.

Lady. I am now, lady, in favour with my uncle and in fair possibility of a good estate, deporting myself (I intend to do) a civil gentleman. To which end (induced as well by reason as by long continued affections) I tender myself to you in the holy condition of marriage. If you vouchsafe your consent (which is my most earnest request), I shall not only declare myself a good husband but the most happy,

George Careless.

Wherein appears the injury to your kinswoman?

Saleware. In flying from his word and deed, madam. He has borne her in hand these two years and used her at his pleasure, detaining her from her choice of many good fortunes, and at last sends her this to make amends for all, and denies his act the next day, sending his man to take the letter from her, pretending 'twas directed to another. [*To Phoebe*] But never the sooner for a hasty word, cousin; we will not be dashed nor 'bashed, I warrant thee.

Lady. Here's the direction: '*To the lily-white hands of Mistress Mariana Gimcrack.*' Is that your name, lady?

Phoebe. I am the sorrowful one that is known by it, madam.

Saleware. Never the sooner for a hasty word, cousin.

Lady [*Aside*]. I conceive the business and find the error, and my great doubt is over.

Saleware. Weep not, I say.

Lady. What would you have me do, Master Saleware?

Saleware. You have discretion, madam, and I made choice of your ladyship, to open this matter unto you rather than to Sir Oliver himself, whom I would not willingly exasperate against his nephew. You may be pleased in a milder way to temper him, and work a satisfaction for my kinswoman. Sir Oliver and yourself, madam, are noble customers to my shop, and for your sakes I would not deal rigorously with your kinsman if a gentle end may be made. But, if you cannot so compound it, the law lies open; money and friends are to be found; a good cause shall not be starved; I will not be dashed nor 'bashed; *sapientia mea mihi* is my word. And so, good madam, you know my mind.

Lady. 'Tis pity a gentlewoman should suffer too much, and I like her so well at first sight that I am easily moved to do good for her. Is she your kinswoman in blood, Master Saleware, or your wife's?

Saleware. Mine, I assure your ladyship. Though my wife can boast as great and noble friends, I thank fortune, as the wife of any tradesman that carries a head in the city (but that's by the by), yet I come of a better house, and am a gentleman born, none dispraised.

Lady. Well, Master Saleware, leave your kinswoman with me a little while; you shall not be seen in my act. I'll try what I can do for her.

Saleware. With all my heart, good madam. And, d'ye hear, Mariana, this is a noble lady; bear yourself discreetly in the business and towards her. You may get a husband by 't, or at least a composition that may purchase one to shoulder you up. But carry it high and worthy of the house I brag of, or—*sapientia mea mihi, stultitia tua tibi.* That's my sentence.

Phoebe. Well, sir, you need not doubt my high carriage.

Lady. Closet.

'Enter Closet.'

[*Closet.*] Madam.

Lady. Take this gentlewoman to your chamber, and I charge you let none see her or take notice of her but yourself and me, till I give order. (*Exeunt* Closet *and* Phoebe.) I shall do something for her, doubt not, Master Saleware.

(*Exit* Lady.)

Saleware. I shall be bound to your ladyship. Now to my shop, to which I thank my wife she has been a wildcat these two days—which must be borne with as we are friends— and from my house all night, and yet no green-goose fair-time. Nor though she were so absent must I be so unfriendly as to question her where or with whom she was. A new article, this, 'twixt man and wife! But *sapientia mea mihi, stultitia sua sibi.* Thus it must be where man and wife are friends, and will continue so in spite of chance, or high-heeled shoes, that will awry sometimes with any woman.

'*The shop discovered*; Alicia *and* Bellamy.' She is not yet come home here. What lady's that, and not my wife there to handle her handsomely for her money? My servants are such asinegos. Stay, are mine eyes perfect? 'Tis she; 'tis my friend-wife, and in the courtly habit, which so long she has longed for. And my Lord Lovely's Ganymed with her. His lordship lay not at home tonight, neither at his lodging. I heard that by the way. I cannot think my lord and she both sat up all night to see the tailors at work and to hasten the finishing of those clothes. If she were with him, which I would not be so unfriendly to enquire for the worth of a wife, 'twas right honourably done of him to send her home as gallantly attended as attired. If she did—a—a—lie with him all night, which I will not be such a beast to believe although I know it—I must come on her with a little wit, though, for which I will precogitate.

Alicia. Once more your story, for I am not satisfied with thrice being told it.

Bellamy. Can a woman take so much delight in hearing of another woman's pleasure taken?

Alicia. As it was given by you, I can, for I am prepared by it to take pleasure from you, and shall with greediness expect it till I have it.

Bellamy. Then know I pleased her so, that she protested —and I believe her—her husband never pleased her so.

Alicia. Or any other man—you should ha' put her to that. Her husband's but a bungler.

Bellamy. How know you that?

Alicia. I do but guess.

Bellamy. Nay, she swore deeply—and I believed her there too—no man besides her husband but myself had e'er enjoyed her. But let me tell you, lady, as she was amply pleased, she may thank you.

Alicia. For sending you—I know she did, and will.

Bellamy. That was the first respect but not the greatest. For in our act of love, our first and second act—

Alicia. Indeed!

Bellamy. In real deed; I can speak now like an emboldened lover.

Alicia. Well, but what in your acts of love?

Bellamy. I had you still in my imagination, and that enabled me to be more grateful to her ladyship, which wrought her thankfulness to you, expressed in a hundred pieces, sent by me, more than I told before, which are your own, she says, since tother morning she was here with you.

Alicia. That token confirms all. Had I the spirit of witchcraft, when putting upon chance for my revenge, to find reward? Have you the money?

Bellamy. Safe at my chamber for you.

Alicia. Oh, you are cunning! Lest I should break with you, you thought to oblige me by 't.

Bellamy. I'll rather run and fetch you twice the sum. I concealed it only to give it you unexpectedly.

Alicia. Sweet Bellamy, I am yours; I could be sorry now I have lost so much of thee. This kiss, and name your time—

Saleware. Would they had done whispering once, that I might enter safe in my manners.

Bellamy. Tomorrow night.

Alicia. Shall you be ready so soon, think you, after your plentiful lady-feast?

Bellamy. Oh, with all fullness both of delight and appetite!

Alicia. And with all faith and secrecy; I am undone else. You know my vows unto my lord.

Bellamy. And can you think I dare be found your mean to break 'em?   [*Saleware comes forward.*]

Alicia. No more; my husband comes.— Pray, sir, return my thanks unto my lord for his right noble bounty, and not mine alone, for so my husband in much duty bound also presents his thanks unto his lordship.

Saleware. Yes, I beseech you, sir.

Bellamy. I am your willing messenger.

Saleware. He is my most honoured lord, and has so many ways obliged me both by my wife and in mine own particular that—

Bellamy. I take my leave.   (*Exit* Bellamy.

Saleware. Still this is an asinego. I can never get him to stand a conference or a compliment with me. But *sapientia mea mihi.* What was that, friend, you made me send thanks for to his lordship? What new favour has he done us beside his counsel? These clothes—the cost was mine, you told me, out of the odd hundred pound you took. What late honour has he done us?

Alicia. Is't not enough I know, friend? Will you ever transgress in your impertinent inquisitions?

Saleware. I cry you mercy, friend; I am corrected justly.

Alicia. Will you never be governed by my judgement and receive that only fit for you to understand which I deliver to you undemanded? Do not I know the weight of your floor, think you? Or do it you on purpose to infringe friendship or break the peace you live in?

Saleware. Never the sooner for a hasty word, I hope, friend.

Alicia. Did you not covenant with me that I should wear what I pleased, and what my lord liked; that I should be as lady-like as I would, or as my lord desired; that I should come and go at mine own pleasure, or as my lord required; and that we should be always friends, and call so, not after the silly manner of citizen and wife, but in the high courtly way?

Saleware. All this, and what you please, sweet courtly friend, I grant as I love courtship. It becomes thee bravely.

Alicia. Oh, does it so?

Saleware. And I am highly honoured, and shall grow fat by the envy of my repining neighbours, that cannot maintain their wives so like court ladies. Some, perhaps, not knowing we are friends, will say she's but Tom Saleware's wife, and she comes by this gallantry the lord knows how, or so. But *sapientia mea mihi*—let the asinegos prate while others shall admire thee, sitting in thy shop more glorious than the maiden head in the Mercers' arms, and say, there is the nonpareil, the paragon of the city, the flower-de-luce of Cheapside, the shop court-lady, or the court shop-mistress, ha, my sweet courtly friend?

Alicia. How do you talk! As if you meant to instruct 'em to abuse me.

Saleware. Sapientia mea mihi.

Alicia. To prevent that, I will remove out of their walk and keep shop no more.

Saleware. Never the less for a hasty word, I hope, friend.

Alicia. Fie, 'tis uncourtly. And now I'll tell you, friend, unasked, what I have done for you besides in my late absence since, and all under one.

Saleware [*Aside*]. Under one! Yes, and I could tell her under whom, if I durst.

Alicia. What's that you say, friend? Methinks you mutter.

Saleware. No, friend, I was guessing what that other thing might be that you have done for me, all under one. You have taken the house, I'll warrant, that my lord liked so.

Alicia. By my lord's favour and direction I have taken it, and I will furnish it so courtly you'll admire.

Saleware. Must I then give up shop, or lie so far remote?

Alicia. No, you must keep your shop, friend, and lie here if your please.

Saleware. And not with you but there?

Alicia. No, not with me at all, friend; that were most uncourtly.

Saleware. But I shall have a chamber in your house, and next to yours. Then in my gown and slippers, friend, at midnight—or the first cock—

Alicia. Softly, for stumbling, friend. I'll do you any honourable offices with my lord, as by obtaining suits for you, for which you must look out and find what you may fitly beg out of his power and by courtly favour. But keep your shop still, friend, and my lord will bring and send you such customs that your neighbours shall envy your wealth and not your wife. You shall have such comings-in abroad and at home that you shall be the first head nominated i' the next sheriff season. But I with my lord will keep you from pricking. Be you a citizen still, friend; 'tis enough I am courtly.

Saleware [*Aside*]. Here's a new courtly humour. I see no remedy unless I run myself out of credit, defy the life of a citizen, and turn courtly too.

Alicia. What's that you say? Do you not mutter now, friend?

Saleware. No, not a syllable, friend. But may not I give up shop and turn courtly too, friend?

Alicia. As you respect my lord and your own profit, you must be a citizen still, and I am no more a citizen's wife else; and she must be a citizen's wife that must do all in all with my lord friends. Though my lord loves the clothes of the court, he loves the diet of the city best, friend. Whatever I wear outwardly, he must find me citizen's wife, which, friend—Oh, he's a sweet lord.

Saleware. Well, it shall be then as the sweet lord will have it. *Sapientia mea mihi.*

(*Exeunt* Saleware *and* Alicia.

ACT IV · SCENE I

'*Enter* Lord Lovely, Crosstill, Bellamy.'

Lord. Lady, 'tis true he is a bashful lover,
Unskill'd to court a widow, has not yet
The art methodical to swear he loves you,
Must and will have you, nor the moving boldness
To stir your blood by putting of you to 't,
Or showing you how 'tis, before the priest
Declares it lawful; but he has love and sweetness,
Which you will find with full and rich content.
And look, look here, what a long middle finger he has,
Which with thin jaws and Roman nose
Are never-failing signs of widows' joys.

Crosstill. Your lordship is dispos'd to mirth.

Lord. It is
My care to put you in a course of mirth,
Nay, of felicity.

Crosstill. In marrying of that stripling!

Lord. Do not think slightly of him, though he appears
Modest and bashfully. If I have any judgement,
He's a fit match for you. His outward fortune
For his estate I will make good to him,
And for his inward virtue, never doubt
He'll make that good to you, however still
He holds his much commended modesty.

Crosstill. My lord, you much commend his modesty
And bashfulness, urging your confidence
Of his strange inward hid abilities.
I hope your lordship's pardon, can you tell
If he has with that bashful modesty
Got any of his mother's maids with child,
Or of his father's tenants' wives or daughters?
I would have some assurance.

Lord. Then I'll tell you.
[*Aside*] These widows love to hear of manly acts,
And choose their husbands by their backs and faces.

Crosstill. My lord, you said you'd tell me.

Lord. Yes, but I would not have you cunningly
To sift discoveries from me to his wrong.

Crosstill. I am loth to speak so plainly to you, my lord,
But by the worst that you can speak of him
I may the better like him.

Lord [*Aside*]. That's her humour.—
Then hark you, widow, to avoid his blushes,
Suppose I tell he has got a bastard.

Crosstill. You may as well suppose I'll say 'twas well.

Lord. What say you to two or three?

Crosstill. The more the merrier.

Lord. He has no less than five old gentlemen's
Young wives with child this moon, but got all in
One week.

Crosstill. Indeed!

Lord. Yes, in good deed, and lusty.

Crosstill. Good deed call you it to get other men's
Children?

Lord. Suppose they have the husbands' consents?

Crosstill. I suppose they are wittols then.

Lord. No, they are wisealls; and 'tis a thing
In much request among landed men, when old
And wanting issue of their own, to keep
Out riotous kindred from inheritance,
Who else would turn the land out of the name.

Crosstill. An excellent policy!

Lord. You know the Lady Thrivewell?

Crosstill. And her old husband, and his riotous kinsman
too.

Lord. You will hear more hereafter. But now to him again
For whom I am spokesman.

Crosstill. In a strange way, methinks.

Lord. He is sent for far and near on those occasions.
He is of so sweet a composure and such
Sure taking mettle that he employs my care
To have him well bestow'd before he begins
To waste.

Crosstill. Is't possible he has done so much
And says so little?

Lord. The deepest waters are most silent.
But he can speak, and well too. Bellamy.

Bellamy. My lord?

Lord. I have made your love known to this lady.

Bellamy. My love, my lord?

Lord. And have begun your suit; follow't yourself.

Bellamy. My suit, my lord, to her? I never mov'd
Your lordship to't, though I presume she may be
A happy fortune to one of my condition,
A poor and younger brother, only made rich
And happy in your lordship's service
And overflowing favours.

Lord. Which I'll take off o' you if you slight my care
In seeking your preferment to this lady,
Of beauty equal with her fair estate,
In both which she is great; and her achievement
Will be the crown and the continuance
Of all my favours to you. You are lost
If you pursue it not. I would thy old uncle
Bellamy saw thy bashfulness.

Crosstill. Your lordship seems now to woo for me, not
him. However I am bound in thanks to your nobleness, in
your fair proportion, I hope I shall not be so poor to require
an advocate when I shall yield to have a husband. But your
mirth becomes your honour, and the young gentleman's
reservedness him. Ha, ha, ha!

Lord. How mean you, Mistress Crosstill?

Crosstill. I do commend your mirth, my lord, for the
lusty strain you spoke him in, that he had got five children
in one week, wherein I may presume you thought you had
moved to my liking. Ha, ha, ha!

Lord. I am glad I have made you merry,
But you will wish, if you reject him—

Crosstill. If I reject one that tenders not himself! Yet
I commend his caution.

Lord. As how, I pray?

Crosstill. As thinking I am one of your cast pieces,
Knowing how well your lordship loves the game,
And now would put me on him.
But you misprise me sinfully, sweet youth,
In such a thought. Howe'er, you should not scorn
To ride in your lord's cast boots, though you be
Gentleman of 's house.

Lord. Come now, he shall have none of you.

Crosstill. I'll hear him say he will not first, by your lordship's leave.

Lord. Spirit of contradiction!

Crosstill. Stay, sir; would you be content to have me?

Bellamy. You heard my lord say I should not.

Crosstill. But say he say again you shall, speak—will you have me?

Lord. Say no—I find her now—that is the way to win her.

Crosstill. Without instructions, good my lord.

Bellamy. Lady, I find so much your scorn already,
That to be wedded to't, I should despair
(My much unworthiness consider'd) to convert it
Ever to love; and 'tis your love, before
Your person or estate, that my affection
Ought to direct me to.
In answer, therefore, to your *will you have me*,
I must say no, till I perceive some sign
Of love in you towards me.

Crosstill. Ay, now he speaks!
Some signs of love in me? How would you have it?
Must I declare it to you before you seek it?

Bellamy. No; I would seek it zealously, but my lord
Is off on't now, and I may lose his favour.

Crosstill. Is your love limited by his favour then?

Bellamy. Not limited, but, as it is as yet
But in its infancy, a little check'd,
Though it still grows and may extend beyond
All limitation to so fair an object
As is yourself. But still my own demerit
Curbs my ambition more than love emboldens.

Crosstill. He speaks within me now.

'*Enter* Saveall, Careless.'

Saveall. Stay, let us retire: here is the Lord Lovely.

Careless. Be he a lord of lords, I'll not retire a foot.

Lord. What servants, Mistress Crosstill, do you keep,
To let intruders in? Oh, Master Saveall.

'*Careless salutes* Crosstill *and puts by* Bellamy.'

Saveall. The humblest of your lordship's servants.

Lord. What gentleman is that you bring with you?

Saveall. It is the nephew of the good knight, Sir Oliver Thrivewell; of which Sir Oliver I have procured unto your lordship the sum which you desired by your servant, Master Bellamy.

Lord. For that I thank him and you. But I could wish you had not brought that nephew hither now.

Saveall. Certes, my lord, I am sorry.

Lord. My reason is, I have entered Bellamy a suitor to the widow.

Saveall. He also comes a suitor.

Lord. And in deep discourse with her already. I'll see fair play.

Careless. But you shall hear me, widow, and that to the point and purpose.

Lord. Lady, at my request, do this gentleman, who made the first approach, the favour to be heard and answered first.

Careless. As his approach was first, my lord, she has heard him first already, and my request is to be heard now; and then let her answer both him or me, or neither—what care I?

Lord. Your name is Careless, I take it?

Careless. I came to talk with this gentlewoman.

Crosstill. Pray, my lord, forbear him and let him speak. What do you say, sir?

Careless. I say I love you, do resolve to marry you, and then to use you as I list.

Crosstill ('*To* Bellamy'). I say I love you, do resolve to marry you, and then to use you as I list.

Bellamy. This to me, lady? I'll take you at your word.

Crosstill. Stay, I do but tell you what he says.

Careless. Take her at her word again, sir, and I shall take you by the lugs. I say again you shall have none but me.

Crosstill ('*To* Bellamy'). I say again you shall have none but me.

Careless. What, do you fool me, or him, yourself, or all?

Crosstill. Pray, sir, how old are you?

Careless. Are you good at that? ('*To* Bellamy') Pray, sir, how old are you?

Lord. You press beyond your privilege, which is only to
speak to the gentlewoman.

Careless. My lord, I am a gentleman.

Lord. You may tell her so.

Saveall. Let me beseech your lordship.

                                        '*Take him aside.*'

Careless. How can you use a gentleman that loves you
Dearer than life, and only bends his study
By all means to deserve you, one that cannot,
Will not, while there are ways to die, live out of
Your favour, with so much despiteful scorn,
That when he speaks his soul to you through his lips,
You make his language yours and give't a boy?

Crosstill. What gentleman's that you speak of?

Careless. The man that speaks it, I am he.

Crosstill. All this, sir, in effect, and more, of my
Affection can I speak to you.

Careless. Oons, but you shall not. You mistake the person
to whom you are, or ought to direct your affection, you
mistake strangely.

Crosstill. No more than once a lover, or at least
A bold pretender, having in civil language
Express'd in writing his affection
To a chaste mistress, seal'd and directed it
To a lewd strumpet, and on the contrary
Courted his virtuous friend in brothel language.
Have I hit you, sir?

Careless. What can I say now? 'Slife, if that anger you
after the error found and confessed, I'll write worse to you,
and in earnest.

Crosstill. Master Bellamy, some other time I shall be glad
to see you.

Careless [*Aside*]. She means that to me now, but I'll take
no notice. I'll find as good a widow in a tavern chimney. Oh,
she's a dainty widow!

Crosstill [*Aside*]. He looks with scorn at me. I must not
lose him,
Yet dare not stay, for fear I tell him so.—
I humbly crave your pardon, good my lord,
For my ill manners and abrupt departure.

The cause is urgent, and, I beseech your mercy,
Question it not.

Lord. Let your will guide you.

Crosstill. Master Saveall, I thank you for my suitor.

Careless. Nay, but lady—

Crosstill. Yes, you shall control me in my own house.

(*Exit* Crosstill.

Careless. Yes, yes, I mean so too, but you shall woo me hard first.

Lord. 'Tis a mad widow. Which of these two now, think you, has the better on't?

Saveall. I think he shall in the end have the best, my lord, that can slight her most.

Lord. 'Tis my opinion too; and hear me—

'[*Takes* Saveall] *aside.*'

Careless. Sir, I have seen you but twice, and it has been at places where I cannot allow of your resorts, first at my aunt's, and now here at my widow's.

Bellamy. Your widow, sir! I thought she had been the widow of one deceased.

Careless. Thou art a witty, pretty, child. But do you here use your wit out of the smell-reach of your lord's perfumed gloves and I shall take you by the nose.

Bellamy. Forbear, sir; I have a handkercher.

Careless. And let me find you there no more, nor here, I charge you.

Bellamy. I hear your charge, sir, but you must leave it to my discretion to obey it or not.

Careless. Trust to your discretion!

Lord. And so commend me to my Lady Thrivewell. Come, Bellamy, away. What's your discourse?

Bellamy. All fair and friendly, my lord.

Careless. Very good.

Lord. So should it be with rivals. Fare you well, Master Careless.   [*Exeunt* Lord Lovely *and* Bellamy.]

Careless. Your lordship's.   '*With a whew.*'

Saveall. Will you walk homewards?

Careless. Excuse me, sir, I pray.

Saveall. It will not be convenient to return this day unto the widow.

Careless. Fear it not, sir; I like her not so well now.

Saveall. Do your pleasure.   (*Exit* Saveall.

Careless. Ha' you cross tricks, Mistress Crosstill? Well, I will go drink your crotchets out of my pate, then home, and do that which mine aunt and I must only know. This is her night of grace, if she keep touch with me.

(*Exit* Careless.

SCENE II

'*Enter* Lady [Thrivewell], Phoebe, Closet.'

Lady. In truth your story is pitiful, but your own folly has brought your scourge upon you.

Phoebe. 'Twas through the blindness of my love and my credulity, madam, wrought by his strong temptations.

Lady. Well, for this once I'll strain a point of honour to you, chiefly, indeed, in answer of his rude unnatural presumption in attempting me. That a villain can still be so barbarously lustful! If in this way I fit him not, and cause him to desist his beastly purpose, I will discover all, to his undoing. Closet, you know my mind and full directions for the conveyance of our design.

Closet. Yes, madam, doubt not. Though I have but a naughty head at most other matters, I dare trust it for a sure one at such conveyances.

Lady. I presume, to further the matter, he'll come home drunk, by his not coming to supper.

Closet. Then he may forget what he so much expected, or sleep away his expectation.

Phoebe. No, he will then be the more vehement till his desire be over.

Lady. You know his humour best, it seems.— Away, away, my husband comes.

(*Exeunt* Phoebe *and* Closet.

'*Enter* Thrivewell *and* Wat.'

Thrivewell. Well, Wat, for this discovery I'll make thy reward worth ten such masters' services. [*Exit* Wat.] Sweetheart, I have a suit to you. But first, what woman's that with nurse?

Lady. A kinswoman of hers whom she would prefer to me. But I have answered her I will not charge your purse with more attendants. Only I have given her leave to entertain and lodge her this night.

Thrivewell. That's my good girl.

Lady. Now, what's your suit, sir (as you are pleased to call it), which I would have to be your free command?

Thrivewell. 'Tis for my absence from thee, to accompany Master Saveall, to bring a dear friend on his way to Gravesend tonight, who is suddenly to depart the land.

Lady. These sudden departures of friends out of the land are so frequent; and that I may believe you intend really, and no feigned excuse; nor will I think, as long as you have good and substantial maid-work at home, that you will seek abroad for any more slight sale-ware.

Thrivewell. No more o' that, sweetheart. Farewell. Expect me early in the morning.   (*Exit* Thrivewell.

Lady. I am glad of his absence tonight, lest there should happen some combustion in the house by his unruly nephew, in case he should discover my deceit in beguiling him with his own wench instead of me. I do even tremble to think upon the unnatural villain, that would offer so to wrong his uncle. I thought I had schooled him sufficiently and beaten him off at his first attempt, and he to assail me again with more forcible temptations, urging me to a promise.

'*Enter* Closet.'

Closet. The young gentleman is come in, madam, and as you foresaw, very high flown, but not so drunk as to forget your promise. He's going to bed in expectation of your approach.

Lady. And have you put his damsel into her night attire?

Closet. Most lady-like, I assure you, madam.

Lady. And let her be sure to steal from him before day.

Closet. Yes, with all silence, madam. She has promised.
                                                      (*Exit* Closet.

Lady. May ladies that shall hear this story told
          Judge mildly of my act, since he's so bold.

SCENE III

'Saleware, Bellamy.'

Saleware. Nay, but look you, Master Bellamy, it is not I protest that I am jealous I make this enquiry for my wife. I jealous? I an asinego then. I am as confident of my wife as that she is in this house, howe'er you deny her to me.

Bellamy. By'r lady, you are not jealous now? If you were not, you would believe me she is not here.

Saleware. Without equivocation, Master Bellamy, she is not here indeed under your foot, but she's here in the house, and under somebody, for aught anybody knows but myself that do confide in her, as I say, and will know no such matter. And so, my lord's will be done with her. I hope I shall see her well tomorrow, and at her own house.

Bellamy. Can such language proceed out of any but a jealous mouth?

Saleware. What an asinego's this! I say again, I do confide in her, nor will I be dashed or 'bashed at what any man says of or against her. And therefore methinks 'tis very strange that you should deny her to me, that comes not to molest her.

Bellamy. There you are again. But since no denial will serve your turn, indeed she is here in this house, and in bed by this time.

Saleware. Away, away! You mock, i'faith. You are a wag. She's no more here than I am. If she were here, can I think you would tell?

Bellamy. How came you to think or dream she was in this house at all?

Saleware. I neither thought it or dreamt it. Ay, but sir, a waterman brought me a letter in haste from one Master Anonymous, intimating that my Ally was with a private friend at this house, and to lie here all night. A very likely matter! What private friend has she but my lord, and that in a right honourable way? I confide in 'em both for that. But at this house, is such a thing—my lord having divers lodgings and she a house of her own at his dispose and command—is that such a thing to be thought or dreamt on?

Bellamy. Why came you to enquire then of such a thing?

Saleware. Why, sir, this Anonymous writ that I should come hastily hither and ask to speak with you, Master Bellamy, and I should know further. Hither I came, here I find you, you deny she is here, and what do I enquire any further?

Bellamy. You hear me say again she is here.

Saleware. Go, you are a wag again. She here? Is my lord here, or any private friend? Alas, alas, you are too young, Master Bellamy, and may as well persuade me I am jealous.

Bellamy. Well, sir, to put you out of all jealousy and doubt (if you be in any), I was the Anonymous that sent you the letter, to draw you hither and declare myself your friend, which shall instantly be manifest to you, if now you have a mind to lie with your own wife before any other man.

Saleware. Then she is here indeed, belike.

Bellamy. Pray come with me into the next chamber.

Saleware. This is some waggery plotted by my wife; I smell it.   (*Exeunt* Bellamy *and* Saleware.

'*The bed put forth*, Alicia *in it. Enter* Bellamy, Saleware, *with light.*'

Bellamy. But you must be sure to say, when she discovers you, that you came of your own accord, unsent for, as inspired or possessed by some dream or vision, to find her here.

Saleware. Well, if this be not my wife's waggery in a main proof of her chastity, I am not here. I will do so, sir.

Bellamy. So then, obscure yourself a while, while I approach her.

Alicia. Who's there?

Bellamy. 'Tis I, your servant, lady.

Alicia. Sweet Bellamy, why come you not to bed?

Saleware. Good.

Alicia. Does the love that was so hot, and the desire that was so fervent begin to cool in you?

Saleware. Good again. As if he, an asinego, had ever made love to her fine waggery!

Alicia. Has my mere consent to satisfy you cloyed you?

Saleware. Consent to my lord's man—a likely matter.

Alicia. Or did you court me to a promise only to try my fidelity to your lord, and then betray me?

Bellamy. Dear lady, think not so, but that I am struck into stone with wonder and amazement at the most unexpected accident that ever crossed a lover.

Saleware. Dainty waggery, this! What little mad rogues are these to plot this to make me jealous!

Alicia. Pray, are you serious? What is the accident?

Bellamy. I will not be so crossed, but kill him rather. To enjoy such a mistress, who would not kill a horned beast? Yet blood is such a horror—

Saleware. Very pretty.

Alicia. Will you not tell me?

Bellamy. Speak lower, gentle lady.

Alicia. Why, prithee? Who can hear us?

Bellamy. I know not by what magic your jealous husband has made discovery of our being here. He wrought, sure, with the devil.

Alicia. I am undone then. He will tell my lord.

Saleware [*Coming forward*]. I shall undo myself, friend. No, *sapientia mea mihi*—. Be not dashed nor 'bashed for that, good friend, if there were any such matter. But this is waggery, fine waggery, plotted betwixt you, to tempt my jealousy. But never the sooner for a hasty word, I warrant you. Master Bellamy, that my wife is here, I thank you; but how I came to know it you shall never know from me. You sent not for me; I am sure you were not the Anonymous. Indeed it should have been Anonyma, friend-wife, for it was thy act, I dare swear. However, you do not hear me say I was sent or writ for at all, more than by a dream or vision. But here I am, and mean to remain tonight. I hope the house can afford you another bed in't, Master Bellamy, and you to leave me to my own friend-wife. I like the lodging most curiously, sweet friend, and, I prithee, let's try heartily what luck we may have in a strange place. I would so fain have a little one like thee.

Bellamy. I'll leave you to your wishes. A good night to you.

Alicia. Pray, sir, a word first. Husband, be farther.

Saleware. Faces about, Tom Saleware, and march forwards.

Alicia. You told me, sir, of a hundred pound that your sweet Lady Thrivewell sent me.

Bellamy. 'Tis true; I have it for you.

Alicia. But she has since countermanded you to keep it, has she, and to mock my expectation of that, and you? Why have you fooled me thus?

Bellamy. I rather should suspect your craft in this prevention. But love forbids me, and I must conclude 'tis witchcraft in your husband.

Alicia. Come, let's kiss friends, and, sweet, tomorrow night I will prevent his witchcraft in the full enjoyment of our free pleasures. Be you true to me.

Bellamy. May all that's man in me forsake me else.

Alicia. Another kiss, and then goodnight.

Saleware. Are you still whispering? No matter; let 'em whisper.

Bellamy. Goodnight.   (*Exit* Bellamy.

Alicia. Now may the spirits of all injured women be added to mine own, for my revenge, which I this night will dream of, slighted and mocked! He and his like shall know,

> That when a yielding woman is so cross'd,
> All thoughts but of revenge are lost.

Saleware. Oh, he's gone.— Ally, friend I would say, and now, I prithee, tell me how or why thou cam'st hither.

Alicia. Will you pardon me?

Saleware. Yes, faith; I were no friend else.

Alicia. 'Twas but to try if I could make thee jealous.

Saleware. In waggery! Did not I say so? When do my prophecies fail?

Alicia. But what brought you hither, think you?

Saleware. A letter from one Anonymous; but I'll eat spiders and break if you sent it not.

Alicia. Give me the letter.

Saleware. Where is it? Facks, I ha' lost it.

Alicia. 'Twas I indeed that sent it.

Saleware. Did not I say so too, and that it should ha' been Anonyma? *Sapientia mea mihi.*— When do my prophecies fail? I'll to bed instantly, while the prophetic spirit is in me, and get a small prophet or a soothsayer.

Alicia. No, I'll have no bed-fellow tonight.

Saleware. Ne'er the less for a hasty word, I hope, friend.

Alicia. I am at a word for that.

Saleware. I'll lie upon thy feet then.

Alicia. Well, you may draw the curtains and sleep by me.

Saleware. *Sapientia mea mihi, stultitia tua tibi.*

'*Puts in the bed, exit.*'

SCENE IV

'Phoebe *passes over the stage in night attire*;
Careless *follows her as in the dark.*'

Careless. Madam, madam, sweet madam, 'twill not be day these three hours. Stay but three minutes longer, but a touch more.— She's whipped into her chamber. Could I but find the door. I know my uncle's from home. Oh, she returns with light. That's well.

'*Enter* Lady, [*with*] *a light.*'

Lady. What ail you? Are you mad?

Careless. Would not any man be mad for losing such a bedfellow? Sweet madam, let us retire without any noise.

Lady. What an insatiate beast are you! Would you undo for ever both me and yourself?

Careless. Not with one do more, I warrant you. Come away, madam; somebody knocks mainly at the gate, and I believe it is my master returned before his time.

'*Enter* Closet.'

Lady. I cannot think 'tis he.

Careless. 'Tis the rogue, my man, I warrant, drunk, and has forgot I turned him away. But he shall spoil no sport. Come away, madam.

Lady. Closet, go your ways down, and hark before you—
[*Whispers to* Closet.]

Closet. I will, madam.   (*Exit* Closet.

Careless. So now come, madam. I commend you in the charge you have given your watch-woman.

Lady. What charge, do you guess?

Careless. Why, to tell my uncle, if he be come, that he must not come near you, that you have had no rest tonight till just now you are fallen asleep, and so forth.

Lady. Go, you are a wicked fellow. I am sorry for any the least favour I have done thee. And do thou dare to attempt me once more, I'll ha' thee turned headlong out of my doors.

Careless [*Aside*]. I have got her with child tonight, with a spark of mine own spirit, and [he] longs already to do me mischief. The boy will be like me; therefore 'tis pity to knock 't o' the head.— But come, madam, tother crash and goodnight. Must I drag you to 't?

Lady. Touch me but with a finger and I'll raise the house.

Careless. You dare not, sure. And now take heed you vex me not. Have you not been my whore?

Lady. You dare not say so, for spoiling your fortune.

Careless. Faith, but I dare; and if you will not obey me in a course of further pleasure tonight, fetch me a hundred pieces to take a course abroad withal. Do ye look? I'll make you fetch me hundred after hundred housewifes when I want it or shall be pleased to call for 't. All comes out else; the gates of your fame flies open, lady; I will proclaim our act.

Lady. Dare you forfeit your own reputation so?

Careless. I shall gain reputation by 't in the company I keep abroad; and if the cuckold, my uncle, come to the knowledge of it at home, I shall possess him that you lust-fully tempted me to it.

Lady. Canst thou be so villainously impudent to destroy thine own fortune to ruin me?

Careless. You may conceal all then, and so will I, and mend my fortune by yours. I will live bravely upon your fortune, and the heir which I have got tonight shall inherit it, my uncle's estate. And therefore, indeed, I would have all concealed for my child's good, or rather for mine own. For it shall go hard if I put him not in to a course in his minority to consume the estate upon me before he come of age.

Lady. I am undone.

Careless. And oh, that ever I did it!

Lady. Thou, villain, hast undone me.

Careless. Come, I'll do you again, and then all's whole again.

'*Enter* Thrivewell, Saveall.'

[*Thrivewell*]. You're both undone! O, you prodigious monsters,

That have betwixt you made me monster too!

What's to be done but that I kill you both,

Then fall upon my sword.

Saveall. Sir, resume you the temper of humanity,

And let the law distinguish you from them.

You neither are to be their executioner

Nor to fall with them.

Thrivewell. Life to me is torment.

Careless. Oh, the devil! What a case am I in now!

Lady. Pray hear me, sir!

Thrivewell. Can more be said to aggravate thy shame

Or my affliction than I have heard already?

Saveall. Let me entreat you hear her.

Lady. What shame did you, or what affliction I

Suffer when you discover'd unto me

Your bargain of a hundred pound in Saleware?

You understand me. How was life a torment

To me then, think you?

Thrivewell. Did not you vow forgements then, and thus

You freely would forgive my act, and thus

Now to revenge it on me to my ruin

And your own endless infamy? Oh, 'tis horrid.

Lady. 'Tis no revenge at all, only a show to startle you, or try your manly temper, and so near to be even with you as to let you know what some wife might perhaps ha' done, being so moved. It was my plot indeed to strain you hither to this false-fire discovery, for which I'll give you reasons.

Thrivewell. Oh, gross dissimulation!

Lady. Master Saveall, you have done many fair offices for his nephew; do this for me: entreat him to a conference a few minutes in my chamber. If I clear not myself in his and your opinion, and that by witnesses, let me be found the shame of all my sex.

Saveall. Sir, my counsels have been prevalent with your judgement; let me persuade you.

Thrivewell. But I will have that friend thrust out of door first.

Lady. I would not that you should, nor give a look or word to him till you have heard me. Then exercise your justice.

Saveall. Sir, be induced to it.

Thrivewell. You have prevailed.

[*Exeunt* Thrivewell *and* Saveall.]

Lady. Go to your bed, George, and sleep; be not afraid of bugbears. (*Exit* Lady.

Careless. How's this? She's come about again and has patched all up already. I hope she'll work mine uncle to reward me for my nightwork, and bring him in time to hold my stirrup while his George mounts her. She's a delicate well-going beast; I know but one to match her in a course. Just the same pace and speed as if I had only had the breaking and managing of her myself. But the mark goes out of Phoebe's mouth now, and I'll play my aunt against all the town. But how she thought to fright me with villain and impudent! And now, go to bed, George.

Ha, ha, ha! I find her drift.

No wit like woman's at a sudden shift. (*Exit* Careless.

ACT V · SCENE I

'*Enter* Old Bellamy, [Lord] Lovely.'

Lord. Bellamy, thou art welcome, and for thy nephew I must ever thank thee; he is my best companion.

Old Bellamy. O my good lord, without boast be it spoken, I have ever been right and straight to your honour and never did you an ill office in man, woman or child. What I have said of 'em they have proved at first, or I have wrought 'em to at last. But what do I speak on't? I have ever been for your lordship. All things I have sworn for you, I have fought for you, I have broked for you, I have pimped for you. But what do I speak on't?

Lord. You need not, Bellamy, for I know all.

Old Bellamy. Oh, the gentlemen's wives and farmers' daughters I have presented to you in your summer progresses and winter journeys about the countries. But what do I speak on't?

Lord. Because thou lov'st to champ upon the bit to please thy old coltish tooth still, thou lov'st the memory of the former sweets which now thou canst not relish.

Old Bellamy. And here i' the city I have pledged more of your several mistresses than in my conscience there be honest women in't. But what do I speak on't?

Lord. I never had so many, man.

Old Bellamy. Or if you had, what do I speak on't? And in my conscience again, I have drunk more to your lordship's health in my days than any wine-cellar in the city at this day contains of Spanish, French, and Rhenish. But what do I speak of that either?

Lord. True, Bellamy; fall then upon some other subject.

Old Bellamy. Yes, my good lord. And I pray your lordship tell me, does not my nephew drink and wench pretty handsomely? I would fain have him take after me and not his drunken father.

Lord. How well he shifts his subject, wicked old fellow.

Old Bellamy. Does he not begin to fall to yet?

Lord. Not he.

Old Bellamy. Not a bit nor a sup? Does he do nothing by example? Or has your lordship left it? Or does he carry it like a gentleman?

Lord. Discreetly and virgin-like.

Old Bellamy. Pretty commendation for a young courtier!

Lord. I would for my deserved love to him have put him upon a fair young widow of a great fortune, but could not make him look upon her like a suitor.

Old Bellamy. Just such a bashful puppy was my brother, his father. I wonder how my mother came by him. My father was right, and she was right, and I have been right—but what do I speak on't?

Lord. True, Bellamy, speak of somewhat else.

Old Bellamy. The boy will ne'er grow up to me. I thought to have left him somewhat; I must discard him.

Lord. If you do, he is in me provided for.

Old Bellamy. What can your lordship love him for?

Lord. Come, I'll tell thee, and be comforted. He has something of thee in him. He will pimp most conveniently.

Old Bellamy. That's something indeed.

Lord. And for his modesty, which is a rare benefit of nature in him, I dare trust him with a mistress as I would an eunuch.

Old Bellamy. Benefit! A defect, I fear. Yet I may hope in time some mistress of your lordship's may tempt and bring him forwards.

Lord. No, I am confident.

'*Enter* Page, *whisper[s to* Lord.]'

Now, your news. Good Bellamy, walk in the gallery a while.

Old Bellamy. Some mistress is coming to him. But what do I speak on't?   (*Exit* Old Bellamy.

[*Lord.*] Go bid her come in.   (*Exit* Page.
What brings her so unseasonably?

'*Enter* Alicia, Saleware.'

Alicia. Stay you at distance yet a while, friend, till I call you.

Saleware. Faces about, Tom Saleware.
                                        (*Exit* Saleware.

Lord. How now! How is it with my love? Ha! How comes a trouble on this face where my delights are ever wont to revel?

Alicia. O my lord—

Lord. Say, who has injured thee? Has thy husband taken up the uncivil boldness to abuse thee? Or be it any other man, it shall be death or an undoing to him.

Alicia. My lord, I am wronged, but would be loth to engage your noble person in my quarrel; some servant of yours may do it.

Lord. Of what condition is thy wrong? Tell me, and who of my servants thou would'st have to right thee.

Alicia. I would have Bellamy. How think you? Is he faithful to you?

Lord. How canst thou question it? Has he not ever been so?

Alicia. Your lordship has well trusted him, I know.

Lord. I do not know the man I trust or love so well.

Alicia. But would your lordship part with any jewel or choice thing you love and have intended only to your own particular use to him, or let him be your own partner in it?

Lord. Troth, I think I should, only thyself excepted. But what's thy wrong, I prithee, or wherein should Bellamy right thee?

Alicia. Bellamy has wronged me to think me so unworthy as to be tempted to his lust. Bellamy has wronged your honour in that ambitious attempt.

Lord. Thou amazest me.

Alicia. And Bellamy must right me, and your honour, or you must cast off him or me.

Lord. Give me at least some circumstance to make this probable.

Alicia. Must not I be believed? You shall have instance then to make it truth.

'*Enter* Saleware.'

Friend Thomas, pray verify unto my lord the discovery you made last night of me and Master Bellamy.

Saleware. 'Twas thus, my lord, an't like your lordship: my wife was forth at evening, an't like your lordship, as she may have often been, an't like your lordship, and may be as oft again, an't like your lordship.

Lord. Well, pray thee, on.

Saleware. Forth she was, an't like your lordship. I stayed supper, and almost bed-time for her, an't like your lordship, and had even given her over for all night, an't like your lordship, as I may of any night, an't like your lordship.

Lord. On, I pray thee.

Saleware. Yes, an't like your lordship. Upon some private notice given to me, an't like your lordship, that she was at a private lodging, an't like your lordship, with a private

friend, an't like your lordship, over I went, and found her
a-bed, an't like your lordship, and Master Bellamy even
ready to go to bed to her, an't like your lordship.

Lord. Is this true?

Saleware. As true as your lordship lives, an't like your
lordship.

Lord. How could you be betrayed so?

Alicia. The villain fetched me forth and lodged me there
as by your appointment, and for your own pleasure. But
when 'twas late, and that your lordship came not, thinking
he had an advantageous opportunity, he soon discovers his
love to me and his treachery to your lordship. I being in
a strait, only (finding happy means to send for my husband
to prevent him) made him a false promise, being secure in
my husband. And what had followed your lordship understands.

Lord. I'll ne'er trust man can blush and weep again.

Saleware. In sooth, an't like your lordship, I thought all
had been but waggery, an't like your lordship, to tempt me
into jealousy. And my wife, knowing well enough that I was
by, bade sweet Bellamy come to bed. O wag!

Lord. What messenger brought you the notice, Master
Saleware?

Saleware. A waterman, my lord, an't like your lordship.
Here's the letter, an't like your lordship.

Alicia. You told me you had lost it when I asked for 't to
burn it.

Saleware. I thought I had, friend, but I found it now, and
[have] given it my lord before I was aware, friend.

Alicia. Hell take that letter!

Saleware. Now, a bots on't for me, if thou beest angry,
friend.

Alicia. You had better ha' swallowed it full of ratsbane.

Saleware. Ne'er the sooner for a hasty word, I hope,
friend.

Lord ('*Reads*'). *Master Saleware, if you will avoid a new
addition of horns, come with this bearer over into Montague's
Close, where you shall find your wife with a private friend, at
a private lodging. Haste hither, and ask for one Bellamy.*

Anonymous.

What riddle's this? This is Bellamy's own hand; I know it.
Why should he send to prevent himself? Or how could she
write his character? This, woman, is not right.

Alicia. Do you note my art, my lord, to write as in a man's
name when I wrought it myself?

Saleware. And did not I tell you, friend, it should ha'
been Anonyma? *Sapientia mea mihi—.*

Lord. Within there, call Bellamy.

'*Enter* Page.'

Page. He's not within, my lord, and has not been tonight.

Alicia. His absence is another circumstance to a proba-
bility, my lord.

[*Page.*] But he was seen this morning to go to Sir Oliver
Thrivewell's.

Lord. Go, let my coach be ready presently. (*Exit* Page.)
He should receive 500l there for me; I trust he will not
furnish himself with it for a flight.

Alicia. My lord, I gave you an inkling of a familiarity
betwixt him and the Lady Thrivewell. He has since declared
their act of lust to me, and urged it for an instance to my
yielding.

Lord. Can you affirm this?

Alicia. Yes, to his face and hers.

'*Enter* Saveall.'

Lord. Oh, Master Saveall! Welcome.

Saveall. My lord, your servant Bellamy is receiving your
money at Sir Oliver Thrivewell's.

Lord. I thank you.

Saveall. But, my lord, there is fallen an unhappy accident
between Sir Oliver, his lady, and his nephew, in which your
servant Bellamy also is concerned. And your lordship is
much, and most humbly, besought by the lady to hear and
examine the difference.

'*Enter* Old Bellamy.'

Lord. I was preparing thither. Oh, Master Bellamy, you
have not eavesdropped, have you?

Old Bellamy. Will you pardon me, my lord?

Lord. Yes, if thou hast.

Old Bellamy. I have, my lord, and am overjoyed to hear so well of my nephew.

Lord. You may hear more anon. Come all along with me.

(*Exeunt omnes except* Old Bellamy.

Old Bellamy. I may hear more anon. Your lordship, though, knows not of what so well as I do know.

(*Exit* Old Bellamy.

SCENE II

'*Enter* [Sir Oliver] Thrivewell, Careless, Lady [Thrivewell], Phoebe, Closet, Wat.'

Thrivewell. I need not cast thee off or bid thee go now and for ever from me; thine own shame will force thee hence.

Careless. You are deceived in that.

Thrivewell. What is thine own take with thee. Here 'tis—Phoebe—all thou ever get'st or canst expect from me.

Careless. She was mine own before your wife became our coupler, in English plain, our bawd.

Thrivewell. Use no uncivil language while you are well.

Careless. For which you have your witnesses—this false traitor, that brought you on.

Lady. By my direction, George.

Wat. No traitor neither, since you left to be my master, wounded and turned me off.

Careless. And this dark-lanthorn here, this old *deceptio visus*, that juggled the wrong party into my bed.

Closet. Ha, ha, ha!

Careless. Do you grin, grim Malkin? But, sweet madam, if your fine springal Bellamy had lain there in my stead, she would ha' brought the right party—your ladyship's lily-white self.

Thrivewell. How's that?

Lady. No more o' that, good George.

Careless. Nay, it shall out. Since you have wrought my ruin, I will be the destruction of you all. And therefore now hear me, O knight, and first resolve to make me rich in my reward, for wonders I'll unfold.

Thrivewell. Canst thou expect reward from me for anything that can by thee be uttered?

Careless. Reward? Why not? Why should not you reward my good offices as well as punish my ill? I must and will rely upon you for all the good that can befall me; or, if I must expect no further from you, I'll give it you *gratis*. And if you be anything but a wittol, hear me.

Lady. What do you mean?

Careless. To set you out livelier than all your paintings. Or, d'ye hear, will you give me a hundred pound a quarter for my silence?

Lady. Not a penny. If you seek my undoing, heaven forgive you.

Thrivewell. What, villain, canst thou speak to her prejudice?

Careless. That which (if you are no wittol) you'll be loth to hear. But you shall have it.

Thrivewell. Dar'st thou talk so?

Careless. And since you hold my attempt at her so heinous, you may be pleased to know I was incited to't by the example of him I named, that smooth-faced Bellamy.

Thrivewell. Dar'st thou accuse her with him?

Careless. You may ask her bolster there, her madam nurse, old Mother Cockbroth.

Closet. Oh me!

Careless. Ay, oh you. Ask her, sir, what she did with him, or he with her, in their two hours privacy in her chamber, when he came to take up five hundred pound for his lord. There was a sweet taking-up, sir. She confessed all to me, and on purpose, I dare be sworn, to embolden me in my attempt to her ladyship.

Closet. I confess?

Thrivewell. What did she confess?

Careless. That he made use of your bed with your wife. What language shall I utter 't in? You were best see it done before you believe it.

Thrivewell. Oh me, most miserable if this be true.

Careless. Well, there's for them two.

[*Lady whispers to* Closet.]

Lady. Go, Closet, till I call you.   (*Exit* Closet.

Careless. Now for that rogue (because I must expect no further good of you but this which is mine own, you say), I'll lay him open to you. You remember how once I ingratiated myself to you by rescuing you from a robbery and murder, as you supposed, for which you took me into favour—

Thrivewell. Yes, and have wished a thousand times since that I had lost the thousand pound I had about me then, and ta'en some wounds for 't in exchange, rather than by that rescue to have taken thy viperous self into my bosom.

Careless. This rogue plotted that business; 'twas a mere trick of his invention. The supposed thieves were his companions, and wrought by him only to scare you and run away when we came to your succour, only to endear me to you. There was no hurt meant but the slap I gave him over the pate to colour the business with [a] little blood. I wish now I had cleft his brains.

Thrivewell. Your wish, though against your will, is a good reward to him, for I love him the better for his wit in that plot and care of his then master.

Careless. Do you so, sir? Then 'twas mine own invention. Let him deny 't if he can.

Wat. Indeed the plot was his, sir; I only found the actors.

Thrivewell. I cannot condemn the conceit, however, and am something taken with the wit on't. Would all the rest were no worse.

Careless. And now I have uttered my whole mind, sir, and you declared I must expect no further good of you, come away, Phib. I have injured thee long; I'll make thee now amends for all. I'll marry thee and sell tobacco with thee.

Lady. Let him not go, sir, I beseech you, in this desperate way, nor till I answer to his accusation.

Thrivewell. Sir, you shall stay, and make yourself good before authority or clear my wife.

Careless. You'll have your house then known to have been a bawdy-house?

Thrivewell. The courts of princes and religious houses may so have been abused.

Careless. Under such governesses.

Thrivewell. You'll anon be silent.

I

'*Enter* Servant.'

What's the matter? We are busy.

Servant. Mistress Crosstill, madam, is come in great haste to visit you, and a kinsman of your ladyship's with her.

Thrivewell. At such a time? Excuse yourself.

Servant. They are here, sir, entered against all resistance.

'*Enter* [Mistress] Crosstill, Fitzgerrard.'

Lady. Mistress Crosstill! You have much honour'd me. Cousin Fitzgerrard, welcome!

Fitzgerrard. I have a private suit to you, madam.

Lady. Pray, Master Thrivewell, entertain the lady.

Careless. Another sprunt youth.

Crosstill. Sir, I perceive some discontent here. I hope your nephew has not again displeased you?

Thrivewell. He is a villain, seeks my utter ruin.

Crosstill. Pray say not so, for fear you force me love him.

Thrivewell. You are undone for ever if you do.

Crosstill. Do not say so, for fear I fly to him.
The thought of him already breaks my sleeps.
I could not rest tonight for thinking of him,
Which made my early haste to unload my mind,
Presuming that your judgement may excuse
A simple woman's weakness.— What is she
That he courts so?

Thrivewell. I tell you she's a whore with child by him, lays claim to him, and I think he'll marry her.

Crosstill. Still you speak better of him, and my love must not see him so lost. Sir, let me speak with you.

Careless. Me, lady? I am busy, I am busy.

Crosstill [*Aside*]. What metal am I of? His scorn's a loadstone;
No courtship like his carelessness to me,
And all dispraise speaks for him.—
Sir, I will speak with you.

Careless. I blush for you. What would you say now, were it not too late?

Crosstill. Nay, only to your ear.

Careless. Stand off a while, Phib.   '*Goes aside.*'

Fitzgerrard. His lordship, madam, shall give me accompt
To each particular.

Lady. You shall do well to put it to him, cousin.—
Husband, I overheard you, and commend you
That though you cast your nephew from all hopes
Of good from you, you will not yet destroy
His fortunes other ways.

Thrivewell. How do you mean?

Lady. For that I find by your reviling him
You more inflame that cross fantastic widow
With eager love to cast herself upon him.

Thrivewell. Had I thought so, I had spoke well of him
Against my conscience.

Lady. No, let me entreat you
Be that way charitable, and speak worse,
The worse the better.

Careless. Tempt me not, good lady,
To your own prejudice, your destruction.
I am one you cannot live and lie withal
A fortnight. You, alas, you're but a grissel,
Weak picking-meat; here's one that will hold me tack
Seven constant ordinaries every night,
Noonings and intermealiary lunchings,
At freedom every day, hold belly hold,
The cupboard never shut.

Crosstill. I understand you not.

Careless. Nor mind me, lady; 'twill be better for you.
You had a thin-chinn'd husband played at doublets with ye,
And that, perhaps, but twice or thrice a week.
You are incapable of better game.
Here's one shall hold me tick-tack night by night,
And neither of us guilty of a why-not.
She's bred up to my hand and knows her play.

Crosstill. Can you so slight me?

Careless. Slight? I honour you,
In caring for you to preserve your life,
And your estate, which I confess myself
Unworthy of. Besides, I am engag'd
To do a poor soul right for my issue's sake
She goes withal.

Crosstill. But say on composition she acquit you?

Careless. Oh, but conscience is conscience.

Crosstill [*Aside*]. I'll die or have him presently.—
Can you refuse me for a prostitute whore?

Careless. Take heed what you say. I'll shake your estate
If you dare call her whore 'fore witnesses.

Crosstill. Call all the world to hear me: madam,
Sir Oliver, and the rest, be all my witnesses.
Give me your hand, sir. Here, before you all
I plight my faith upon this gentleman.
He is my husband, and I am his wife.

Thrivewell. You are then undone.

Crosstill. I care not, sir, for your ill will; no more shall
he.

Careless. Are you catch'd, widow? *Foutre* for uncles now!

Crosstill. Why answer you not me in troth-plight?

Careless. I do, but yet I tell you again, conscience
Is conscience. The woman's not compounded with.

Crosstill. I'll give her a brace of hundred pounds.

Phoebe. The woman will not take it.

Wat. The woman shall take it, for now know, sir, I love
you not so ill as to undo you. This woman has been mine as
much as yours. She has done as much with me, for offices
and service I have done her, as she has done with you for
love and money. Let her deny 't.

Careless. I have lately suspected so.

Wat. And if her friends will make her brace of hundreds
a leash, I'll marry and honestify her.

Lady. Honest Wat in good earnest! Gentlewoman, with
your hand give him your consent, and I'll supply you with
the odd hundred pound, for Wat's love to his master.

Thrivewell. Will you?

Lady. Yes, and with your allowance, it shall be in lieu of
the hundred I took in commodity of her kinswoman, Mistress Saleware, which would never thrive with me (as it may
properly with them), as 'twas the price of lust. You know it
was, and how untowardly things have chanced amongst us
since it was so. And now that I have declined it, you shall see
how sweetly all will be reconciled.

Thrivewell. Do as you please.

Lady. Go get you to the priest presently, and bring him hither for thy master, Wat.   (*Exeunt* Wat *and* Phoebe.

'*Enter* Lord Lovely, Old Bellamy, Saveall, Saleware, Alicia.'

Lord. Madam, you sent for me, though I had former cause to require a conference with you.

Lady. My cause, my lord, is almost ended among ourselves; pray let your former, therefore, be determined first. Your lordship may be pleased to sit.

Lord. I desire first, by good Sir Oliver's patience, madam, a word with you in absence of all the rest, except this gentlewoman.

Thrivewell. With all respect, my lord.

Lady. No, you shall stay, and all the rest. Speak openly, my lord, I do beseech you.

Lord. My modesty forbids.

Lady. I'll speak it for you then. Good my lord, sit judge. This woman comes to accuse me with incontinency with your servant Bellamy, is it not so?

Old Bellamy. Ay, marry, does she, madam, to make her word good to my lord that he would have lain with her too; and says that Bellamy affirmed to her that he did; ay, marry, did he, with your ladyship.

Lady. Ha, ha, ha! I have a nephew here affirmed as much.

Careless. I am sorry I said so much; 'twas but my suspicion in the days of my wickedness. I am honest now, and can think no such matter.

'*Enter* Wat, *whispers* [*to* Careless].'

                              Oh, is the parson come?
                              (*Exeunt* Careless, Crosstill, Wat.

Thrivewell. I fear I shall be wretched.

Saveall. You are wretched in your fear. Note your wife's confidence; can guilt look with that face?

Lord. I understand that Bellamy is in your house.

Lady. Forth coming, my good lord. Good Master Bellamy, fetch your nephew; you'll find him in my chamber.
                              (*Exit* Old Bellamy.

Fitzgerrard. And in this respect you shall give me leave,
My lord, to call your honour into question.

Lord. You're very round with me, Master Fitzgerrard.
What is your question?

Fitzgerrard. Where is my sister Amy?

Lord. Ask you me?

Fitzgerrard. Yes, and in honour you're to answer me.
It is too evident your courtship won
Her virgin honour.

Lord. Then I forc'd her not.

Fitzgerrard. The blame of that lay therefore on herself.
That loss I seek not after; but I ask
Her life and being—if she live or be—
Of you, my lord, since it is manifest
She left her friends and country shortly after
Her folly had betray'd her into shame,
To be at your dispose, as we presume
She is since in her two years absence. We
Have sought all other ways in vain. You shall
Do therefore well, my lord, to render her
Or give me leave to urge you t' an accompt
Of what's become of her.

Lord. You cannot, sure,
Compel me, sir.

Fitzgerrard. To hazard of my life I will, my lord.

Lord. That she is lost I am griev'd;
But for your stout demand I'll answer you
At weapons, time and place convenient.

'*Enter* Old Bellamy, *and* Bellamy *in a
woman's habit*, Closet.'

Old Bellamy. I'll end your difference, cousin Fitzgerrard.
Here is your sister Amy. My lord, here is your servant
Bellamy, whom I preferred to you as my nephew, to be
a go-betwixt you and mistresses, which quality I now abhor,
as I could wish your lordship would leave wenching, for
this inconstant woman's sake, that would be prostitute unto
your servant. 'Twas a flat bargain, and but a flat one; but
for the non-performance her husband may thank their
parity of sex, not his wife's want of desire.

Saleware. Ne'er the sooner for a hasty word, I hope.

Old Bellamy. What further end she had to serve your lordship she may relate herself.

Bellamy. Lost to myself and friends, being made unfit
In any other region to appear,
And more unable to live other where
Than in the presence of my loved lord
(Although not as myself), I did assume
That masculine boldness so to let you know,
My lord, that I more fully could subsist
By the mere sight of you and so contain
Myself, than she, your more respected mistress,
Could in the rich and plentiful enjoyments
Of your most real and essential favours.

Lord. Sweet, let us speak aside.

Saleware. What ails my friend? Is not all this now but a plot to make me jealous?

Alicia. I am discovered and undone.   '*Chafes.*'

Saleware. Ne'er the sooner for a hasty word, I hope, friend. Come, leave your waggery. Is not all this but a plot now to make me jealous?

Lady. Your plot, good Mistress Saleware, would not hold.

Saleware. Nor shall it hold, good madam. I cannot be jealous. *Sapientia mea mihi—*.

Lady. Yet the young gentleman (such as you see he is) has lain with me of old, before I was married. Do not look so dismayedly; I will not detect you with my husband for a hundred pound.

Saleware. Nor will I be jealous for a thousand, madam. Your plot's too weak, facks. But where's my injured kinswoman, madam?

Lady. Oh, Phoebe Gimcrack! She is by this time righted, that is, married.

Saleware. *Sapientia mea mihi* again then for that. That was my plot, and it held, madam.

Lord. My dear, dear Amy, and my Bellamy,
I do commend your vow of future chastity,
Vowing the same myself; and here before
Your brother and these friends, to help your marriage,

I freely give you two hundred pounds a year
During your life.

Saveall. Now do you note the effect of all, Sir Oliver?

Thrivewell. I do, with much joy.

Lord. And Mistress Saleware, for your falsehood,
(Which I forgive, because you are a woman),
I quit familiarity with you, and advise you
To love your husband, giving him no cause
Of fear or jealousy.

Alicia. Your lordship counsels well.

Saleware. Hang fears and jealousies! I would there were
no greater in the kingdom than in Tom Saleware's coxcomb.
But, by your favour, friend, we will be friends no more, but
loving man and wife henceforward.

Alicia. That shall be as you please.   '*Music.*'

'*Enter* Careless, Crosstill, Wat, Phoebe.'

Lady. See, new-married couples. Please your lordship to
take notice?   '[Lord] Lovely *salutes the brides.*'

Careless. Uncle and madam, I am come to call you to my
house to dinner, and your lordship, if you please, and all
the rest here. I want one, my rival Bellamy. Where is he?
We'll be all friends today, and at night, sweetheart—at
night, at night, at night—,
We'll get the boy that shall become a knight.

Crosstill. You promise lustily.

Wat. And, Phoebe, if thou beest not better provided
already, if I get not thee with squire, let me turn clown.

Careless. But where's this Bellamy? What new lady's
that?

Old Bellamy. This new lady, sir, is that Bellamy you
enquire for.

Saveall. The same gentleman that you accused your aunt
with.

Closet. That I confess had lain with her.

Careless. Ha! Is't so, i'faith? And, now I think on't, in
troth I thought so. Would I have taxed her, think you, but
with a woman? Pray, Master Bellamy, let me salute your
lips. And, good uncle, now we are at neighbours and both
good housekeepers, let us not be strangers to one another.

Thrivewell. Well, sir, as I shall find you by your wife's report, I shall be still your uncle.

Careless. I shall be his heir in spite o' the devil and all his works and mine.

Lord. Come, madam, I find here's music. Let's lead the brides a dance to stir their appetites to dinner.

'*Dance.*'

Careless. And now, my lord, to grace our wedding feast,
As you in honour are the greatest guest,
You have full power to welcome all the rest.

FINIS.

Epilogue.

Well! Had your mirth enough? Much good may 't do you.
If not, 'tis more than I did promise to you.
'Tis your own fault, for it is you, not we,
Make a play good or bad. And if this be
Not answerable to your expectation,
Ye are the free-born people of this nation,
And have the power to censure worth and wit.
But we must suffer for what you commit.
Yet we're resolv'd to bear your gentle hands,
And if you will tie us in any bands,
Let us be bound to serve you. And that's thus,
To tell you truth, as long as you serve us.

THE
ANTIPODES:

A COMEDIE.

Acted in the yeare 1638. by the Queenes
Majesties Servants, at *Salisbury*
Court in Fleet-street.

The Author *Richard Brome.*

Hic totus volo rideat Libellus. Mart.

LONDON:

Printed by *J. Okes,* for *Francis Constable,* and
are to be sold at his shops in Kings-
street at the signe of the Goat,
and in Westminster-hall. 1640.

The Epistle Dedicatory

To the Right Honourable, William, Earl of Hertford, etc:

My Lord:

The long experience I have had of your Honour's favourable intentions towards me hath compelled me to this presumption; but I hope your goodness will be pleased to pardon what your benignity was the cause of, viz., the error of my dedication. Had your candour not encouraged me, in this I had been innocent: yet, I beseech you, think not I intend it any other than your recreation at your retirement from your weighty employments, and to be the declaration of your gracious encouragements towards me, and the testimony of my gratitude. If the public view of the world entertain it with no less welcome than that private one of the stage already has given it, I shall be glad the world owes you the thanks. If it meet with too severe construction, I hope your protection. What hazards soever it shall justle with, my desires are it may pleasure your Lordship in the perusal, which is the only ambition he is conscious of, who is,

My Lord,
Your Honour's humbly devoted

RICHARD BROME

The Prologue

Opinion, which our author cannot court,
   (For the dear daintiness of it) has of late
From the old way of plays possess'd a sort
   Only to run to those that carry state
In scene magnificent and language high,
   And clothes worth all the rest, except the action.
And such are only good, those leaders cry;
   And into that belief draw on a faction,
      That must despise all sportive, merry wit,
      Because some such great play had none in it.

But it is known (peace to their memories)
   The poets late sublimed from our age,
Who best could understand and best devise
   Works that must ever live upon the stage,
Did well approve and lead this humble way
   Which we are bound to travel in tonight;
And, though it be not trac'd so well as they
   Discover'd it by true Phoebean light,
      Pardon our just ambition yet, that strive
      To keep the weakest branch o' th' stage alive.

I mean the weakest in their great esteem
   That count all slight that's under us, or nigh,
And only those for worthy subjects deem
   Fetch'd or reach'd at (at least) from far or high;
When low and home-bred subjects have their use
   As well as those fetch'd from on high or far;
And 'tis as hard a labour for the Muse
   To move the earth, as to dislodge a star.
      See yet those glorious plays; and let their sight
      Your admiration move, these your delight.

THE PERSONS IN THE PLAY

Blaze, *an herald painter.*

Joyless, *an old country gentleman.*

Hughball, *a doctor of physic.*

Barbara, *wife to Blaze.*

Martha, *wife to Peregrine.*

Letoy, *a fantastic Lord.*

Quailpipe, *his curate.*

Peregrine, *son to Joyless.*

Diana, *wife to Joyless.*

Byplay, *a conceited servant to Letoy.*

Truelock, *a close friend to Letoy.*

Followers *of the Lord Letoy's, who are actors in the by-play.*

[Scene: London.]

THE ANTIPODES

ACT I · SCENE I

'Blaze, Joyless.'

Blaze. To me, and to the city, sir, you are welcome,
And so are all about you; we have long
Suffer'd in want of such fair company.
But now that time's calamity has given way
(Thanks to high providence) to your kinder visits,
We are (like half-pin'd wretches, that have lain
Long on the planks of sorrow, strictly tied
To a forc'd abstinence from the sight of friends)
The sweetlier fill'd with joy.

Joyless. Alas, I bring
Sorrow too much with me to fill one house,
In the sad number of my family.

Blaze. Be comforted, good sir: my house, which now
You may be pleas'd to call your own, is large
Enough to hold you all; and for your sorrows,
You came to lose 'em. And I hope the means
Is readily at hand. The doctor's coming,
Who, as by letters I advertis'd you,
Is the most promising man to cure your son
The kingdom yields. It will astonish you
To hear the marvels he hath done in cures
Of such distracted ones as is your son,
And not so much by bodily physic (no!
He sends few recipes to th' apothecaries),
As medicine of the mind, which he infuses
So skilfully, yet by familiar ways,
That it begets both wonder and delight
In his observers, while the stupid patient
Finds health at unawares.

Joyless. You speak well of him;

Yet I may fear my son's long-grown disease
Is such he hath not met with.
    Blaze. Then I'll tell you, sir,
He cur'd a country gentleman that fell mad
For spending of his land before he sold it;
That is, 'twas sold to pay his debts. All went
That way, for a dead horse, as one would say:
He had not money left to buy his dinner
Upon that wholesale day. This was a cause
Might make a gentleman mad, you'll say; and him
It did, as mad as landless squire could be.
This doctor by his art remov'd his madness,
And mingled so much wit among his brains,
That, by the overflowing of it merely,
He gets and spends five hundred pound a year now,
As merrily as any gentleman
In Derbyshire. I name no man; but this
Was pretty well, you'll say.
    Joyless. My son's disease
Grows not that way.
    Blaze. There was a lady mad—
I name no lady, but stark mad she was,
As any in country, city, or almost
In court could be—
    Joyless. How fell she mad?
    Blaze. With study,
Tedious and painful study. And for what
Now, can you think?
    Joyless. For painting, or new fashions;
I cannot think for the philosophers' stone.
    Blaze. No, 'twas to find a way to love her husband,
Because she did not, and her friends rebuk'd her.
    Joyless. Was that so hard to find, if she desir'd it?
    Blaze. She was seven years in search of it, and could not,
Though she consum'd his whole estate by it.
    Joyless. 'Twas he was mad then.
    Blaze. No, he was not born
With wit enough to lose; but mad was she
Until this doctor took her into cure;
And now she lies as lovingly on a flock-bed

With her own knight as she had done on down,
With many others—but I name no parties.
Yet this was well, you'll say.

Joyless. Would all were well.

Blaze. Then, sir, of officers and men of place,
Whose senses were so numb'd they understood not
Bribes from due fees, and fell on *praemunires*,
He has cur'd diverse, that can now distinguish
And know both when and how to take of both,
And grow most safely rich by't. Tother day
He set the brains of an attorney right,
That were quite topsy-turvy overturn'd
In a pitch o'er the bar, so that, poor man,
For many moons he knew not whether he
Went on his heels or 's head, till he was brought
To this rare doctor. Now he walks again,
As upright in his calling as the boldest
Amongst 'em. This was well, you'll say.

Joyless. 'Tis much.

Blaze. And then for horn-mad citizens, my neighbours,
He cures them by the dozens, and we live
As gently with our wives as rams with ewes.

Joyless. We, do you say? Were you one of his patients?

Blaze [*Aside*]. 'Slid, he has almost catch'd me.—No,
    sir, no;
I name no parties, I, but wish you merry.
I strain to make you so, and could tell forty
Notable cures of his to pass the time
Until he comes.

Joyless. But pray, has he the art
To cure a husband's jealousy?

Blaze. Mine, sir, he did. [*Aside*] 'Sfoot, I am catch'd
    again.

Joyless. But still you name no party. Pray how long,
Good Master Blaze, has this so famous doctor,
Whom you so well set out, been a professor?

Blaze. Never in public; nor endures the name
Of doctor, though I call him so, but lives
With an odd lord in town, that looks like no lord—
My doctor goes more like a lord than he.

'*Enter* Doctor [Hughball].'

O welcome, sir! I sent mine own wife for you;
Ha' you brought her home again?
    Doctor. She's in your house,
With gentlewomen, who seem to lodge here.
    Blaze. Yes, sir, this gentleman's wife, and his son's wife.
They all ail something, but his son, 'tis thought,
Is falling into madness, and is brought
Up by his careful father to the town here
To be your patient. Speak with him about it.
    Doctor. How do you find him, sir? Does his disease
Take him by fits, or is it constantly
And at all times the same?
    Joyless. For the most part
It is only inclining still to worse
As he grows more in days. By all the best
Conjectures we have met with in the country,
'Tis found a most deep melancholy.
    Doctor. Of what years is he?
    Joyless. Of five and twenty, sir.
    Doctor. Was it born with him? Is it natural,
Or accidental? Have you or his mother
Been so at any time affected?
    Joyless. Never;
Not she unto her grave, nor I, till then,
Knew what a sadness meant; though since, I have,
In my son's sad condition, and some crosses
In my late marriage, which at further time
I may acquaint you with.
    Blaze [*To* Doctor]. The old man's jealous
Of his young wife; I find him by the question
He put me to ere while.
    Doctor. Is your son married?
    Joyless. Diverse years since; for we had hope a wife
Might have restrain'd his travelling thoughts, and so
Have been a means to cure him; but it fail'd us.
    Doctor. What has he in his younger years been most
Addicted to? What study, or what practice?

Joyless. You have now, sir, found the question which I
   think
Will lead you to the ground of his distemper.
   Doctor. That's the next way to the cure. Come, quickly,
      quickly.
   Joyless. In tender years he always lov'd to read
Reports of travels and of voyages;
And when young boys like him would tire themselves
With sports and pastimes, and restore their spirits
Again by meat and sleep, he would whole days
And nights (sometimes by stealth) be on such books
As might convey his fancy round the world.
   Doctor. Very good, on.
   Joyless. When he grew up towards twenty,
His mind was all on fire to be abroad;
Nothing but travel still was all his aim.
There was no voyage or foreign expedition
Be said to be in hand but he made suit
To be made one in it. His mother and
Myself oppos'd him still in all, and strongly
Against his will still held him in, and won
Him into marriage, hoping that would call
In his extravagant thoughts. But all prevail'd not,
Nor stay'd him, though at home, from travelling
So far beyond himself that now too late
I wish he had gone abroad to meet his fate.
   Doctor. Well, sir, upon good terms I'll undertake
Your son. Let's see him.
   Joyless. Yet there's more—his wife, sir.
   Doctor. I'll undertake her too. Is she mad too?
   Blaze. They'll ha' mad children then.
   Doctor. Hold you your peace.
   Joyless. Alas, the danger is they will have none:
He takes no joy in her, and she no comfort
In him; for though they have been three years wed,
They are yet ignorant of the marriage-bed.
   Doctor. I shall find her the madder of the two then.
   Joyless. Indeed she's full of passion, which she utters
By the effects, as diversely as several
Objects reflect upon her wand'ring fancy,

Sometimes in extreme weepings, and anon
In vehement laughter; now in sullen silence,
And presently in loudest exclamations.

Doctor. Come, let me see 'em, sir. I'll undertake
Her too. Ha' you any more? How does your wife?

Joyless. Some other time for her.

Doctor. I'll undertake
Her too. And you yourself, sir, (by your favour,
And some few yellow spots which I perceive
About your temples) may require some counsel.

'*Enter* Barbara.'

Blaze [*Aside*]. So, he has found him.

Joyless. But my son, my son, sir?

Blaze. Now, Bab, what news?

Barbara. There's news too much within
For any home bred Christian understanding.

Joyless. How does my son?

Barbara. He is in travail, sir.

Joyless. His fit's upon him?

Barbara. Yes. Pray, Doctor Hughball,
Play the man-midwife, and deliver him
Of his huge tympany of news—of monsters,
Pygmies and giants, apes and elephants,
Griffons and crocodiles, men upon women,
And women upon men, the strangest doings,
As far beyond all Christendom as 'tis to't.

Doctor. How, how?

Barbara. Beyond the moon and stars I think,
Or mount in Cornwall either.

Blaze. How prettily like a fool she talks!
An she were not mine own wife, I could be
So taken with her.

Doctor. 'Tis most wondrous strange.

Barbara. He talks much of the kingdom of Cathaya,
Of one great Caan, and goodman Prester John,
(Whate'er they be) and says that Caan's a clown
Unto the John he speaks of, and that John
Dwells up almost at paradise. But sure his mind
Is in a wilderness, for there he says

Are geese that have two heads a-piece, and hens
That bear more wool upon their backs than sheep—
    Doctor. O Mandeville! Let's to him. Lead the way, sir.
    Barbara. And men with heads like hounds.
    Doctor. Enough, enough.
    Barbara. You'll find enough within, I warrant ye.
                       (*Exeunt* Joyless, Doctor *and* Blaze.

'*Enter* Martha.'

And here comes the poor mad gentleman's wife,
Almost as mad as he. She haunts me all
About the house to impart something to me.
Poor heart, I guess her grief, and pity her.
To keep a maidenhead three years after marriage,
Under wedlock and key! Insufferable, monstrous!
It turns into a wolf within the flesh,
Not to be fed with chickens and tame pigeons.
I could wish maids be warn'd by't not to marry
Before they have wit to lose their maidenheads,
For fear they match with men whose wits are past it.
What a sad look, and what a sigh was there!
Sweet Mistress Joyless, how is't with you now?
    Martha. When I shall know, I'll tell. Pray tell me first,
How long have you been married?
    Barbara [*Aside*]. Now she is on it.—Three years, for-
        sooth.
    Martha. And truly so have I. We shall agree, I see.
    Barbara. If you'll be merry.
    Martha. No woman merrier, now I have met with one
Of my condition. Three years married, say you? Ha, ha, ha!
    Barbara. What ails she, trow?
    Martha. Three years married! Ha, ha, ha!
    Barbara. Is that a laughing matter?
    Martha. 'Tis just my story. And you have had no child.
That's still my story. Ha, ha, ha!
    Barbara. Nay, I have had two children.
    Martha. Are you sure on't,
Or does your husband only tell you so?
Take heed o' that, for husbands are deceitful.

Barbara. But I am o' the surer side. I am sure
I groan'd for mine and bore 'em, when at best
He but believes he got 'em.

Martha.				Yet both he
And you may be deceiv'd, for now I'll tell you,
My husband told me, fac'd me down and stood on't,
We had three sons, and all great travellers,
That one had shook the great Turk by the beard.
I never saw 'em, nor am I such a fool
To think that children can be got and born,
Train'd up to men, and then sent out to travel,
And the poor mother never know nor feel
Any such matter. There's a dream indeed!

Barbara. Now you speak reason, and 'tis nothing but
Your husband's madness that would put that dream
Into you.

Martha. He may put dreams into me, but
He ne'er put child nor anything towards it yet
To me to making. Something sure belongs			'*Weep.*'
To such a work; for I am past a child
Myself to think they are found in parsley beds,
Strawberry banks, or rosemary bushes, though
I must confess I have sought and search'd such places,
Because I would fain have had one.

Barbara [*Aside*]. 'Las, poor fool.

Martha. Pray tell me, for I think nobody hears us,
How came you by your babes? I cannot think
Your husband got them you.

Barbara [*Aside*]. Fool, did I say?
She is a witch, I think.—Why not my husband?
Pray can you charge me with another man?

Martha. Nor with him neither. Be not angry, pray now;
For were I now to die, I cannot guess
What a man does in child-getting. I remember
A wanton maid once lay with me, and kiss'd
And clipt, and clapt me strangely, and then wish'd
That I had been a man to have got her with child.
What must I then ha' done, or, good now, tell me,
What has your husband done to you?

Barbara [*Aside*]. Was ever

Such a poor piece of innocence? Three years married!—
Does not your husband use to lie with you?

   Martha. Yes, he does use to lie with me, but he does not
Lie with me to use me as he should, I fear;
Nor do I know to teach him. Will you tell me?
I'll lie with you and practise, if you please.
Pray take me for a night or two; or take
My husband and instruct him, but one night.
Our country folks will say you London wives
Do not lie every night with your own husbands.

   Barbara. Your country folks should have done well to ha'
      sent
Some news by you; but I trust none told you there
We use to leave our fools to lie with madmen.

   Martha. Nay, now again you're angry.

   Barbara. No, not I,
But rather pity your simplicity.
Come, I'll take charge and care of you.

   Martha. I thank you.

   Barbara. And wage my skill against my doctor's art,
Sooner to ease you of these dangerous fits
Than he shall rectify your husband's wits.

   Martha. Indeed, indeed, I thank you.

                   (*Exeunt* Martha *and* Barbara.

[SCENE II]

'Letoy, Blaze.'

   Letoy. Why, brought'st thou not mine arms and pedigree
Home with thee, Blaze, mine honest herald's painter?

   Blaze. I have not yet, my lord, but all's in readiness,
According to the herald's full directions.

   Letoy. But has he gone to the root? Has he deriv'd me
Ex origine, ab antiquo? Has he fetch'd me
Far enough, Blaze?

   Blaze. Full four descents beyond
The conquest, my good lord, and finds that one
Of your French ancestry came in with the conqueror.

   Letoy. Jeffrey Letoy, 'twas he—from whom the English

Letoys have our descent; and here have took
Such footing that we'll never out while France
Is France and England England,
And the sea passable to transport a fashion.
My ancestors and I have been beginners
Of all new fashions in the court of England
From before *primo Ricardi Secundi*
Until this day.
    Blaze. I cannot think, my lord,
They'll follow you in this, though.
    Letoy. Mark the end.
I am without a precedent for my humour.
But is it spread, and talk'd of in the town?
    Blaze. It is, my lord, and laugh'd at by a many.
    [*Letoy.*] I am more beholding to them than all the rest.
Their laughter makes me merry; others' mirth,
And not mine own it is that feeds me, that
Battens me as poor men's cost does usurers.
But tell me, Blaze, what say they of me, ha?
    Blaze. They say, my lord, you look more like a pedlar
Than like a lord, and live more like an emperor.
    Letoy. Why, there they ha' me right. Let others shine
Abroad in cloth o' bodkin; my broadcloth
Pleases mine eye as well, my body better;
Besides, I'm sure 'tis paid for (to their envy)—
I buy with ready money; and at home here
With as good meat, as much magnificence,
As costly pleasures, and as rare delights,
Can satisfy my appetite and senses,
As they with all their public shows and braveries.
They run at ring, and tilt 'gainst one another;
I and my men can play a match at football,
Wrastle a handsome fall, and pitch the bar,
And crack the cudgels, and a pate sometimes,
'Twould do you good to see 't.
    Blaze. More than to feel 't.
    Letoy. They hunt the deer, the hare, the fox, the otter,
Polecats, or harlots, what they please; whilst I
And my mad grigs, my men, can run at base,
And breathe ourselves at barley break and dancing.

Blaze. Yes, my lord, i' th' country, when you are there.

Letoy. And now I am here i' th' city, sir, I hope
I please myself with more choice home delights
Than most men of my rank.

Blaze. I know, my lord,
Your house in substance is an amphitheatre
Of exercise and pleasure.

Letoy. Sir, I have
For exercises, fencing, dancing, vaulting;
And for delight, music of all best kinds;
Stage-plays and masques are nightly my pastimes—
And all within myself. My own men are
My music and my actors. I keep not
A man or boy but is of quality;
The worst can sing or play his part o' th' viols,
And act his part, too, in a comedy;
For which I lay my bravery on their backs;
And where another lord undoes his followers,
I maintain mine like lords. And there's my bravery.

> '*Hautboys. A service as for dinner pass over the stage,
> borne by many servitors, richly apparelled, doing honour
> to* Letoy *as they pass.*'

Now tell me, Blaze, look these like pedlar's men?

Blaze. Rather an emperor's, my lord.

Letoy. I tell thee,
These lads can act the emperors' lives all over,
And Shakespeare's chronicled histories to boot;
And were that Caesar, or that English earl,
That lov'd a play and players so well, now living,
I would not be outvied in my delights.

Blaze. My lord, 'tis well.

Letoy. I love the quality of playing, ay; I love a play with
        all
My heart, a good one, and a player that is
A good one too, with all my heart. As for the poets,
No men love them, I think, and therefore
I write all my plays myself, and make no doubt
Some of the court will follow
Me in that too. Let my fine lords
Talk o' their horse-tricks and their jockeys that

Can out-talk them; let the gallants boast
Their May-games, play-games, and their mistresses—
I love a play in my plain clothes, ay,
And laugh upon the actors in their brave ones.

'*Enter* Quailpipe.'

Quailpipe. My lord, your dinner stays prepar'd.
Letoy. Well, well,
Be you as ready with your grace as I
Am for my meat, and all is well.   (*Exit* Quailpipe.
                                   Blaze, we have rambled
From the main point this while. It seems by his letter
My doctor's busy at thy house. I know who's there
Beside. Give him this ring; tell him it wants
A finger. Farewell, good Blaze.   [*Exit* Letoy.]
Blaze. Tell him it wants a finger! My small wit
Already finds what finger it must fit.   [*Exit* Blaze.]

[SCENE III]

'*Enter* Doctor, Peregrine, *a book in his hand*,
Joyless, Diana.'

Doctor. Sir, I applaud your noble disposition,
And even adore the spirit of travel in you,
And purpose to wait on it through the world,
In which I shall but tread again the steps
I heretofore have gone.
Peregrine. All the world o'er ha' you been already?
Doctor. Over and under, too.
Peregrine. In the Antipodes?
Doctor. Yes, through and through;
No isle nor angle in that nether world
But I have made discovery of. Pray, sir, sit.
[*To* Joyless] And, sir, be you attentive; I will warrant
His speedy cure without the help of Galen,
Hippocrates, Avicen, or Dioscorides.
Diana. A rare man! Husband, truly I like his person
As well as his rare skill.

Joyless. Into your chamber!
I do not like your liking of men's persons.

Doctor. Nay, lady, you may stay. Hear and admire,
If you so please, but make no interruptions.

Joyless. And let no looser words or wand'ring look
Bewray an intimation of the slight
Regard you bear your husband, lest I send you
Upon a further pilgrimage than he
Feigns to convey my son.

Diana. O jealousy!

Doctor. Do you think, sir, to th' Antipodes such a journey?

Peregrine. I think there's none beyond it, and that
    Mandeville,
Whose excellent work this is, was th' only man
That e'er came near it.

Doctor. Mandeville went far.

Peregrine. Beyond all English legs that I can read of.

Doctor. What think you, sir, of Drake, our famous
    countryman?

Peregine. Drake was a dydapper to Mandeville.
Ca'ndish, and Hawkins, Furbisher, all our voyagers
Went short of Mandeville. But had he reach'd
To this place here—yes, here—this wilderness,
And seen the trees of the sun and moon, that speak,
And told King Alexander of his death, he then
Had left a passage ope for travellers
That now is kept and guarded by wild beasts,
Dragons, and serpents, elephants, white and blue
Unicorns, and lions of many colours,
And monsters more, as numberless as nameless.

Doctor. Stay there.

Peregrine. Read here else. Can you read?
Is it not true?

Doctor. No truer than I ha' seen 't.

Diana. Ha' you been there, sir? Ha' you seen those trees?

Doctor. And talk'd with 'em, and tasted of their fruit.

Peregrine. Read here again then. It is written here
That you may live four or five hundred year.

Diana. Brought you none of that fruit home with you,
sir?

Joyless. You would have some of 't, would you, to have hope
T' outlive your husband by 't?

Diana. I'd ha' 't for you,
In hope you might outlive your jealousy.

Doctor. Your patience both, I pray; I know the grief
You both do labour with, and how to cure it.

Joyless. Would I had given you half my land 'twere done.

Diana. Would I had given him half my love to settle
The tother half free from incumbrances
Upon my husband.

Doctor [*To* Peregrine]. Do not think it strange, sir;
I'll make your eyes witnesses of more
Than I relate, if you'll but travel with me.
You hear me not deny that all is true
That Mandeville delivers of his travels,
Yet I myself may be as well believ'd.

Peregrine. Since you speak reverently of him, say on.

Doctor. Of Europe I'll not speak—'tis too near home.
Who's not familiar with the Spanish garb,
Th' Italian shrug, French cringe, and German hug?
Nor will I trouble you with my observations
Fetch'd from Arabia, Paphlagonia,
Mesopotamia, Mauritania,
Syria, Thessalia, Persia, India—
All still is too near home. Though I have touch'd
The clouds upon the Pyrenean mountains,
And been on Paphos isle, where I have kiss'd
The image of bright Venus—all is still
Too near home to be boasted.

Diana. That I like well in him too: he will not boast of kissing
A woman too near home.

Doctor. These things in me are poor; they sound
In a far traveller's ear
Like the reports of those that beggingly
Have put out, on returns from Edinburgh,
Paris, or Venice, or perhaps Madrid,
Whither a Milaner may with half a nose
Smell out his way; and is not near so difficult

As for some man in debt, and unprotected,
To walk from Charing Cross to th' old Exchange.
No, I will pitch no nearer than th' Antipodes,
That which is farthest distant, foot to foot
Against our region.
    Diana. What, with their heels upwards?
Bless us! How 'scape they breaking o' their necks?
    Doctor. They walk upon firm earth, as we do here,
And have the firmament over their heads,
As we have here.
    Diana. And yet just under us!
Where is hell then? If they whose feet are towards us,
At the lower part of the world, have heaven too
Beyond their heads, where's hell?
    Joyless. You may find that
Without enquiry. Cease your idle questions.
    Diana. Sure hell's above ground then, in jealous husbands.
    Peregrine. What people, sir, (I pray proceed) what people
Are they of the Antipodes? Are they not such
As Mandeville writes of, without heads or necks,
Having their eyes plac'd on their shoulders, and
Their mouths amidst their breasts?
    Diana. Ay so, indeed;
Though heels go upwards and their feet should slip,
They have no necks to break.
    Doctor. Silence, sweet lady;
Pray give the gentleman leave to understand me.
The people through the whole world of Antipodes,
In outward feature, language, and religion,
Resemble those to whom they are supposite:
They under Spain appear like Spaniards,
Under France Frenchmen, under England English,
To the exterior show; but in their manners,
Their carriage, and condition of life,
Extremely contrary. To come close to you,
What part o' th' world's Antipodes shall I now
Decipher to you, or would you travel to?
    Peregrine. The furthest off.
    Doctor. That is th' Antipodes of England.
The people there are contrary to us,

As thus: here (heaven be prais'd) the magistrates
Govern the people; there the people rule
The magistrates.

 Diana. There's precious bribing then.

 Joyless. You'll hold your peace.

 Doctor. Nay, lady, 'tis by nature.
Here generally men govern the women—

 Joyless. I would they could else.

 Diana. You will hold your peace.

 Doctor. But there the women over-rule the men.
If some men fail here in their power, some women
Slip their holds there. As parents here, and masters,
Command, there they obey the child and servant.

 Diana. But pray, sir, is't by nature or by art
That wives o'ersway their husbands there?

 Doctor. By nature.

 Diana. Then art's above nature, as they are under us.

 Doctor. In brief, sir, all
Degrees of people, both in sex and quality,
Deport themselves in life and conversation
Quite contrary to us.

 Diana. Why then, the women
Do get the men with child—and put the poor fools
To grievous pain, I warrant you, in bearing.

 Joyless. Into your chamber! Get you in, I charge you.

 Doctor. By no means, as you tender your son's good.
No, lady, no; that were to make men women,
And women men. But there the maids do woo
The bachelors, and 'tis most probable
The wives lie uppermost.

 Diana. That is a trim
Upside-down Antipodean trick indeed.

 Doctor. And then at christenings and gossips' feasts
A woman is not seen; the men do all
The tittle-tattle duties, while the women
Hunt, hawk, and take their pleasure.

 Peregrine. Ha' they good game, I pray, sir?

 Doctor. Excellent;
But by the contraries to ours: for where
We hawk at pheasant, partridge, mallard, heron,

With goshawk, tarcel, falcon, laneret,
Our hawks become their game, our game their hawks.
And so the like in hunting: there the deer
Pursue the hounds, and (which you may think strange),
I ha' seen one sheep worry a dozen foxes
By moonshine in a morning before day.
They hunt trainsents with oxen, and plough with dogs.
   Peregrine. Hugh, hugh, hugh.
   Diana. Are not their swans all black and ravens white?
   Doctor. Yes, indeed are they; and their parrots teach
Their mistresses to talk.
   Diana. That's very strange.
   Doctor. They keep their cats in cages,
From mice that would devour them else, and birds;
Teach 'em to whistle, and cry, Beware the rats, puss.
But these are frivolous nothings. I have known
Great ladies ride great horses, run at tilt,
At ring, races, and hunting matches, while
Their lords at home have painted, pawn'd their plate
And jewels to feast their honourable servants;
And there the merchants' wives do deal abroad
Beyond seas, while their husbands cuckold them
At home.
   Diana. Then there are cuckolds too, it seems,
As well as here.
   Joyless. Then you conclude here are.
   Diana. By hearsay, sir. I am not wise enough
To speak it on my knowledge yet.
   Joyless. Not yet!
   Doctor. Patience, good sir.
   Peregrine. Hugh, hugh, hugh.
   Doctor. What, do you laugh, that there is cuckold-making
In the Antipodes? I tell you, sir,
It is not so abhorr'd here as 'tis held
In reputation there: all your old men
Do marry girls, and old women boys,
As generation were to be maintain'd
Only by cuckold-making.
   Joyless. Monstrous!
   Doctor. Pray, your patience.

There's no such honest men there in their world
As are their lawyers: they give away
Their practice, and t'enable 'em to do so,
Being all handicrafts or labouring men,
They work (poor hearts, full hard) in the vacations,
To give their law for nothing in the term times.
No fees are taken; which makes their divines,
Being generally covetous, the greatest wranglers
In lawsuits of a kingdom. You have not there
A gentleman in debt, though citizens
Haunt them with cap in hand to take their wares
On credit.

   Diana. What fine sport would that be here now!

   Doctor. All wit and mirth and good society
Is there among the hirelings, clowns and tradesmen,
And all their poets are puritans.

   Diana. Ha' they poets?

   Doctor. And players too; but they are all the sob'rest,
Precisest people pick'd out of a nation.

   Diana. I never saw a play.

   Doctor. Lady, you shall.

   Joyless. She shall not.

   Doctor. She must, if you can hope for any cure.
Be govern'd sir; your jealousy will grow
A worse disease than your son's madness else.
You are content I take the course I told you of
To cure the gentleman?

   Joyless. I must be, sir.

   Doctor. Say, Master Peregrine, will you travel now
With me to the Antipodes, or has not
The journey wearied you in the description?

   Peregrine. No, I could hear you a whole fortnight, but
                         '*A bowl on the table.*'
Let's lose no time; pray talk on as we pass.

   Doctor. First, sir, a health to auspicate our travels,
And we'll away.

   Peregrine. Gi' me't.

                 '*Enter* Blaze.'

What's he? One sent,

I fear, from my dead mother, to make stop
Of our intended voyage.
    Doctor. No, sir; drink.
    Blaze [*To* Doctor]. My lord, sir, understands the course
        you're in
By your letters, he tells me; and bade me gi' you
This ring, which wants a finger here, he says.
    Peregrine. We'll not be stay'd.
    Doctor. No, sir; he brings me word
The mariner calls away; the wind and tide
Are fair, and they are ready to weigh anchor,
Hoist sails, and only stay for us. Pray drink, sir.
    Peregrine. A health then to the willing winds and seas,
And all that steer towards th' Antipodes.
    Joyless. He has not drunk so deep a draught this twelve-
        month.
    Doctor. 'Tis a deep draught indeed; and now 'tis down,
And carries him down to the Antipodes—
I mean but in a dream.
    Joyless. Alas, I fear.
See, he begins to sink.
    Doctor. Trust to my skill.
Pray take an arm, and see him in his cabin.
[*To* Diana] Good lady, save my ring that's fallen there.
    Diana. In sooth, a marvellous neat and costly one!
    Blaze [*Aside*]. So, so, the ring has found a finger.
    Doctor. Come, sir, aboard, aboard, aboard, aboard.
                            [*Exeunt all except Blaze.*]
    Blaze. To bed, to bed, to bed. I know your voyage,
And my dear lord's dear plot; I understand
Whose ring hath pass'd here by your sleight of hand.
                                  [*Exit Blaze.*]

ACT II · SCENE I

'Letoy, Doctor.'

Letoy. Tonight say'st thou, my Hughball?
Doctor. By all means;
And if your play takes to my expectation,
As I not doubt my potion works to yours,
Your fancy and my cure shall be cried up
Miraculous. O you're the lord of fancy!
Letoy. I'm not ambitious of that title, sir.
No, the Letoys are of antiquity,
Ages before the fancys were begot,
And shall beget still new to the world's end.
But are you confident o' your potion, doctor?
Sleeps the young man?
Doctor. Yes, and has slept these twelve hours,
After a thousand mile an hour outright,
By sea and land; and shall wake anon
In the Antipodes.
Letoy. Well, sir, my actors
Are all in readiness, and I think all perfect
But one, that never will be perfect in a thing
He studies; yet he makes such shifts extempore,
(Knowing the purpose what he is to speak to)
That he moves mirth in me 'bove all the rest.
For I am none of those poetic furies,
That threats the actor's life in a whole play
That adds a syllable or takes away.
If he can fribble through, and move delight
In others, I am pleas'd.
Doctor. It is that mimic fellow which your lordship
But lately entertain'd?
Letoy. The same.
Doctor. He will be wondrous apt in my affair,
For I must take occasion to interchange
Discourse with him sometimes amidst their scenes,
T' inform my patient, my mad young traveller,
In diverse matters.

Letoy. Do, put him to 't; I use 't myself sometimes.

Doctor. I know it is your way.

Letoy. Well, to the business.
Hast wrought the jealous gentleman, old Joyless,
To suffer his wife to see our comedy?

Doctor. She brings your ring, my lord, upon her finger,
And he brings her in 's hand. I have instructed her
To spur his jealousy off o' the legs.

Letoy. And I will help her in 't.

Doctor. The young distracted
Gentlewoman too, that 's sick of her virginity,
Yet knows not what it is, and Blaze and 's wife,
Shall all be your guests tonight, and not alone
Spectators, but (as we will carry it), actor[s]
To fill your comic scenes with double mirth.

Letoy. Go fetch 'em then, while I prepare my actors.

(*Exit* Doctor.

Within there, ho!

[*Servants*] ('*Within*')	1. This is my beard and hair. 2. My lord appointed it for my part. 3. No, this is for you; and this is yours, this grey one. 4. Where be the foils and targets for the women? 1. Here, can't you see?

Letoy. What a rude coil is there! But yet it pleases me.

('*Within*')	1. You must not wear that cloak and hat. 2. Who told you so? I must— In my first scene, and you must wear that robe.

Letoy. What a noise make those knaves! Come in, one of you.

'*Enter* Quailpipe, *three* Actors *and* Byplay.'

Are you the first that answers to that name?

Quailpipe. My lord.

Letoy. Why are not you ready yet?

Quailpipe. I am not to put on my shape before
I have spoke the prologue; and for that, my lord,
I yet want something.

Letoy. What, I pray, with your grave formality?

Quailpipe. I want my beaver shoes and leather cap
To speak the prologue in, which were appointed
By your lordship's own direction.

Letoy. Well, sir, well;
There they be for you. I must look to all.

Quailpipe. Certes, my lord, it is a most apt conceit,
The comedy being the world turn'd upside-down,
That the presenter wear the capital beaver
Upon his feet, and on his head shoe-leather.

Letoy. Trouble not you your head with my conceit,
But mind your part. Let me not see you act now
In your scholastic way you brought to town wi' ye,
With see-saw sack-a-down, like a sawyer;
Nor in a comic scene play Hercules Furens,
Tearing your throat to split the audients' ears.
And you, sir, you had got a trick of late
Of holding out your bum in a set speech,
Your fingers fibulating on your breast,
As if your buttons or your band-strings were
Helps to your memory. Let me see you in 't
No more, I charge you. No, nor you, sir, in
That one action of the legs I told you of,
Your singles and your doubles—look you, thus—
Like one o' th' dancing masters o' the Bear Garden;
And when you have spoke, at end of every speech,
Not minding the reply, you turn you round
As tumblers do, when betwixt every feat
They gather wind by firking up their breeches.
I'll none of these absurdities in my house,
But words and action married so together,
That shall strike harmony in the ears and eyes
Of the severest, if judicious critics.

Quailpipe. My lord, we are corrected.

Letoy.   Go, be ready.

[*Exeunt* Quailpipe *and* Actors.]

[*To* Byplay] But you, sir, are incorrigible, and
Take licence to yourself to add unto
Your parts your own free fancy, and sometimes
To alter or diminish what the writer

With care and skill compos'd; and when you are
To speak to your co-actors in the scene,
You hold interlocutions with the audients.

Byplay. That is a way, my lord, has been allow'd
On elder stages to move mirth and laughter.

Letoy. Yes, in the days of Tarleton and Kempe,
Before the stage was purg'd from barbarism,
And brought to the perfection it now shines with.
Then fools and jesters spent their wits, because
The poets were wise enough to save their own
For profitabler uses. Let that pass.
Tonight I'll give thee leave to try thy wit
In answering my doctor and his patient
He brings along with him to our Antipodes.

Byplay. I heard of him, my lord. Blaze gave me light
Of the mad patient, and that he never saw
A play in 's life. It will be possible
For him to think he is in the Antipodes
Indeed, when he is on the stage among us,
When 't has been thought by some that have their wits
That all the players i' th' town were sunk past rising.

Letoy. Leave that, sir, to th' event. See all be ready,
Your music, properties, and—

Byplay. All, my lord;
Only we want a person for a mute.

Letoy. Blaze when he comes shall serve. Go in;
My guests I hear are coming.   (*Exit* Byplay.

'*Enter* Blaze, Joyless, Diana, Martha, Barbara.'

Blaze. My lord, I am become your honour's usher
To these your guests: the worthy Master Joyless,
With his fair wife and daughter-in-law.

Letoy. They're welcome;
And you in the first place, sweet Mistress Joyless.
You wear my ring, I see; you grace me in it.

Joyless. His ring! What ring? How came she by't?

Blaze [*Aside*]. 'Twill work.

Letoy. I sent it as a pledge of my affection to you;
For I before have seen you, and do languish
Until I shall enjoy your love.

Joyless. He courts her!

Letoy. Next, lady—you—I have a toy for you too.

Martha. My child shall thank you for it, when I have one.
I take no joy in toys since I was married.

Letoy. Prettily answer'd! I make you no stranger,
Kind Mistress Blaze.

Barbara. Time was your honour us'd
Me strangely too, as you'll do these, I doubt not.

Letoy. Honest Blaze,
Prithee go in; there is an actor wanting.

Blaze. Is there a part for me? How shall I study't?

Letoy. Thou shalt say nothing.

Blaze. Then if I do not act
Nothing as well as the best of 'em, let me be hiss'd.

(*Exit* Blaze.

Joyless. I say restore the ring, and back with me.

Diana. To whom shall I restore it?

Joyless. To the lord that sent it.

Diana. Is he a lord? I always thought and heard
I' th' country lords were gallant creatures. He
Looks like a thing not worth it. 'Tis not his;
The doctor gave it me, and I will keep it.

Letoy. I use small verbal courtesy, Master Joyless,
You see, but what I can in deed I'll do.
You know the purpose of your coming, and
I can but give you welcome. If your son
Shall receive ease in 't, be the comfort yours,
The credit of 't my doctor's. You are sad.

Joyless. My lord, I would entreat we may return;
I fear my wife's not well.

Letoy. Return! Pray slight not so my courtesy.

Diana. Besides, sir, I am well; and have a mind,
(A thankful one), to taste my lord's free bounty.
I never saw a play, and would be loath
To lose my longing now.

Joyless [*Aside*]. The air of London
Hath tainted her obedience already;
And should the play but touch the vices of it,
She'd learn and practise 'em.—Let me beseech
Your lordship's re-acceptance of the un-

Merited favour that she wears here, and
Your leave for our departure.
    Letoy. I will not
Be so dishonour'd; nor become so ill
A master of my house to let a lady
Leave it against her will and from her longing.
I will be plain wi' ye, therefore: if your haste
Must needs post you away, you may depart;
She shall not, not till the morning, for mine honour.
    Joyless. Indeed 'tis a high point of honour in
A lord to keep a private gentleman's wife
From him.
    Diana [*Aside*]. I love this plain lord better than
All the brave gallant ones that e'er I dreamt on.
    Letoy. 'Tis time we take our seats. So, if you'll stay,
Come sit with us; if not, you know your way.
    Joyless. Here are we fallen through the doctor's fingers
Into the lord's hands. Fate deliver us!   (*Exeunt omnes.*

[SCENE II]

'*Enter, in sea-gowns and caps*, Doctor, *and* Peregrine *brought
    in a chair by two sailors. Cloaks and hats brought in.*'

    Doctor. Now the last minute of his sleeping fit
Determines. Raise him on his feet. So, so.
Rest him upon mine arm. Remove that chair.
Welcome ashore, sir, in th' Antipodes.
    Peregrine. Are we arriv'd so far?
    Doctor. And on firm land.
Sailors, you may return now to your ship.

                                             (*Exeunt* Sailors.

    Peregrine. What worlds of lands and seas have I pass'd
        over,
Neglecting to set down my observations.
A thousand thousand things remarkable
Have slipp'd my memory, as if all had been
Mere shadowy phantasms, or fantastic dreams.
    Doctor. We'll write as we return, sir. And 'tis true
You slept most part o' th' journey hitherward,

The air was so somniferous; and 'twas well—
You 'scap'd the calenture by 't.

    Peregrine. But how long do you think I slept?

    Doctor. Eight months and some odd days,
Which was but as so many hours and minutes
Of one's own natural country sleep.

    Peregrine. Eight months?

    Doctor. 'Twas nothing for so young a brain.
How think you one of the seven Christian champions,
David by name, slept seven years in a leek bed?

    Peregrine. I think I have read it in their famous history.

    Doctor. But what chief thing of note now in our travels
Can you call presently to mind? Speak like a traveller.

    Peregrine. I do remember, as we pass'd the verge
O' th' upper world, coming down, down hill,
The setting sun, then bidding them goodnight,
Came gliding easily down by us, and struck
New day before us, lighting us our way;
But with such heat, that till he was got far
Before us, we even melted.

    Doctor [*Aside*]. Well wrought, potion!—Very well
        observ'd, sir.
But now we are come into a temperate clime
Of equal composition of elements
With that of London, and as well agreeable
Unto our nature as you have found that air.

    Peregrine. I never was at London.

    Doctor. Cry you mercy.
This, sir, is Anti-London—that's the Antipodes
To the grand city of our nation,
Just the same people, language, and religion,
But contrary in manners, as I ha' told you.

    Peregrine. I do remember that relation
As if you had but given it me this morning.

    Doctor. Now cast your sea weeds off, and do'n fresh
        garments.
Hark, sir, their music.   '*Shift.*'

    '*Hautboys. Enter* Letoy, Joyless, Diana, Martha, Barbara
      in masks. They sit at the other end of the stage.'

    Letoy. Here we may sit, and he not see us.

Doctor. Now see one of the natives of this country;
Note his attire, his language, and behaviour.

'*Enter* Quailpipe, Prologue.'

Quailpipe. Our far-fetch'd title over lands and seas
Offers unto your view th' Antipodes.
But what Antipodes now shall you see?
Even those that foot to foot 'gainst London be,
Because no traveller that knows that state
Shall say we personate or imitate
Them in our actions; for nothing can,
Almost, be spoke, but some or other man
Takes it unto himself and says the stuff,
If it be vicious or absurd enough,
Was woven upon his back. Far, far be all
That bring such prejudice mix'd with their gall.
This play shall no satiric timist be,
To tax or touch at either him or thee,
That art notorious. 'Tis so far below
Things in our orb, that do among us flow,
That no degree, from Caesar to the clown,
Shall say this vice or folly was mine own.
    Letoy. This had been well now, if you had not dreamt
Too long upon your syllables.   (*Exit* Quailpipe.
    Diana. The prologue call you this, my lord?
    Barbara. 'Tis my lord's reader, and as good a lad
Out of his function as I would desire
To mix withal in civil conversation.
    Letoy. Yes, lady, this was prologue to the play,
As this is to our sweet ensuing pleasures.   '*Kiss.*'
    Joyless [*Aside*]. Kissing indeed is prologue to a play,
Compos'd by th' Devil, and acted by the children
Of his black revels. May hell take ye for 't.
    Martha. Indeed I am weary, and would fain go home.
    Barbara. Indeed but you must stay, and see the play.
    Martha. The play? What play? It is no children's play,
Nor no child-getting play, pray, is it?
    Barbara. You'll see anon. Oh, now the actors enter.
                                              '*Flourish.*'

'*Enter two* Sergeants, *with swords drawn, running before
a* Gentleman.'

Gentleman. Why do you not your office, courteous friends?
Let me entreat you stay, and take me with you.
Lay but your hands on me; I shall not rest
Until I be arrested. A sore shoulder-ache
Pains and torments me till your virtuous hands
Do clap or stroke it.
    1st Sergeant. You shall pardon us.
    2nd Sergeant. And I beseech you pardon our intent,
Which was indeed to have arrested you;
But sooner shall the charter of the city
Be forfeited, than varlets, like ourselves,
Shall wrong a gentleman's peace. So fare you well, sir.
                        (*Exeunt* Sergeants.

    Gentleman. Oh, you're unkind.
    Peregrine. Pray what are those?
    Doctor. Two catchpoles
Run from a gentleman, it seems, that would
Have been arrested.

'*Enter* Old Lady *and* Byplay, *like a Serving-man.*'

    Lady. Yonder's your master;
Go take him you in hand, while I fetch breath.
    Byplay. Oh, are you here? My lady and myself
Have sought you sweetly—
    Letoy. You and your lady, you
Should ha' said, puppy.
    Byplay. For we heard you were
To be arrested. Pray, sir, who has bail'd you?
I wonder who of all your bold acquaintance
That knows my lady durst bail off her husband.
    Gentleman. Indeed, I was not touch'd.
    Byplay. Have you not made
An end by composition, and disburs'd
Some of my lady's money for a peace
That shall beget an open war upon you?
Confess it if you have, for 'twill come out.
She'll ha' you up, you know. I speak it for your good.

Gentleman. I know 't, and I'll entreat my lady wife
To mend thy wages tother forty shillings
A year, for thy true care of me.

    Lady. 'Tis well, sir.
But now (if thou hast impudence so much
As face to face to speak unto a lady
That is thy wife and supreme head) tell me
At whose suit was it, or upon what action?
Debts I presume you have none; for who dares trust
A lady's husband who is but a squire,
And under covert barne? It is some trespass—
Answer me not till I find out the truth.

    Gentleman. The truth is—

    Lady. Peace!
How dar'st thou speak the truth
Before thy wife? I'll find it out myself.

    Diana. In truth she handles him handsomely.

    Joyless. Do you like it?

    Diana. Yes, and such wives are worthy to be lik'd,
For giving good examples.

    Letoy. Good! Hold up
That humour by all means.

    Lady. I think I ha' found it.
There was a certain mercer sent you silks
And cloth of gold, to get his wife with child;
You slighted her, and answer'd not his hopes;
And now he lays to arrest you; is 't not so?

    Gentleman. Indeed, my lady wife, 'tis so.

    Lady. For shame,
Be not ingrateful to that honest man,
To take his wares, and scorn to lie with his wife.
Do't, I command you. What did I marry you for?
The portion that you brought me was not so
Abundant, though it were five thousand pounds,
(Considering, too, the jointure that I made you)
That you should disobey me.

    Diana. It seems the husbands
In the Antipodes bring portions, and
The wives make jointures.

    Joyless. Very well observ'd.

Diana. And wives, when they are old and past child-
    bearing,
Allow their youthful husbands other women.

Letoy. Right; and old men give their young wives like
    licence.

Diana. That I like well. Why should not our old men
Love their young wives as well?

Joyless. Would you have it so?

Letoy. Peace, Master Joyless, you are too loud. Good,
    still.

Byplay. Do as my lady bids; you got her woman
With child at half these words.

Gentleman. Oh, but another's
Wife is another thing. Far be it from
A gentleman's thought to do so, having a wife
And handmaid of his own, that he loves better.

Byplay. There said you well; but take heed, I advise you,
How you love your own wench or your own wife
Better than other men's.

Diana. Good Antipodean counsel.

Lady. Go to that woman; if she prove with child,
I'll take it as mine own.

Gentleman. Her husband would
Do so. But from my house I may not stray.

Martha. If it be me your wife commends you to,
You shall not need to stray from your own house.
I'll go home with you.

Barbara. Precious! What do you mean?
Pray keep your seat; you'll put the players out.

Joyless. Here's goodly stuff! She's in the Antipodes too.

Peregrine [*Seeing* Letoy *and his guests*]. And what are
    those?

Doctor. All Antipodeans.
Attend, good sir.

Lady. You know your charge; obey it.

        '*Enter* Waiting-woman *great bellied.*'

Woman. What is his charge, or whom must he obey,
Good madam, with your wild authority?
You are his wife, 'tis true, and therein may,

According to our law, rule and control him;
But you must know withal, I am your servant,
And bound by the same law to govern you,
And be a stay to you in declining age,
To curb and qualify your headstrong will,
Which otherwise would ruin you. Moreover,
Though you're his wife, I am a breeding mother
Of a dear child of his, and therein claim
More honour from him than you ought to challenge.

 Lady. In sooth she speaks but reason.

 Gentleman. Pray let's home, then.

 Woman. You have something there to look to, one would
  think,
If you had any care how well you saw
Your father at school today, and knowing how apt
He is to play the truant.

 Gentleman. But is he not
Yet gone to school?

 Woman. Stand by, and you shall see.

   '*Enter three* Old Men *with satchels, &c.*'

 Old Men. Domine, domine, duster,
   Three knaves in a cluster, *&c.*

 Gentleman. O this is gallant pastime. Nay, come on,
Is this your school? Was that your lesson, ha?

 1st Old Man. Pray now, good son, indeed, indeed—

 Gentleman. Indeed
You shall to school. Away with him, and take
Their wagships with him, the whole cluster of 'em.

 2nd Old Man. You shan't send us now, so you shan't.

 3rd Old Man. We be none of your father, so we beant.

 Gentleman. Away with 'em, I say, and tell their school-
  mistress
What truants they are, and bid her pay 'em soundly.

 Old Men. Oh, oh, oh!

 Byplay. Come, come, ye gallows-clappers.

 Diana. Alas, will nobody beg pardon for
The poor old boys?

 Doctor. Sir, gentle sir, a word with you.

 Byplay. To strangers, sir, I can be gentle.

Letoy. Good.
Now mark that fellow—he speaks extempore.
    Diana. Extempore call you him? He's a dogged fellow
To the three poor old things there. Fie upon him!
    Peregrine. Do men of such fair years here go to school?
    Byplay. They would die dunces else.
    Peregrine. Have you no young men scholars, sir, I pray,
When we have beardless doctors?
    Doctor [*Aside*]. He has wip'd my lips.—You question very
        wisely, sir.
    Byplay. So, sir, have we—and many reverend teachers,
Grave counsellors at law, perfect statesmen,
That never knew use of razor, which may live,
For want of wit, to lose their offices.
These were great scholars in their youth; but when
Age grows upon men here, their learning wastes,
And so decays, that if they live until
Threescore, their sons send them to school again.
They'd die as speechless else as new-born children.
    Peregrine. 'Tis a wise nation, and the piety
Of the young men most rare and commendable.
Yet give me as a stranger leave to beg
Their liberty this day, and what they lose by't,
My father, when he goes to school, shall answer.
    Joyless. I am abus'd on that side too.
    Byplay. 'Tis granted.
Hold up your heads and thank the gentleman
Like scholars, with your heels now.
    Old Men. Gratias, gratias, gratias.   (*Exeunt* Old Men.
    Diana. Well done, son Peregrine. He's in his wits, I hope.
    Joyless. If you lose yours the while, where's my advantage?
    Diana. And trust me, 'twas well done too of Extempore
To let the poor old children loose. And now
I look well on him, he's a proper man.
    Joyless. She'll fall in love with the actor, and undo me.
    Diana. Does not his lady love him, sweet my lord?
    Letoy. Love? Yes, and lie with him, as her husband does
With 's maid. It is their law in the Antipodes.
    Diana. But we have no such laws with us.
    Joyless. Do you approve of such a law?

Diana. No, not so much
In this case, where the man and wife do lie
With their inferior servants; but in the other,
Where the old citizen would arrest the gallant
That took his wares and would not lie with 's wife,
There it seems reasonable, very reasonable.

Joyless. Does it?

Diana. Make 't your own case: you are an old man;
I love a gentleman; you give him rich presents
To get me a child, because you cannot—must not
We look to have our bargain?

Joyless. Give me leave
Now to be gone, my lord, though I leave her
Behind me. She is mad, and not my wife,
And I may leave her.

Letoy. Come, you are mov'd, I see.
I'll settle all; but first, prevail with you
To taste my wine and sweetmeats. The comedians
Shall pause the while. This you must not deny me.

     (*Exeunt* Letoy, Martha, Diana, Barbara.

Joyless. I must not live here always; that's my comfort.

         (*Exit* Joyless.

Peregrine. I thank you, sir, for the poor men's release;
It was the first request that I have made
Since I came in these confines.

Byplay. 'Tis our custom
To deny strangers nothing; yea, to offer
Of anything we have that may be useful
In courtesy to strangers. Will you therefore
Be pleas'd to enter, sir, this habitation,
And take such viands, beverage, and repose,
As may refresh you after tedious travels?

Doctor. Thou tak'st him right, for I am sure he's hungry.

Peregrine. All I have seen since my arrival are
Wonders, but your humanity excels.

Byplay. Virtue in the Antipodes only dwells.

      (*Exeunt* Doctor, Byplay, Peregrine.

———————

ACT III · SCENE I

'Letoy, Joyless, Diana, Martha, Barbara.'

Letoy. Yet, Master Joyless, are you pleas'd? You see
Here's nothing but fair play, and all above board.

Joyless. But it is late, and these long intermissions
By banquetting and courtship 'twixt the acts
Will keep back the catastrophe of your play
Until the morning light.

Letoy. All shall be short.

Joyless. And then, in midst of scenes
You interrupt your actors and tie them
To lengthen time in silence, while you hold
Discourse by th' by.

Letoy. Pox o' thy jealousy,
Because I give thy wife a look or word
Sometimes! What if I kiss—thus; I'll not eat her.

Joyless. So, so, his banquet works with him.

Letoy. And for my actors, they shall speak, or not speak,
As much, or more, or less, and when I please.
It is my way of pleasure, and I'll use it.
So, sit. They enter. 'Flourish.'

'Enter Lawyer, and Poet.'

Lawyer. Your case is clear; I understand it fully,
And need no more instructions. This shall serve
To firk your adversary from court to court.
If he stand out upon rebellious legs
But till Octavus Michaelis next,
I'll bring him on submissive knees.

Diana. What's he?

Letoy. A lawyer, and his client there's a poet.

Diana. Goes law so torn, and poetry so brave?

Joyless. Will you but give the actors leave to speak,
They may have done the sooner.

Lawyer. Let me see,
This is your bill of parcels.

Poet. Yes, of all
My several wares, according to the rates
Deliver'd unto my debitor.

Diana. Wares, does he say?

Letoy. Yes, poetry is good ware
In the Antipodes, though there be some ill payers,
As well as here. But law there rights the poets.

Lawyer. Deliver'd too, and for the use of the right
    worshipful
Master Alderman Humblebee, as followeth: *Imprimis—*
                                       '*Reads.*'
Umh, I cannot read your hand; your character
Is bad, and your orthography much worse.
Read it yourself, pray.

Diana. Do aldermen
Love poetry in Antipodean London?

Letoy. Better than ours do custards; but the worst
Paymasters living there, worse than our gallants,
Partly for want of money, partly wit.

Diana. Can aldermen want wit and money too?
That's wonderful.

Poet. *Imprimis*, sir, here is
For three religious madrigals to be sung
By th' holy vestals in Bridewell, for the
Conversion of our city wives and daughters,
Ten groats a-piece—it was his own agreement.

Lawyer. 'Tis very reasonable.

Poet. *Item:* twelve hymns
For the twelve sessions during his shrievalty,
Sung by the choir of Newgate, in the praise
Of city clemency (for in that year
No guiltless person suffer'd by their judgement),
Ten groats a-piece also.

Lawyer. So, now it rises.

Diana. Why speaks your poet so demurely?

Letoy. Oh,
'Tis a precise tone he has got among
The sober sisterhood.

Diana. Oh, I remember,
The doctor said poets were all puritans

In the Antipodes. But where's the doctor?
And where's your son, my Joyless?
 Letoy. Do not mind him.
 Poet. Item:
A distich graven in his thumb-ring
Of all the wise speeches and sayings of all
His alder predecessors and his brethren
In two kings' reigns.
 Lawyer. There was a curious piece!
 Poet. Two pieces he promis'd to me for it.
Item: inscriptions in his hall, and parlour,
His gallery, and garden, round the walls,
Of his own public acts, between the time
He was a common council man and shriefe,
One thousand lines put into wholesome verse.
 Lawyer. Here's a sum towards indeed! A thousand verses?
 Poet. They come to, at the known rate of the city,
(That is to say, at forty pence the score),
Eight pounds, six shillings, eightpence.
 Lawyer. Well, sir, on.
 Poet. Item: an elegy for Mistress Alderwoman
Upon the death of one of her coach-mares
She priz'd above her daughter, being crooked—
 Diana. The more beast she.
 Martha. Ha, ha, ha!
 Barbara. Enough, enough, sweetheart.
 Martha. 'Tis true; for I should weep for that poor
    daughter;
'Tis like she'll have no children. Pray now, look,
Am not I crooked too?
 Barbara. No, no; sit down.
 Poet. Item: a love epistle for the aldermanikin his son,
And a book of the godly life and death
Of Mistress Katherine Stubbs, which I have turn'd
Into sweet metre, for the virtuous youth
To woo an ancient lady widow with.
 Lawyer. Here's a large sum in all, for which I'll try
His strength in law, till he *peccavi* cry;
When I shall sing, for all his present bigness,
Iamque opus exegi quod nec Iovis ira, nec ignis.

Diana. The lawyer speaks the poet's part.

Letoy. He thinks
The more; the poets in th' Antipodes
Are slow of tongue, but nimble with the pen.

Poet. The counsel and the comfort you have given
Me requires a double fee.   '*Offers money.*'

Lawyer. Will you abuse me therefore?
I take no fees, double nor single, I.
Retain your money; you retain not me else.
Away, away, you'll hinder other clients.

Poet. Pray give me leave to send them to your wife.

Lawyer. Not so much as a posy for her thimble,
For fear I spoil your cause.

Poet. You've warn'd me, sir.   (*Exit* Poet.

Diana. What a poor honest lawyer's this.

Letoy. They are all so
In th' Antipodes.

'*Enter a spruce young Captain*' [*with a feather in his hat*].

Lawyer. You're welcome, captain.
In your two causes I have done my best.

Captain. And what's the issue, pray, sir?

Lawyer. Truly, sir,
Our best course is not to proceed to trial.

Captain. Your reason? I shall then recover nothing.

Lawyer. Yes, more by composition than the court
Can lawfully adjudge you, as I have labour'd.
And, sir, my course is, where I can compound
A difference, I'll not toss nor bandy it
Into the hazard of a judgement.

Diana. Still
An honest lawyer, and though poor, no marvel.

Letoy. A kiss for thy conceit.

Joyless. A sweet occasion!

Captain. How have you done, sir?

Lawyer. First you understand
Your several actions and your adversaries:
The first a battery against a coachman
That beat you sorely.

Diana. What hard-hearted fellow
Could beat so spruce a gentleman, and a captain?

Captain. By this fair hilt, he did, sir, and so bruis'd
My arms, so crush'd my ribs and stitch'd my sides,
That I have had no heart to draw my sword since;
And shall I put it up, and not his purse
Be made to pay for 't?

Lawyer. It is up already, sir,
If you can be advis'd. Observe, I pray,
Your other actions 'gainst your feathermaker,
And that of trespass for th' incessant trouble
He puts you to by importunate requests
To pay him no money, but take longer day.

Captain. Against all human reason; for although
I have bought feathers of him these four years,
And never paid him a penny, yet he duns me
So desperately to keep my money still,
As if I ought him nothing. He haunts and breaks my sleeps.
I swear, sir, by the motion of this I wear now,

                                                    '*Shakes it.*'

I have had twenty better feathers of him, and as ill paid for,
Yet still he duns me to forbear my payment,
And to take longer day,
More than at first. I ha' not said my prayers in
Mine own lodging, sir, this twelve-months day
For sight or thought of him. And how can you
Compound this action, or the other of
That ruffian coachman that durst lift a hand
'Gainst a commander?

Lawyer. Very easily, thus:
The coachman's poor, and scarce his twelve-months wages,
Though 't be five marks a year, will satisfy.

Captain. Pray name no sum in marks—I have had too
      many
Of 's marks already.

Lawyer. So you owe the other
A debt of twenty pound, the coachman now
Shall for your satisfaction beat you out
Of debt.

Captain. Beat me again?

Lawyer. No, sir, he shall beat
For you your feather-man till he take his money.
    Captain. So I'll be satisfied, and help him to
More customers of my rank.
    Lawyer. Leave it to me then.
It shall be by posterity repeaten,
That soldiers ought not to be dunn'd or beaten.
Away, and keep your money.
    Captain. Thank you, sir.   [*Exit* Captain.]
    Diana. An honest lawyer still! How he considers
The weak estate of a young gentleman
At arms.—But who comes here? A woman?

'*Enter* Buff Woman.'

Letoy. Yes, that has taken up the newest fashion
Of the town militasters.
    Diana. Is it buff,
Or calfskin, trow? She looks as she could beat
Out a whole tavern garrison before her
Of mill tasters, call you 'em? If her husband
Be an old jealous man now, and can please her
                '*Lawyer reads on papers.*'
No better than most ancient husbands can,
I warrant she makes herself good upon him.
    Joyless. 'Tis very good; the play begins to please me.
    Buff. I wait to speak wi' ye, sir, but must I stand
Your constring and piercing of your scribblings?
    Lawyer. Cry mercy, lady.
    Diana. Lady, does he call her?
    Lawyer. Thus far I have proceeded in your cause
I'th' marshall's court.
    Buff. But shall I have the combat?
    Lawyer. Pray observe
The passages of my proceedings, and
The pros and contras in the windings, workings,
And carriage of the cause.
    Buff. Fah on your passages,
Your windy workings, and your fislings at
The bar. Come me to th' point. Is it decreed
A combat?

Lawyer. Well, it is; and here's your order.

Buff. Now thou hast spoken like a lawyer.
And here's thy fee.

Lawyer. By no means, gentle lady.

Buff. Take it, or I will beat thy carcase thinner
Than thou hast worn thy gown here.

Lawyer. Pardon me.

Buff. Must I then take you in hand?

Lawyer. Hold, hold; I take it.

Diana. Alas, poor man, he will take money yet
Rather than blows; and so far he agrees
With our rich lawyers, that sometimes give blows,
And shrewd ones, for their money.

Buff. Now victory
Afford me, fate, or bravely let me die.

(*Exit* Buff Woman.

Letoy. Very well acted, that.

Diana. Goes she to fight now?

Letoy. You shall see that anon.

> '*Enter a* Beggar, *and a* Gallant.'

Diana. What's here, what's here?
A courtier, or some gallant practising
The beggar's trade, who teaches him, I think.

Letoy. You're something near the subject.

Beggar. Sir, excuse me, I have
From time to time supplied you without hope
Or purpose to receive least retribution
From you, no, not so much as thanks or bare
Acknowledgement of the free benefits
I have conferr'd upon you.

Gallant. Yet, good uncle—

Beggar. Yet do you now, when that my present store
Responds not my occasions, seek to oppress me
With vain petitionary breath, for what I may not
Give without fear of dangerous detriment?

Diana. In what a phrase the ragged orator
Displays himself.

Letoy. The beggars are the
Most absolute courtiers in th' Antipodes.

Gallant. If not a piece, yet spare me half a piece,
For goodness sake, good sir. Did you but know
My instant want, and to what virtuous use
I would distribute it, I know you would not
Hold back your charity.

Diana. And how feelingly
He begs! Then as the beggars are the best
Courtiers, it seems the courtiers are best beggars
In the Antipodes. How contrary in all
Are they to us!

Beggar. Pray to what virtuous uses
Would you put money to now, if you had it?

Gallant. I would bestow a crown in ballads,
Love-pamphlets, and such poetical rarities,
To send down to my lady grandmother.
She's very old, you know, and given much
To contemplation. I know she'll send me for 'em,
In puddings, bacon, souse and pot-butter,
Enough to keep my chamber all this winter.
So shall I save my father's whole allowance
To lay upon my back, and not be forc'd
To shift out from my study for my victuals.

Diana. Belike he is some student.

Beggar. There's a crown.

Gallant. I would bestow another crown in
Hobby-horses and rattles for my grandfather,
Whose legs and hearing fail him very much;
Then, to preserve his sight, a Jack-a-Lent,
In a green sarsnet suit. He'll make my father
To send me one of scarlet, or he'll cry
His eyes out for 't.

Diana. Oh politic young student!

Beggar. I have but just a fee left for my lawyer;
If he exact not that, I'll give it thee.

Diana. He'll take no fee (that's sure enough, young man)
Of beggars; I know that.

Letoy. You are deceiv'd.

Diana. I'll speak to him myself else, to remit it.

Joyless. You will not, sure. Will you turn actor too?
Pray do; be put in for a share amongst 'em!

Diana. How must I be put in?

Joyless. The players will quickly
Show you, if you perform your part. Perhaps
They may want one to act the whore among'st 'em.

Letoy. Fie, Master Joyless, you're too foul.

Joyless. My lord,
She is too fair, it seems, in your opinion,
For me. Therefore, if you can find it lawful,
Keep her; I will be gone.

Letoy. Now I protest,
Sit, and sit civilly, till the play be done.
I'll lock thee up else, as I am true Letoy.

Joyless. Nay, I ha' done.

> *'Whistles "Fortune my Foe."'*

Lawyer. Give me my fee; I cannot hear you else.

Beggar. Sir, I am poor, and all I get is at
The hands of charitable givers. Pray, sir—

Lawyer. You understand me, sir: your cause is to be
Pleaded today, or you are quite o'erthrown in 't.
The judge by this time is about to sit.
Keep fast your money, and forego your wit.

> *(Exit* Lawyer.

Beggar. Then I must follow, and entreat him to it.
Poor men in law must not disdain to do it.

> *(Exit* Beggar.

Gallant. Do it then; I'll follow you and hear the cause.

> *(Exit* Gallant.

Diana. True Antipodeans still! For as with us
The gallants follow lawyers, and the beggars them,
The lawyer here is follow'd by the beggar,
While the gentleman follows him.

Letoy. The moral is, the lawyers here prove beggars,
And beggars only thrive by going to law.

Diana. How takes the lawyers then the beggars' money,
And none else by their wills?

Letoy. They send it all
Up to our lawyers, to stop their mouths
That curse poor clients that are put upon 'em
In forma pauperis.

Diana. In truth, most charitable.

But sure that money's lost by th' way sometimes.
Yet, sweet my lord, whom do these beggars beg of,
That they can get aforehand so for law?
Who are their benefactors?

   Letoy. Usurers, usurers.

   Diana. Then they have usurers in th' Antipodes too?

   Letoy. Yes, usury goes round the world, and will do,
Till the general conversion of the Jews.

   Diana. But ours are not so charitable, I fear.
Who be their usurers?

   Letoy. Soldiers and courtiers chiefly,
And some that pass for grave and pious churchmen.

   Diana. How finely contrary th' are still to ours!

'Enter Byplay.'

   Letoy. Why do you not enter? What, are you asleep?

   Byplay. My lord, the mad young gentleman—

   Joyless. What of him?

   Byplay. He has got into our tiring house amongst us,
And ta'en a strict survey of all our properties,
Our statues and our images of Gods;
Our planets and our constellations;
Our giants, monsters, furies, beasts, and bugbears;
Our helmets, shields and vizors, hairs and beards;
Our paste-board marchpanes, and our wooden pies.

   Letoy. Sirrah, be brief; be not you now as long in
Telling what he saw as he surveying.

   Byplay. Whether he thought 'twas some enchanted castle
Or temple, hung and pil'd with monuments
Of uncouth and of various aspects,
I dive not to his thoughts. Wonder he did
Awhile, it seem'd, but yet undaunted stood;
When on the sudden, with thrice knightly force,
And thrice, thrice puissant arm he snatcheth down
The sword and shield that I play'd Bevis with,
Rusheth amongst the foresaid properties,
Kills monster after monster; takes the puppets
Prisoners, knocks down the Cyclops, tumbles all
Our jigambobs and trinkets to the wall.
Spying at last the crown and royal robes

I' th' upper wardrobe, next to which by chance
The devils' vizors hung, and their flame-painted
Skin coats, those he remov'd with greater fury,
And, having cut the infernal ugly faces
All into mammocks, with a reverend hand
He takes the imperial diadem and crowns
Himself king of the Antipodes, and believes
He has justly gain'd the kingdom by his conquest.

    Letoy. Let him enjoy his fancy.

    Byplay. Doctor Hughball
Hath sooth'd him in 't, so that nothing can
Be said against it. He begins to govern
With purpose to reduce the manners
Of this country to his own. H'as constituted
The doctor his chief officer, whose secretary
I am to be. You'll see a court well order'd.

    Letoy. I see th' event already, by the aim
The doctor takes. Proceed you with your play,
And let him see it in what state he pleases.

                            '*Letoy whispers with* Barbara.'

    Byplay. I go, my lord.   (*Exit* Byplay.

    Diana. Trust me, this same Extempore
(I know not 's tother name) pleases me better
For absolute action than all the rest.

    Joyless. You were best beg him of his lord.

    Diana. Say you so?
He 's busy, or I'd move him.

    Letoy. Prithee do so,
Good Mistress Blaze. ('*To* Martha') Go with her, gentle lady.
Do as she bids you; you shall get a child by 't.

    Martha. I'll do as anybody bids me for a child.

    Joyless. Diana, yet be wise; bear not the name
Of sober chastity to play the beast in.

    Diana. Think not yourself nor make yourself a beast
Before you are one; and when you appear so,
Then thank yourself. Your jealousy durst not trust me
Behind you in the country, and since I'm here,
I'll see and know, and follow th' fashion. If
It be to cuckold you, I cannot help it.

    Joyless. I now could wish my son had been as far

In the Antipodes as he thinks himself,
Ere I had run this hazard.
    Letoy [*To* Barbara]. You're instructed.
    Barbara. And I'll perform 't, I warrant you, my lord.
                          (*Exeunt* Barbara, Martha.
    Diana. Why should you wish so? Had you rather lose
Your son than please your wife? You show your love both
    ways.
    Letoy. Now what's the matter?
    Joyless. Nothing, nothing—
    Letoy. Sit; the actors enter.   '*Flourish.*'

'*Enter* Byplay *the* Governor, Mace-bearer, Sword-bearer,
Officer. *The mace and sword laid on the table, the* Governor
sits.'

    Diana. What's he? A king?
    Letoy. No, 'tis the city governor,
And the chief judge within their corporation.
    Joyless. Here's a city
Like to be well govern'd then.

            '*Enter* Peregrine *and* Doctor.'

    Letoy. Yonder's a king; do you know him?
    Diana. 'Tis your son,
My Joyless. Now you're pleas'd.
    Joyless. Would you were pleas'd
To cease your huswifry in spinning out
The play at length thus.
    Doctor. Here, sir, you shall see
A point of justice handled.
    Byplay. Officer.
    Officer. My lord.
    Byplay. Call the defendant and the plaintiff in.
    Sword-bearer. Their counsel and their witnesses.
    Byplay. How now!
How long ha' you been free o'th' point-makers,
Good master hilt and scabbard carrier—
Which is in my hands now? Do you give order
For counsel and for witnesses in a cause
Fit for my hearing, or for me to judge, haw?

I must be rul'd and circumscrib'd by lawyers, must I,
And witnesses, haw? No, you shall know
I can give judgement, be it right or wrong,
Without their needless proving and defending.
So bid the lawyers go and shake their ears,
If they have any, and the witnesses
Preserve their breath to prophesy of dry summers.
Bring me the plaintiff and defendant only,
But the defendant first; I will not hear
Any complaint before I understand
What the defendant can say for himself.   [*Exit* Officer.]
  Peregrine. I have not known such downright equity.
If he proceeds as he begins, I'll grace him.

'*Enter* Gentleman, *and* Officer.'

  Byplay. Now, sir, are you the plaintiff or defendant, haw?
  Gentleman. Both, as the case requires, my lord.
  Byplay. I cannot
Hear two at once. Speak first as you're defendant.
  Gentleman. Mine adversary doth complain—
  Byplay. I will hear no
Complaint. I say speak your defence.
  Gentleman. For silks and
Stuffs receiv'd by me.
  Byplay. A mercer is he, haw?
  Gentleman. Yes, my good lord. He doth not now complain—
  Byplay. That I like well.
  Gentleman. For money nor for wares
Again, but he complains—
  Byplay. Complains again? Do you double with me, haw?
  Gentleman. In his wife's cause.
  Byplay. Of his wife, does he, haw? That, I must confess,
Is many a good man's case. You may proceed.
  Gentleman. In money I tender him double satisfaction,
With his own wares again unblemish'd, undishonour'd.
  Byplay. That is, unworn, unpawn'd.
  Diana. What an odd
Jeering judge is this!

Gentleman. But unto me
They were deliver'd upon this condition,
That I should satisfy his wife.
    Byplay. He'll have
Your body for her then, unless I empt
My breast of mercy to appease her for you.
Call in the plaintiff. Sir, stand you aside.   (*Exit* Officer.
    Diana. Oh, 'tis the flinching gentleman that broke
With the kind citizen's wife. I hope the judge
Will make him an example.

'*Enter* Citizen, *and* Officer.'

    Byplay. Come you forwards—
Yet nearer, man. I know my face is terrible,
And that a citizen had rather lose
His debt than that a judge should truly know
His dealings with a shop-keeper. Yet speak;
Repeat without thy shop-book now, and without
Fear it may rise in judgement here against thee,
What is thy full demand? What satisfaction
Requirest thou of this gentleman?
    Citizen. An't please you, sir—
    Sword-bearer. Sir! You forget yourself.
    Byplay. 'Twas well said, sword-bearer.
Thou knowest thy place, which is to show correction.
    Citizen. My lord, an't please you, if it like your honour—
    Byplay. Ha! an intelligent citizen, and may grow
In time himself to sit in place of worship.
    Citizen. I ask no satisfaction of the gentleman,
But to content my wife. What her demand is,
'Tis best known to herself. Please her, please me,
An't please you, sir—my lord, an't like your honour.
But before he has given her satisfaction,
I may not fall my suit nor draw my action.
    Byplay. You may not?
    Citizen. No, alack a day, I may not,
Nor find content, nor peace at home, an't please you,
My lord, an't like your honour, I would say.
An't please you, what's a tradesman that

Has a fair wife without his wife, an't please you?
And she without content is no wife, considering
We tradesmen live by gentlemen, an't please you,
And our wives drive a half trade with us. If the gentlemen
Break with our wives, our wives are no wives to us,
And we but broken tradesmen, an't please you,
An't like your honour, my good lord, an't please you.

    Byplay. You argue honestly.
    Citizen.   Yet gentlemen,
Alack a day, an't please you, an't like your honour,
Will not consider our necessities,
And our desire in general through the city,
To have our sons all gentlemen like them.
    Byplay. Nor, though a gentlemen consume
His whole estate among ye, yet his son
May live t' inherit it?
    Citizen. Right, right, an't please you,
Your honour, my good lord, an't please you.
    Byplay. Well,
This has so little to be said against it,
That you say nothing. Gentleman, it seems
You're obstinate, and will stand out—
    Gentleman. My lord,
Rather than not to stand out with all men's wives,
Except mine own, I'll yield me into prison.
    Citizen. Alack a day!
    Diana. If our young gentlemen
Were like those of th' Antipodes, what decay
Of trade would here be, and how full the prisons!
    Gentleman. I offer him any other satisfaction:
His wares again, or money twice the value,
    Byplay. That's from the point.
    Citizen. Ay, ay, alack a day,
Nor do I sue to have him up in prison.
Alack a day, what good, good gentleman,
Can I get by his body?
    Byplay. Peace, I should
Now give my sentence, and for your contempt,
(Which is a great one, such as if let pass
Unpunish'd, may spread forth a dangerous

Example, to the breach of city custom,
By gentlemen's neglect of tradesmen's wives)
I should, [I] say, for this contempt commit you
Prisoner from sight of any other woman,
Until you give this man's wife satisfaction,
And she release you. Justice so would have it;
But as I am a citizen by nature,
(For education made it so) I'll use
Urbanity in your behalf towards you;
And as I am a gentleman by calling,
(For so my place must have it) I'll perform
For you the office of a gentleman
Towards his wife. I therefore order thus:
That you bring me the wares here into court
(I have a chest shall hold 'em as mine own),
And you send me your wife. I'll satisfy her
Myself. I'll do 't, and set all straight and right.
Justice is blind, but judges have their sight.
      Diana. And feeling, too, in the Antipodes,
Ha'n't they, my lord?
      Joyless. What's that to you, my lady?
      [*Voice*] ('*Within*'). Dismiss the court.
      Letoy. Dismiss the court. Cannot you hear the prompter?
Ha' you lost your ears, judge?
      Byplay. No. Dismiss the court.
Embrace you friends, and, to shun further strife,
See you send me your stuff, and you your wife.
      Peregrine. Most admirable justice!
      Diana. Protest, Extempore play'd the judge, and I
Knew him not all this while.
      Joyless. What oversight
Was there!
      Diana. He is a properer man, methinks,
Now than he was before. Sure I shall love him.
      Joyless. Sure, sure, you shall not, shall you?
      Diana. And I warrant,
By his judgement speech e'en now, he loves a woman well;
For he said, if you noted him, that he
Would satisfy the citizen's wife himself.
Methinks a gentlewoman might please him better.

Joyless. How dare you talk so?

'*Byplay kneels and kisses Peregrine's hand.*'

Diana. What's he a-doing now, trow?

Peregrine. Kneel down,
Again. Give me a sword somebody.

Letoy. The king's about to knight him.

Byplay. Let me pray
Your Majesty be pleased yet to with-hold
That undeserved honour, till you first
Vouchsafe to grace the city with your presence,
Accept one of our hall-feasts, and a freedom,
And freely use our purse for what great sums
Your majesty will please.

Diana. What subjects there are
In the Antipodes!

Letoy. None in the world so loving.

Peregrine. Give me a sword, I say. Must I call thrice?

Letoy. No, no, take mine, my liege.

Peregrine. Yours! What are you?

Doctor. A loyal lord, one of your subjects too.

Peregrine. He may be loyal—he's a wondrous plain one.

Joyless. Prithee, Diana, yet let's slip away
Now while he's busy.

Diana. But where's your daughter-in-law?

Joyless. Gone home I warrant you, with Mistress Blaze.
Let them be our example.

Diana. You are cozen'd.

Joyless. You're an impudent whore.

Diana. I know not what I may be
Made by your jealousy.

Peregrine. I'll none o' this;
Give me that princely weapon.

Letoy. Give it him.

Sword-bearer. It is a property you know, my lord,
No blade, but a rich scabbard with a lath in 't.

Letoy. So is the sword of Justice for aught he knows.

Peregrine. It is enchanted.

Byplay. Yet on me let it fall,
Since 'tis Your Highness' will, scabbard and all.

Peregrine. Rise up, our trusty well-beloved knight.

Byplay. Let me find favour in your gracious sight
To taste a banquet now, which is prepar'd,
And shall be by your followers quickly shar'd.
   Peregrine. My followers? Where are they?
   Letoy. Come, sirs, quickly.   '*Enter* 5 *or* 6 *Courtiers.*'
   Peregrine. 'Tis well; lead on the way.
         [*Exeunt* Peregrine, Doctor *and* Courtiers.]
   Diana. And must not we
Go to the banquet too?
   Letoy. He must not see
You yet; I have provided otherwise
For both you in my chamber, and from thence
We'll at a window see the rest o'th' play;
Or if you needs, sir, will stay here, you may.
                  (*Exeunt* Letoy *and* Diana.
   Joyless. Was ever man betray'd thus into torment?
                      (*Exit* Joyless.

ACT IV · SCENE I

'*Enter* Doctor *and* Peregrine.'

   Doctor. Now, sir, be pleas'd to cloud your princely raiment
With this disguise. Great kings have done the like,
To make discovery of passages
                  '*Puts on a cloak and hat.*'
Among the people. Thus you shall perceive
What to approve and what correct among 'em.
   Peregrine. And so I'll cherish, or severely punish.

'*Enter an* Old Woman, *reading* [*a handbill*]; *to her,
a young* Maid [*with a book*].'

   Doctor. Stand close, sir, and observe.
   Old Woman [*Reading*]. 'Royal pastime, in a great match

between the tanners and the butchers, six dogs of a side, to
play single at the game bear, for fifty pound, and a ten pound
supper for their dogs and themselves. Also, you shall see two
ten-dog courses at the great bear.'

 Maid. Fie, granny, fie! Can no persuasions,
Threat'nings, nor blows prevail, but you'll persist
In these profane and diabolical courses,
To follow bear baitings, when you can scarce
Spell out their bills with spectacles?
 Old Woman. What though
My sight be gone beyond the reach of spectacles
In any print but this, and though I cannot,
         'Strikes down her book.'
No, no, I cannot read your meditations,
Yet I can see the royal game play'd over and over,
And tell which dog does best without my spectacles.
And though I could not, yet I love the noise;
The noise revives me, and the Bear Garden scent
Refresheth much my smelling.
 Maid. Let me entreat you
Forbear such beastly pastimes; they're Satanical.
 Old Woman. Take heed, child, what you say: 'tis the
  king's game.
 Peregrine. What is my game?
 Doctor. Bear-baiting, sir, she means.
 Old Woman. A bear's a princely beast, and one side
  venison,
Writ a good author once. You yet want years,
And are with baubles pleas'd; I'll see the bears.
           (*Exit* Old Woman.
 Maid. And I must bear with it. She's full of wine,
And for the present wilful; but in due
Season I'll humble her. But we are all
Too subject to infirmity.

  'Enter a young Gentleman *and an old* Serving-man.'

 Gentleman. Boy, boy.
 Serving-man. Sir.
 Gentleman. Here, take my cloak.

Peregrine. Boy did he say?

Doctor. Yes, sir; old servants are
But boys to masters, be they ne'er so young.

Gentleman. 'Tis heavy, and I sweat.

Serving-man. Take mine, and keep you warm then;
I'll wear yours.

Gentleman. Out, you varlet!
Dost thou obscure it, as thou meant'st to pawn it?
Is this a cloak unworthy of the light?
Publish it, sirrah—oh, presumptuous slave,
Display it on one arm—oh, ignorance!

Serving-man. Pray load your ass yourself, as you would
have it.

Gentleman. Nay, prithee, be not angry. Thus—and now
Be sure you bear't at no such distance but
As 't may be known appendix to this book.

Peregrine. This custom I have seen with us.

Doctor. Yes, but
It was deriv'd from the Antipodes.

Maid [*Aside*]. It is a dainty creature, and my blood
Rebels against the spirit. I must speak to him.

Serving-man. Sir, here's a gentlewoman makes towards
you.

Gentleman. Me? She's deceiv'd; I am not for her mowing.

Maid. Fair sir, may you vouchsafe my company?

Gentleman. No, truly I am none of those you look for.
The way is broad enough. Unhand me, pray you.

Maid. Pray, sir, be kinder to a lass that loves you.

Gentleman. Some such there are, but I am none of those.

Maid. Come, this is but a copy of your countenance.
I ha' known you better than you think I do.

Gentleman. What ha' you known me for?

Maid. I knew you once
For half a piece, I take it.

Gentleman. You are deceiv'd,
The whole breadth of your nose. I scorn it.

Maid. Come, be not coy, but send away your servant,
And let me gi' you a pint of wine.

Gentleman. Pray keep
Your courtesy; I can bestow the wine

Upon myself, if I were so dispos'd.
To drink in taverns—fagh!
   Maid. Let me bestow 't
Upon you at your lodging then, and there
Be civilly merry.
   Gentleman. Which if you do,
My wife shall thank you for it. But your better
Course is to seek one fitter for your turn;
You'll lose your aim in me; and I befriend you
To tell you so.
   Maid. Gip, gaffer shotten, fagh!
Take that for your coy counsel.   [*She*] '*kicks*' [*him.*]
   Gentleman. Help, oh help!
   Serving-man. What mean you, gentlewoman?
   Maid. That to you, sir.   '*Kicks.*'
   Gentleman. O murder, murder.
   Serving-man. Peace, good master,
And come away.
   [*Maid.*] Some cowardly jade, I warrant,
That durst not strike a woman.

'Enter Constable and Watch.'

   Constable. What's the matter?
   Serving-man. But and we were your match—
   Watch. What would you do?
Come, come afore the constable. Now if
You were her match, what would you do, sir?
   Maid. Do?
They have done too much already, sir. A virgin   '*Weeps.*'
Shall not pass shortly, for these street walkers,
If some judicious order be not taken.
   Gentleman. Hear me the truth.
   Constable. Sir, speak to your companions;
I have a wife and daughters, and am bound
By hourly precepts to hear women first,
Be 't truth or no truth. Therefore, virgin, speak,
And fear no bugbears. I will do thee justice.
   [*Maid.*] Sir, they assail'd me, and with violent hands,
When words could not prevail, they would have drawn me
Aside unto their lust, till I cried murder.

Gentleman. Protest, sir, as I am a gentleman,
And as my man's a man, she beat us both,
Till I cried murder.

Serving-man. That's the woeful truth on't.

Constable. You are a party, and no witness, sir.
Besides, you're two, and one is easier
To be believ'd. Moreover, as you have the odds
In number, what were justice if it should not support
The weaker side? Away with them to the Counter!

Peregrine. Call you this justice?

Doctor. In th' Antipodes.

Peregrine. Here's much to be reform'd. [*Coming forward*]
Young man, thy virtue
Hath won my favour. Go; thou art at large.

Doctor [*Aside*]. Be gone.

Gentleman [*Aside*]. He puts me out—my part is now
To bribe the Constable.

Doctor [*Aside*]. No matter, go.

(*Exeunt* Gentleman *and* Servant.

Peregrine. And you, sir, take that sober-seeming wanton
And clap her up, till I hear better of her;
I'll strip you of your office and your ears else.

Doctor. At first show mercy.

Peregrine. They are an ignorant nation,
And have my pity mingled with correction;
And therefore, damsel—for you are the first
Offender I have noted here, and this
Your first offence, for aught I know—

Maid. Yes, truly.

Doctor. That was well said.

Peregrine. Go, and transgress no more;
And as you find my mercy sweet, see that
You be not cruel to your grandmother
When she returns from bear-baiting.

Doctor. So, all be gone.

(*Exeunt all except* Peregrine *and* Doctor.

'*Enter* Buff Woman, *her head and face bleeding,
and many women, as from a prize.*'

Peregrine. And what are these?

Doctor. A woman fencer, that has play'd a prize,
It seems, with loss of blood.

Peregrine. It doth amaze me.   '*They pass over.*'
What can her husband be, when she's a fencer?

Doctor. He keeps a school, and teacheth needlework,
Or some such arts which we call womanish.

Peregrine. 'Tis most miraculous and wonderful.

Man-scold ('*Within*'). Rogues, varlets, harlots, ha' you
            done
Your worst, or would you drown me? Would you take my
            life?

Women ('*Within*'). Duck him again, duck him again.

Peregrine. What noise is this?

Doctor. Some man, it seems, that's duck'd for scolding.

Peregrine. A man, for scolding?

Doctor. You shall see.

'*Enter* Women *and* Man-Scold.'

[*1st*] *Woman.* So, so,
Enough, enough; he will be quiet now.

Man-scold. How know you that, you devil-ridden witch,
            you?
How quiet? Why quiet? Has not the law pass'd on me,
Over and over me, and must I be quiet?

1st Woman. Will you incur the law the second time?

Man-scold. The law's the river, is 't? Yes, 'tis a river,
Through which great men and cunning wade or swim,
But mean and ignorant must drown in't. No,
You hags and hell-hounds, witches, bitches, all,
That were the law, the judge and executioners,
To my vexation, I hope to see
More flames about your ears than all the water
You cast me in can quench.

3rd Woman. In with him again. He calls us names.

2nd Woman. No, no; I charge ye, no.

Man-scold. Was ever harmless creature so abus'd?
To be drench'd under water, to learn dumbness
Amongst the fishes, as I were forbidden
To use the natural members I was born with,

And of them all, the chief that man takes pleasure in—
The tongue. Oh me, accursed wretch.   '*Weeps.*'
   Peregrine. Is this a man?
I ask not by his beard, but by his tears.
   1st Woman. This shower will spend the fury of his tongue,
And so the tempest's over.
   2nd Woman. I am sorry for 't;
I would have had him duck'd once more.
But somebody will shortly raise the storm
In him again, I hope, for us to make
More holiday sport of him.   (*Exeunt* Women.
   Peregrine. Sure, these are dreams,
Nothing but dreams.
   Doctor. No, doubtless we are awake, sir.
   Peregrine. Can men and women be so contrary
In all that we hold proper to each sex?
   Doctor [*Aside*]. I'm glad he takes a taste of sense in that
    yet.
   Peregrine. 'Twill ask long time and study to reduce
Their manners to our government.
   Doctor. These are
Low things and easy to be qualified—
But see, sir, here come courtiers. Note their manners.

   '*Enter a Courtier*' [*another following behind*].

   1st Courtier. This was three shillings yesterday. How now!
All gone but this? Sixpence for leather soles
To my new green silk stockings, and a groat
My ordinary in pompions bak'd with onions.
   Peregrine. Do such eat pompions?
   Doctor. Yes, and clowns musk-melons.
   1st Courtier. Threepence I lost at ninepins; but I got
Six tokens towards that at pigeon holes.
'Snails, where's the rest? Is my poke bottom broke?
   2nd Courtier [*Coming forward*]. What, Jack! A pox o'er-
    take thee not. How dost?   '*Kick.*'
   1st Courtier. What with a vengeance ailst? Dost think my
    breech
Is made of bell-metal? Take that.   '*Box o' th' ear.*'
   2nd Courtier. In earnest?

1st Courtier.   Yes, till more comes.

2nd Courtier. Pox rot your hold! Let go my lock! D'ye think
You're currying of your father's horse again?

1st Courtier. I'll teach you to abuse a man behind
Was troubled too much afore.   '*They buffet.*'

'*Enter* 3rd Courtier.'

3rd Courtier. Hey! There, boys, there.
Good boys are good boys still. There, Will; there, Jack.
Not a blow now he's down!

2nd Courtier. 'Twere base; I scorn 't.

1st Courtier. There's as proud fall as stand in court or city.

3rd Courtier. That's well said, Will. Troth, I commend
    you both.
How fell you out? I hope in no great anger.

2nd Courtier. For mine own part I vow I was in jest.

1st Courtier. But I have told you twice and once, Will,
    jest not
With me behind. I never could endure,
Not of a boy, to put up things behind;
And that my tutor knew; I had been a scholar else.
Besides, you know my sword was nock'd i' th' fashion,
Just here behind, for my back-guard and all;
And yet you would do 't.
I had as lief you would take a knife—

3rd Courtier.   Come, come,
You're friends. Shake hands. I'll give you half a dozen
At the next alehouse, to set all right and straight,
And a new song, a dainty one—here 'tis.

'[*Shows*] *a ballad.*'

1st Courtier. Oh, thou art happy that canst read.
I would buy ballads too, had I thy learning.

2nd Courtier. Come, we burn daylight, and the ale may
    sour.

(*Exeunt* Courtiers.

Peregrine. Call you these courtiers? They are rude silken
    clowns,
As coarse within as watermen or carmen.

Doctor. Then look on these: here are of those conditions.

'*Enter* Carman *and* Waterman.'

Waterman. Sir, I am your servant.
Carman. I am much oblig'd,
Sir, by the plenteous favours your humanity
And noble virtue have conferr'd upon me,
To answer with my service your deservings.
Waterman. You speak what I should say. Be therefore pleas'd
T'unload, and lay the weight of your commands
Upon my care to serve you.
Carman. Still your courtesies,
Like waves of a spring tide, o'erflow the banks
Of your abundant store; and from your channel,
Or stream of fair affections, you cast forth
Those sweet refreshings on me (that were else
But sterile earth), which cause a gratitude
To grow upon me, humble, yet ambitious
In my devoir to do you best of service.
Waterman. I shall no more extend my utmost labour
With oar and sail to gain the livelihood
Of wife and children, than to set ashore
You and your faithful honourers at the haven
Of your best wishes.
Carman. Sir, I am no less
Ambitious to be made the happy means,
With whip and whistle, to draw up or drive
All your detractors to the gallows.

'*Enter* Sedan-man.'

Waterman. See,
Our noble friend.
Sedan-man. Right happily encountered!
I am the just admirer of your virtues.
Waterman. ⎫
Carman. ⎬ We are, in all, your servants.
Sedan-man. I was in quest
Of such elect society, to spend
A dinnertime withal.

Waterman.⎫
Carman. ⎬ Sir, we are for you.

Sedan-man. Three are the golden number in a tavern;
And at the next of best, with the best meat
And wine the house affords (if you so please)
We will be competently merry. I
Have receiv'd, lately, letters from beyond seas,
Importing much of the occurrences
And passages of foreign states. The knowledge
Of all I shall impart to you.

Waterman.   And I
Have all the new advertisements from both
Our universities, of what has pass'd
The most remarkably of late.

Carman.   And from
The court I have the news at full
Of all that was observable this progress.

Peregrine.   From court?

Doctor. Yes, sir; they know not there they have
A new king here at home.

Sedan-man.   'Tis excellent!
We want but now the news-collecting gallant
To fetch his dinner and materials
For his this week's despatches.

Waterman.   I dare think,
The meat and news being hot upon the table,
He'll smell his way to 't.

Sedan-man. Please you to know yours, sir?

Carman.   Sir, after you.

Sedan-man. Excuse me.

Waterman.   By no means, sir.

Carman. Sweet sir, lead on.

Sedan-man.   It shall be as your servant
Then, to prepare your dinner.

Waterman.   Pardon me.

Carman. In sooth, I'll follow you.

Waterman.   Yet 'tis my obedience.

                    (*Exeunt* Waterman, Carman, Sedan-man.

Peregrine. Are these but labouring men, and tother
      courtiers?

Doctor. 'Tis common here, sir, for your waterman
To write most learnedly, when your courtier
Has scarce ability to read.
   Peregrine.   Before. I reign
A month among them, they shall change their notes,
Or I'll ordain a course to change their coats.
I shall have much to do in reformation.
   Doctor. Patience and counsel will go through it, sir.
   Peregrine. What if I crav'd a counsel from New England?
The old will spare me none.
   Doctor [*Aside*]. Is this man mad?
My cure goes firmly on.—Do you marvel that
Poor men outshine the courtiers? Look you, sir:
A sick man giving counsel to a physician;
And there's a puritan tradesman, teaching a
Great traveller to lie; that ballad-woman
Gives light to the most learned antiquary
> '*These persons pass over the stage in couples according*
> *as he describes them.*'

In all the kingdom.
   Ballad-woman. Buy new ballads, come.
   Doctor. A natural fool, there, giving grave instructions
T' a lord ambassador; that's a schismatic,
Teaching a scrivener to keep his ears;
A parish clerk, there, gives the rudiments
Of military discipline to a general;
And there's a basket-maker confuting Bellarmine.
   Peregrine. Will you make me mad?
   Doctor.   We are sail'd, I hope,
Beyond the line of madness.

> '*Enter* Byplay *like a statesman, 3 or 4*
> Projectors *with bundles of papers.*'

                     Now, sir, see
A statesman studious for the commonwealth
Solicited by projectors of the country.
   Byplay. Your projects are all good; I like them well,
Especially these two: this for th' increase of wool,
And this for the destroying of mice. They're good,
And grounded on great reason. As for yours,

For putting down the infinite use of jacks
(Whereby the education of young children,
In turning spits, is greatly hinder'd),
It may be look'd into. And yours against
The multiplicity of pocket-watches—
Whereby much neighbourly familiarity,
By asking, 'What d'ye guess it is a'clock?'
Is lost, when every penny clerk can carry
The time o'th' day in 's breeches—this, and these
Hereafter may be look'd into. For present,
This for the increase of wool—that is to say,
By flaying of live horses and new covering them
With sheepskins—I do like exceedingly;
And this, for keeping of tame owls in cities
To kill up rats and mice, whereby all cats
May be destroy'd, as an especial means
To prevent witchcraft and contagion.

 Peregrine. Here's a wise business!

 Projector. Will your honour now
Be pleas'd to take into consideration
The poor men's suits for briefs, to get relief
By common charity throughout the kingdom,
Towards recovery of their lost estates?

 Byplay. What are they? Let me hear.

 Projector. First, here's a gamester that sold house and land,
To the known value of five thousand pounds,
And by misfortune of the dice lost all,
To his extreme undoing, having neither
A wife or child to succour him.

 Byplay.   A bachelor?

 Projector. Yes, my good lord.

 Byplay.   And young and healthful?

 Projector. Yes.

 Byplay.   Alas, 'tis lamentable; he deserves much pity.

 Peregrine. How's this?

 Doctor.   Observe him further, pray, sir.

 Projector. Then, here's a bawd, of sixty-odd years standing.

Byplay. How old was she when she set up?

Projector. But four

And twenty, my good lord. She was both ware
And merchant, flesh and butcher, as they say,
For the first twelve years of her housekeeping.
She's now upon fourscore, and has made markets
Of twice four thousand choice virginities,
And twice their number of indifferent gear—
No riff-raff was she ever known to cope for.
Her life is certified here by the justices,
Adjacent to her dwelling—

Byplay. She is decay'd?

Projector. Quite trade-fallen, my good lord, now in her
  dotage,
And desperately undone by riot.

Byplay.   'Las, good woman.

Projector. She has consum'd in prodigal feasts and
  fiddlers,
And lavish spendings to debauch'd comrades
That suck'd her purse, in jewels, plate, and money,
To the full value of six thousand pounds.

Byplay. She shall have a collection, and deserves it.

Peregrine. 'Tis monstrous, this!

Projector. Then here are divers more,
Of panders, cheaters, house and highway robbers,
That have got great estates in youth and strength,
And wasted all as fast in wine and harlots,
Till age o'ertook 'em and disabled them
For getting more.

Byplay. For such the law provides
Relief within those counties where they practis'd.

Peregrine. Ha! What, for thieves?

Doctor. Yes, the law punisheth
The robb'd, and not the thief, for surer warning
And the more safe prevention. I have seen
Folks whipt for losing of their goods and money,
And the pick-pockets cherish'd.

Byplay. The weal public,
As it severely punisheth their neglect,
Undone by fire ruins, shipwrack and the like

With whips, with brands, and loss of careless ears,
Imprisonment, banishment, and sometimes death,
And carefully maintaineth houses of correction
For decay'd scholars and maim'd soldiers,
So doth it find relief and alms-houses
For such as liv'd by rapine and by cosenage.

   Peregrine. Still worse and worse! Abominable! Horrid!

   Projector. Yet here is one, my lord, 'bove all the rest,
Whose services have generally been known,
Though now he be a spectacle of pity.

   Byplay.   Who's that?

   Projector. The captain of the cutpurses, my lord,
That was the best at's art that ever was,
Is fallen to great decay by the dead palsy
In both his hands, and craves a large collection.

   Byplay. I'll get it him.

   Peregrine [*Coming forward*]. You shall not get it him.
Do you provide whips, brands, and ordain death
For men that suffer under fire or shipwrack
The loss of all their honest gotten wealth,
And find relief for cheaters, bawds, and thieves?
I'll hang ye all.

   Byplay.   Mercy, great king!

   Omnes.   O mercy!

   Byplay. Let not our ignorance suffer in your wrath
Before we understand your highness' laws.
We went by custom, and the warrant which
We had in your late predecessor's reign.
But let us know your pleasure, you shall find
The state and commonwealth in all obedient,
To alter custom, law, religion, all,
To be conformable to your commands.

   Peregrine. 'Tis a fair protestation, and my mercy
Meets your submission. See you merit it
In your conformity.

   Byplay.   Great sir, we shall.
In sign whereof we lacerate these papers
And lay our necks beneath your kingly feet.

                 'Letoy, Diana, Joyless *appear above.*'

   Peregrine. Stand up; you have our favour.

Diana. And mine too.
Never was such an actor as Extempore!
 Joyless. You were best to fly out of the window to him.
 Diana. Methinks I am even light enough to do it.
 Joyless. I could find in my heart to quoit thee at him.
 Diana. So he would catch me in his arms, I car'd not.
 Letoy. Peace, both of you, or you'll spoil all.
 Byplay.   Your grace
Abounds—abounds—your grace—I say, abounds.
 Letoy. Pox o' your mumbling chops! Is your brain dry?
Do you pump?
 Diana.   He has done much, my lord, and may
Hold out a little.
 Letoy.   Would you could hold your peace
So long.
 Diana. Do you sneap me too, my lord?
 Joyless. Ha, ha, ha!
 Letoy [*To* Byplay]. Blockhead!
 Joyless. I hope his hotter zeal to 's actors
Will drive out my wife's love-heat.
 Diana.   I had
No need to come hither to be sneap'd.
 Letoy. Hoyday! The rest will all be lost. We now give over
The play, and do all by Extempore,
For your son's good, to soothe him into 's wits.
If you'll mar all, you may. [*To* Byplay] Come nearer,
  coxcomb.
Ha' you forgotten, puppy, my instructions
Touching his subjects and his marriage?
 Byplay. I have all now, my lord.
 Peregrine.   What voice was that?
 Byplay. A voice out of the clouds, that doth applaud
Your highness' welcome to your subjects' loves.
 Letoy. So, now he's in. Sit still; I must go down
And set out things in order.   (*Exit* Letoy.
 Byplay. A voice that doth inform me of the tidings,
Spread through your kingdom, of your great arrival,
And of the general joy your people bring
To celebrate the welcome of their king.
             '*Shouts within.*'

Hark how the country shouts with joyful votes,
Rending the air with music of their throats.

                                        '*Drum and trumpets.*'

Hark how the soldier, with his martial noise,
Threatens your foes, to fill your crown with joys.
Hark how the city, with loud harmony,   '*Hautboys.*'
Chants a free welcome to your majesty.
Hark how the court prepares your grace to meet

                                        '*Soft music.*'

With solemn music, state and beauty sweet.

> '*The soft music playing, enter, by two and two, divers courtiers,* Martha *after them, like a queen, between two boys, in robes, her train borne up by* Barbara. *All the lords kneel, and kiss* Peregrine's *hand.* Martha *approaching, he starts back, but is drawn on by* Byplay *and the* Doctor. Letoy *enters and mingles with the rest, and seems to instruct them all.*'

Diana. O here's a stately show! Look, Master Joyless:
Your daughter-in-law presented like a queen
Unto your son. I warrant now he'll love her.

Joyless. A queen?

Diana.   Yes, yes, and Mistress Blaze is made
The mother of her maids, if she have any;
Perhaps the Antipodean court has none.
See, see, with what a majesty he receives 'em.

Song.

> Health, wealth, and joy our wishes bring,
>   All in a welcome to our king;
>   May no delight be found
>   Wherewith he be not crown'd.
>   Apollo with the Muses,
>   Who arts divine infuses,
> With their choice garlands deck his head;
> Love and the graces make his bed;
> And to crown all, let Hymen to his side
> Plant a delicious, chaste, and fruitful bride.

Byplay. Now, sir, be happy in a marriage choice
That shall secure your title of a king.
See, sir, your state presents to you the daughter,

The only child and heir apparent of
Our late deposed and deceased sovereign,
Who with his dying breath bequeath'd her to you.

Peregrine. A crown secures not an unlawful marriage,
I have a wife already.

    Doctor.   No, you had, sir,
But she's deceas'd.

    Peregrine.   How know you that?

    Doctor. By sure advertisement, and that her fleeting
    spirit
Is flown into and animates this princess.

Peregrine. Indeed she's wondrous like her.

    Doctor.   Be not slack
T'embrace and kiss her, sir.

                           '*He kisses her and retires.*'

    Martha. He kisses sweetly;
And that is more than e'er my husband did.
But more belongs than kissing to child-getting;
And he's so like my husband, if you note him,
That I shall but lose time and wishes by him.
No, no, I'll none of him.

    Barbara. I'll warrant you he shall fulfil your wishes.

    Martha. O but try him you first, and then tell me.

    Barbara. There's a new way indeed to choose a husband!
Yet 'twere a good one to bar fool-getting.

    Doctor. Why do you stand aloof, sir?

    Peregrine.   Mandeville writes
Of people near the Antipodes, call'd Gadlibriens,
Where on the wedding night the husband hires
Another man to couple with his bride,
To clear the dangerous passage of a maidenhead.

    Doctor [*Aside*]. 'Slid, he falls back again to Mandeville
    madness.

    Peregrine. She may be of that serpentine generation
That stings oft times to death, as Mandeville writes.

    Doctor. She's no Gadlibrien, sir, upon my knowledge.
You may as safely lodge with her as with
A maid of our own nation. Besides,
You shall have ample counsel. For the present,
Receive her, and entreat her to your chapel.

Byplay. For safety of your kingdom, you must do it.
Letoy. So, so, so, so. This may yet prove a cure.
 '*Hautboys. Exit in state as* Letoy *directs. Manet* Letoy.'
Diana. See, my lord now is acting by himself.
Letoy. And Letoy's wit cried up triumphant, ho.
Come, Master Joyless and your wife, come down
Quickly; your parts are next.

                              [*Exeunt above* Joyless *and* Diana.]

                  '*Enter* Quailpipe *in a fantastical shape.*'

                                      I had almost
Forgot to send my chaplain after them.
You, domine, where are you?
Quailpipe. Here, my lord.
Letoy. What, in that shape?
Quailpipe.   'Tis for my part, my lord,
Which is not all perform'd.
Letoy. It is, sir, and the play for this time. We
Have other work in hand.
Quailpipe.   Then have you lost
Action (I dare be bold to speak it) that
Most of my coat could hardly imitate.
Letoy. Go, shift your coat, sir, or, for expedition,
Cover it with your own, due to your function.
Follies, as well as vices, may be hid so;
Your virtue is the same. Despatch, and do
As Doctor Hughball shall direct you. Go.

                                      (*Exit* Quailpipe.

                     '*Enter* Joyless, Diana.'

Now, Master Joyless, do you note the progress
And the fair issue likely to ensue
In your son's cure? Observe the doctor's art:
First, he has shifted your son's known disease
Of madness into folly, and has wrought him
As far short of a competent reason as
He was of late beyond it. As a man

Infected by some foul disease is drawn
By physic into an anatomy
Before flesh fit for health can grow to rear him,
So is a madman made a fool before
Art can take hold of him to wind him up
Into his proper centre, or the medium
From which he flew beyond himself. The doctor
Assures me now, by what he has collected
As well from learned authors as his practice,
That his much troubled and confused brain
Will, by the real knowledge of a woman,
Now opportunely ta'en, be by degrees
Settled and rectified, with the helps beside
Of rest and diet, which he'll administer.

    Diana. But 'tis the real knowledge of the woman
(Carnal I think you mean) that carries it.

    Letoy. Right, right.

    Diana. Nay, right or wrong, I could even wish,
If he were not my husband's son, the doctor
Had made my flesh his recipe to be the means
Of such a cure.

    Joyless.   How, how?

    Diana. Perhaps that course might cure your madness too,
Of jealousy, and set all right on all sides.
Sure, if I could but make him such a fool,
He would forego his madness and be brought
To Christian sense again.

    Joyless. Heaven grant me patience,
And send us to my country home again!

    Diana. Besides, the young man's wife's as mad as he.
What wise work will they make!

    Letoy. The better, fear 't not,
Bab Blaze shall give her counsel, and the youth
Will give her royal satisfaction.
Now, in this kingly humour, I have a way
To cure your husband's jealousy myself.

    Diana. Then I am friends again. Even now I was not
When you sneap'd me, my lord.

    Letoy. That you must pardon.
Come, Master Joyless, the new married pair

Are towards bed by this time; we'll not trouble them,
But keep a house-side to ourselves. Your lodging
Is decently appointed.

 Joyless.   Sure your lordship
Means not to make your house our prison?

 Letoy. By
My lordship but I will for this one night.
See, sir, the keys are in my hand. You're up,
As I am true Letoy. Consider, sir,
The strict necessity that ties you to 't,
As you expect a cure upon your son.
Come, lady, see your chamber.

 Diana.   I do wait
Upon your lordship.   (*Exeunt* Letoy *and* Diana.

 Joyless. I both wait, and watch.
Never was man so master'd by his match.   (*Exit* Joyless.

ACT V · SCENE I

'Joyless *with a light in his hand.*'

 Joyless. Diana! Ho! Where are you? She is lost.
Here is no further passage. All's made fast.
This was the bawdy way by which she 'scap'd
My narrow watching. Have you privy posterns
Behind the hangings in your strangers' chambers?
She's lost from me, for ever. Why then seek I?
O my dull eyes, to let her slip so from ye,
To let her have her lustful will upon me!
Is this the hospitality of lords?
Why, rather, if he did intend my shame
And her dishonour, did he not betray me
From her out of his house, to travail in
The bare suspicion of their filthiness,
But hold me a nose-witness to its rankness?
No, this is sure the lordlier way, and makes
The act more glorious in my sufferings. O   [*Kneels.*]

May my hot curses on their melting pleasures
Cement them so together in their lust,
That they may never part but grow one monster!

'*Enter* Barbara.'

Barbara. Good gentleman! He is at his prayers now
For his mad son's good night-work with his bride.
Well fare your heart, sir; you have pray'd to purpose;
But not all night, I hope. Yet sure he has—
He looks so wild for lack of sleep. You're happy, sir.
Your prayers are heard, no doubt, for I'm persuaded
You have a child got you tonight.
   Joyless.   Is't gone
So far, do you think?
   Barbara.   I cannot say how far;
Not fathom deep, I think; but to the scantling
Of a child-getting, I dare well imagine;
For which, as you have pray'd, forget not, sir,
To thank the lord o' th' house.
   Joyless.   For getting me
A child? Why, I am none of his great lordship's tenants,
Nor of his followers, to keep his bastards.
Pray stay a little.
   Barbara. I should go tell my lord
The news; he longs to know how things do pass.
   Joyless. Tell him I take it well, and thank him.
I did before despair of children, I.
But I'll go wi' ye, and thank him.
   Barbara [*Aside*].   Sure his joy
Has madded him. Here's more work for the doctor.
   Joyless [*Drawing his dagger*]. But tell me first: were you
      their bawd that speak this?
   Barbara. What mean you with that dagger?
   Joyless. Nothing; I
But play with 't. Did you see the passages
Of things? I ask, were you their bawd?
   Barbara. Their bawd?
I trust she is no bawd that sees and helps,
If need require, an ignorant lawful pair
To do their best.

Joylesss.   Lords' actions all are lawful.
And how? And how?

Barbara. These old folks love to hear.
I'll tell you, sir—and yet I will not neither.

Joyless. Nay, pray thee out with 't.

Barbara.   Sir, they went to bed.

Joyless. To bed! Well, on.

Barbara. On? They were off, sir, yet,
And yet a good while after. They were both
So simple that they knew not what nor how,
For she's, sir, a pure maid.

Joyless. Who dost thou speak of?

Barbara. I'll speak no more, 'less you can look more
tamely.

Joyless. Go bring me to 'em then. Bawd, will you go?

Barbara. Ah—

'*Enter* Byplay *and holds* Joyless.'

Byplay. What ail you, sir? Why bawd? Whose bawd is
she?

Joyless. Your lord's bawd, and my wife's.

Byplay. You are jealous mad.
Suppose your wife be missing at your chamber,
And my lord too at his, they may be honest.
If not, what's that to her, or you, I pray,
Here in my lord's own house?

Joyless. Brave, brave, and monstrous!

Byplay. She has not seen them. I heard all your talk.
The child she intimated is your grandchild
In *posse*, sir, and of your son's begetting.

Barbara. Ay, I'll be sworn I meant, and said so too!

Joyless. Where is my wife?

Byplay. I can give no account.
If she be with my lord I dare not trouble 'em,
Nor must you offer at it, no, nor stab yourself.

'Byplay *takes away his dagger*.'
But come with me; I'll counsel, or at least
Govern you better. She may be, perhaps,
About the bride-chamber, to hear some sport,
For you can make her none, 'las, good old man—

Joyless. I'm most insufferably abus'd.
   Byplay.   Unless
The killing of yourself may do 't; and that
I would forbear, because perhaps 'twould please her.
   Joyless. If fire, or water, poison, cord, or steel,
Or any means be found to do it, I'll do it,
Not to please her, but rid me of my torment.
                              (Exit Joyless.
   Byplay. I have more care and charge of you than so.
                              (Exit Byplay.
   Barbara. What an old desperate man is this! To make
Away yourself for fear of being a cuckold!
If every man that is, or that but knows
Himself to be o' th' order, should do so,
How many desolate widows would here be.
They are not all of that mind. Here's my husband.

       'Enter Blaze *with a habit in his hand.'*

   Blaze. Bab! Art thou here?
   Barbara. Look well. How think'st thou, Tony?
Hast not thou neither slept tonight?
   Blaze.   Yes, yes,
I lay with the butler. Who was thy bedfellow?
   Barbara. You know I was appointed to sit up.
   Blaze. Yes, with the doctor in the bride-chamber.
But had you two no waggery? Ha!
   Barbara. Why, how now, Tony?
   Blaze. Nay, facks, I am not jealous;
Thou know'st I was cur'd long since, and how.
I jealous! I an ass! A man shan't ask
His wife shortly how such a gentleman does,
Or how such a gentleman did, or which did best,
But she must think him jealous!
   Barbara. You need not; for
If I were now to die on 't, nor the doctor
Nor I came in a bed tonight—I mean
Within a bed.
   Blaze. Within or without, or over or under,
I have no time to think o' such poor things.
   Barbara. What's that thou carriest, Tony?

Blaze. Oho, Bab,
This is a shape.

Barbara. A shape? What shape, I prithee, Tony?

Blaze. Thou'lt see me in 't anon, but shalt not know me
From the stark'st fool i' th' town. And I must dance
Naked in 't, Bab.

Barbara. Will here be dancing, Tony?

Blaze. Yes, Bab; my lord gave order for 't last night.
It should ha' been i' th' play, but because that
Was broke off, he will ha 't today.

Barbara. O Tony,
I did not see thee act i' th' play.

Blaze.   Oh, but
I did, though, Bab—two mutes.

Barbara. What, in those breeches?

Blaze. Fie, fool, thou understand'st not what a mute is.
A mute is a dumb speaker in the play.

Barbara. Dumb speaker! That's a bull. Thou wert the
    bull
Then in the play. Would I had seen thee roar.

Blaze. That's a bull, too, as wise as you are, Bab.
A mute is one that acteth speakingly,
And yet says nothing. I did two of them,
The sage man-midwife, and the basket-maker.

Barbara. Well, Tony, I will see thee in this thing—
And 'tis a pretty thing.

Blaze. Prithee, good Bab,
Come in, and help me on with 't in our tiring-house;
And help the gentlemen, my fellow dancers,
And thou shalt then see all our things, and all
Our properties, and practise to the music.

Barbara. O Tony, come; I long to be at that. (*Exeunt.*

[SCENE II]

'Letoy *and* Diana.'

Diana. My lord, your strength and violence prevail not:
There is a providence above my virtue,
That guards me from the fury of your lust.
  Letoy. Yet, yet, I prithee, yield. Is it my person
That thou despisest? See, here's wealthy treasure,
                        '*A table set forth, covered with treasure.*'
Jewels that Cleopatra would have left
Her Marcus for.
  Diana. My lord, 'tis possible
That she who leaves a husband may be bought
Out of a second friendship.
  Letoy. Had stout Tarquin
Made such an offer, he had done no rape,
For Lucrece had consented, sav'd her own,
And all those lives that follow'd in her cause.
  Diana. Yet then she had been a loser.
  Letoy. Would'st have gold?
Mammon, nor Plutus' self, should overbid me,
For I'd give all. First, let me rain a shower
To outvie that which overwhelm'd Danäe,
And after that another; a full river
Shall from my chests perpetually flow
Into thy store.
  Diana. I have not much lov'd wealth,
But have not loath'd the sight of it till now,
That you have soil'd it with that foul opinion
Of being the price of virtue. Though the metal
Be pure and innocent in itself, such use
Of it is odious, indeed damnable,
Both to the seller and the purchaser;
Pity it should be so abus'd. It bears
A stamp upon 't, which but to clip is treason.
'Tis ill us'd there, where law the life controls;
Worse, where 'tis made a salary for souls.
  Letoy. Deny'st thou wealth? Wilt thou have pleasure,
    then,

Give and ta'en freely, without all condition?
I'll give thee such as shall, if not exceed,
Be at the least comparative with those
Which Jupiter got the demi-gods with, and
Juno was mad she miss'd.

 Diana. My Lord, you may
Gloze o'er and gild the vice, which you call pleasure,
With god-like attributes, when it is, at best,
A sensuality, so far below
Dishonourable that it is mere beastly,
Which reason ought to abhor; and I detest it
More than your former hated offers.

 Letoy.   Lastly,
Wilt thou have honour? I'll come closer to thee
(For now the flames of love grow higher in me,
And I must perish in them, or enjoy thee):
Suppose I find by power, or law, or both,
A means to make thee mine, by freeing
Thee from thy present husband—

 Diana. Hold, stay there.
Now should you utter volumes of persuasions,
Lay the whole world of riches, pleasures, honours
Before me in full grant, that one last word,
Husband, and from your own mouth spoke, confutes
And vilifies even all. The very name
Of husband, rightly weigh'd and well remember'd,
Without more law or discipline, is enough
To govern womankind in due obedience,
Master all loose affections, and remove
Those idols which, too much, too many love,
And you have set before me, to beguile
Me of the faith I owe him. But, remember
You grant I have a husband; urge no more.
I seek his love; 'tis fit he loves no whore.

 Letoy. This is not yet the way. You have seen, lady,
My ardent love, which you do seem to slight,
Though to my death, pretending zeal to your husband.
My person nor my proffers are so despicable
But that they might, had I not vow'd affection
Entirely to yourself, have met with th' embraces

Of greater persons, no less fair, that can,
Too, if they please, put on formality,
And talk in as divine a strain as you.
This is not earnest. Make my word but good,
Now, with a smile, I'll give thee a thousand pound.
Look i' my face—come, prithee look, and laugh not—
Yes, laugh, an' dar'st. Dimple this cheek a little—
I'll nip it else.
　　Diana. I pray forbear, my lord;
I'm past a child, and will be made no wanton.
　　Letoy. How can this be? So young, so vigorous,
And so devoted to an old man's bed!
　　Diana. That is already answer'd. He's my husband.
You are old, too, my lord.
　　Letoy. Yes, but of better mettle.
A jealous old man, too, whose disposition
Of injury to beauty and young blood
Cannot but kindle fire of just revenge
In you, if you be woman, to requite
With your own pleasure his unnatural spite.
You cannot be worse to him than he thinks you,
Considering all the open scorns and jeers
You cast upon him, to a flat defiance;
Then, the affronts I gave, to choke his anger;
And lastly, your stol'n absence from his chamber;
All which confirms (we have as good as told him)
That he's a cuckold. Yet you trifle time,
As 'twere not worth the doing.
　　Diana. Are you a lord?
Dare you boast honour and be so ignoble?
Did not you warrant me upon that pawn
(Which can take up no money), your blank honour,
That you would cure his jealousy, which affects him
Like a sharp sore, if I, to ripen it,
Would set that counterfeit face of scorn upon him,
Only in show of disobedience; which
You won me to, upon your protestation
To render me unstain'd to his opinion,
And quit me of his jealousy for ever?
　　Letoy. No, not unstain'd, by your leave, if you call

Unchastity a stain. But for his yellows,
Let me but lie with you, and let him know it,
His jealousy is gone, all doubts are clear'd,
And for his love and good opinion,
He shall not dare deny 't. Come, be wise,
And this is all. All is as good as done
To him already; let 't be so with us;
And trust to me, my power, and your own,
To make all good with him. If not—now mark:
To be reveng'd for my lost hopes (which yet I
Pray thee save), I'll put thee in his hands,
Now in his heat of fury, and not spare
To boast thou art my prostitute, and thrust ye
Out of my gates, to try 't out by yourselves.
  Diana. This you may do, and yet be still a lord;
This can I bear, and still be the same woman.
I am not troubled now: your wooing oratory,
Your violent hands, made stronger by your lust,
Your tempting gifts, and larger promises
Of honour and advancements were all frivolous,
But this last way of threats ridiculous
To a safe mind, that bears no guilty grudge.
My peace dwells here, while yonder sits my judge,
And in that faith I'll die.

'*Enter* Joyless *and* Byplay.'

  Letoy. She is invincible!
Come, I'll relate you to your husband.
  Joyless.   No,
I'll meet her with more joy than I receiv'd
Upon our marriage-day. My better soul,
Let me again embrace thee.
  Byplay.   Take your dudgeon, sir;
I ha' done you simple service.
  Joyless.   O my lord,
My lord, you ha' cur'd my jealousy. I thank you;
And more, your man for the discovery;
But most, the constant means, my virtuous wife,
Your medicine, my sweet lord.

Letoy.   She has ta'en all
I mean to give her, sir. [*To* Byplay] Now, sirrah, speak.

Byplay. I brought you to the stand from whence you saw
How the game went.

Joyless.   O my dear, dear Diana.

Byplay. I seem'd to do it against my will, by which I
          gain'd
Your bribe of twenty pieces.

Joyless.   Much good do thee.

Byplay. But I assure you my lord gave me order
To place you there after, it seems, he had
Well put her to't within.

Joyless.   Stay, stay, stay, stay.
Why may not this be then a counterfeit action,
Or a false mist to blind me with more error?
The ill I fear'd may have been done before,
And all this but deceit to daub it o'er.

                              [*Joyless* draws his dagger.]

Diana. Do you fall back again?

Joyless.   Shugh, give me leave.

Byplay. I must take charge, I see, o' th' dagger again.

Letoy. Come, Joyless, I have pity on thee. Hear me:
I swear upon mine honour she is chaste.

Joyless. Honour! An oath of glass.

Letoy.   I prithee hear me.
I tried and tempted her for mine own ends
More than for thine.

Joyless.   That's easily believ'd.

Letoy. And had she yielded, I not only had
Rejected her (for it was ne'er my purpose—
Heaven, I call thee to witness—to commit
A sin with her), but laid a punishment
Upon her greater than thou could'st inflict.

Joyless. But how can this appear?

Letoy. Do you know your father, lady?

Diana. I hope I am so wise a child.

Letoy [*To* Byplay].   Go call
In my friend Truelock.

Byplay.   Take your dagger, sir;
Now I dare trust you.

Letoy.   Sirrah, dare you fool
When I am serious? Send in Master Truelock.

(*Exit* Byplay.

Diana. That is my father's name.
Joyless.   Can he be here?
Letoy. Sir, I am neither conjuror nor witch,
But a great fortune-teller, that you'll find
You are happy in a wife, sir, happier—yes,
Happier by a hundred thousand pound
Than you were yesterday.
Joyless.   So, so, now he's mad.
Letoy. I mean in possibilities—provided that
You use her well, and never more be jealous.
Joyless. Must it come that way?
Letoy.   Look you this way, sir,
When I speak to you; I'll cross your fortune else,
As I am true Letoy.
Joyless.   Mad, mad, he's mad.
Would we were quickly out on's fingers yet.
Letoy. When saw you your wife's father? Answer me!
Joyless. He came for London four days before us.
Letoy. 'Tis possible he's here then. Do you know him?

'*Enter* Truelock.'

Diana. Oh, I am happy in his sight. Dear sir.
                    '*She kneels.*'
Letoy. 'Tis but so much knee-labour lost. Stand up,
Stand up, and mind me.
Truelock. You are well met, son Joyless.
Joyless. How have you been conceal'd, and [in] this house?
Here's mystery in this.
Truelock.   My good lord's pleasure—
Letoy. Know, sir, that I sent for him, and for you,
Instructing your friend Blaze, my instrument,
To draw you to my doctor with your son.
Your wife I knew must follow. What my end
Was in't shall quickly be discover'd to you,
In a few words of your supposed father.
Diana. Supposed father!

Letoy.   Yes. Come, Master Truelock,
My constant friend of thirty years acquaintance,
Freely declare with your best knowledge now
Whose child this is.
     Truelock.   Your honour does as freely
Release me of my vow, then, in the secret
I lock'd up in this breast these seventeen years
Since she was three days old?
     Letoy.   True, Master Truelock,
I do release you of your vow. Now speak.
     Truelock. Now she is yours, my lord, your only daughter.
And know you, Master Joyless, for some reason
Known to my lord—and large reward to me—
She has been from the third day of her life
Reputed mine; and that so covertly,
That not her lady mother nor my wife
Knew to their deaths the change of my dead infant,
Nor this sweet lady. 'Tis most true we had
A trusty nurse's help and secrecy,
Well paid for, in the carriage of our plot.
     Letoy. Now shall you know what mov'd me, sir. I was
A thing beyond a madman, like yourself,
Jealous, and had that strong distrust, and fancied
Such proofs unto myself against my wife,
That I conceiv'd the child was not mine own,
And scorn'd to father it. Yet I gave to breed her
And marry her as the daughter of this gentleman—
Two thousand pound I guess you had with her.
But since your match, my wife upon her deathbed
So clear'd herself of all my foul suspicions
(Blest be her memory), that I then resolv'd
By some quaint way (for I am still Letoy)
To see and try her throughly; and so much
To make her mine as I should find her worthy.
And now thou art my daughter, and [thou] mine heir,
Provided still (for I am still Letoy)
You honourably love her, and defy
The cuckold-making fiend, foul jealousy.
     Joyless. My lord, 'tis not her birth and fortune, which
Do jointly claim a privilege to live

Above my reach of jealousy, shall restrain
That passion in me, but her well-tried virtue,
In the true faith of which I am confirm'd,
And throughly cur'd.

    Letoy. As I am true Letoy,
Well said. I hope thy son is cur'd by this too.

'Enter Barbara.'

Now, Mistress Blaze! Here is a woman now!
I cur'd her husband's jealousy, and twenty more
I'th' town, by means I and my doctor wrought.

    Barbara. Truly, my lord, my husband has ta'en bread
And drink upon 't, that under heaven he thinks
You were the means to make me an honest woman,
Or, at the least, him a contented man.

    Letoy. Ha' done, ha' done.

    Barbara.   Yes, I believe you have done;
And if your husband, lady, be cur'd, as he should be,
And as all foolish jealous husbands ought to be,
I know what was done first, if my lord took
That course with you as me—

    Letoy. Prithee what cam'st thou for?

    Barbara. My lord, to tell you, as the doctor tells me,
The bride and bridegroom both are coming on
The sweetliest to their wits again.

    Letoy.   I told you.

    Barbara. Now you are a happy man, sir, and I hope a
       quiet man,

    Joyless. Full of content and joy.

    Barbara. Content! So was my husband when he knew
The worst he could by his wife. Now you'll live quiet, lady.

    Letoy. Why flyest thou off thus, woman, from the subject
Thou wert upon?

    Barbara. I beg your honour's pardon;
And now I'll tell you. Be it by skill or chance,
Or both, was never such a cure as is
Upon that couple. Now they strive which most
Shall love the other.

    Letoy.   Are they up and ready?

    Barbara. Up! Up, and ready to lie down again.

There is no ho with them;
They have been in th' Antipodes to some purpose,
And now are risen, and return'd themselves.
He's her dear Per, and she is his sweet Mat.
His kingship and her queenship are forgotten,
And all their melancholy and his travails past,
And but suppos'd their dreams.
 Letoy.   'Tis excellent.
 Barbara. Now, sir, the doctor (for he is become
An utter stranger to your son, and so
Are all about 'em) craves your presence,
And such as he's acquainted with.
 Letoy.   Go, sir,
And go you, daughter.
 Barbara [*Aside*]. Daughter! That's the true trick
Of all old whoremasters, to call their wenches daughters.
 Letoy. Has he known you, friend Truelock, too?
 Truelock. Yes, from his childhood.
 Letoy.   Go then and possess him,
Now he is sensible, how things have gone:
What art, what means, what friends have been employ'd
In his cure; and win him by degrees
To sense of where he is. Bring him to me,
And I have yet an entertainment for him,
Of better settle-brain than drunkard's porridge,
To set him right. As I am true Letoy,
I have one toy left. Go, and go you. Why stay'st thou?
        (*Exeunt* Joyless, Diana, Truelock.
 Barbara. If I had been a gentlewoman born,
I should have been your daughter too, my lord.
 Letoy. But never as she is.
You'll know anon.
 Barbara. Neat city-wives' flesh yet may be as good
As your coarse country gentlewoman's blood.
           (*Exit* Barbara.
 Letoy. Go with thy flesh to Turnbull shambles! Ho!
Within there!

     '*Enter* Quailpipe.'

 Quailpipe. Here, my lord.

Letoy. The music, songs and dance I gave command for, are they ready?

Quailpipe. All, my good lord; and in good sooth, I cannot enough applaud your honour's quaint conceit in the design: so apt, so regular, so pregnant, so acute, and so, withal, *poetice* legitimate, as I may say justly with Plautus—

Letoy. Prithee say no more, but see upon my signal given they act as well as I designed.

Quailpipe. Nay, not so well, my exact lord, but as they may, they shall.   (*Exit* Quailpipe.

Letoy. I know no flatterer in my house but this;
But for his custom I must bear with him.
'Sprecious, they come already. Now, begin.

> '*A solemn lesson upon the recorders. Enter* Truelock,
> Joyless *and* Diana, Peregrine *and* Martha, Doctor
> *and* Barbara. Letoy *meets them.* Truelock *presents*
> Peregrine *and* Martha *to him. He salutes them. They
> seem to make some short discourse. Then* Letoy *appoints
> them to sit.* Peregrine *seems something amazed. The
> music ceases.*'

Letoy. Again you are welcome, sir, and welcome all.

Peregrine. I am what you are pleased to make me, but withal so ignorant of mine own condition, whether I sleep, or wake, or talk, or dream; whether I be or be not, or if I am, whether I do or do not anything; for I have had, if I now wake, such dreams, and been so far transported in a long and tedious voyage of sleep, that I may fear my manners can acquire no welcome where men understand themselves.

Letoy. This is music. Sir, you are welcome; and I give full power unto your father, and my daughter here, your mother, to make you welcome.

> 'Joyless *whispers* Peregrine.'

Peregrine. How! Your daughter, sir?

Doctor. My lord, you'll put him back again if you trouble his brain with new discoveries.

Letoy. Fetch him you on again then. Pray, are you Letoy or I?

Joyless. Indeed it is so, son.

Doctor. I fear your show will but perplex him too.

Letoy. I care not, sir; I'll have it to delay your cure a

while, that he recover soundly. Come, sit again; again you
are most welcome.

'*A most untunable flourish. Enter* Discord, *attended by*
Folly, Jealousy, Melancholy *and* Madness.'

There's an unwelcome guest—uncivil Discord, that trains
into my house her followers, Folly and Jealousy, Melancholy
and Madness.

Barbara. My husband presents Jealousy, in the black and
yellow jaundiced suit there, half like man, and tother half
like woman, with one horn and ass-ear upon his head.

Letoy. Peace, woman, mark what they do. [*To* Peregrine]
But by the way, conceive you me this show, sir, and device?

Peregrine. I think so.

Letoy. How goes he back again now, doctor? Sheugh!

'*Song in untunable notes.*'

Discord. Come forth, my darlings, you that breed
    The common strifes that Discord feed:
    Come in the first place, my dear Folly;
    Jealousy next, then Melancholy;
    And last come Madness; thou art he
    That bear'st th' effects of all those three.
    Lend me your aids; so Discord shall you crown,
    And make this place a kingdom of our own.

            '*They dance.*'
'*After a while, they are broke off by a flourish and the
approach of* Harmony *followed by* Mercury, Cupid,
Bacchus *and* Apollo. Discord *and her faction fall down.*'

Letoy. See, Harmony approaches, leading on
'Gainst Discord's factions four great deities,
Mercury, Cupid, Bacchus, and Apollo:
Wit against Folly, Love against Jealousy,
Wine against Melancholy, and 'gainst Madness, Health.
Observe the matter and the method.

Peregrine. Yes.

Letoy.   And how, upon the approach of Harmony,
Discord and her disorders are confounded.

Song.

Harmony. Come Wit, come Love, come Wine, come
                Health,
            Maintainers of my commonwealth,
        'Tis you make Harmony complete;
        And from the spheres, her proper seat,
        You give her power to reign on earth,
            Where Discord claims a right by birth.
        Then let us revel it while we are here,
        And keep possession of this hemisphere.

'*After a strain or two*, Discord *cheers up her faction.
They all rise and mingle in the dance with Harmony
and the rest. Dance.*'

Letoy. Note there how Discord cheers up her disorders,
To mingle in defiance with the Virtues.
                    '*Exit* Discord' [and her faction].
But soon they vanish, and the mansion quit
Unto the Gods of health, love, wine and wit,
Who triumph in their habitation new,
Which they have taken, and assign to you;
In which they now salute you—bid you be
            '[Harmony *and her followers*] *salute* [Peregrine *and*] *exeunt.*'
Of cheer, and for it lay the charge on me.
And unto me you're welcome, welcome all.
Meat, wine, and mirth shall flow, and what I see
Yet wanting in your cure supplied shall be.

Peregrine. Indeed I find me well.

Martha.   And so shall I,
After a few such nights more.

Barbara.   Are you there?
Good madam, pardon errors of my tongue.

Diana. I am too happy made to think of wrong.

Letoy. We will want nothing for you that may please,
Though we dive for it to th' Antipodes.

The Epilogue.

Doctor. Whether my cure be perfect yet or no,
It lies not in my doctorship to know.

Your approbation may more raise the man
Than all the College of Physicians can;
And more health from your fair hands may be won
Than by the strokings of the seventh son.
    Peregrine. And from our travels in th' Antipodes
We are not yet arriv'd from off the seas,
But on the waves of desperate fears we roam
Until your gentler hands do waft us home.

FINIS.

Courteous Reader: you shall find in this book more than was presented upon the stage, and left out of the presentation for superfluous length, as some of the players pretended. I thought good all should be inserted according to the allowed original, and as it was at first intended for the Cockpit Stage, in the right of my most deserving friend, Mr. William Beeston, unto whom it properly appertained. And so I leave it to thy perusal, as it was generally applauded and well acted at Salisbury Court. Farewell.

Ri. Brome.

THE
VVITTS.

A Comedie,

PRESENTED AT THE
Private Houſe in *Blacke Fryers*,
by his Majeſties Servants.

The Authour VVilliam D'Avenant,
Servant to Her Majeſtie.

LONDON,
Printed for Richard Meighen, next
to the Middle Temple in Fleetſtreet.
1 6 3 6.

To the chiefly beloved of all that are ingenious and noble, Endymion Porter, of His Majesty's bed-chamber.

Sir,

Though you covet not acknowledgements, receive what belongs to you by a double title: your goodness hath preserved life in the author, then rescued his work from a cruel faction, which nothing but the forces of your reason and your reputation could sub-due. If it become your pleasure now, as when it had the advantage of presentation on the stage, I shall be taught to boast some merit in myself, but with this inference: you still (as in that doubtful day of my trial) endeavour to make show of so much justice as may countenance the love you bear to

> *Your most obliged and thankful humble servant,*

WILLIAM DAVENANT

To the reader of Master William Davenant's play.

It hath been said of old that plays are feasts,
Poets the cooks, and the spectators guests,
The actors waiters. From this simile
Some have deriv'd an unsafe liberty
To use their judgements as their tastes, which choose
Without control this dish, and that refuse.
But wit allows not this large privilege:
Either you must confess or feel its edge;
Nor shall you make a current inference
If you transfer your reason to your sense.
Things are distinct, and must the same appear
To every piercing eye or well-tun'd ear.
Though sweets with yours, sharps best with my taste meet,
Both must agree this meat's or sharp or sweet.
But if I scent a stench or a perfume,
Whilst you smell naught at all, I may presume
You have that sense imperfect. So you may
Affect a sad, merry, or humorous play,
If, though the kind distaste or please, the good
And bad be by your judgement understood.
But if, as in this play, where with delight
I feast my epicurean appetite
With relishes so curious as dispense
The utmost pleasure to the ravish'd sense,
You should profess that you can nothing meet
That hits your taste, either with sharp or sweet,
But cry out 'tis insipid, your bold tongue
May do its master, not the author wrong;
For men of better palate will by it
Take the just elevation of your wit.

                                        T. CAREW

THE PERSONS OF THE COMEDY

Pallatine the elder, *richly landed, and a wit.*

Pallatine the younger, *a wit too, but lives on his exhibition in town.*

Sir Morglay Thwack, *a humorous rich old knight.*

Sir Tyrant Thrift, *guardian to the* Lady Ample.

Meager, *a soldier, newly come from Holland.*

Pert, *his comrade.*

Engine, *steward to* Sir Tyrant Thrift.

The Lady Ample, *an inheretrix, and ward to* Sir Tyrant Thrift.

Lucy, *mistress to the younger* Pallatine.

Ginet, *woman to the* Lady Ample.

Snore, *a constable.*

Mistress Snore, *his wife.*

Mistress Queasy, *her neighbour.*

Watchmen, &c.

The Scene: London

THE WITS

The Prologue

Bless me, you kinder stars! How are we throng'd!
Alas, whom hath our long-sick poet wrong'd,
That he should meet together in one day
A session and a faction at his play,
To judge and to condemn? For 't cannot be
Amongst so many here all should agree.
Then 'tis to such vast expectation rais'd
As it were to be wonder'd at, not prais'd.
And this, good faith, Sir Poet (if I've read
Customs or men), strikes you and your muse dead!
Conceive now too how much, how oft each ear
Hath surfeited in this our hemisphere
With various, pure, eternal wit, and then,
My fine young comic sir, you're kill'd again.
But 'bove the mischief of these fears, a sort
Of cruel spies (we hear) intend a sport
Among themselves. Our mirth must not at all
Tickle or stir their lungs, but shake their gall.
So this, join'd with the rest, makes me again
To say, you and your lady muse within
Will have but a sad doom; and your trim brow,
Which long'd for wreaths, you must wear naked now,
'Less some resolve, out of a courteous pride,
To like and praise what others shall deride.
So they've their humour too; and we, in spite
Of our dull brains, will think each side i' th' right.
Such is your pleasant judgements upon plays,
Like par'llels that run straight, though sev'ral ways.

ACT I · SCENE I

'*Enter* Young Pallatine, Meager, Pert.'

Young Pall. Welcome o' shore, Meager! Give me thy
  hand!
'Tis a true one, and will no more forsake
A bond or bill than a good sword, a hand
That will shift for the body till the laws
Provide for both.
  Meager. Old wine and new clothes, sir,
Make you wanton. D'you not see Pert, my comrade?
  Young Pall. Ambiguous Pert, hast thou danc'd to the
  drum too?
Could a taff'ta scarf, a long estridge wing,
A stiff iron doublet and a brazil pole
Tempt thee from cambric sheets, fine active thighs,
From caudles where the precious amber swims?
  Pert. Faith, we have been to kill we know not whom
Nor why, led on to break a commandment
With the consent of custom and the laws.
  Meager. Mine was a certain inclination sir,
To do mischief where good men of the jury
And a dull congregation of greybeards
Might urge no tedious statute 'gainst my life.
  Young Pall. Nothing but honour could seduce thee, Pert;
Honour, which is the hope of the youthful,
And the old soldier's wealth, a jealousy
To the noble, and myst'ry to the wise.
  Pert. It was, sir, no geographical fancy
('Cause in our maps I lik'd this region here
More than that country lying there) made me
Partial which to fight for.
  Young Pall. True, sage Pert.
What is't to thee whether one Don Diego,
A prince, or Hans von Holme, fritter-seller
Of Bombell, do conquer that parapet,
Redoubt or town, which thou ne'er saw'st before?
  Pert. Not a brass thimble to me. But honour—

Young Pall. Why, right. Else wherefore shouldst thou
    bleed for him
Whose money, wine, nor wench thou ne'er hast us'd?
Or why destroy some poor root-eating soldier,
That never gave thee the lie, denied to pledge
Thy cockatrice's health, ne'er spit upon
Thy dog, jeer'd thy spur-leather, or return'd
Thy toothpick ragged which he borrowed whole?
    Pert. Never to my knowledge.
    Meager. Comrade, 'tis time—
    Young Pall. What, to unship your trunks at Billingsgate?
Fierce Meager, why such haste? Do not I know
That a mouse yok'd to a peascod may draw
With the frail cordage of one hair your goods
About the world?
    Pert. Why, we have linen, sir.
    Young Pall. As much, sir, as will fill a tinder box
Or make a frog a shirt. I like not, friends,
This quiet, modest posture of your shoulders.
Why stir you not as you were practising
To fence? Or do you hide your cattle lest
The skipper make you pay their passage over?
    Pert. Know, Pallatine, truth is a naked lady;
She will show all. Meager and I have not—
    Young Pall. The treasure of St. Mark's, I believe, sir,
Though you are as rich as cast servingmen
Or bawds led thrice into captivity.
    Pert. Thou hast a heart of the right stamp: I find
It is not comely in thine eyes to see
Us sons of war walk by the pleasant vines
Of Gascony as we believ'd the grapes
Forbidden fruit; sneak through a tavern with
Remorse as we had read the Alcoran
And made it our best faith.
    Meager. And abstain flesh
As if our English beef were all reserv'd
For sacrifice.
    Pert. Whilst colon keeps more noise
Than mariners at plays, or apple-wives
That wrangle for a sieve.

Meager. Contribute, come!

Young Pall. Stand there, close, on your lives! Here in
    this house
Lives a rich old hen whose young egg (though not
Of her own laying) I have in the embers.
She may prove a morsel for a discreet mouth,
If the kind fates have but the leisure to
Betray the old one.

Pert.   Pallatine,
No plots upon generation! We two
Have fasted so long that we cannot think
Of begetting anything unless
Like cannibals we might eat our own issue.

Young Pall. I say, close; shrink in your morions! Go!

Meager. Why hidden thus? A soldier may appear.

Young Pall. Yes, in a sutler's hut on the pay-day.
But do you know the silence of this house,
The gravity and the awe? Here dwells a lady
That hath not seen a street since good King Harry
Call'd her to a masque. She is more devout
Than a weaver of Banbury that hopes
T'entice heaven by singing to make him lord
Of twenty looms. I never saw her yet,
And to arrive at my preferment first
In your sweet company will, I take it,
Add but little to my hopes. Retire, go!
      'They step aside, whilst he calls between the hangings.'

Pert. We shall obey; but do not tempt us now
With sweetmeats for the nether palate; do not!

Young Pall. What, Lucy! Luce! Now is the old beldame
Misleading her to a cushion, where she
Must pray and sigh, and fast until her knees
Grow smaller than her knuckles. Lucy! Luce!
No hope, she is undone! She'll number o'er
As many orisons as if she had
A bushels of beads to her rosary.
Lucy, my April love, my mistress, speak!

             'Enter Lucy.'

Lucy. Pallatine, for heaven's sake keep in your voice!
My cruel aunt will hear, and I am lost.
   Young Pall. What can she hear, when her old ears are
      stuff'd
With as much warm wax as will seal nine leases?
What a pox does she list'ning upon earth?
Is't not time for her t'affect privacy,
To creep into a close dark vault, there gossip
With worms and such small tame creatures as heaven
Provided to accompany old people?
   Lucy. Still better'd unto worse! But that my heart
Consents not to disfigure thee, thou wouldst be torn
To pieces numberless as sand, or as
The doubts of guilt or love in cowards are.
   Young Pall. How now, Luce! From what strange coast
      this storm, ha?
   Lucy. Thou dost outdrink the youth of Norway at
Their marriage feasts, outswear a puny gamester
When his first misfortune rages; outquarrel
One that rides post and is stopp'd by a cart.
Thy walking hours are later in the night
Than those which drawers, traitors or constables
Themselves do keep, for watchmen know thee better
Than their lanthorn. And here's your surgeon's bill;
Your kind thrift (I thank you) hath sent it me
To pay, as if the poor exhibition
My aunt allows for aprons would maintain
You in cerecloths.   *'Gives him a paper.'*
   Meager. Can the daughters of Brabant
Talk thus when younker-gheek leads 'em to a stove?
   Pert. I say, Meager, there is a small parcel
Of man that rebels more than all the rest
Of his body, and I shall need, if I
Stay here, no elixir of beef to exalt
Nature, though I were leaner than a groat.
   Young Pall. This surgeon's a rogue, Luce, a fellow, Luce,
That hath no more care of a gentleman's
Credit than of the lint he hath twice us'd.
   Lucy. Well, sir, but what's that instrument he names?
   Young Pall. He writes down here for a tool of injection,

Luce, a small water-engine which I bought
For my tailor's child to squirt at prentices.

Lucy. Ay, sir, he sins more against wit than heaven
That knows not how t'excuse what he hath done.
I shall be old at twenty, Pallatine;
My grief to see thy manners and thy mind
Hath wrought so much upon my heart.

Young Pall. I'd as lieve keep our marriage supper
In a churchyard and beget our children
In a coffin as hear thee prophesy.
Luce, thou art drunk, Luce, far gone in almond-milk.
Kiss me.

Pert. Now I dissolve like an eryngo.

Meager. He's ploughing o'th' Indies; good gold appear.

Young Pall. I am a new man, Luce; thou shalt find me
In a Geneva band that was reduc'd
From an old alderman's cuff, no more hair left
Than will shackle a flea. This debosh'd whinyard
I will reclaim to comely bow and arrows,
And shoot with haberdashers at Finsbury,
And be thought the grandchild of Adam Bell.
And more, my Luce, hang at my velvet girdle
A book wrapp'd in a green dimity bag,
And squire thy untooth'd aunt to an exercise.

Lucy. Nothing but strict laws and age will tame you.

Young Pall. What money hast thou, Luce?

Lucy. Ay, there's your business.

Young Pall. It is the business of the world: injuries grow
To get it, justice sits for the same end;
Men are not wise without it, for it makes
Wisdom known; and to be a fool and poor
Is next t'old aches and bad fame; 'tis worse
Than to have six new creditors, they each
Twelve children, and not bread enough to make
The landlord a toast when he calls for ale
And rent. Think on that, and rob thy aunt's trunks
Ere she hath time to make an inventory.

Pert. A cunning pioneer! He works to th' bottom.

Lucy. Hast thou no taste of heaven? Wert thou begot
In a prison and bred up in a galley?

Young Pall. Luce, I speak like one that hath seen the book
Of fate. I'm loth for thy sake to mount a coach
With two wheels, whilst the damsels of the shop
Cry out, A goodly straight-chin'd gentleman!
He dies for robbing an attorney's cloak-bag
Of copper seals, foul nightcaps, together
With his wife's bracelet of mill-testers!

Lucy. There, sir—   *'Flings him a purse.'*
'Tis gold—my pendants, carcanets and rings,
My christ'ning caudle-cup and spoons
Are dissolv'd into that lump. Nay, take all!
And with it as much anger as would make
Thy mother write thee illegitimate.
See me no more! I will not stay to bless
My gift lest I should teach my patience suffer
Till I convert it into sin.   (*Exit* Lucy.

Young Pall. Temptations will not thrive. This baggage
    sleeps
Cross-legg'd, and the devil has no more power
O'er that charm than dead men o'er their lewd heirs.
I must marry her, and spend my revenue
In cradles, pins and soap! That's th' end of all
That 'scape a deep river and a tall bough.

Meager. Pallatine, how much?

Pert. Honorable Pall.

Young Pall. Gentlemen, you must accept without 'gaging
Your corporal oaths to repay in three days.

Pert. Not we, Pall, in three jubilees! Fear not.

Young Pall. Nor shall you charge me with loud vehe-
    mence
(Thrice before company) to wait you in
My chamber such a night, for then a certain
Drover of the south comes to pay you money.

Meager. On our new faiths!

Pert. On our allegiance, Pall!

Young Pall. Go then; shift, and brush your skins well,
    d'you hear.
Meet me at the new play fair and perfum'd.
There are strange words hang on the lips of rumour.

Pert. Language of joy, dear Pall!

Young Pall. This day is come
To town the minion of the womb, my lads,
My elder brother, and he moves like some
Assyrian prince; his chariots measure leagues;
Witty as youthful poets in their wine,
Bold as a centaur at a feast, and kind
As virgins that were ne'er beguil'd with love.
I seek him now. Meet, and triumph!

Meager. ⎱
Pert.   ⎰ King Pall!   (*Exeunt* omnes.

[SCENE II]

'*Enter* Sir Morglay Thwack, Elder Pallatine, *new and
richly clothed, buttoning themselves.*'

Elder Pall. Sir Morglay, come! The hours have wings,
    and you
Are grown too old t' overtake them. The town
Looks, methinks, as it would invite the country
To a feast.
    Thwack. At which sergeants and their yeomen
Must be no waiters, Pallatine, lest some
O' the guests pretend business. How dost like me?
    Elder Pall. As one old women shall no more avoid
Than they can warm furs and muscadel.
    Thwack. Pallatine, to have a volatile ache,
That removes oftener than the Tartar's camp;
To have a stitch that sucks a man awry,
Till he show crooked as a chestnut bough,
Or stand in the deform'd guard of a fencer;
To have these hid in flesh that has liv'd sinful
Fifty long years, yet husband so much strength
As could convey me hither four score miles
On a design of wit and glory may
Be register'd for a strange northern act.
    Elder Pall. I cannot boast those noble maladies
As yet; but time, dear knight, as I have heard,
May make man's knowledge bold upon himself.
We travel in the grand cause. These smooth rags,

These jewels too, that seem to smile ere they
Betray, are certain silly snares in which
Your lady-wits and their wise compeers-male
May chance be caught.

'*Enter* Young Pallatine.'

   Young Pall. Your welcome, noble brother,
Must be hereafter spoke, for I have lost
With glad haste to find you much of my breath.
   Elder Pall. Your joy becomes you; it hath courtship in't.
   Young Pall. Sir Morglay Thwack! I did expect to see
The archer Cymbeline or old King Lud
Advance his fauchion here again ere you
'Mongst so much smoke, diseases, law, and noise.
   Thwack. What your town gets by me let 'em lay up
For their orphans and record in their annals.
I come to borrow where I'll never lend,
And buy what I'll never pay for.
   Young Pall. Not your debts?
   Thwack. No, sir, though to a poor Brownist's widow,
Though she sigh all night and have the next morning
Nothing to drink but her own tears.
   Elder Pall. Nor shalt thou lend money to a sick friend,
Though the sad worm lie mortgag'd in his bed
For the hire of his sheets.
   Young Pall. These are resolves
That give me newer wonder than your clothes.
Why in such shining trim, like men that come
From rifled tents, loaden with victory?
   Elder Pall. Yes, brother, or like eager heirs new dipp'd
In ink, that seal'd the day before in haste
Lest parchment should grow dear. Know, youth, we come
To be the business of all eyes, to take
The wall of our St. George on his feast day.
   Thwack. Yes, and then embark at Dover and do
The like to St. Denis. All this, young sir,
Without charge too,—I mean to us. We bring
A humorous odd philosophy to town
That says, pay nothing.

Young Pall. Why, where have I liv'd?

Elder Pall. Brother, be calm and edify. But first
Receive a principle: never hereafter,
From this warm breathing till your last cold sigh,
Will I disburse for you again, never!

Young Pall. Brother mine, if that be your argument,
I deny the major.

Thwack.   Resist principles?

Elder Pall. Good faith, though you should send me more
    epistles
Than young factors in their first voyage write
Unto their short-hair'd friends, than absent lovers
Pen near their marriage week t' excuse the slow
Arrival of the license and the ring,
Not one clipp'd penny should depart my reach.

Young Pall. This doctrine will not pass. How shall I live?

Elder Pall. As we intend to do, by our good wits.

Young Pall. How, brother, how?

Elder Pall. Truth is a pleasant knowledge,
Yet you shall have her cheap. Sir Morglay here,
My kind disciple, and myself have leas'd
Out all our rents and lands for pious uses.

Young Pall. What, co-founders! Give legacies ere death!
Pallatine the pious and St. Morglay!
Your names will sound but ill i' th' calendar.
How long must this fierce raging zeal continue?

Elder Pall. Till we subsist here no more by our wit.
Then we'll renounce the town and patiently
Vouchsafe to reassume our mother earth,
Lead on our ploughs into their rugged walks
Again, grope our young heifers in the flank,
And swagger in the wool we shall borrow
From our own flocks.

Thwack.   But ere we go, we may
From the vast treasure purchas'd by our wit
Leave here some monument to speak our fame.
I have a strong mind to re-edify
The decays of Fleet Ditch, from whence I hear
The roaring vestals late are fled through heat
Of persecution.

Young Pall. What a small star have I,
That never yet could light me to this way!
Live by our wits?
    Elder Pall.   So live that usurers
Shall call their monies in, remove their bank
T' ordinaries, Spring Garden and Hyde Park,
Whilst their glad sons are left seven for their chance
At hazard, hundred and all made at sant,
Three motley cocks o'th' right Derby strain
Together with a foal of Beggibrigge.
    Thwack. Sir, I will match my Lord Mayor's horse, make
        jockeys
Of his hench-boys and run 'em through Cheapside.
    Elder Pall. What beauties, girls of feature, govern now
I'th' town? 'Tis long since we did traffic here
In midnight whispers, when the dialect
Of love's loose wit is frighted into signs,
And secret laughter stifled into smiles,
When nothing 's loud but the old nurse's cough.
Who keeps the game up, ha? Who misled now?
    Thwack. Not, sir, that if we woo, we'll be at charge
For looks, or if we marry, make a jointure.
Entail land on women? Entail a back,
And so much else of man as nature did
Provide for the first wife.
    Elder Pall.   I could keep thee,
Thy future pride, thy surfeits and thy lust
(I mean in such a garb as may become
A christian gentleman), with the sole tithe
Of tribute I shall now receive from ladies.
    Thwack. Your brother and myself have seal'd to cove-
        nants:
The female youth o'th' town are his, but all
From forty to fourscore mine own. A widow,
You'll say, is a wise, solemn, wary creature;
Though she hath liv'd to th' cunning of dispatch,
Clos'd up nine husbands' eyes, and have the wealth
Of all their testaments, in one month, sir,
I will waste her to her first wedding smock,
Her single ring, bodkin, and velvet muff.

Young Pall. Your rents expos'd at home for pious uses
Must expiate your behaviour here. Tell me,
Is that the subtle plot you have on heaven?

   Thwack. The worm of your worship's conscience would
      appear
As big as a conger, but a good eye
May chance to find it slender as a grig.

   Young Pall. Amazement knows no ease but in demands.
Pray tell me, gentlemen, to all this vast
Designment (which so strikes my ear), deduct
You naught from your revenue, naught that may
Like fuel feed the flame of your expense?

   Elder Pall. Brother, not so much as will find a Jew
Bacon to his eggs. These gay tempting weeds,
These eastern stones of cunning foil, bespoke
'Gainst our arrival here, together with
A certain stock of crowns in either's purse,
Is all the charge that from our proper own
Begins or furthers the magnific plot;
And of these crowns not one must be usurp'd
By you.

   Thwack. No relief but wit and good counsel.

   Elder Pall. The stock my father left you, if your care
Had purpos'd so discreet a course, might well
Have set you up i'th' trade. But we spend light;
Our coach is yet unwheel'd. Sir Morglay, come.
Let's suit those Friesland horse with our own strain.

   Young Pall. Why, gentlemen, will the design keep horses?

   Thwack. Maybe, sir, they shall live by their wits too.

   Young Pall. Their masters are bad tutors else. Well, how
You'll work the ladies and weak gentry here
By your fine gilded pills, a faith that is
Not old may guess without distrust. But, sirs,
The city (take't on my experiment)
Will not be gull'd.

   Thwack.   Not gull'd? They dare not be
So impudent. I say they shall be gull'd,
And trust, and break, and pawn their charter too.

   Young Pall. Is it lawful, brother, for me to laugh
That have no money?

Elder Pall.   Yes, sir, at yourself.

Young Pall. Two that have tasted nature's kindness, arts,
And men; have shin'd in moving camps; have seen
Courts in their solemn business and vain pride;
Convers'd so long i'th' town here that you know
Each sign and pebble in the streets; for you,
After a long retirement, to lease forth
Your wealthy pleasant lands to feed John Crump
The cripple, Widow Needy and Abraham
Sloth the beadsman of Moredale; then, forsooth,
Persuade yourselves to live here by your wits!

Thwack. Where we ne'er cheated in our youth, we resolve
To cozen in our age.

Elder Pall.   Brother, I came
To be your wise example in the arts
That lead to thriving glory and supreme life,
Not through the humble ways wherein dull lords
Of lands and sheep do walk—men that depend
On the fantastic winds, on fleeting clouds,
On seasons more uncertain than themselves,
When they would hope or fear. But you are warm
In another's silk, and make your tame ease
Virtue, call it content and quietness.

Thwack. Write letters to your brother, do, and be
Forsworn in every long parenthesis
For twenty pound sent you in butcher's silver.

Elder Pall. Rebukes are precious; cast them not away.
            [*Exeunt* Elder Pallatine *and* Thwack.]

Young Pail. Neither of these philosophers were born
To above five senses; why then should they
Have hope to do things greater and more new
I' th' world than I? This devil plenty thrusts
Strange boldness upon men. Well, you may laugh
With so much violence till it consume
Your breath. Though sullen want, the enemy
Of wit, have sunk her low, if pregnant wine
Can raise her up, this day she shall be mine.
                 (*Exit* Young Pallatine.

ACT II · SCENE I

'Enter the Lady Ample, Engine, Ginet.*'*

Ample. My guardian hors'd? This evening, say'st thou,
Engine?
　Engine. It's an hour, madam, since he smelt the town.
　Ample. Saw'st thou his slender empty leg in th' stirrup,
His iv'ry box on his smooth ebon staff
New civeted and tied to's gouty wrist,
With his warp'd face close button'd in his hood,
That men may take him for a monk disguis'd
And fled post from a pursuivant?
　Engine. Madam, beware, I pray, lest th' age and cunning
He is master of prepare you a revenge,
And such as your fine wit shall ne'er entreat
Your patience to digest. Tomorrow night
Th' extremest minute of your wardship is
Expir'd, and we magicians of the house
Believe this hasty journey he hath ta'en
Is to provide a husband for your sheets.
　Ample. And such a one as judgement and mine eyes
Must needs dislike, that's composition may
Grow up to his own thrifty wish.
　Engine. 　　　　　　　　Madam,
Your arrow was well aim'd. I call him master
But I am servant unto truth and you.
　Ample. He choose a husband, fit to guide and sway
My beauty's wealthy dowry, and my heart?
I'll make election to delight myself.
What composition strictest laws will give
His guardianship may take from the rich bank
My father left, and not devour my land.
　Ginet. Your ladyship has liv'd six years beneath
His roof, therefore may guess the colour
Of his heart and what his brains do weigh.
But Engine, madam, is your humble creature.
　Ample. I have bounty, Engine,
And thou shalt largely taste it when the next

Fair sun is set, for then my wardship ends.

'*Knocking within.*'

That speaks command or haste; open the door.

'*Enter* Lucy.'

Lucy! Weeping, my wench, melting thine eyes,
As they had trespass'd against light, and thou
Wouldst give them darkness for a punishment?

Lucy. Undone, madam, without all hope but what
Your pity will vouchsafe to minister!

Ample. Hast thou been struck by infamy, or com'st
A mourner from the funeral of love?

Lucy. I am the mourner and the mourn'd, dead to
Myself, but left not rich enough to buy a grave.
My cruel aunt hath banish'd me her roof,
Expos'd me to the night, the winds, and what
The raging elements on wand'rers lay,
Left naked as first infancy or truth.

Ginet. I could ne'er endure that old moist-ey'd lady;
Methought she pray'd too oft.

Ample.   A mere receipt
To make her longwinded, which our devout
Physicians now prescribe to defer death.
But, Lucy, can she urge no cause for this
Strange wrath that you would willingly conceal?

Lucy. Suspicions of my chastity, which heaven
Must needs resist as false, though she accus'd
Me even in dream, where thoughts commit by chance,
Not appetite.

Ample.   What ground had her suspect?

Lucy. Young Pallatine (that woo'd my heart until
He gather'd fondness where he planted love),
Was fall'n into such want as eager blood
And youth could not endure and keep the laws
Inviolate. I, to prevent my fear,
Sold all my jewels and my trifling wealth,
Bestow'd them on him, and she thinks a more
Unholy consequence attends the gift.

Ample. This, Luce, is such apostasy in wit
As nature must degrade herself in woman to
Forgive. Shall love put thee to charge? Could'st thou
Permit thy lover to become thy pensioner?

Engine. Her sense will now be tickled till it ache.

Ample. Thy feature and thy wit are wealth enough
To keep thee high in all those vanities
That wild ambition or expensive pride
Perform in youth, but thou invert'st their use.
Thy lover, like the foolish adamant,
The steel, thou fiercely dost allure and draw,
To spend thy virtue, not to get by it.

Lucy. This doctrine, madam, is but new to me.

Ample. How have I liv'd, think'st thou? E'en by my wits.
My guardian's contribution gave us gowns,
But cut from th' curtains of a carrier's bed;
Jewels we wore, but such as potters' wives
Bake in the furnace for their daughters' wrists;
My woman's smocks so coarse as they were spun
O'th' tackling of a ship.

Ginet.   A coat of mail
Quilted with wire was soft sarsnet to 'em.

Ample. Our diet scarce so much as is prescrib'd
To mortify: two eggs of emmets poach'd,
A single bird no bigger than a bee,
Made up a feast.

Ginet.   He had starv'd me but that
The green sickness took away my stomach.

Ample. Thy disease, Ginet, made thee in love with
mortar,
And thou eat'st him up two foot of an old wall.

Engine. A privilege my master only gave
Unto her teeth; none else o'th' house durst do't.

Ample. When, Lucy, I perceiv'd this straiten'd life,
Nature, my steward, I did call t' accompt
And took from her exchequer so much wit
As has maintain'd me since. I led my fine
Trim-bearded males in a small subtle string
Of my soft hair; made 'em to offer up
And bow, and laugh'd at the idolatry.

Ginet. A jewel for a kiss, and that half ravish'd.

Lucy. I feel I am inclin'd t' endeavour in
A calling; madam, I'd be glad to live.

Ample. Know, Luce, this is no hospital for fools.
My bed is yours, but on condition, Luce,
That you redeem the credit of your sex;
That you begin to tempt, and when the snare
Hath caught the fowl, you plume him till you get
More feathers than you lost to Pallatine.

Lucy. I shall not waste my hours in winding silk
Or sheeling peascods with your ladyship.

Ample. Frost on my heart! What, give unto a suitor?
Know, I would fain behold that silly monarch,
Bearded man, that durst woo me with half
So impudent a hope.

Engine.   Madam, you are
Not far from the possession of your wish.
There is no language heard, no business now
In town but what proclaims th' arrival here,
This morn, of th' elder Pallatine, brother
To him you nam'd, and with him such an old
Imperial buskin knight as th' isle ne'er saw.

Ample. What's their design?

Engine.   They will immure themselves
With diamonds, with all refulgent stones
That merit price. Ask 'em who pays? Why, ladies.
They'll feast with rich provincial wines. Who pays?
Ladies. They'll shine in various habit, like
Eternal bridegrooms of the day. Ask 'em
Who pays. Ladies. Lie with those ladies too,
And pay 'em but with issue-male, that shall
Inherit nothing but their wit, and do
The like to ladies when they grow to age.

Lucy. My ears receiv'd a taste of them before.

Ample. Engine, how shall we see them? Bless me, Engine,
With thy kind voice.

Engine.   Though miracles are ceas'd,
This, madam, 's in the power of thought and time.

Ample. I would kiss thee, Engine, but for an odd
Nice humour in my lips—they blister at

Inferior breath. This ring and all my hopes
Are thine. Dear Engine, now project, and live.
   Ginet. I'd lose my wedding to behold these dagonets.
   Ample. My guardian's out of town. Let us triumph
Like Caesars till tomorrow night. Thou know'st
I'm then no more o'th' family. I would,
Like a departing lamp, before I leave
You in the dark, spread in a glorious blaze.
   Engine. Madam, command the keys, the house, and me.
   Ample. Spoke like the bold Cophetua's son.
Let us contrive within to tempt 'em hither.
Follow, my Luce; restore thyself to fame.

                (*Exeunt* Engine, Ample, Ginet.

     'Young Pallatine *beckons* Lucy *from between the*
             hangings as she is going.'

   Young Pall. Luce! Luce!
   Lucy. Death on my eyes, how came you hither?
   Young Pall. I'm, Luce, a kind of peremptory fly
Shifts houses still to follow the sunbeams;
I must needs play in the flames of thy beauty.
   Lucy. You've us'd me with a Christian care, have you
     not?
   Young Pall. Come, I know all. I've been at thy aunt's
     house
And there committed more disorder than
A storm in a ship or a cannon bullet
Shot through a kitchen among shelves of pewter.
   Lucy. This madness is not true, I hope.
   Young Pall.   Yes, faith.
Witness a shower of Malmsey lees, dropp'd from
Thy aunt's own urinal on this new morion.
   Lucy. Why, you have seen her then?
   Young Pall. Yes, and she looks like the old slut of
     Babylon
Thou hast read of. I told her she must die,
And her beloved velvet hood be sold
To some Dutch brewer of Ratcliffe to make
His Yeu Frow slippers.
   Lucy. Speak low! I am depriv'd

By thy rash wine of all atonement now
Unto her after-legacies or love.

Young Pall. My Luce, be magnified! I am all plot.
All stratagem. My brother is in town;
My lady Ample's fame hath caught him, girl.
I'm told he means an instant visit hither.

Lucy. What happiness from this?

Young Pall. As he departs
From hence, I've laid two instruments, Meager
And Pert, that shall encounter his long ears.
With tales less true than those of Troy they shall
Endanger him maugre his active wits,
And mount thee, little Luce, that thou may'st reach
To dandle fate, to soothe them till they give
Us leave to make or alter destinies.

Lucy. You are too loud; whisper your plots within.

(*Exeunt* Young Pallatine *and* Lucy.

[SCENE II]

'*Enter* Engine, Elder Pallatine, Thwack.'

Engine. You call and govern, gentlemen, as if
Your business were above your haste. But know
You where you are?

Elder Pall. Sir Tyrant Thrift dwells here,
The Lady Ample is his ward, she is
Within, and we must see her. No excuses!
She is not old enough to be lock'd up
To 'say new perukes or purge for rheum.

Thwack. Tell her that a young devout knight, made grey
By a charm (t' avoid temptation in others),
Would speak with her.

Engine. I shall deliver you both.
[*Aside*] These tigers hunt their prey with a strange nostril!
Come unsent for so aptly to our wish! (*Exit* Engine.

Elder Pall. But this, Sir Morglay, will not do; in troth
You break our covenants.

Thwack. Why, hear me plead.

N

Elder Pall. From forty to fourscore, the written law
Runs so. This lady's in her nonage yet,
And you to press into my company,
Where visitations are decreed mine own,
Argues a heat that my rebukes must cool.

 Thwack. What should I do? Wouldst have me keep my
  chamber
And mend dark lanthorns, invent steel mattocks
Or weigh gunpowder? Solitude leads me
To nothing less than treason. I shall conspire
To dig and blow up all rather than sit still.

 Elder Pall. Follow your task. You see how early I
Have found this young inheretrix; go seek
The aged out. Bones unto bones! Like cards
Ill pack'd, shuffle yourselves together till
You each dislike the game.

 Thwack.   'Tis the cause I
Come for: a wither'd midwife, or a nurse
Who draws her lips together, like an eye
That gives the cautionary wink, are those
I would find here, so they be rich and fat.

       'Enter Ginet.'

 Ginet. My lady understands your haste, and she
Herself consults now in affairs of haste,
But yet will hastily approach to see
You gentlemen and then in haste return. (*Exit* Ginet.

 Elder Pall. What's this, the superscription of a packet?

 Thwack. Now does my blood wamble. You! Sucket-
  eater!

   'Offers to follow her; [Elder] *Pallatine stays him.'*

 Elder Pall. These covenants, knight, will never be ob-
  serv'd.
I'll sue the forfeiture, leave you so poor
Till for preferment you become an eunuch
And sing a treble in a chantry, knight.

 'Enter [Lady] *Ample, Lucy, Ginet.* Elder Pallatine *and*
  Thwack *address to kiss them and are thrust back.'*

Ample. Stay, gentlemen! Good souls, they have seen, Lucy,
The country turtles bill, and think our lips
I' th' town and court are worn for the same use.

Lucy. Pray, how do the ladies there? Poor villagers,
They churn still, keep their dairies, and lay up
For embroider'd mantles against the heir's birth.

Ample. Who is begot i' th' Christmas holidays.

Elder Pall. Yes, surely, when the spirit of mince-pie
Reigns in the blood.

Ample.   What, penny gleek I hope's
In fashion yet, and the treacherous foot
Not wanting on the table-frame to jog
The husband lest he lose the noble that
Should pay the grocer's man for spice and fruit.

Lucy. The good old butler shares too with his lady
In the box, bating for candles that were burnt
After the clock struck ten.

Thwack.   He doth indeed.
Poor country madams, they're in subjection still;
The beasts their husbands make 'em sit on three-
Legg'd stools, like homely daughters of an hospital,
To knit socks for their cloven feet.

Elder Pall. And when these tyrant husbands too grow old
(As they have still th' impudence to live long),
Good ladies, they are fain to waste the sweet
And pleasant seasons of the day in boiling
Jellies for them and rolling little pills
Of cambric lint to stuff their hollow teeth.

Lucy. And the evenings, warrant ye, they spend
With mother Spectacle the curate's wife,
Who does inveigh 'gainst curling and dyed cheeks,
Heaves her devout impatient nose at oil
Of jessamine, and thinks powder of Paris more
Profane than th' ashes of a Romish martyr.

Ample. And in the days of joy and triumph, sir,
Which come as seldom to them as new gowns,
Then, humble wretches, they do frisk and dance
In narrow parlours to a single fiddle
That squeaks forth tunes like a departing pig.

Lucy. Whilst the mad hinds shake from their feet more
    dirt
Than did the cedar roots that danc'd to Orpheus.
    Ample. Do they not pour their wine too from an ewer
Or small gilt cruse, like orange-water kept
To sprinkle holiday beards?
    Lucy. And when a stranger comes, send seven miles post
By moonshine for another pint?
    Elder Pall. All these indeed are heavy truths, but what
Do you, th' exemplar madams of the town?
Play away your youth, as our hasty gamesters
Their light gold, not with desire to lose it,
But in a fond mistake that it will fit
No other use.
    Thwack. And then reserve your age
As superstitious sinners' ill-got wealth,
Perhaps for th' Church, perhaps for hospitals.
    Elder Pall. If rich you come to court, there learn to be
At charge to teach your paraquitoes French
And then allow them their interpreters,
Lest the sage fowl should lose their wisdom on
Such pages of the presence and the guard
As have not pass'd the seas.
    Thwack.   But if you're poor,
Like wanton monkeys chain'd from fruit,
You feed upon the itch of your own tails.
    Lucy. Rose-vinegar to wash that ruffian's mouth!
    Ample. They come to live here by their wits; let them
use 'em.
    Lucy. They have so few, and those they spend so fast,
They will leave none remaining to maintain them.
    Elder Pall. You shall maintain us, a community
The subtle have decreed of late: you shall
Endow us with your bodies and your goods,
Yet use no manacles call'd dull matrimony
To oblige affection against wise nature,
Where it is lost, perhaps through a disparity
Of years, or justly through distaste of crimes.
    Ample. Most excellent resolves!
    Elder Pall. But if you'll needs marry,

Expect not a single turf for a jointure,
Not so much land as will allow a grasshopper
A salad.

   Thwack. I would no more doubt t' enjoy
You two in all variety of wishes
(Were't not for certain covenants that I lately
Sign'd to in my drink) than I would fear usury
In a small poet or a cast corporal.

   Ample.   You would not.

   Thwack. But look to your old widows;
There my title's good. See they be rich too,
Lest I shall leave their twins upon the parish,
To whom the deputy o' th' ward will deny
Blue coats at Easter, loaves at funerals,
'Cause they were sons of an old country wit.

   Ample. Why all for widows, sir? Can nothing that
Is young affect your mouldy appetite?

   Thwack. No, in sooth; damsels at your years are wont
To talk too much over their marmalade;
They can't fare well but all the town must hear 't.
Their love's so full of praises and so loud,
A man may with less noise lie with a drum.

   Ample. Think you so, sir?

   Thwack. Give me an old widow that commits sin
With the gravity of a corrupt judge,
Accepts of benefits i'th' dark, and can
Conceal them from the light.

                     '*Ample takes* Elder Pallatine *apart.*'

   Ample. Pray, sir, allow me but your ear aside.
Though this rude Clym i'th' Clough presume
In his desires more than his strength can justify,
You should have nobler kindness than to think
All ladies relish of an appetite
Bad as the worst your evil chance hath found.

   Elder Pall. All are alike to me; at least I'll make
Them so, with thin persuasions and a short
Expense of time.

   Ample. Then I have cast away
My sight. My eyes have look'd themselves into
A strong disease; but they shall bleed for it.

Elder Pall. Troth, lady mine, I find small remedy.

Ample. Why came you hither, sir? She that shall sigh
Her easy spirits into wind for you
Must not have hope the kindness of your breath
Will e'er recover her.

Lucy. What do I hear? Hymen defend!
But three good corners to your little heart,
And two already broiling on love's altar?
Does this become her, Ginet? Speak.

Ginet. As age and half a smock would become me.

Thwack. Thou'st caught her, Pallatine, insinuate rogue!

Lucy. Love him? You must recant, or the small god
And I shall quarrel when we meet i'th' clouds.

Thwack. 'Slight, see how she stands. Speak to her.

Elder Pall. Peace, knight. It is apt cunning that we go.
Disdain is like to water pour'd on ice,
Quenches the flame a while to raise it higher.

'Enter Engine.'

Lucy. Engine, show them their way.

Engine. It lies here, gentlemen.

Elder Pall. There needs small summons; we are gone.
But, d'you hear,
We will receive no letters, we, though sent
By th' incorporeal spy your dwarf, or Audrey
Of the chamber, that would deliver them
With as much caution as they were attachments
Upon money newly paid.

Thwack.   Nor no message
From the old widow your mother (if you
Have one), no, though she send for me when she
Is giving up her testy ghost and lies
Half drown'd in rheum, those floods of rheum, in which
Her maids do daily dive to seek the teeth
She cough'd out last.

                    (*Exeunt* Engine, Elder Pallatine, Thwack.

Lucy. 'Las, good old gentleman,
We shall see him shortly in as many nightcaps
As would make sick Mahomet a turban
For the winter.

Ample. Are they gone, Luce?

Lucy. Not like the hours, for they'll return again
Ere long. Oh, you carried your false love rarely!

Ample. How impudent these country fellows are!

Lucy. He thinks you're caught. He has you between 's
  teeth
And intends you for the very next bit
He means to swallow.

Ample. Luce, I have a thousand thoughts
More than a kerchief can keep in. Quick, girl,
Let us consult, and thou shalt find what silly snipes
These witty gentlemen shall prove, and in
Their own confession too, or I'll cry flounders else,
And walk with my petticoat tuck'd up like
A long maid of Almainy. (*Exeunt omnes.*)

[SCENE III]

'*Enter* Young Pallatine, Meager, Pert, *the two last being
new clothed.*'

Young Pall. Don Meager and Don Pert, you neither
  found
These embroider'd skins in your mother's womb;
Surely nature's wardrobe is not thus lac'd.

Pert. We flourish, Pall, by th' charter of thy smiles,
A little magnified with show and thought
Of our new plot.

Meager. The chamber's bravely hung.

Pert. To thy own wish, a bed and canopy
Prepar'd all from our number'd pence. If it
Should fail, Meager and I must creep into
Our quondam rags, a transmigration, Pall,
Which our divinity can ill endure.

Meager. If I have more left to maintain a large stomach
And a long bladder than one comely shilling,
Together with a single ounce of hope,
I am the son of a carman.

Young Pall. Do you suspect my prophecies,
That am your mint, your grand exchequer?

Pert. Pall, no suspicions, Pall; but we that embark
Our whole stock in one vessel would be glad
To have all pirates o'shore and the winds
In a calm humour.

Meager.   How fares th' intelligence?

Young Pall. I left 'em at the Lady Ample's house.
This street they needs must pass if they reach home.

Pert. Oh, I would fain project 'gainst the old knight.
Can we not share him too?

Young Pall.   This wheel must move
Alone. Sir Morglay Thwack's too rugged yet;
He'd interrupt the course. A little more
O'th' file will smooth him fit to be screw'd up.

Pert. Shrink off, Pall; I hear 'em.

'*Enter* Thwack, Elder Pallatine.'

Elder Pall. Thou'st not the art of patient leisure to
Attend the aptitude of things. Wouldst thou
Run on like a rude bull, on every object that
Doth heat the blood? This cunning abstinence
Will make her passions grow more violent.

Thwack. But, Pallatine, I do not find I have
The cruelty or grace to let a lady
Starve for a warm morsel.

'*Pert and* Meager *take the* Elder Pallatine *aside.*'

Young Pall. Now, my fine Pert.

Pert. Sir, we have business for your ear. It may
Concern you much; therefore 'tis fit it be
Particular.

Elder Pall. From whom?

Meager. A young lady, sir.
It is a secret will exact much care
And wisdom i'th' delivery. You should
Dismiss that gentleman.

Elder Pall.   A young lady! Good!
All the best stars i' th' firmament are mine.
[*To* Thwack] Our coach attends us, knight, i'th' bottom of
The hither street; you must go home alone.

Thwack. I'll sooner kill a sergeant, choose my jury
In the city, and be hang'd from a tavern bush.

Elder Pall. Wilt ruin all our destinies hath built?

Thwack. Come, what are those sly silk-worms there that creep
So close into their wool as they would spin
For none but their dear selves? I heard 'em name a lady.

Elder Pall. You heard them say then she was young. And what
Our covenants are, remember.

Thwack.   Young? How young?
She left her wormseed and her coral whistle
But a month since—do they mean so?

Elder Pall. Morglay, our covenants is all I ask.

Thwack. Maybe she hath a mind to me, for there's
A reverend humour in the blood which thou
Ne'er knew'st. Perhaps she would have boys begot
Should be deliver'd with long beards. Till thou
Arrive at my full growth, thou'lt yield the world
Naught above dwarf or page.

Elder Pall. Our covenants still, I cry.

Thwack. Faith, I'll stride my mule tomorrow and away
To th' homely village in the north!

Elder Pall.   Why so?

Thwack. Alas, these silly covenants you know
I seal'd to in my drink, and certain fears
Lurk in a remote corner of my head
That say the game will all be yours.

Elder Pall. But what success canst thou expect, since we've
Not yet enjoy'd the city a full day?

Thwack. I say, let me have woman. Be she young
Or old, grandam or babe, I must have woman.

Elder Pall. Carry but thy patience like a gentleman
And let me singly manage this adventure.
It will tomorrow cancel our old deeds
And leave thee to subscribe to what thy free
Pleasure shall direct.

Thwack.   We'll equally enjoy
Virgin, wife, and widow, the younger kerchief with
The aged hood.

Elder Pall. What I have said, if I had leisure now,
I'd ratify with oaths of thy own choosing.

Thwack. Go, propagate! Fill the shops with thy notch'd
Issue, that when our money's spent we may
Be trusted, break, and cozen in our own tribe.

Elder Pall. Leave me to fortune.

Thwack.   D'you hear, Pallatine,
Perhaps this young lady has a mother.

Elder Pall. No more; goodnight.   (*Exit* Thwack.
I have obey'd you, gentlemen: no ears
Are near us but our own. What's your affair?

Meager. We'll lead you to the lady's mansion, sir;
'Tis hard by.

Elder Pall. Hard by!

Pert. So near that if your lungs be good
You may spit thither. That is the house.

Elder Pall [*Aside*]. These appear gentlemen,
And of some rank. I will in.
                        (*Exeunt* Elder Pallatine, Meager, Pert.

Young Pall. So, so! The hook has caught him by the gills,
And it is fasten'd to a line will hold
You, sir, though your wits were stronger than your purse.
Sir Morglay Thwack's gone home. His lodging I
Have learn'd, and there are certain gins prepar'd
In which his wary feet may chance to be
Ensnar'd though he could wear his eyes upon his toes.
I must follow the game close. He is enter'd,
And ere this amaz'd at the strange complexion
Of the house, but 'twas the best our friendship
And our treasure could procure.   (*Exit* Young Pallatine.

'[*Enter*] Elder Pallatine, Meager, Pert, *with lights*.'

Elder Pall. Gentlemen, if you please, lead me no further.
I have so little faith to believe this
The mansion of a lady that I think
'Tis rather the decays of hell, a sad
Retirement for the fiend to sleep in when
He's sick with drinking sulphur.

Pert. Sir, you shall see this upper room is hung.

Elder Pall. With cobwebs, sir, and those so large they may
Catch and ensnare dragons instead of flies,

Where sit a melancholy race of old
Norman spiders that came in wi' th' Conqueror.

Meager. This chamber will refresh your eyes when you
Have cause to enter it.

> *'Leads him to look in 'tween the hangings.'*

Elder Pall. A bed, and canopy!
There's shew of entertainment there indeed.
There lovers may have place to celebrate
Their warm wishes and not take cold. But, gentlemen,
How comes the rest of this blind house so naked,
So ruinous and deform'd?

Pert. Pray, sir, sit down.
If you have seen aught strange or fit for wonder,
It but declares the hasty shifts to which
The poor distressed lady is expos'd
In pursuit of your love. She hath good fame,
Great dignity and wealth, and would be loth
To cheapen these by making her dull family
Bold witnesses of her desires with you.
Therefore, t' avoid suspicion, to this place
Sh'ath sent part of her neglected wardrobe.

Meager. And will, ere time grows older by an hour,
Gild all this homely furniture at charge
Of her own eyes. Her beams can do it, sir.

Elder Pall. My manners will not suffer me to doubt.

Pert. We hope so too. Besides, though ev'ry one
That hath a heart of 's own may think his pleasure,
We should be loth your thoughts should throw mistakes
On us, that are the humble ministers
Of your kind stars. For sure, though we look not
Like men that make plantation on some isle
That's uninhabited, yet you believe
We would teach sexes mingle, to increase men.

Meager. Squires of the placket we know you think us.

Elder Pall. Excuse my courage, gentlemen! Good faith,
I am not bold enough to think you so.

Pert. Nor will you yet be wooed to such mistake?

Elder Pall. Not all the art nor flattery you have
Can render you to my belief worse than
Myself. Panders and bawds! Good gentlemen,

I shall be angry if you persuade me to
So vile a thought.

    Pert.   Sir, you have cause.
And in good faith, if you should think us such,
We would make bold to cut that slender throat.

    Elder Pall. How, sir?

    Pert. That very throat through which the lusty grape
And sav'ry morsel in the gamester's dish
Steal down so leisurely with kingly gust.

    Meager. Sir, it should be open wide as th' widest oyster
I' th' Venetian lake.

    Elder Pall.   Gentlemen, it should.
It is a throat I can so little hide
In such a cause that I would whet your razor for 't
On my own shoe.

    Pert.   Enough, you shall know all!
This lady hath a noble mind, but 'tis
So much o'ermaster'd by her blood, we fear
Nothing but death, or you, can be her remedy.

    Elder Pall. And she is young?

    Meager. Oh, as the April bud.

    Elder Pall. 'Twere pity, faith, she should be cast away.

    Pert. You have a soft and blessed heart, and to
Prevent so sad a period of her sweet breath,
Ourselves, this house, the habit of this room,
The bed within, and your fair person we
Have all assembled in a trice.

    Elder Pall.   Sure, gentlemen,
In my opinion more could not be done
Were she inheretrix of all the east.

    Pert. But, Sir, the excellence of your pure fame
Hath given us boldness to make suit that if
You can reclaim her appetite with chaste
And wholesome homilies, such counsel as
Befits your known morality, you will
Be pleas'd to save her life and not undo her honour.

    Meager. We hope you will afford her med'cine by
Your meek and holy lectures rather than
From any manly exercise, for such
In troth, sir, you appear to our weak sight.

Elder Pall. Brothers and friends—a style more distant now
Cannot be given—though you were in compass
Thick as the Alps, I must embrace you both.
You've hit the very centre unto which
The toils and comforts of my studies tend.

Pert. Alas, we drew our arrow but by aim.

Elder Pall. Why, gentlemen, I have converted more
Than ever gold or Aretine misled.
I've disciples of all degrees in nature,
From your little punk in purple to your
Tall canvas girl; from your satin slipper
To your iron patten and your Norway shoe.

Pert. And can you mollify the mother, sir,
In a strong fit?

Elder Pall.   Sure, gentlemen, I can,
If books penn'd with a clean and wholesome spirit
Have any might to edify. Would they
Were here.

Meager. What, sir?

Elder Pall.   A small library,
Which I am wont to make companion to
My idle hours, where some, I take it, are
A little consonant unto this theme.

Pert. Have they not names?

*Elder Pall. A Pill to Purge Phlebotomy, A Balsamum
For the Spiritual Back, A Lozenge Against Lust,*
With divers others, sir, which, though not penn'd
By dull platonic Greeks or Memphian priests,
Yet have the blessed marks of separation,
Of authors silenc'd for wearing short hair.

Pert. But, sir, if this chaste means cannot restore
Her to her health and quiet peace, I hope
You will vouchsafe your lodging in yon bed
And take a little pains—.   *'Points to the bed within.'*

Elder Pall. Faith, gentlemen, I was
Not bred on Scythian rocks; tigers and wolves
I've heard of, but ne'er suck'd their milk; and sure
Much would be done to save a lady's longing.

Meager. 'Tis late, sir; pray uncase.
                        'They help to unclothe him.'

Pert. Your boot—believe 't, it is my exercise.

Elder Pall. Well, 'tis your turn to labour now and mine
Anon—for your dear sakes, gentlemen, I profess—

Pert. My friend shall wait upon you to your sheets,
Whilst I go and conduct the lady hither;
Whom if your holy doctrine cannot well
Reclaim, pray hazard not her life. You have
A body, sir.

Elder Pall. Oh, think me not cruel.

(*Exeunt* Meager, Elder Pallatine.

'*Enter* Young Pallatine.'

Pert. Pall! Come in, Pall.

Young Pall.   Is he in bed?

Pert.   Not yet,
But stripping in more haste than an old snake
That hopes for a new skin.

Young Pall.   If we could laugh
In our coffin, Pert, this would be a jest
Long after death. He is so eager in
His witty hopes that he suspects nothing.

Pert. Oh, all he swallows, sir, is melting conserve
And soft Indian plum.

'*Enter* Meager.'

                        Meager, what news?

Meager. Laid! Gently laid! He is all virgin, sure,
From the crown of 's head to his very navel.

Young Pall. Where are his breeches? Speak! His hat-
    band too;
'Tis of grand price; the stones are roseal and
Of the white rock.

Meager.   I hung 'em purposely
Aside; they're all within my reach. Shall I in?

Young Pall. Soft! Softly, my false fiend. Remember,
    rogue,
You tread on glasses, eggs, and gouty toes!

        '*Meager takes out his hat and breeches. The pockets
        and hatband rifled, they throw 'em in again.*'

Meager. Hold, Pall! Th' exchequer is thine own; we will
Divide when thou art gracious and well pleas'd.

Young Pall. All gold! The stalls of Lombard Street
    pour'd into a purse!

Pert. These, dear Pall, are thy brother's goodly herds.

Young Pall. Yes, and his proud flocks; but you see what
    they
Come to? A little room contains them all
At last. So, so, convey them in again.
Because he is my elder brother,
My mother's maidenhead and a country wit,
He shall not be expos'd to bare thighs and a
Bald crown. What noise is that?

                    'Knocking within; Pert *looks at door.'*

Pert. Death! There's old Snore
The constable, his wife, a regiment of halberds
And Mistress Queasy too, the landlady
That owns this house.

Meager.   Belike they've heard our friend
The bawd fled hence last night, and now they come
To seize on moveables for rent.

Young Pall. The bed within and the hangings that we
    hir'd
To furnish our design are all condemn'd;
My brother, too. They'll use him with as thin
Remorse as an old gamester would an alderman's heir.

Pert. No matter, our adventure's paid. Follow,
Pall, and I'll lead you a back way, where you
Shall climb o'er tiles like cats when they make love.

Young Pall. Now I shall laugh at those that heap up
    wealth
By lazy method and slow rules of thrift.
I'm grown the child of wit and can advance
Myself by being votary to chance.   (*Exeunt omnes.*

ACT III · SCENE I

'*Enter* Snore, Mistress Snore, Queasy, *and* Watchmen.'

Mistress Snore. Days o' my breath, I have not seen the
like.
What would you have my husband do? 'Tis past
One by Bow, and the bellman has gone twice.
Queasy. Good Master Snore, you are the constable;
You may do it, as they say, be it right or wrong.
'Tis four years' rent come Childermas eve next.
Snore. You see, neighbour Queasy, the doors are open;
Here's no goods, no bawd left; I'ld see the bawd.
Mist. Snore. Ay, or the whores. My husband's the king's
officer
And still takes care, I warrant ye, of bawds
And whores. Show him but a whore at this time
O' night, good man, you bring [him] abed i'faith.
Queasy. I pray, Mistress Snore, let him search the parish;
They are not gone far. I must have my rent.
I hope there are whores and bawds in the parish.
Mist. Snore. Search now? It is too late. A woman had
As good marry a colestaff as a constable,
If he must nothing but search and search, follow
His whores and bawds all day and never comfort
His wife at night. I prithee, lamb, let us to bed.
Snore. It must be late, for gossip Nock the nailman
Had catechized his maids and sung three catches
And a song ere we set forth.
Queasy. Good Mistress Snore, forbear your husband but
Tonight, and let the search go on.
Mist. Snore. I will not forbear. You might ha' let your
house
To honest women, not to bawds. Fie upon you!
Queasy. Fie upon me! 'Tis well known I'm the mother
Of children. Scurvy fleak! 'Tis not for naught
You boil eggs in your gruel. And your man Sampson
Owes my son-in-law the surgeon ten groats
For turpentine, which you have promis'd to pay
Out of his Christmas box.

Mist. Snore.   I defy thee.
Remember thy first calling: thou set'st up
With a peck of damsons and a new sieve
When thou brok'st at Dowgate corner 'cause the boys
Flung down thy ware.
    Snore. Keep the peace, wife, keep the peace!
    Mist. Snore. I will not peace. She took my silver thimble
To pawn when I was a maid. I paid her
A penny a month use.
    Queasy.   A maid? Yes, sure,
By that token goody Tongue the midwife
Had a dozen napkins o' your mother's best
Diaper to keep silence, when she said
She left you at St. Peter's fair, where you
Long'd for pig.
    Snore.   Neighbour Queasy, this was not
In my time. What my wife hath done since I
Was constable and the king's officer
I'll answer. Therefore, I say, keep the peace.
And when we've search'd the two back rooms, I'll to bed.
Peace, wife, not a word.
    (*Exeunt* Snore, Mistress Snore, Queasy, *and* Watchmen.)

'*Enter* Elder Pallatine *clothing himself in haste.*'

    Elder Pall. 'Tis time to get on wings and fly.
Here's a noise of thunder, wolves, women, drums,
All that's confus'd and frights the ear. I heard
Them cry out bawds. The sweet young lady is
Surpris'd, sure, by the nice slave her husband
Or some old frosty matron of near kin,
And the good gentlemen sh' employ'd to me
Are tortur'd and call'd bawds. If I am ta'en,
I'll swear I purpos'd her conversion.

'*Enter* Snore, Mistress Snore, Queasy, *and* Watchmen.'

    Snore. Here's a room hung and a fair bed within.
I take it there's the he-bawd too.
    Queasy. Seize on the lewd thing!
I pray, Master Snore, seize on the goods too.
    Mist. Snore. Who would not be a bawd? They've
      proper men

To their husbands, and she maintains him
Like any parish deputy.
    Elder Pall.   What are you?
    Snore. I am the constable.
    Elder Pall.   Good. The constable.
I begin to stroke my long ears, and find
I am an ass! Such a dull ass as deserves
Thistles for provender, and sawdust too,
Instead of grains. Oh, I am finely gull'd!
    Mist. Snore. Truly as proper a bawd as a woman
Would desire to use!
    Elder Pall.   Master Constable,
Though these your squires o' th' blade and bill seem to
Be courteous gentlemen and well taught, yet
I would know why they embrace me.
    Snore. You owe my neighbour, Mistress Queasy, four
        years' rent.
    Queasy. Yes, and for three bed ticks and a brass pot,
Which your wife promis'd me to pay this term,
For now, she said, sh' expects her country customers.
    Elder Pall. My wife! Have I been led to th' altar
        too
By some doughty deacon, ta'en woman by
The pretty thumb, and given her a ring
With my dear self for better and for worse,
And all in a forgotten dream? But for whom
Do you take me?
    Snore.   For the he-bawd.
    Elder Pall. Good faith, you may as soon
Take me for a whale, which is something rare,
You know, o' this side the bridge.
    Mist. Snore.   'Tis indeed!
Yet our Paul was in the belly of one,
In my Lord Mayor's show; and, husband, you remember,
He beckon'd you, out o' the fish's mouth,
And you gave him a pippin, for the poor soul
Had like t' have chok'd for very thirst.
    Elder Pall. I saw it, and cried out
O' th' city, 'cause they would not be at charge
To let the fish swim in a deeper sea.

Mist. Snore. Indeed; why, I was but a tiny girl then.
I pray, how long have you been a bawd here?
  Elder Pall. Again! How the devil
Am I chang'd since my own glass render'd me
A gentleman. Well, Master Constable,
Though ev'ry stall's your worship's wooden throne,
Here you are humble, and o' foot. Therefore,
I will put on my hat; pray reach it me.
                            '*Misses his diamond hatband.*'
Death! My hatband! A row of diamonds
Worth a thousand marks! Nay, it is time then
To doubt, and tremble too. My gold, my gold!
                                 '*Searches his pockets.*'
And precious stones!
  Mist. Snore. Do you suspect my husband?
He hath no need o' your stones, I praise heaven.
  Elder Pall. A plague upon your courteous midnight
    leaders!
Good silly saints, they are dividing now
And minist'ring, no doubt, unto the poor!
This will decline the reputation of
My wit till I be thought to have a less head
Than a Justice o' peace. If Morglay hear 't,
He'll think me dull as a Dutch mariner!
No medicine now from thought? Good! 'Tis design'd!
  Snore. Come along, 'tis late.
  Elder Pall. Whither must I go?
  Queasy. To the counter, sir, unless my rent be paid.
  Snore. And for being a bawd.
  Elder Pall. Confin'd in wainscot walls too,
Like a liquorish rat, for nibbling
Unlawfully upon forbidden cheese:
This to the other sauce is aloes and myrrh.
But, Master Constable, do you behold this ring?
It is worth all the bells in your church steeple,
Though your sexton and side-men hung there too
To better the peal.
  Snore.   Well, what's your request?
  Elder Pall. Marry, that you will let me go to fetch
The bawd, the very bawd, that owes this rent;

Who being brought, you shall restore my ring
And believe me to be an arrant gentleman,
Such as in 's scutcheon gives horns, hounds, and hawks,
Hunting nags, with tall eaters in blue coats,
Sans number.
 Queasy. Pray let him go, Master Snore.
We'll stay and keep the goods.
 Mist. Snore. Yes, let him, husband,
For I would fain see a very he-bawd.
 Snore. Come, neighbours, light him out! (*Exeunt omnes.*

[SCENE II]

'*Enter* Young Pallatine, [Lady] Ample, Pert, Lucy,
Ginet, Engine, *with lights.*'

 Ample. A forest full of palms thy lover, Luce,
Merits in garlands for his victory.
I'm wild with joy! Why, there was wit enough
In this design to bring a ship o' fools
To shore again and make them all good pilots.
 Young Pall. Madam, this gentleman deserves to share
In your kind praise. He was a merry agent
In the whole plot, and would exalt himself
To your ladyship's service—if you please,
For my humble sake, unto your lips too! '*Pert salutes her.*'
 Ample. Sir, you are friend to Pallatine,
And that entitles you unto much worth.
 Pert. The title will be better'd, madam, when
I am become a servant to your beauty.
 Lucy. Why, your confederate Pert is courtly too;
He will out-tongue a favourite of France.
But didst thou leave thy brother surfeiting
On lewd hopes?
 Young Pall. He believes all womankind
Dress'd and ordain'd for th' mercy of his tooth.
 Ample. And now lies stretch'd in his smooth slippery
   sheets!
 Young Pall. Oh, like a wanton snake on camomile,
And rifled to so sad remains of wealth,

That if his resolution still disdain
Supplement from his lands, and he resolve
To live here by his wits, he will ere long
Betroth himself to raddish-women for
Their roots, pledge children in their sucking bottles,
And in dark winter mornings rob small schoolboys
Of their honey and their bread.

 Pert. Faith, Meager and I us'd him with as much
Remorse as our occasions could allow.
'Las, he must think we shreds of time
Have our occasions too.

 Young Pall. What, madam, need he care?
For let him but prove kind unto his bulls,
Bring them their heifers when their crests are high,
Stroke his fair ewes and pimp a little
His rams, they straight will multiply; and then
The next great fair prepares him fit again
For th' city's view and our surprise.

 Ample. Why, this young gentleman hath relish in't!
Yet when you understand the dark and deep
Contrivements which myself, Engine, and Luce
Have laid for this great witty villager,
To whom you bow as foremost of your blood,
You will degrade yourselves from all prerogatives
Above our sex, and all those pretty marks
Of manhood (your trim beards) singe off with tapers,
As a just sacrifice to our supremacy.

 Lucy. If Sir Tyrant Thrift, your phlegmatic guardian,
Leave but this mansion ours till the next sun,
We'll make your haughty brother tremble at
The name of woman, and blush behind a fan
Like a yawning bride that hath foul teeth.

 Engine. Madam, 'tis time you were abed, for sure, besides
The earnest invitation which I left
Writ in his chamber, these afflictions will
Disturb his rest and bring him early hither
To recover his sick hopes.

'*Enter* Meager.'

 Young Pall. Meager! What news? Madam, the homage of

Your lip again—a man o' war, believe 't,
One that hath fasted in the face of 's foe,
Seen Spinola entrench'd, sometimes hath spread
His butter at the States' charge, sometimes, too,
Fed on a salad that hath grown upon
The enemy's own land, but, pardon me,
Without or oil or vinegar.

Ample. Sir, men in choler may do anything.

Meager. Your ladyship will excuse his new plenty;
It hath made him pleasant.

    Young Pall. Meager, what news? How do our spies
        prosper?

Meager. Sir, rare discoveries! I've trac'd your brother;
You shall hear more anon.

Ginet. Your ladyship forgets how early your
Designs will waken you.

Engine.   Madam, I'd fain be
Bold, too, to hasten you unto your rest.

Ample. 'Tis late indeed. The silence of the night
And sleep be with you, gentlemen.

          (*Exeunt* Lady Ample, Ginet, Engine.

    Young Pall. Madam, goodnight. But our heads never were
Ordain'd to so much trivial leisure as
To sleep: you may as soon entreat
A sexton sleep in 's belfry when the plague reigns,
An aged sinner in a tempest, or
A jealous statesman when his prince is dying.

Lucy. Pray dismiss your friends; I would speak with you.

Young Pall. Men o' the puissant pike, follow the lights.

          (*Exeunt* Meager, Pert.

Lucy. You are as good natur'd to me, Pall,
As the wife of a silenc'd minister
Is to a monarchy or to lewd gallants
That have lost a nose.

Young Pall.   And why so, dame Luce?

Lucy. So many yellow images at once
Assembled in your fist, and jewels too
Of goodly price, all this free booty got
In lawful war, and I no tribute, Pall?

    Young Pall. What need it, Luce? A virgin may live cheap;

They'r maintain'd with as small charge as a wren
With maggots in a cheesemonger's shop.

 Lucy. Well, Pall, and yet you know all my extremes:
How for a little taffeta to line
A mask I'm fain to mollify my mercer
With a soft whisper and a tim'rous blush;
To sigh unto my milliner for gloves,
That they may trust, and not complain unto my aunt,
Who is as jealous of me as their wives—and all
Through your demeanour, Pall, whose kindness, I
Perceive, will raise me to such dignity
That I must teach children in a dark cellar,
Or work coifs in a garret for crack'd groats
And broken meat!

 Young Pall. Luce, I will give thee, Luce, to buy—
 Lucy. What, Pall?
 Young Pall. An ounce of ars'nic to mix in thy aunt's
  caudles.
This aunt I must see cold and grinning, Luce,
Seal'd t' her last wink, as if she clos'd her eyes
T'avoid the sight of feathers, coaches, and short cloaks.

 Lucy. How many angels of your family
Are there in heaven? But few I fear; and how
You'll be the first that shall entitle them
To such high calling is to me a doubt.

 Young Pall. Why is there never a pew there, Luce, but for
Your coughing aunt and you?

 Lucy. Hadst thou eyes like flaming beacons, crooked
  horns,
A tail three yards long, and thy feet cloven,
Thou couldst not be more a fiend than thou art now;
But to advance thy sins with being hard
And costive unto me!

 Young Pall. You lie, Luce, you lie! '*Flings her a purse.*'
There's gold! The fairies are thy mint-men, girl.
Of this thou shalt have store enough to make
The hungry academics mention thee
In evening lectures with applause and prayer.
A foundress thou shalt be.

 Lucy.   Of hospitals

For your decayed self, Meager, and Pert,
Those wealthy usurers, your poor friends.
  Young Pall. A nunn'ry, Luce, where all the female issue
Of our decay'd nobility shall live
Thy pensioners. It will preserve them from
Such want as makes them quarter arms with th' city
And match with saucy haberdashers' sons,
Whose fathers liv'd in alleys and dark lanes.
  Lucy. Goodnight, Pall. Your gold I'll lay up, though but
T'encounter the next surgeon's bill. Yet know
Our wits are ploughing too, and in a ground
That yields as fair a grain as this.
  Young Pall. Farewell, and let me hear thy aunt is stuck
With more bayleaves and rosemary than a
Westphalia gammon.   (*Exeunt* Lucy *and* Young Pallatine.

[SCENE III]

'*Enter* Elder Pallatine *and* Thwack, *dressing himself*.'

  Elder Pall. Quick, dispatch, knight! Thou art as tedious in
Thy dressing as a court bride: two ships might
Be rigg'd for the Straits in less space than thou
Careen'st that same old hulk. Can it be thought
That one so fill'd with hope and wise designs
Could be subdued with sleep? What, dull and drowsy?
Keep earlier hours than a roost hen in winter?
  Thwack. Pallatine, the design grew all dream, magic
And alchemy to me. I gave it lost,
Clove to my soft pillow like a warm Justice,
And slept there with less noise than a dead lawyer
In a monument.
  Elder Pall. This is the house. Dispatch, that I may knock.
  Thwack. 'Slight, stay. Thou think'st I've the dexterity
Of a spaniel, that with a yawn, a scratch
On his left ear and stretching his hind legs
Is ready for all day. Oh, for the Biscay sleeve
And Boulogne hose I wore when I was shrieve
In '88.

Elder Pall.   Faith, thou art comely, knight!
And I already see the town girls melt
And thaw before thee.
   Thwack.   We must be content.
Thou know'st all men are bound to wear their limbs
I' th' same skin that nature bestows upon them,
Be it rough or be it smooth. For my part,
If she to whom you lead me now like not
The grain of mine, I will not flay myself
T' humour the touch of her ladyship's fingers.
   Elder Pall. Well, I had thought t' have carried it with
      youth,
But when I came to greet her beauties with
The eyes of love and wonder, she despis'd me,
Rebuk'd those haughty squires, her servants, that
Conveyed me thither in mistake, and cried
She meant the more authentic gentleman,
The reverend monsieur, she.
   Thwack.   The reverend monsieur?
Why, does she take me for a French dean?
   Elder Pall. Her confessor at least: her secrets are
Thine own; but by what charms attain'd
Let him determine that has read Agrippa.
   Thwack. Charms? Yes, sir, if this be a charm—or this—
Or here again—t' advance th' activity   *'Leaps and frisks.'*
Of a poor old back.
   Elder Pall.   No ape, Sir Morglay,
After a year's obedience to the whip,
Is better qualified.
   Thwack.   Limber and sound, sir.
Besides, I sing *Little Musgrove*, and then
For *The Chevy Chase* no lark comes near me.
If she be ta'en with these, why, at her peril be't.
   Elder Pall. Come, sir, dispatch. I'll knock, for here's the
      house.
   Thwack. Stay, stay. This lane, sure, has no great renown.
The house, too, if the moon reveal 't aright,
May for its small magnificence be left,
For aught we know, out of the city map.
   Elder Pall. Therein consists the miracle; and when

The doors shall ope, and thou behold how lean
And ragged ev'ry room appears, till thou
Hast reach'd the sphere where she, illustrious, moves,
Thy wonder will be more perplex'd. For know
This mansion is not hers, but a conceal'd
Retirement, which her wisdom safely chose
To hide her loose love.

 Thwack. Give me a baggage that has brains! But, Pallatine,
Did not I at first persuade thee those two
Trim gentlemen, her squires, might happily
Mistake the person unto whom the message was
Dispos'd, and that myself was he?

 Elder Pall. Thou didst, and thou hast got, knight, by this hand,
I think, the Mogul's niece, she cannot be
Of less descent; the height and strangeness of
Her port denote her foreign, and of great blood.

 Thwack. What should the Mogul's niece do here?

 Elder Pall. 'Las, thy ears are buried in a woolsack;
Thou hear'st no news. 'Tis all the voice in court
That she is sent hither in disguise, to learn
To play on the guitar and make almond-butter.
But whether this great lady that I bring
Thee to be she is yet not quite confirm'd.

 Thwack. Thou talk'st o'th' high and strange comportment
Thou found'st her in.

 Elder Pall. Right, sir! She sat on a rich Persian quilt,
Threading a carcanet of pure round pearl.
Bigger than pigeon's eggs.

 Thwack.   Those I will sell.

 Elder Pall. Her maids, with little rods of rosemary
And stalks of lavender, were brushing ermines' skins.

 Thwack. Furs for the winter! I'll line my breeches with them.

 Elder Pall. Her young smooth pages lay round at her feet,
Cloth'd like the Sophy's sons, and all at dice;
The caster six wedges a cubit long,
Cries one; another comes a tun of pisotets,
And then is cover'd with an argosy
Laden with indigo and cochineal.

Thwack. This must be the great Mogul's niece.

Elder Pall. As for her grooms, they all were planted on
Their knees, carousing their great lady's health
In perfum'd wines, and then straight qualified
Their wild voluptuous heats with cool sherbet,
The Turks' own julep.

Thwack. Knock, Pallatine!
Quick, rogue! I cannot hold. Little thought I
The Thwacks of the north should inoculate
With the Moguls of the south. '*Pallatine knocks.*'

'*Enter* Snore.'

Elder Pall. Speak softly, Master Constable; I've brought
The very he-bawd.

Snore. Blessing on your heart, sir!
My watch are above at Tray-trip for a
Black-pudding and a pound o' Suffolk cheese.
They'll ha' done straight. Pray fetch him to me.
I'll call them down, and lead him to a by-room.

Thwack. Pallatine, what's he?

Elder Pall. The lady's steward, sir,
A sage philosopher, and a grave pander,
One that hath writ bawdy sonnets in Hebrew,
And those so well that if the Rabbins were
Alive, 'tis thought he would corrupt their wives.
Follow me, knight!—

Thwack. Pallatine,
Half the large treasure that I get is yours.

Elder Pall. Good faith, my friend, when you are once
    possess'd
Of all, 'tis as your conscience will vouchsafe.

Thwack. Dost thou suspect? I'll stay here till thou fetch
A bible and a cushion, and swear kneeling.

Elder Pall. My faith shall rather cozen me. Walk in
With this philosopher. No words, for he's
A Pythagorean and professes silence.
My ring, Master Constable.
        '*Snore gives him his ring, then exit with* Thwack.'
Here yet my reputation's safe. Should he
Have heard of my mischance, and not accompanied

With this defeat upon himself, his mirth
And tyranny had been 'bove human sufferance.
Now for the Lady Ample. She, I guess,
Looks on me with strong fervent eyes. She's rich,
And could I work her into profit, 'twould
Procure my wit immortal memory.
But to be gull'd, and by such trifles too,
Dull, humble gentlemen that ne'er drunk wine
But on some coronation day, when each
Conduit pisses claret at the town charge!—
Well, though 'tis worse than steel or marble to
Digest, yet I have learn'd, one stop in a
Career taints not a rider with disgrace,
But may procure him breath to win the race.

(*Exit* Elder Pallatine.

ACT IV · SCENE I

'*Enter* Young Pallatine, Engine, Meager, Pert,
Pallatine *richly clothed*.'

Engine. Your brother's in the house. The letter which
I sent to tempt him hither wrought above
The reach of our desires. My lady, sir,
He does believe is sick to death, and all
In languishment for his dear love.
    Young Pall. Pert and Meager, though you have both
    good faces,
They must not be seen here. There is below
A brother o' mine, whom I take it, you
Have us'd not overtenderly.
    Meager. 'Slight, he must needs remember us.
    Pert. We'll sooner stay t' outface a basilisk.
Whither shall we go?
    Young Pall. To Snore the constable. Morglay is still
A pris'ner in his house. Take order for's
Release, as I projected, but, d'you hear,
He must not free him till I come.

Pert. Pall, will the dull ruler of the night, Pall,
Obey thy edict?

Young Pall. His wife will, and she's his constable.
Name me but to her, and she does homage.

Meager. Enough, we will attend thee there.

Engine. This way, gentlemen.

> (*Exeunt* Engine, Pert, Meager.

'*Enter* Elder Pallatine.'

Elder Pall. What 's this, an apparition, a ghost embroider'd?
Sure he has got the devil for his tailor.

Young Pall. Good morrow, brother, 'morrow!

Elder Pall. You are in glory, sir; I like this flourishing.
The lily, too, looks handsome for a month,
But you, I hope, will last out the whole year.

Young Pall. What flourishing? Oh, sir, belike you mean
My clothes. They're rags, coarse homely rags, believ't.
Yet they will serve for the winter, sir, when I
Ride post in Sussex ways.

Elder Pall. This gaiety denotes
Some solitary treasure in the pocket,
And so you may become a lender too.
You know I'm far from home.

Young Pall. I'll lend nothing but good counsel and wit.

Elder Pall. Why, sure, you have no factors, sir, in Delph,
Leghorn, Aleppo or th' Venetian isles,
That by their traffic can advance you thus,
Nor do you trade i'th' city by retail
In our small wares. All that you get by law
Is but a doleful execution
After arrest; and for your power in court,
I know, your stockings being on, you are
Admitted in the presence.

Young Pall. What does this infer, brother?
Men of design are chary of their minutes;
Be quick and subtle.

Elder Pall. The inf'rence is
You prosper by my documents, and what
You have achiev'd must be by your good wits.

Young Pall. If you had had a sibyl to your nurse,
You could not, sir, have aim'd nearer the truth.
I saw your ears and bags were shut to all
Intents of bounty; therefore was enforc'd
Into this way; and 'twas at first somewhat
Against my conscience too.

 Elder Pall.   If not to vex
The zealous spirit in you, I would know why.

 Young Pall. Good faith, I've search'd records and cannot
  find
That *Magna Charta* does allow a subject
To live by his wits; there is no statute for 't.

 Elder Pall. Your common lawyer was no antiquary.

 Young Pall. And then, credit me, sir, the canons of
The Church authorize no such thing.

 Elder Pall. You have met with a dull civilian too.

 Young Pall. Yet, brother, these impediments cannot
Choke up my way. I must still on.

 Elder Pall. And you believe the stories of young heirs
Enforc'd to sign at midnight to appease
The sword-man's wrath may be outdone by you.

 Young Pall. I were unkind else to my own good parts.

 Elder Pall. And that your wit has power to tempt from the
Severe grave bench the aldermen themselves,
To rifle where you please for scarfs, feathers,
And for race nags.

 Young Pall.   It is believ'd, sir, in a trice.

 Elder Pall. And that your wit can lead our rev'rend
  matrons
And testy widows of fourscore to seal
(And in their smocks) for frail commodities
To elevate your punk?

 Young Pall.   All this, sir, is so easy,
My faith would swallow 't though 't had a sore throat.

 Elder Pall. Give me thy hand! This day I'll cut off the
  entail
Of all my lands and disinherit thee.

 Young Pall. Will you, sir? I thank ye.

 Elder Pall. But mark me, brother, for there's justice in 't
Admits of no reproof: what should you do

With land, that have a portion in your brain
Above all legacies or heritage?

   Young Pall. I conceive you.

   Elder Pall. Oh, to live here, i'th' fair metropolis
Of our great isle, a free inheritor
Of ev'ry modest or voluptuous wish
Thy young desires can breathe, and not oblig'd
To th' ploughman's toils or lazy reaper's sweat;
To make the world thy farm, and ev'ry man
Less witty than thyself tenant for life!
These are the glories that proclaim a true
Philosophy and soul in him that climbs
To reach them with neglect of fame and life.

   Young Pall. [*Aside*]. He carries it bravely, as he had felt
Nothing that fits his own remorse.—But know,
Sir Eagle, th' higher that you fly, the less
You will appear to us dim-sighted fowl
That flutter here below. Brother, farewell!
They say the lady of this house groans for
Your love. The tame sick fool is rich; let not
Your pride beguile your profit!   (*Exit* Young Pallatine.

   Elder Pall. I suspect him. Not all the skill I have
In reason or in nature can pronounce
Him free from the defeat upon my gold
And jewels. 'Twas like a brother! But for
His two confederates, though I should meet
Them in a mist darker than night or southern fens
Produce, my eyes would be so courteous, sure,
To let me know them.

     '*Enter* [Lady] Ample, *carried in as sick in a couch*,
              Lucy, Engine, Ginet.'

   Engine. Room! More air! If heav'nly ministers
Have leisure to consider or assist
The best of ladies, let them show it now.

   Lucy. How do you, madam? Oh, I shall lose
The chief example of eternal love,
Of gentle grace and feature, that the world
Did ever show to dignify our sex!

Engine [*Aside*]. Work on! I must stand sentinel beneath.

                        (*Exit* Engine.

   Elder Pall. [*Aside*]. Is her disease grown up to such
     extremity?
Then it is time I seem to suffer too,
Or else my hopes will prove sicker than she.
   Lucy. More cruel than the panther on his prey!
Why speak you not? No comfort from your lips?
You, sir, that are the cause of this sad hour!
   Ginet. He stands as if his legs had taken root,
A very mandrake!
   Elder Pall. How comes it, lady, all these beauties, that
But yesterday did seem to teach
The spring to flourish and rejoice, so soon
Are wither'd from our sight?
   Ample. It is in vain t'enquire the reason of
That grief whose remedy is past. Had you
But felt so much remorse or softness in
Your heart as would have made you nobly just
And pitiful, the mourners of this day
Had wanted then their dead to weep upon.
   Elder Pall. Am I the cause? Forbid it, gentle heaven!
The virgins of our land, when this is told,
Will raze the monumental building where
My buried flesh shall dwell, and throw my dust
Before the sportive winds till I am blown
About in parcels less than eyesight can
Discern.
   Lucy. She listens to you, sir.
   Elder Pall. If I am guilty of neglect,
Give me a taste of duty, name how far
I shall submit to love. The mind hath no
Disease above recovery if we
Have courage to remove despair.
   Ample. O sir, the pride and scorns with which you
     first
Did entertain my passions and regard
Have worn my easy heart away. My breast
Is emptier than my eyes, that have distill'd
Their balls to funeral dew. It is too late.

Lucy. Ginet, my fears have in them too much prophecy;
I told thee she would ne'er recover.

Ginet. For my poor part, I wish no easier bed
At night than the cold grave where she must lie.

Ample. Luce, Luce, entreat the gentleman to sit.

Lucy. Sit near her, sir. You hear her voice grows weak.

Ample. That you may see your scorns could not persuade
My love to thoughts of anger or revenge,
The faint remainder of my breath I'll waste
In legacies—and, sir, to you. You shall
Have all the laws will suffer me to give.

Elder Pall. Who, I? Sweet saint, take heed of your last
    deeds!
Your bounty carries cunning murder in't:
I shall be kill'd with kindness, and depart
Weeping, like a fond infant, whom the nurse
Would soothe too early to his bed.

Lucy. Nay, sir, no remedy, you must have all;
Though you procur'd her death, the world shall not
Report she died beholding to you.

Ginet. Go to her, sir; she'd speak with you again.

Ample. Sir, if mine eyes in all their health and glory
Had not the power to warm you into love,
Where are my hopes now they are dim, and have
Almost forgot the benefit of light?

Elder Pall. Not love! Lady! Queen of my heart! What
    oaths
Or execrations can persuade your faith
From such a cruel jealousy?

Ample. I'd have some testimony, sir; if but
T' assure the world my love and bounty at
My death were both conferr'd on one that show'd
So much requital as declares he was
Of gentle humane race.

Elder Pall. What shall I do?
Prescribe me dangers now, horrid as those
Which midnight fires beget in cities overgrown,
Or winter storms produce at sea, and try
How far my love will make me venture to
Augment th' esteem of yours.

Ample. That trial of your love which I request
Implies no danger, sir. 'Tis not in me
T' urge anything but what your own desires
Would choose.

Elder Pall. Name it! Like eager mastiffs chain'd
From the encounter of their game, my hot
Fierce appetite diminisheth my strength.

Ample. 'Tis only this: for fear some other should
Enjoy you when I'm cold in my last sleep,
I would entreat you to sit here, grow sick,
Languish, and die with me.

Elder Pall. How! Die with you!   '*Takes* Lucy *aside.*'
'Twere fit you hasten'd her to write down all
She can bestow, and in some form of law:
I fear she's mad. Her senses are so lost,
She'll never find them to her use again.

Lucy. I pray, sir, why?

Elder Pall. Did you not hear what a fantastic suit
She makes, that I would sit and die with her?

Lucy. Does this request seem strange? You will do
little
For a lady, that deny to bring her
Onward her last journey. Or is't your thrift?
Alas, you know, souls travel without charge.

Elder Pall. [*Aside*]. Her little skull is tainted too.

Ample. Is he not willing, Luce?

Elder Pall. My best dear lady, I am willing to
Resign myself to anything but death.
Do not suspect my kindness now. In troth
I've business upon earth will hold me here
At least a score or two of years. But when
That's done, I am content to follow you.

Ample. If this persuasion cannot reach at your
Consent, yet let me witness so much love
In you as may enforce you languish and
Decay, for my departure from your sight.

Lucy. Can you do less than languish for her death?
Sit down here and begin. True sorrow, sir,
If you have any in your breast, will quickly
Bring you low enough.

Elder Pall. Alas, good ladies, do you think my languish-
  ment
And grief is to begin upon me now?
Heaven knows how I have pin'd and groan'd since first
Your letter gave me knowledge of the cause.

 Lucy. It is not seen, sir, in your face.

 Elder Pall. My face I grant you: I bate inwardly.
I'm scorch'd and dried with sighing to a mummy.
My heart and liver are not big enough
To choke a daw. A lamb laid on the altar for
A sacrifice hath much more entrails in 't.

 Lucy. Yet still your sorrow alters not your face?

 Elder Pall. Why no, I say. No man that ever was
Of nature's making hath a face moulded
With less help for hypocrisy than mine.

 Ginet. Great pity, sir!

 Elder Pall. Though I endur'd the diet and the flux;
Lay seven days buried up to th' lips like a
Diseas'd sad Indian in warm sand, whilst his
Afflicted female wipes his salt foam off
With her own hair, feeds him with buds of guacum
For his salad and pulp of salsa for
His bread; I say, all this endur'd would not
Concern my face. Nothing can decline that.

 Ample. Yet you are us'd, sir, to bate inwardly!

 Elder Pall. More than heirs unlanded or unjointur'd wives.

'Enter Engine.'

 Engine. What shall we do? Sir Tyrant Thrift's come
  home!

 Elder Pall. Sir Tyrant Thrift?

 Lucy.   My lady's guardian, sir.

 Ample. He meets th' expected hour, just to my wish.

 Lucy. What, hath he brought a husband for my lady?

 Engine. There is a certain one-legg'd gentleman,
Whose better half of limbs is wood, for whom
Kind nature did provide no hands, to prevent
Stealing; and, to augment his gracefulness,
He's crooked as a witch's pin.

 Lucy.   Is he so much wood?

Engine. So much, that if my lady were in health
And married to him, as her guardian did
Propose, we should have an excellent generation
Of bed-staves.

    Lucy.   When does he come?

    Engine. Tonight, if his slow litter will consent;
For they convey him tenderly, lest his
Sharp bones should grate together. Sir Pallatine,
I wish you could escape my master's sight.

    Elder Pall. Is he coming hither?

    Engine. He's at the door! My lady's sickness was
No sooner told him but he straight projects
To proffer her a will of his own making.
He means, sir, to be heir of all. If he
Should see you here, he would suspect my loyalty
And doubt you for some cunning instrument
That means to interrupt his covetous hopes.

    Elder Pall. Then I'll be gone.

    Engine. No, sir; he needs must meet you in
Your passage down. Besides, it is not fit
For you and your great hopes, with my dependency
On both, to have you absent when my lady dies.
I know you must have all. Sir, I could wish
That we might hide you here.
Draw out the chest within; that's big enough
To hold you. It were dangerous to have
My lady's guardian to find you, sir.

                        '*They draw in a chest.*'

    Elder Pall. How! Laid up like a brush'd gown, under lock
And key! By this good light, not I!

    Lucy. O sir, if but to save the honour of
Your mistress's fame. What will he think to see
So comely and so straight a gentleman
Converse here with a lady in her chamber,
And in a time that makes for his suspicion too,
When he's from home!

    Elder Pall.   I hate enclosure, I;
It is the humour of a distress'd rat!

    Ginet. It is retirement, sir, and you'll come forth
Again so sage!

Ample.   Sir Pallatine!

Lucy. Your lady calls, sir. To her, and be kind!

Ample. Will you permit the last of all my hours
Should be defil'd with infamy, proclaim'd
By lewder tongues to be unchaste ev'n at
My death? What will my guardian guess, to find
You here?

Elder Pall. No more; I'll in! But think on't, gentle lady:
First to bate inwardly, and then to have
My outward person shut thus and enclos'd
From daylight and your company. I say
But think if 't be not worse than death!

'He enters the chest.'

Ample. Lock him up, Luce, safe as thy maidenhead!

'Enter Sir Tyrant Thrift.'

Thrift. Engine, where's my charge, Engine, my dear
        charge?

Engine. Sick, as I told you, sir, and lost to all
The hope that earthly med'cine can procure!
Her physicians have taken their last fees,
And then went hence shaking their empty heads,
As they had left less brain than hope.

Thrift. Alas, poor charge! Come, let me see her, Engine.

Lucy. At distance, sir, I pray, for I have heard
Your breath is somewhat sour with overfasting, sir,
On holy-day eves.

Thrift.   Ha! What is she, Engine?

Engine. A pure good soul, one that your ward desir'd,
For love and kindred's sake, t' have near her at
Her death. She'll outwatch a long rush candle,
And reads to her all night the posy of
Spiritual flowers.

Thrift.   Does she not gape for legacies?

Engine. Fie, no! There's a cornelian ring, perhaps,
She aims at, cost ten groats, or a wrought smock
My lady made now 'gainst her wedding, sir,
Trifles which maids desire to weep upon
With fun'ral tales after a midnight posset.

Thrift. Thou said'st below she hath made me her heir.

Engine. Of all, ev'n to her slippers and her pins.

Ample. Luce, methought, Luce, I heard my guardian's
voice.

Engine. It seems her senses are grown warm again.
Your presence will recover her.

Thrift. Will it recover her? Then I'll be gone.

Engine. No, sir; she'll straight grow cold again. On! On!
She looks that you would speak to her.

Thrift. Alas, poor charge! I little thought to see
This doleful day.

Ample.   We are all mortal, sir.

Thrift. I've taken care and labour to provide
A husband for thee. He's in 's litter now,
Hastening to town, a fine young gentleman,
Only a little rumpled in the womb
With falls his mother took after his making.

Ample. Death is my husband now! But yet I thank
You for your tender pains, and wish you would
Continue it in quiet governing my legacies,
When I am past the power to see it, sir.
You shall enjoy all.

Thrift. This will occasion more church building
And raising of new hospitals. There were
Enow before; but, charge, you'll have it so.

Ample. I'll make, sir, one request, which I have hope
You'll grant in thankfulness to all my bounty.

Thrift. O dear charge, anything! Your cousin here
Shall witness the consent and act.

Ample. Because I would not have my vanities
Remain as fond examples to persuade
An imitation in those ladies that
Succeed my youthful pride i' th' town, my plumes,
Fantastic flowers and chains, my haughty rich
Embroideries, my gaudy gowns and wanton jewels
I have lock'd within a chest.

Lucy. There, sir, there the chest stands.

Ample. And I desire it may be buried with me.

Thrift. Engine, take care, Engine, to see it done.

Ample. Now, sir, I beseech you leave me, for 'twill
But make my death more sorrowful thus to

Continue my converse with one I so
Much love and must forsake at last.

Thrift. Alack, alack! Bury her tonight, Engine.

Engine. Not, sir, unless she dies. Her ancestors
Have sojourn'd long here in St. Barthol'mews,
And there's a vault i'th' parish church kept only
For her family. She must be buried there.

Thrift. Ay, Engine, ay. And let me see—the church,
Thou know'st, joins to my house—a good prevention
From a large walk: 'twill save the charge of torchlight.

Engine. What fun'ral guests? The neighbours, sir, will
    look
To be invited.

Thrift.   No more than will suffice
To carry down the corpse—and thou know'st, Engine,
She is no great weight.

Engine. And what to entertain them, sir?

Thrift. A little rosemary, which thou mayst steal
From th' Temple garden, and as many comfits
As might serve to christen a watchman's bastard.
'Twill be enough.

Engine.   This will not do; your citizen
Is a most fierce devourer, sir, of plums:
Six will destroy as many as can make
A banquet for an army.

Thrift. I'll have no more, Engine,
I'll have no more! Nor, d'you hear, no burnt wine.
I do not like this drinking healths to th' memory
O'th' dead; it is profane.

Engine.   You are obey'd.
But, sir, let me advise you now to trust
The care and benefit of all your fate
Presents you in this house to my discretion;
And get you instantly to horse again.

Thrift. Why, Engine? Speak.

Engine. In brief, you know that all
The writings which concern your ward's estate
Lie at her lawyer's, fifteen miles from hence.
Your credit—he not knowing, sir, she's sick—
Will easily tempt them to your own possession;

Which, once enjoy'd, you're free from all litigious suits
His envy might incense her kindred to.

    Thrift. Enough, Engine; I am gone.

    Engine. If you should meet the crooked lover in
His litter, sir (as 'tis in your own road),
You may persuade him move like a crab, backward;
For here 's no mixture but with worms.

    Thrift. 'Tis well thought on, Engine. Farewell, Engine!
Be faithful, and be rich.

    Engine.   My breeding and
Good manners, sir, teach me t'attend your bounty.

    Thrift. But, Engine, I could wish she would be sure
To die tonight.

    Engine.   Alas, good soul! I'll undertake
She shall do anything to please you, sir,   (*Exit* Thrift

    Ample. Engine, thou hast wrought above the power
Of accident or art.

    Engine.   If you consider 't with a just
And lib'ral brain: first, to prevent
Th' access and tedious visits of the fiend,
His lovesick monster, and then rid him hence
Upon a journey to preserve this house
Empty and free to celebrate the rest
Of our designs!

    Lucy. This, Engine, is thy holiday!

                         '*Luce knocks at the chest.*'
What hoa! Sir Pallatine, are you within?

    Elder Pall. Is Sir Tyrant Thrift gone? Open, lady, open!

    Lucy. The casement, sir, I will, a little to
Increase your witship's allowance of air.

               '*Opens a wicket at the end of the chest.*'
But th' troth for liberty of limbs, you may
As soon expect it in a galley, sir,
After six murders and a rape.

    Elder Pall. How, lady of the lawn!

    Lucy.   Sir Launcelot,
You may believe 't, if your discreet faith please.
This tenement is cheap; here you shall dwell,
Keep home, and be no wanderer.

    Elder Pall. The pox take me if I like this! Sure when

Th' advice of th' ancients is but ask'd, they'll say
I am now worse than in the state of a bawd.
  Engine. D'you know this lady, sir?
  Elder Pail. The Lady Ample!
Her veil's off, too! And in the lusty garb
Of health and merriment! Now shall I grow
As modest as a snail, that in 's affliction
Shrinks up himself and 's horns into his shell,
Asham'd still to be seen.
  Ample. Could'st thou believe,
Thou bearded babe, thou dull engenderer,
Male rather in the back than in the brain,
That I could sicken for thy love, for th' cold
Society of a thin northern wit!
  Elder Pall. Then Trojans wail with great remorse,
                       'Elder Pallatine *sings.*'
The Greeks are lock'd i'th' wooden horse!

        '*Enter* Young Pallatine.'

  Lucy. Pall, come in, Pall! 'Tis done. The spacious man
Of land is now contented with his own length.
  Ample. Your brother 's come to see you, sir.
  Elder Pall. Brother! Mad girls, these. Couldst thou
    believe 't, sirrah,
I am coffin'd up like a salmon pie
New sent from Dev'nshire for a token. Come,
Break up the chest.
  Young Pall.   Stay, brother. Whose chest is it?
  Elder Pall. Thou'lt ask more questions than a constable
In 's sleep. Prithee, dispatch.
  Young Pall.   Brother, I can
But mark the malice and the envy of
Your nature: I am no sooner exalted
To rich possessions and a glorious mean,
But straight you tempt me to a forfeiture
Of all: to commit felony, break open chests!
  Elder Pall. Oh, for dame Patience, the fool's mistress.
  Young Pall. Brother, you have pray'd well; heaven send
    her you!

You must forsake your own fair fertile soil
To live here by your wits!
   Lucy.   And dream, sir, of
Enjoying goodly ladies six yards high,
With satin trains behind them ten yards long.
   Ample. Cloth'd all in purple, and embroider'd with
Embossments wrought in imag'ry, the works
O'th' ancient poets drawn into similitude
And cunning shape.
   Ginet.   And this attain'd, sir, by your wits!
   Young Pall. Nothing could please your haughty palate but
The Muscatelli and Frontiniac grape,
Your Turin and your Tuscan veal, with red-
Legg'd partridge of the Genoa hills.
   Engine. With your broad liver o'th' Venetian goose,
Fatten'd by a Jew, and your aged carp,
Bred i'th' Geneva lake.
   Ample.
   Lucy.   } All this maintain'd, sir, by your wits!
   Ginet.
   Engine. And then you talk'd, sir, of your snails ta'en from
The dewy marble quarries of Carrara,
And sous'd in Lucca oil; with cream of Switzerland
And Genoa paste.
   Young Pall.   Your angelots of Brie,
Your Marsolini, and Parmesan of Lodi;
Your Malamucca melons and Sicilian dates!
And then to close your proud voluptuous jaw,
Marmalade made by the cleanly nuns of Lisbon!
   Ample.
   Lucy.   } And still thus feasted by your wits!
   Ginet.
   Elder Pall. Deafen'd with tyranny! Is there no end?
   Ample. Yes, sir, an end of you: you shall be now
Convey'd into a close dark vault, there keep
My silent grandsire company, and all
The music of your groans engross to your own ears.
   Elder Pall. How! Buried, and alive?
   Young Pall. Brother, your hand!
Farewell! I'm for the north! The fame of this

Your voluntary death will there be thought
Pure courtesy to me. I mean to take
Possession, sir, and patiently converse
With all those hinds, those herds and flocks
That you disdain'd in fulness of your wit.

   Lucy. Help, Pall, to carry him. He takes it heavily.

   Elder Pall. I'll not endure it! Fire! Murder! Fire!
Treason
Murder! Treason! Fire!

   Ample.   Alas, you are not heard.
The house contains none but ourselves.

                  (Exeunt omnes, 'carrying out the chest.'

[SCENE II]

'Enter Thwack, Pert, Meager.'

   Pert. We bring you, sir, commends from Pallatine.

   Thwack. I had as lieve you'd brought it from the devil,
Together with his horns boil'd to a jelly
For a cordial against lust.

   Meager. We mean the younger Pallatine; one, sir,
That loves your person and laments this chance
Which his false brother hath expos'd you to.

   Pert. And as we told you, sir, by his command
We have compounded with the constable,
In whose dark house you're now a prisoner.
But, sir, take 't on my faith, you must disburse.
For gold is a restorative, as well
To liberty as health.

   Thwack.   And you believe,
It seems, that your small tiny officer
Will take his unction in the palm as lovingly
As your exalted grandee, that awes all
With hideous voice and face!

   Pert. Even so the moderns render it!

   Thwack. But, gentlemen, you ask a hundred pounds;
'Tis all I've left.

Pert.   Sir, do but think what a
Prodigious blemish it will be, both to
Your ingenuity and fame, to be
Betray'd by one that is believ'd no wittier than
Yourself, and lie imprison'd for a bawd.

Thwack. Sir, name it not! You kill me through the ear!
I'd rather, sir, you'd take my mother from
Her grave and put her to do penance in
Her winding-sheet. There is the sum.

Meager. I'll in, sir, and discharge you.   (*Exit* Meager.

Thack. These carnal mulcts and tributes are design'd
Only to such vain people as have land.
Are you and your friend landed, sir?

Pert. Such land as we can share, sir, in the map.

Thwack. Lo you there now! These live by their wits!
Why should not I take the next key I meet
And open this great head to try if there
Be any brains left but sour curds and plum-broth!
Cozen'd in my youth, cozen'd in my age!
Sir, do you judge if I have cause to curse
This false inhuman town! When I was young,
I was arrested for a stale commodity
Of nut-crackers, long-gigs and casting-tops;
Now I am old, imprison'd for a bawd!

Pert. These are sad tales.

Thwack. I will write down to th' country, to dehort
The gentry from coming hither, letters
Of strange dire news—you shall disperse them, sir—

Pert. Most faithfully.

Thwack. That there are Lents six years long proclaim'd by
         th' state;
That our French and Deal wines are poison'd so
With brimstone by the Hollander that they
Will only serve for med'cine to recover
Children of the itch; and there is not left
Sack enough to mull for a parson's cold.

Pert. This needs must terrify.

Thwack. That our theatres are raz'd down; and where
They stood, hoarse midnight lectures preach'd by wives
Of comb-makers and midwives of Tower Wharf!

Pert. 'Twill take impregnably.

Thwack. And that a new plantation, sir (mark me),
Is made i'th' Covent Garden from the sutlery
O'th' German camps and the suburbs of Paris,
Where such a salt disease reigns as will make
Sassafras dearer than unicorn's horn.

Pert. This cannot choose but fright the gentry hence
And more impoverish the town than a
Subversion of the Fair of Barthol'mew,
The absence of the terms and court!

Thwack. You shall (if my projections thrive), in less,
Sir, than a year, stable your horses in
The New Exchange, and graze them in the Old.

'*Enter* Young Pallatine, Meager, Queasy, Snore,
Mistress Snore.'

Pert. Jog off! There's Pall, treating for your liberty.

Young Pall. The canopy, the hangings and the bed
Are worth more than your rent. Come, you're overpaid.
Besides, the gentleman's betray'd. He is no bawd.

Snore. Truly, a very civil gentleman.
'Las, he hath only roar'd and sworn and curs'd
Since he was ta'en; no bawdry, I'll assure ye.

Mistress Snore. Gossip Queasy, what a goodyear would
ye have?

Queasy. I am content if you and I were friends.

Young Pall. Come, come, agree! 'Tis I that ever bleed
And suffer in your wars.

Mistress Snore. Sweet Master Pallatine, hear me but speak.
Have I not often said, Why, neighbour Queasy,
Come to my house. Besides, your daughter Mall,
You know, last pompion time din'd with me thrice,
When my child's best yellow stockings were missing,
And a new pewter porringer mark'd with a P.L.

Snore. Ay, for Elizabeth Snore!

Mistress Snore. The pewterer that mark'd it was my
uncle.

Queasy. Why, did my daughter steal your goods?

Mistress Snore. You hear me say nothing. But there is

As bad as this (I warrant ye) learnt at
The bakehouse. I'll have an oven o' mine own shortly.

  Young Pall. Come, no more words! There's to reconcile
    you
In burnt wine and cake. Go, get you all in!
I'm full of business and strange mystery.

       (*Exeunt* Snore, Mistress Snore, Queasy.

  Meager. A hundred, Pall! 'Twas all his store. It lies
Here, my brave boy, warm and secure in pouch.

  Pert. We'll share 't anon.—What need you blush, Sir
    Morglay,
Like a maid newly undone in a dark
Entry? There are disasters, sure, as bad
As yours recorded in the city annals.

  Thwack. Your brother is a gentleman of a
Most even and blessed composition, sir;
His very blood is made of holy water,
Less salt than almond-milk.

  Young Pall. My silly reprehensions were despis'd;
You'd be his disciple and follow him
In a new path, unknown to his own feet.
Yet I've walk'd in it since, and prosper'd as
You see, without or land or tenement.

  Thwack. 'Tis possible to live b' our wits; that is
As evident as light. No human learning
Shall advise me from that faith.

  Young Pall. Sir Knight, what will you give worthy my
    brain
And me, if, after a concealment of
Your present shame, I can advise you how
T'achieve such store of wealth and treasure as
Shall keep you here, th' exemplar glory of
The town, a long whole year, without relief
Or charge from your own rents? This, I take it,
Was the whole pride at which, some few days since,
Your fancy aim'd.

  Thwack. This was, sir, in the hours
Of haughtiness and hope; but now—

  Young Pall. I'll do 't, whilst my poor brother too, low and
Declin'd, shall see and envy it.

Thwack. Live in full port, observ'd and wonder'd at?
Wine ever flowing in large Saxon romekins
About my board, with your soft sarsnet smock
At night, and foreign music to entrance?

Young Pall. All this, and more than thy invention can
Invite thee to.

Thwack. I'll make thee heir of my
Estate! Take my right hand, and your two friends
For witnesses!

Young Pall. Enough! Hear me with haste!
The Lady Ample 's dead. Nay, there are things
Have chanc'd since your concealment far more fit
For wonder, sir, than this: out of a silly piety,
T' avoid a thirst of gold and gaudy pride
I'th' world, sh'ath buried with her in a chest
Her jewels and her clothes; besides, as I'm
Inform'd by Luce, my wise intelligence,
Five thousand pounds in gold, a legacy
Left by her aunt more than her guardian knew.

Thwack. Well, what of this?

Young Pall. Yourself and I, join'd, sir, in a most firm
And loyal league, may rob this chest.

Thwack. Marry, and will!

Young Pall. Then when your promise is but ratified,
Take all the treasure for your own expense.

Thwack. Come, let us go. My fingers burn till they
Are telling it. The night will grow upon's.
Only you and I—I'll not trust new faces.
Dismiss these gentlemen!

Young Pall. At the next street, sir.

Thwack. This is at least a girn of fortune, if
Not a fair smile. I'm still for my old problem.
Since the living rob me, I'll rob the dead.

Young Pall. On, my delicious Pert! Now is the time
To make our purses swell and spirits climb.

(*Exeunt omnes.*

ACT V · SCENE I

'*Enter* Young Pallatine, [Lady] Ample, Lucy,
Engine, *with a torch.*'

Young Pall. Engine, draw out the chest and ope the
    wicket.
Let us not hinder him the air, since 'tis
Become his food.
    Elder Pall.   Who's there? What are you? Speak.
    Ample. A brace of mourning virgins, sir, that, had
You died in love, and in your wits, would now
Have brought roses and lilies, buds of the brier
And summer pinks to strew upon your hearse.
    Elder Pall. Then you resolve me dead.
    Lucy. 'Twere good that you would so resolve yourself.
    Young Pall. She counsels you to wise and severe thoughts.
Why, you are no more mortified than men
That are about to dance the morris.
    Elder Pall. Ladies, and brother too (whom I begin
To worship now, for tenderness of heart),
Can you believe I am so leaden, stupid,
And so very a fish, to think you dare
Thus murder me in bravery of mirth?
You have gone far; part of my suff'rance I
Confess a justice to me.
    Ample.   Oh, do you so?
Hath your heart and brain met upon that point
And render'd you silly to your own thoughts?
    Elder Pall. Somewhat mistaken i'th' projection of
My journey hither. Three hours in a chest
Among the dead will profit more than three
Years in a study 'mongst fathers, schoolmen
And philosophers.
    Young Pall. And you're persuaded now that there is,
    relative
To th' maintaining of a poor younger brother,
Something beside his wits?
    Elder Pall.   'Tis so conceiv'd.

Ample. And that we ladies of the town or court
Have not such waxen hearts that ev'ry beam
From a hot lover's eye can melt them through
Our breasts?

Elder Pall. Faith, 'tis imagin'd too.

Lucy. That though th'unruly appetites of some
Perverted few of our frail sex have made
Them yield their honours to unlawful love,
Yet there is no such want of you male sinners
As should constrain them hire you to 't with gold?

Elder Pall. You've taught me a new music; I am all
Consent and concordance.

Engine. And that the nimble packing hand, the swift
Disorder'd shuffle or the slur, or his
More base employment that with youth and an
Eternal back engenders for his bread,
Do all belong to men that may be said
To live, sir, by their sins, not by their wits?

Elder Pall. Sir, whom I love not nor desire to love;
I am of your mind too.

Young Pall. Madam, a fair conversion. 'Tis now fit
I sue unto you for his liberty.

Ample. Alas, he hath so profited in this
Retirement that I fear he will not willingly
Come out.

Elder Pall. O lady, doubt it not! Open the chest!

Ample. A little patience, sir.

'*Enter* Ginet.'

Ginet. Madam, we are undone. Your guardian is
At door, knocking as if he meant to wake
All his dead neighbours in the church.

Ample. So soon return'd! It is not midnight yet.

Engine. I know the bait that tempts him back with such
Strange haste, and have according to your will
Provided, madam, to betray his hopes.

Ample. Excellent Engine!

Engine. This key conveys you through the chancel to
The house gall'ry. My way lies here. I'll let
Him in and try how our design will relish.   (*Exit* Engine.

Ample. Come, sir, it is decreed in our wise counsel
You must be laid some distance from this place.

Elder Pall. Pray save your labour, madam; I'll come forth.

Ample. No, sir, not yet.

Elder Pall.   Brother, a cast of your voice!

Young Pall. She hath the key, brother. 'Tis but an hour's
Dark contemplation more.

Elder Pall. Madam, hear me speak.

Ample. Nay, no beginning of orations now;
This is a time of great dispatch and haste.
We have more plots than a general in a siege.

> (*Exeunt* Young Pallatine, Lady Ample, Ginet '*carry-
> ing out the chest.*'

> '*Enter* Thrift, Engine.'

Engine. None of the writings, sir, and yet perplex
Yourself with so much speed in a return!

Thrift. The lawyer was from home. But, Engine, I
Had hope to have prevented by my haste
Though not her fun'ral, yet the fun'ral of
The chest. Ah, dear Engine, tell me but why
So much pure innocent treasure should be
Thus thrown into a dark forgetfulness.

Engine [*Aside*]. I thought I had encounter'd his intents.—
All, sir, that law allow'd her bounty to
Bestow is yours; but for the chest, trust me,
'Tis buried, sir. The key is here, sir,—of no use.

Thrift. Ha, Engine! Give it me.

Engine. And, sir, to vex your meditation more,
Though not with manners yet with truth, know there
Is hidden in that chest a plenteous heap
Of gold, together with a rope of most
Inestimable pearl, left by her late
Dead aunt by will, and kept from your discovery.

Thrift. Is this true, Engine?

Engine. That precise chit Luce, her cousin-Puritan,
Was at th' interring of 't, conceal'd it till
The funeral forms were past, and then, forsooth,
She boasted that it was a pious means
To avoid covetous desires i'th' world.

Thrift. These fun'ral tales, Engine, are sad indeed,
Able to melt an eye, though harder than
That heart which did consent to so much cruelty
Upon the harmless treasure.
   Engine.   I mourn within, sir, too.
   Thrift. Give me the key that leads me from my house
Unto the chancel door.
   Engine. 'Tis very late, sir; whither will you go?
   Thrift. Never too late to pray. My heart is heavy.
   Engine. Where shall I wait you, sir?
   Thrift. At my low gall'ry door. I may chance stay long.
                        (*Exit* Sir Tyrant Thrift.
   Engine. This takes me more than all the kindness fortune
Ever show'd me. A decent transmutation:
I am no more your steward but your spy.   (*Exit* Engine.

[SCENE II]

'*Enter* Young Pallatine, Pert, Meager, Snore, *and*
Watchmen.'

   Young Pall. There, there's more money for your watch.
   Methinks
They've not drunk wine enough: they do not chirp.
   Snore. Your wine mates them; they understand it not.
But they have very good capacity in ale.
Ale, sir, will heat 'em more than your beef brewis.
   Young Pall. Well, let them have ale then.
   Snore. O sir, 'twill make 'em sing like the silk-knitters
Of Cock Lane.
   Young Pall. Meager, go you to Sir Tyrant Thrift's house.
Luce and the lady are alone; they will
Have cause to use your diligence. Make haste!
   Meager. Your dog, tied to a bottle, shall not outrun me.
                        (*Exit* Meager.
   Young Pall. Pert, stay you here with Master Constable,
And when occasion calls, see that you draw
Your lusty bill-men forth, bravely advanc'd
Under the colours of Queen Ample and
Myself, her general.

Pert. If ale can fortify, fear not! Where 's Sir Morglay?

Young Pall. I'm now to meet him i'th' churchyard. Th'
    old blade
Skulks there like a tame filcher, as he had
Ne'er stol'n 'bove eggs from market women,
Robb'd an orchard or a cheese loft.

Snore. We'll wait your worship in this corner.

Young Pall. No stirring, till I either come or send.

Snore. Pray, sir, let 's not stay long; 'tis a cold night
And I have nothing on my bed at home
But a thin coverlet and my wife's sey petticoat.
She'll never sleep, poor soul, till I come home
To keep her warm.

Young Pall.   You shall be sent for straight.
Be merry, my dull sons o'th' night, and chirp.

                        (*Exit* Young Pallatine.

Snore. Come, neighbour Runlet, sighing pays no rent,
Though the landlady be in love. Sing out!

                    '*They sing a catch in four parts.*'

Watchmen. With lanthorn on stall, at Tray-trip we play,
For ale, cheese and pudding, till it be day.
And for our breakfast, after long sitting,
We steal a street pig, o'th' Constable's getting.

'*Enter* Engine.'

Engine. Sir, draw down your watch into the church,
And let 'em lie hid close by the vestry door.

Pert. Is he there already?

Engine. Fat carriers, sir, make not more haste to bed
Nor lean philosophers to rise. I've so
Prepar'd things that he'll find himself mistaken.

Pert. Close by the vestry door.

Engine.   Right, sir.
I'll to my lady and expect th' event of your surprise.

Pert. Follow, Master Constable, one and one,
All in a file.   (*Exeunt* Pert, Snore, *and* Watchmen.

'*Enter* Thrift, *with a candle.*'

Thrift. I cannot find where they have laid her coffin.

But there's the chest. I'll draw it out, that I
May have more room to search and rifle it.
The weight seems easy to me though my strength
Be old. How long, thou bright all-powerful mineral,
Might'st thou lie hid ere the dull dead, that are
Entomb'd about thee here, could reach the sense
To turn wise thieves and steal thee from oblivion!

'Opens it and finds a halter.'

How! A halter! What fiend affronts me with
This emblem? Is this the rope of orient pearl?

'Enter Pert, Snore, Watchmen.'

Pert. Now I have told you, Master Constable,
The entire plot. Mark but how like that chest
Is to the other, where the elder Pallatine
Lies a perdu. Engine contriv'd them both.
   Thrift. Ha! What are these, the constable and watch?
   Pert. Seize on him for no less than sacrilege.
   Thrift. Why, neighbours, gentlemen!
   Pert.   Away with him!
   Snore. We shall know now who stole the wainscot cover
From the font and the vicar's surplice.
   Pert. Alas, grave sir, become a forfeiture
To th' king for sacrilege?
   Thrift.   Hear me but speak!
   Snore. No, not in a cause against the king.
   Pert. Lead to 's own house. He shall be pris'ner there,
And lock'd up safe enough.
   Thrift. Undone for ever!
            (*Exeunt* Pert, Snore, Thrift, *and* Watchmen.

'Enter Young Pallatine, Thwack, *with an iron crow and
dark lanthorn.*'

   Thwack. Why, this was such a firk of piety
I ne'er heard of. Bury her gold with her?
'Tis strange her old shoes were not interr'd too
For fear the days of Edgar should return,
When they coin'd leather.
   Young Pall. Come, sir, lay down your instrument.
   Thwack.   Why so?

Young Pall. I'm so taken with thy free, jolly nature,
I cannot for my heart proceed to more
Defeat upon thy liberty. All that
I told thee were rank lies.

Thwack.   How! No treasure trovar?

Young Pall. Not so much as will pay for that small
    candle-light
We waste to find it out.

Thwack. I thank you, sir.

                        'Flings down the crow of iron.'

Young Pall. You shall have cause, when you hear more.
    To this
Dark region, sir, solemn and silent as
Your thoughts must be ere they are mortified,
Have I now brought you, to perceive what an
Immense large ass (under your favour, knight)
You are, to be seduc'd to such vain stratagems
By that more profound fop, your friend, my brother.

Thwack. How had I been serv'd if I'd brought my scales
Hither to weigh this gold? But on! Your brother,
Whose name (let me tell you first) sounds far worse
To me than does a sergeant to a young
Indebted lover that's arrested in his coach,
And with his mistress by him.

Young Pall. You are believ'd. But will you now confirm
Me to your grace and love if I shall make 't
Appear that in a kind revenge of what
You suffer'd, sir, I've made this false and great
Seducer of mankind to suffer more?

Thwack. The Legend, Talmud, nor the Alcoran
Have not such doubtful tales as these. But make 't
Appear—I would have evidence.

Young Pall. Then take 't on my religion, sir, he was
Laid up in durance for a bawd before
He betray'd you to the same preferment.

Thwack. Shall this be justified when my disgrace
Comes to be known? Wilt thou then witness it?

Young Pall. With a deep oath. And, sir, to tempt more of
Your favour on poor me, that ever mourn'd
For all your sufferings, know you shall now

See him enclos'd in a blind chest, where he
Lies bath'd, sir, in a greater sweat than e'er
Cornelius took in his own tub.

 Thwack. Here, amongst sepulchres and melancholy
   bones!
Let me but see 't, and I will die for joy,
To make thee instantly my heir.

 Young Pall. You shall; and yet, ere the sun rise, find him
Enthralled too in a new distress.

 Thwack. Dost want money? Bring me to parchment and
A scriv'ner; I'll seal out two pound of wax.

       '*Young Pallatine knocks at the chest.*'

 Young Pall. You, sir, my nearest ally, are you asleep?

 Elder Pall. O brother, art thou come? Quick, let me forth!

 Young Pall. Here is a certain friend of yours presents
His loving visit, sir.   '*Opens the wicket.*'

 Elder Pall. Sir Morglay Thwack!
I had rather have seen my sister naked!

 Thwack. What, like a bashful badger do you draw
Your head into your hole again? Come, sir,
Out with that sage noddle, that has contriv'd
So cunningly for me and your dear self.

 Elder Pall. Here, take my eyelids, knight, and sew 'em up!
I dare not see thy face.

 Thwack.   But what think you
Of a new journey from the north, to live
Here by your wits, or midnight visits, sir,
To the Mogul's niece?

 Elder Pall.   I have offended, knight.
Whip me with wire, headed with rowels of
Sharp Ripon spurs. I'll endure anything
Rather than thee.

 Thwack. We have (I thank your bounteous brain)
Been entertain'd with various consorts, sir,
Of whisp'ring lutes, to soothe us into slumbers,
Spirits of clare to bathe our temples in,
And then the wholesome womb of woman too
That never teem'd—all this for nothing, sir.

 Young Pall. Come, I'll let him forth.

 Thwack. Rogue, if thou lov'st me,

Nay, let him be confin'd thus one short month.
I'll send him down to country fairs for a
New motion made b' a German engineer.
   Young Pall. 'Las, he is my brother.
   Thwack.   Or for a solitary ape,
Led captive thus by th' Hollander, because
He came aloft for Spain and would not for the States.
   Young Pall. Sir Morglay, leave your lanthorn here, and
      stay
My coming at your door. I'll let him out.
But for the new distress I promis'd on
His person, take it on my manhood, sir,
He feels it straight.
   Thwack.   Finely ensnar'd again, and instantly!
   Young Pall. Have a good faith and go.   (*Exit* Thwack.
   Elder Pall. Dear brother, wilt thou give me liberty?
   Young Pall. Upon condition, sir, you kiss these hilts,
Swear not to follow me but here remain
Until the Lady Ample shall consent
To th' freedom I bestow.   '*He kisses the hilts.*'
   Elder Pall. 'Tis done. A vow inviolate.
             '*He opens the chest and lets him out.*'
   Young Pall. Now silence, brother; not one curse, nor
      thanks.   (*Exit* Young Pallatine.
   Elder Pall. Fate and a good star speed me! Though I have
Long since amaz'd myself e'en to a marble,
Yet I have courage left to ask what this
Might mean. Was ever two-legg'd man thus us'd?

         '*Enter* Pert, Snore, *and* Watchmen.'

   Pert. Pall and his friend are gone. I must not stay
His sight. But after you have seiz'd upon him,
Lead him a prisoner to the lady too.   (*Exit* Pert.
   Snore. Warrant ye, though he were Gog or Hildebrand.
            '*They lay hold on him.*'
   Elder Pall. How now! What mean you, sirs?
   Snore. Yield to the Constable.
   Elder Pall. 'Tis yielded, sir, that you are Constable.
But where have I offended?

Snore. Here, sir, you have committed sacrilege
And robb'd an alderman's tomb, of himself
And his two sons kneeling in brass.

Elder Pall. How! Flay monuments of their brazen skins?

Snore. Look, a dark lanthorn and an iron crow!
Fine evidence for a jury.

Elder Pall. I like this plot. The Lady Ample and
My brother have most rare triumphant wits.
Now by this hand, I am most eagerly
In love with both. I find I have deserv'd all,
And am resolv'd t' hug them and their designs.
Though they afflict me more and more. Whither must I go?

Snore. Away with him! Saucy fellow! Examine
The king's constable! *(Exeunt omnes.*

[SCENE III]

'*Enter* Young Pallatine, Thwack, [Lady] Ample,
Lucy, Meager.'

Meager. I am become your guardian's jailer, lady;
He's safe lock'd in the parlour, and there howls
Like a dog that sees a witch flying.

Thwack. I long to hear how my wise tutor thrives
I'th' new defeat.

Ample. 'Tis well you are converted.
Believe 't, that gentleman deserves your thanks.

Thwack. Lady, seal my conversion on your lip;
'Tis the first leading kiss, that I intend
For after chastity. '*Kisses her.*'

Young Pall. Luce, see you make the proposition good
Which I shall give my brother from this lady,
Or I'll so swaddle your small bones.

Lucy. Sweet Pall, thou shalt. Madam, you'll please to
    stand
To what I lately mention'd to your own desire?

Ample. To ev'ry particle, and more.

'*Enter* Pert.'

Pert. Your brother's come. This room must be his prison.

Young Pall. 'Way, Luce, away! Stand in the closet, madam,
That you may hear us both and reach my call.

Thwack. I'll stay and see him.

Young Pall. No, knight; you are decreed Sir Tyrant's judge.
Go that way, sir, and force him to compound.

Thwack. I'll fine him soundly,
Till 's purse shrink like a bladder in the fire!

(*Exeunt* Lady Ample, Lucy, Thwack, Meager, Pert.)

'*Enter* Snore, Elder Pallatine.'

Snore. Here, sir, this is your jail, too good for such
A great offender.

Elder Pall. Sacrilege! Very well.
Now all the pulpit cushions, all the hearse-cloths
And winding-sheets that have been stol'n about
The town this year will be laid to my charge.

Young Pall. Pray leave us, Master Constable, and look
Unto your other bondman in the parlour.   (*Exit* Snore.

Elder Pall. This is the wittiest offspring that our name
E'er had. I love him beyond hope or lust.
My father was no poet, sure; I wonder
How he got him.

Young Pall.   I know you curse me now.

Elder Pall. Brother, in troth you lie, and whoe'er believes it.

Young Pall. Indeed you do. Conjurers in a circle,
That have rais'd up a wrong spirit, curse not
So much nor yet so inwardly.

Elder Pall.   I've a great mind to kiss thee.

Young Pall. You have not, sure?

Elder Pall. I shall do 't, and eat up thy lips so far,
Till thou'st nothing left to cover thy teeth.

Young Pall. And can you think all the afflictions you
Endur'd were merited: first, for misleading
Morglay, your old friend; then, neglect of me
And haughty overvaluing yourself?

Elder Pall. Brother, I murmur not. The traps that you

Have laid were so ingenious, I could wish
To fall in them again.

Young Pall. The Lady Ample, sir,
There is the great contriver that hath weav'd
These knots so intricate and safe. 'Las, I
Was but her lowly instrument.

Elder Pall. Ah, that lady! Were I a king, she should
Sit with me under my best canopy,
A silver sceptre in her hand, with which
I'd give her leave to break my head for ev'ry fault
I did commit.

Young Pall. But say I bring this lady, sir, unto
Your lawful sheets, make her your bosom wife?
Besides the plenty of her heritage,
How would it sound that you had conquer'd her
Who hath so often conquer'd you?

Elder Pall. Dear brother, no new plots.

Young Pall. Six thousand pounds, sir, is your yearly rent,
A fair temptation to a discreet lady.
Luce hath fill'd both mine ears with hope. Besides,
I heard her say she ne'er should meet a man
That she could more subdue with wit and government.

Elder Pall. That I'll venture.

Young Pall. Well, my first bounty is your freedom, sir,
For th' Constable obeys no law but mine.
And now, madam, appear!

'*Enter* [Lady] Ample, Lucy.'

Ample. You're welcome 'mongst the living, sir!

Elder Pall. Lady, no words. If you've but so much mercy
As could secure one that your eyes affect—

Ample. Why, you're grown arrogant again! D'you think
They are so weak to affect you?

Elder Pall. I have a heart so kind unto myself
To wish they could. Oh, we should live—

Ample. Not by our wits.

Elder Pall. No, no, but with such soft content, still in
Conspiracy how to betray ourselves
To new delights, keep harmony, with no

More noise than what the upper motions make;
And this so constant too, turtles themselves,
Seeing our faith, shall slight their own, and pine
With jealousy.

 Ample. Luce, the youth talks sense now; no med'cine for
The brain like to captivity in a dark chest.

 Young Pall. O madam, you are cruel.

 Ample. Well, my sad convertite, joy yet at this:
I've often made a vow to marry on
That very day my wardship is expir'd;
And two hours since, that liberty begun.

 Lucy. Nay, hear her out; your wishes are so saucy, sir.

 Ample. And know, my glory is dispatch. My ancestors
Were of the fiery French, and taught me love,
Hot eagerness and haste.

 Elder Pall.   Let me be rude
A while: lie with your judgement and beget
Sages on that! My dearest, chiefest lady!

 Ample. Your brain 's yet foul, and will recoil again.

 Elder Pall. No more; I'll swallow down my tongue.

 Ample. If, sir, your nature be so excellent
As your kind brother hath confirm'd to Luce
And me, follow, and I'll present you straight
With certain writings you shall seal to, hoodwink'd,
And purely ignorant of what they are.
This is the swiftest and the easiest test
That I can make of your bold love. Do this,
Perhaps I may vouchsafe to marry you.
The writings are within.

 Elder Pall.   Lead me to trial! Come!

 Ample. But, sir, if I should marry you, it is
In confidence I have the better wit,
And can subdue you still to quietness,
Meek sufferings and patient awe.

 Elder Pall. You rap me still anew.

 Young Pall. In, Luce; our hopes grow strong and giantly.

              (*Exeunt omnes.*

[SCENE IV]

'*Enter* Thrift, Snore, Mistress Snore, Queasy, Ginet.'

Ginet. To him Mistress Snore; 'tis he has kept
Your husband from his bed so long, to watch
Him for a church robbery.

    Mistress Snore. Ah, thou Judas! I thought what thou'ldst
      come to!
Remember the warrant thou sent'st for me
Into Duck Lane, 'cause I call'd thy maid trot,
When I was fain t' invite thy clerk to a
Fee pie, sent me b' a Temple cook, my sister's sweetheart!

    Queasy. Nay, and remember who was brought to bed
Under thy coach-house wall, when thou denied'st
A wad of straw, and wouldst not join thy halfpenny
To send for milk for the poor chrisom!

    Snore. Now you may sweeten me with sugar-loaves
At New Year's-tide, as I have you, sir.

'*Enter* Thwack, Pert, Meager, Engine.'

    Thwack. We'll teach you to rob churches. 'Slight, here-
      after
We of the pious shall be afraid to go
To a long exercise for fear our pockets should
Be pick'd. Come, sir, you see already how
The neighbours throng to find you. Will you consent?
'Tis but a thousand pounds apiece to these
Two gentlemen, and five hundred more t' Engine.
Your crime is then conceal'd and yourself free.

    Meager. No, he may choose, he'll trust to th' kind-
      hearted law.

    Pert. Let him, and to dame Justice too, who though
Her Ladyship be blind, will grope hard, sir,
To find your money-bags.

    Engine. Sir, you are rich; besides, you know what you
Have got by your ward's death. I fear you will
Be begg'd at court unless you come off thus.

    Thrift. There is my closet key. Do what you please.

    Engine. Gentlemen, I'll lead you to it. Follow me.

Thwack. D'you use to find such sums as these beneath
An oak, after a long march? I think, sure,
The wars are not so plentiful.

   Pert.   We think so too.

   Thwack. You'd better trail a bodkin, gentlemen,
Under the Lady Ample than a pike
Under a German general.

   Pert. We'll in for th' money, sir, and talk anon.

                     (*Exeunt* Engine, Pert, Meager.

'*Enter* Elder Pallatine, Young Pallatine, [Lady] Ample,
Lucy.'

   Young Pall. Sir Tyrant Thrift, here is your ward, come
    from
The dead t' indict you for a robbery
Upon her ghost.

   Thrift.   Ha! Is she alive too?

   Lucy. Yes, and her wardship out, before you've prof-
    ferr'd her
A husband, sir. So the best benefit
Of all your guardianship is lost.

   Ample. In seven long years you could not, sir, provide
A man deform'd enough to offer me
For your own ends.

   Thrift. Cozen'd of wealth, of fame! Dog Engine!

                        (*Exit* Thrift.

   Thwack. We must have you enclos'd again: you're very
Forward with the lady.

   Elder Pall.   I will be, sir,
Until she groan. This priest stays somewhat long.

   Thwack. How's this? Troth, I shall forgive thee then
    heartily.

   Ample. I've ta'en him i'th' behalf of health, to chide
And jeer, for recreation sake; 'twill keep
Me, sir, in breath, now I am past growing.

   Elder Pall. Hark, knight, here's relish for your ears. I
    chose
None of your dull country madams, that spend
Their time in studying receipts to make
Marchpane and preserve plums; that talk

Of painful childbirths, servants' wages, and
Their husbands' good complexion and his leg.

Thwack. New wonders yet!

Elder Pall. What was that, mistress, which I seal'd to, hoodwink'd,
A simple trial of my confidence and love?

Ample. Your brother has it; 'tis a gift to him
Of one fair manor 'mongst those many that you
Have in possession, sir; and in this bond
You're witness to three thousand pounds I give to Luce.

Lucy. Yes, sir, for Pall and I must marry too.

Young Pall. I were an eunuch else, and th' world should know't.

Elder Pall. Thou couldst not have betray'd me to a bounty
I more love. Brother, give thee joy!

> '*Thwack takes* Young Pallatine *aside.*'

Thwack. You are the cause of all these miracles;
Therefore I desire you to be my heir.
By this good day, you must; for I've ta'en order,
Though I love your wit, you shall not live by it.

Young Pall. My kind thanks, sir, the poor man's gratitude.

Mistress Snore. Give you joy, sweet Master Pallatine, and
Your brother too!

Queasy.   And send you more such wives,
Ev'ry year as many as shall please heaven!

Snore. 'Tis day. I'll not to bed, sir, now; my watch
Shall be drunk at your worship's wedding.

Young Pall. They shall, and there is gold enough to keep
Them so until thy reign be out.

> '*Enter* Pert, Meager, Engine, *with money-bags.*'

Pert. Loaden with composition, Pall—

Meager. 'Tis for your sake we groan under these burdens—

Young Pall. The offal of Sir Tyrant's trunks! Brother,
Pray know these gentlemen; they owe you more
Money than they mean to pay now.

Elder Pall. I remember 'em. But no words, my cavaliers,
And you are safe. Where shall we dine today?

Young Pall. At Lucy's aunt's. We'll make her costive
  beldamship
Come off when she beholds a goodly jointure
And our fair hopes.
    Elder Pall.   First, to the church, lady;
I'll make your skittish person sure. Some of
Your pleasant arts upon me may become
A wise example and a moral too,
Such as their haughty fancy well befits
That undertake to live here by their wits.   (*Exeunt omnes.*

FINIS

Epilogue

The office of an epilogue is now
To smoothe and stroke the wrinkles from each brow;
To guide severer judgements (if we could
Be wise enough) until they thought all good
Which they perhaps dislike. And sure, this were
An overboldness, rais'd from too much fear.
You have a freedom, which we hope you'll use,
T' advance our youthful poet and his muse
With a kind doom; and he'll tread boldly then
In 's best new comic socks this stage again.

THE
Parsons Wedding,
A
COMEDY.

The Scene *LONDON.*

WRITTEN AT

Basil in Switzerland:

BY

THOMAS KILLIGREW.

DEDICATED

TO THE

LADY *URSULA BARTU,*
WIDOW.

LONDON:
Printed by *J. M.* for *Henry Herringman,* and are to be
sold at his Shop at the sign of the *Blew Anchor,* in
the lower Walk of the *New-Exchange.* 1663.

P

DRAMATIS PERSONAE

Master Careless, *a gentleman, and a wit.*

Master Wild, *a gentleman, nephew to the* Widow.

Master Jolly, *a humorous gentleman, and a courtier.*

Captain, *a leading wit, full of designs.*

Parson, *a wit also, but over-reached by the* Captain *and his* Wanton.

Master Constant ⎱ *two dull suitors to the* Lady Widow *and*
Master Sadd ⎰ Mistress Pleasant.

Lady Wild, *a rich (and somewhat youthful) widow.*

Mistress Pleasant, *a handsome young gentlewoman, of a good fortune.*

Mistress Secret, *her (indifferent honest) woman.*

Lady Love-all, *an old stallion-hunting widow.*

Faithful, *her (errant honest) woman.*

Mistress Wanton, *the* Captain's *livery punk, married to the* Parson *by confederacy.*

Bawd, [*maid to* Mistress Wanton.]

[Cropp, *a scrivener.*]

[A Tailor.]

[Boy, *servant to the* Captain.]

Servants.

Drawers.

Fiddlers.

[Watch.]

[The Scene: London.]

THE PARSON'S WEDDING

ACT I · SCENE I

'*Enter the* Captain *in choler, and* Wanton.'

Captain. No more! I'll sooner be reconciled to want or sickness than that rascal; a thing that my charity made sociable; one that when I smiled would fawn upon me and wag his stern, like starved dogs; so nasty, the company cried foh! upon him, he stunk so of poverty, ale, and bawdry; so poor and despicable when I relieved him he could not avow his calling for want of a cassock, but stood at corners of streets and whispered gentlemen in the ear as they passed and so delivered his wants like a message; which being done, the rogue vanished, and would dive at Westminster like a dab-chick and rise again at Temple-gate. The ingenuity of the rascal, his wit being snuffed by want, burnt clear then and furnished him with a bawdy jest or two to take the company, but now the rogue shall find he has lost a patron.

Wanton. As I live, if I had thought you would have been in such a fury, you should never have known it.

Captain. Treacherous rogue, he has always railed against thee to me as a danger his friendship ought to give me warning of, and nightly cried, 'Yet look back, and hunt not with good nature and the beauties of thy youth that false woman, but hear thy friend, that speaks from sad experience.'

Wanton. Did he say this?

Captain. Yes, and swears ye are as unsatiate as the sea, as covetous and as ungrateful; that you have your tempest too, and calms more dangerous than it.

Wanton. Was the slave so eloquent in his malice?

Captain. Yes, faith, and urged you (for your part) were never particular and seldom sound.

Wanton. Not sound! Why, he offered to marry me and swore he thought I was chaste, I was so particular; and proved it, that consent was full marriage, by the first institution; and that those that love and lie together and tell have fulfilled all ceremonies now.

Captain. Did he offer to marry thee?

Wanton. Yes, yes.

Captain. If ever then I deserved from thee, or if thou be'st dear to thyself, as thou hast anything thou hop'st shall be safe or sound about thee, I conjure thee, take my counsel: marry him, to afflict him.

Wanton. Marry him?

Captain. If I have any power I shall prevail. Thou know'st he has a fat benefice, and leave me to plague him till he give it me to be rid of thee.

Wanton. Will you not keep me then?

Captain. I keep thee! Prithee, wilt thou keep me? I know not why men are such fools to pay: we bring as much to the sport as women. Keep thee? I'd marry thee as soon. Why, that's wedding sin. No, no keeping, I. That you are not your own is all that prefers you before wives.

Wanton. I hope this is not real.

Captain. Art thou such a stranger to my humour? Why, I tell thee I should hate thee if I could call thee mine, for I loathe all women within my knowledge, and 'tis six to four if I knew thy sign I'd come there no more. A strange mistress makes every night a new, and these are your pleasing sins. I had as lief be good as sin by course.

Wanton. Then I am miserable.

Captain. Not so, if you'll be instructed and let me pass like a stranger when you meet me.

Wanton. But have you these humours?

Captain. Yes, faith; yet if you will observe them, though you marry him, I may perchance be your friend. But you must be sure to be coy, for to me the hunting is more pleasure than the quarry.

Wanton. But if I observe this, will you be my friend hereafter?

Captain. Firm as the day. ('*The* Parson *calls within.*') Hark, I hear him. I knew he would follow me. I gave him a small touch that wakened his guilt. Resolve to endear yourself to him, which you may easily do by taking his part when

I have vexed him. No dispute; resolve it, or, as I live, here I disclaim thee for ever.

Wanton. 'Tis well; something I'll do.   (*Exit* Wanton.

Captain [*Following* Wanton *to the door*]. Open the door, I say, and let me in. Your favourite and his tithes shall come no more here.

'*Enter* Parson [*by another door*].'

Parson. Yes, but he shall. 'Tis not you nor your braced drum shall fright me hence who can command the souls of men. I have read divine Seneca; thou know'st nothing but the earthly part, and can'st cry to that, 'Faces about.'

Captain. Thou read Seneca! Thou steal his cover to clothe thee, naked and wicked, that for money wouldst sell thy share of the twelve, and art allowed by all that know thee fitter to have been Judas than Judas was for his treachery.

Parson. Rail, do rail, my illiterate Captain, that can only abuse by memory; and should I live [till] thou couldst read my sentence, I should never die.

Captain. No, ingrateful, live till I destroy thee. And, thankless wretch, did all my care of thee deserve nothing but thy malice and treacherous speaking darkly still, with thy fine, 'No, not he,' when any malicious discourse was made of me. and by thy false, faint, 'No, faith, confess,' in thy denials, whilst thy smiling excuses stood a greater and more dangerous evidence against me than my enemies' affidavits could have done?

Parson. I'll lie for never a lean soldier of you all.

Captain. I have, for thee, slave, when I have been wondered at for keeping company with such a face. But they were such as know thee not, all which thy looks deceived as they did me. They are so simple they'd cozen a jury, and a judge that had wit would swear thou lied'st shouldst thou confess what I know to be true, and award Bedlam for thee. 'Tis so strange and so new a thing to find so much rogue lodge at the sign of the fool.

Parson. Leave this injurious language or I'll lay off my cassock, for nothing shall privilege your bragger's tongue to abuse me, a gentleman and a soldier ancienter than thyself.

Captain. Yes, thou wert so; and now I think on't, I'll

recount the cause, which it may be thou hast forgot through thy variety of sins: it was a hue and cry that followed thee a scholar and found thee a soldier.

Parson. Thou li'st. Thou and scandal have but one tongue; hers dwells with thy coward's teeth.

Captain. Oh, do you rage? Nay, I'll put the cause in print too. I am but a scurvy poet, yet I'll make a ballad shall tell how, like a faithful disciple, you followed your poor whore till her martyrdom in the suburbs.

Parson. I'll be revenged for this scandal.

Captain. Then shall succeed your flight from the university, disguised into captain—only the outside was worse buff and the inside more atheist than they—furnished with an insolent faith, uncharitable heart, envious as old women, cruel and bloody as cowards. Thus armed at all points thou went'st out, threatening God and trembling at men.

Parson. I'll be revenged, thou poor man of war, I'll be revenged.

'*Enter* Wanton.'

Wanton. And why so bitter? Whose house is this? Who dares tell this story?

Captain. Why, sweet, hath he not treacherously broke into our cabinet and would have stolen thee thence? By these hilts, I'll hang him, and then I can conclude my ballad with, 'Take warning all Christian people by the same.' I will, you lean slave; I'll prosecute thee till thou art fain to hide in a servitor's gown again and live upon crumbs with the robin redbreasts that haunt the hall, your old messmates. Do you snarl? I'll do 't, I will, and put thee to fight with the dogs for the bones that but smell of meat, those that your hungry students have polished with their teeth.

Wanton. If you do this, good Captain, lieutenant and company—for all your command, I think, is within your reach—I say, if you dare do this, I shall sing a song of one that bade stand and made a carrier pay a dear rent for a little ground upon his majesty's highway.

Captain. How now, Mistress Wanton! What's this? What's this?

Parson. This? 'Tis matter for a jury, I'll swear, and positively. I'll hang thee, I'll do 't, by this hand. Let me alone to swear the jury out of doubt.

Captain. But you are in jest, Mistress Wanton, and will confess (I hope) this is no truth.

Wanton. Yes, sir, as great a truth as that you are in your unpaid-for scarlet. Fool! Didst think I'd quit such a friend and his staid fortune to rely upon thy dead pay and hopes of a second covenant?

Captain. His fortune? What is 't? Th' advowson of Tyburn deanery?

Parson. No, nor rents brought in by long-staff speeches that asks alms with frowns till thy looks and speech have laid violent hands upon men's charity.

Wanton. Let him alone; I'll warrant he'll never be indicted for drawing anything but his tongue against a man.

Captain. Very good.

Parson. Dear Mistress Wanton, you have won my heart, and I shall live to dote upon you for abusing this impetuous captain. Will you listen to my old suit? Will you marry me and vex him? Say, dare you do 't, without more dispute?

Captain. 'Twas a good question: she that dares marry thee dares do anything. She may as safely lie with the great bell upon her—and his clapper is less dangerous than thine.

Wanton. Why, I pray?

Captain. What a miserable condition wilt thou come to: his wife cannot be an honest woman; and if thou shouldst turn honest, would it not vex thee to be chaste and poxed—a saint without a nose? What calendar will admit thee by an incurable slave that's made of rogue's flesh? Consider that.

Wanton. Why, that's something yet; thou hast nothing but a few scars and a little old fame to trust to, and that scarce thatches your head.

Captain. Nay then, I see thou'rt base and this plot not accident. And now I do not grudge him thee. Go together; 'tis pity to part you, whore and parson, as consonant—

Wanton. As whore and captain.

Captain. Take her; I'll warrant her a breeder. I'll prophesy she shall lie with thy whole congregation and bring an heir to thy parish, one that thou mayst enclose the common by his title and recover it by common law.

Parson. That's more than thy dear dam could do for thee, thou son of a thousand fathers, all poor soldiers, rogues that ought mischiefs, no midwives, for their birth. But I cry thee mercy, my patron has an estate of old iron by his side, with the farm of old ladies he scrapes a dirty living from.

Wanton. He earn from an old lady? Hang him, he's only wicked in his desires, and for adultery he cannot be condemned though he should have the vanity to betray himself. God forgive me for belying him so often as I have done. The weak-chinned slave hired me once to say I was with child by him.

Captain. This is pretty. Farewell, and may the next pig thou farrow'st have a promising face, without the dad's fool or gallows in 't, that all may swear at first sight, 'That's a bastard'; and it shall go hard but I'll have it called mine. I have the way—'tis but praising thee and swearing thou art honest before I am asked; you taught me the trick.

Parson. Next levy I'll preach against thee and tell them what a piece you are. Your drum and borrowed scarf shall not prevail, nor shall you win with charms half-ell long (hight ferret-riband) the youth of our parish as you have done.

Captain. No, lose no time, prithee study and learn to preach and leave railing against the surplice now thou hast preached thyself into linen. Adieu, Abigail, adieu, heir-apparent to Sir Oliver Martext. To church, go. I'll send a beadle shall sing your epithalamium.

Parson. Adieu, my captain of a tame band. I'll tell your old lady how you abused her breath and swore you earned your money harder than those that dig in the mines for 't.

(*Exit* Captain.

A fart fill thy sail, captain of a galley foist. He's gone. Come, sweet, let's to church immediately, that I may go and take my revenge. I'll make him wear thin breeches.

Wanton. But if you should be such a man as he says you are, what would my friends say when they hear I have cast myself away?

Parson. He says? Hang him, lean mercenary, provant rogue! I knew his beginning, when he made the stocks lousy and swarmed so with vermin we were afraid he would have brought that curse upon the county. He says? But what's [the] matter what he says? A rogue, by sire and dam! His father was a broad fat pedlar, a what-do-you-lack-sir, that haunted good houses and stole more than he bought. His dam was a gypsy, a pilfering canting sibyl in her youth and she suffered in her old age for a witch. Poor stromwell, the rogue was a perpetual burden to her—she carried him longer at her back than in her belly. He dwelt there till she lost him one night in the great frost, upon our common, and there he was found in the morning, candied in ice. A pox of their charity that thawed him! You might smell a rogue then in the bud. He is now run away from his wife.

Wanton. His wife?

Parson. Yes, his wife. Why, do you not know he's married according to the rogue's liturgy? A left-handed bridegroom; I saw him take the ring from a tinker's dowager.

Wanton. Is this possible?

Parson. Yes, most possible, and you shall see how I'll be revenged on him: I will immediately go seek the ordinance against reformadoes.

Wanton. What ordinance?

Parson. Why, they do so swarm about the town and are so destructive to trade and all civil government that the state has declared no person shall keep above two colonels and four captains of what trade soever in his family; for now the war is done, broken-breech, wood-monger, ragman, butcher, and link-boy (comrades that made up the ragged regiment in this holy war) think to return and be admitted to serve out their times again.

Wanton. Your ordinance will not touch the Captain, for he is a known soldier.

Parson. He a captain? An apocryphal modern one, that went convoy once to Brainford with those troops that conducted the contribution puddings in the late holy war, when the city ran mad after their russet Levites, apron rogues with horn hands. Hang him, he's but the sign of a soldier, and I hope to see him hanged for that commission when the king comes to his place again.

Wanton. You abuse him now he's gone, but—

Parson. Why, dost thou think I fear him? No, wench, I

know him too well for a cowardly slave that dares as soon eat his fox as draw it in earnest. The slave's noted to make a conscience of nothing but fighting.

Wanton. Well, if you be not a good man and a kind husband—

Parson. Thou know'st the proverb, As happy as the parson's wife during her husband's life.

[*Exeunt* Parson *and* Wanton.]

SCENE II

'*Enter* Mistress Pleasant, Widow Wild, *her aunt, and* Secret, *her woman, above in the music room, as dressing her. A glass, a table, and she in her night-clothes.*'

Pleasant. Secret, give me the glass and see who knocks.

[*Enter* Widow.]

Widow. Niece, what, shut the door? As I live this music was meant to you. I know my nephew's voice.

Pleasant. Yes, but you think his friend's has more music in 't.

Widow. No, faith, I can laugh with him or so, but he comes no nearer than my lace.

Pleasant. You do well to keep your smock betwixt.

Widow. Faith, wench, so wilt thou an thou beest wise— from him and all of them. And be ruled by me, we'll abuse all the sex till they put a true value upon us.

Pleasant. But dare you forbid the travelled gentlemen and abuse them, and your servant, and swear with me not to marry in a twelvemonth though a lord bait the hook, and hang out the sign of a court cupid whipped by a country widow? Then I believe we may have mirth cheaper than at the price of ourselves and some sport with the wits that went to lose themselves in France.

Widow. Come, no dissembling, lest I tell your servant when he returns how much you're taken with the last new fashion.

Secret. Madam, 'tis almost noon; will you not dress yourself today?

Widow. She speaks as if we were boarders. Prithee, wench, is not the dinner our own? Sure, my cook shall lay by my own roast till my stomach be up.

Pleasant. But there may be company, and they will say we take too long time to trim. Secret, give me the flowers my servant sent me; he sware 'twas the first the wench made of the kind.

Widow. But when he shall hear you had music sent you today, 'twill make him appear in his old clothes.

Pleasant. Marry, I would he would take exception; he should not want ill usage to rid me of his trouble. As I live, custom has made me so acquainted with him that I now begin to think him not so displeasing as at first; and if he fall not out with me, I must with him, to secure myself. Sure, aunt, he must find sense and reason absent, for when a question knocks at his head the answer tells that there is nobody at home. I asked him th' other day if he did not find a blemish in his understanding and he sware a great oath, Not he. I told him 'twas very strange, for fool was so visible an eyesore that neither birth nor fortune could reconcile [him] to me.

Widow. Faith, methinks his humour is good, and his purse will buy good company, and I can laugh and be merry with him sometimes.

Pleasant. Why, pray, aunt, take him to yourself and see how merry we will be; I can laugh at anybody's fool but mine own.

Widow. By my troth, but that I have married one fool already you should not have him. Consider, he asks no portion and yet will make a great jointure. A fool with these conveniences, a kind, loving fool, and one that you may govern, makes no ill husband. Niece, there are other arguments, too, to bid a fool welcome, which you will find without teaching. Think of it, niece: you may lay out your affection to purchase some dear wit or judgement of the city and repent at leisure a good bargain in this fool.

Pleasant. Faith, aunt, fools are cheap in the butchery and dear in the kitchen; they are such unsavoury, insipid things that there goes more charge to the sauce than the fool is worth ere a woman can confidently serve him, either to her bed or board. Then if he be a loving fool, he troubles all the world a-days and me all night.

Secret. Friendship-love, madam, has a remedy for that.

Pleasant. See if the air of this place has not inclined Secret to be a bawd already. No, Secret, you get no gowns that way, upon my word. If I marry, it shall be a gentleman that has wit and honour, though he has nothing but a sword by his side. Such a one naked is better than a fool with all his trappings, bells and baubles.

Widow. Why, as I live, he's a handsome fellow, and merry; mine is such a sad soul, and tell me stories of lovers that died in despair and of the lamentable end of their mistresses (according to the ballad), and thinks to win me by example.

Pleasant. Faith, mine talks of nothing but how long he has loved me, and those that know me not think I am old; and still finds new causes (as he calls them) for his love. I asked him the other day if I changed so fast or no.

Widow. But what think'st thou, Secret? My nephew dances well, and has a handsome house in the Piazza.

Pleasant. Your nephew? Not I, as I live! He looks as if he would be wooed. I'll warrant you, he'll never begin with a woman till he has lost the opinion of himself. But since you are so courteous, I'll speak to his friend and let him know how you suffer for him.

Widow. Hum! Marry, God bless all good women from him! Why, he talks as if the dairymaid and all her cows could not serve his turn. Then they wear such bawdy breeches 'twould startle an honest woman to come in their company for fear they should break and put her to count from the fall of them, for I'll warrant the year of the Lord would sooner out of her head than such a sight.

Pleasant. I am not such an enemy now to his humour as to your nephew's. He rails against our sex and thinks by beating down the price of women to make us despair of merchants, but if I had his heart-strings tied on a true lover's knot I would so firk him till he found physic in a rope.

Secret. He's a scurvy-tongued fellow, I'm sure of that, and if I could have got a staff, I had marked him.

Widow. What did he do to thee, Secret?

Pleasant. Why, he swore he had a better opinion of her than to think she had her maidenhead; but if she were that fool and had preserved the toy, he swore he would not take the pains of fetching it to have it. I confess I would fain be revenged on them because they are so blown up with opinion of their wit.

Widow. As I live, my nephew travels still; the sober, honest Ned Wild will not be at home this month.

Pleasant. What say you? Will you abuse them and all the rest and stand to my first proposition?

Widow. Yes, faith, if it be but to bury my servant Sadd, for he cannot last above another fall. And how, think you, will your servant take it?

Pleasant. Mine? Oh, God help me, mine's a healthy fool. I would he were subject to pine and take things unkindly— there were some hope to be rid of him, for I'll undertake to use him as ill as anybody.

Widow. As I live, I am easily resolved, for if I would marry, I know neither who nor what humour to choose.

Secret. By my troth, madam, you are hard to please; else the courtier might have served turn.

Widow. Serve turn! Prithee, what haste, Secret, that I should put myself to bed with one I might make a shift with? When I marry thou shalt cry, 'Ay, marry, madam, this is a husband,' without blushing, wench, and none of your so-so husbands. Yet he might [have] half overcome my aversion, I confess.

Pleasant. Overcome! I think so; he might have won a city his way; for when he saw you were resolved he should not eat with you, he would set himself down as if he meant to besiege us and had vowed never to rise until he had taken us in; and because our sex forbade force, he meant to do it by famine. Yet you may stay, and miss a better market; for, hang me, I am of Secret's opinion: he had but two faults—a handsome fellow, and too soon denied.

Widow. 'Tis true he was a handsome fellow, and a civil; that I shall report him, for as soon as it was given him to understand I desired he would come no more, I never saw him since but by chance.

Pleasant. Why did you forbid him?

Widow. There were divers exceptions, but that which angered me then was, he came with the king's letters patents as if he had been to take up a wife for his majesty's use.

Pleasant. Alas, was that all? Why, 'tis their way at court, a common course among them, and was it not one the king had a great care of? When my mother was alive I had such a packet from the court directed unto me; I bid them pay the post and make the fellow drink, which he took as ill as I could wish, and has been ever since such a friendly enemy.

Widow. Nay, as I live, she was for the Captain too—his scarf and feather won his heart.

Secret. Truly, madam, never flatter yourself, for the gentleman did not like you so well as to put you to the trouble of saying no.

Pleasant. Lord, how I hated and dreaded that scarf and buff coat!

Secret. Why, Mistress Pleasant, a captain is an honourable charge.

Widow. Prithee, Secret, name them no more, Colonel and Captain, Commissioner, Free-quarters, Ordnance and Contribution. When Buff utters these words I tremble and dread the sound; it frights me still when I do but think on them. Cuds body, they're twigs of the old rod, wench, that whipped us so lately.

Pleasant. Ay, ay, and they were happy days, wench, when the captain was a lean, poor, humble thing, and the soldier tame, and durst not come within the city for fear of a constable and a whipping-post. They knew the penal statutes give no quarter. Then Buff was out of countenance and skulked from alehouse to alehouse, and the city had no militia but the sheriff's men. In those merry days a bailiff trod the streets with terror, when all the chains in the city were rusty but Master Sheriff's, when the people knew no evil but the constable and his watch. Now every committee has as much power and as little manners and examines with as much ignorance, impertinence, and authority as a constable in the king's key.   *'People talking without.'*

Widow. See who's that so loud.

Secret. The men you talk'd of newly come to town.

                                        (*Exeunt omnes.*

SCENE III

'*Enter* Jack Constant, Will Sadd, Jolly, *and a footman.*
They comb their heads and talk.'

Jolly. Remember our covenants: get them that can all
friends and be sure to despatch the plot to carry them into
the country lest the brace of new-come monsieurs get them.

Constant. Those flesh-flies! I'll warrant thee for them.
Yet 'twas foolishly done of me to put on this gravity; I shall
break out and return to myself if you put me to a winter's
wooing.

Sadd. A little patience does it, and I am content to suffer
anything till they're out of town. Secret says they think my
pale face proceeds from my love.

Jolly. Does she? That shall be one hint to advance your
designs and my revenge, for so she be cozened I care not who
does it, for scorning me, who by this hand loved her parlously.

Footman. Sir, what shall I do with the horses?

Sadd. Carry them to Brumsted's.

Footman. What shall I do with your worship's?

Jolly. Mine? Take him, hamstring him, kill him—anything to make him away, lest having such a conveniency I be
betrayed to another journey into the country. Gentlemen,
you are all welcome to my country house. Charing Cross, I
am glad to see thee, with all my heart!

Constant. What, not reconciled to the country yet?

Sadd. He was not long enough there to see the pleasure
of it.

Jolly. Pleasure? What is 't called? Walking or hawking, or
shooting at butts?

Constant. You found other pleasures or else the story of
the meadow is no gospel.

Jolly. Yes, a pox upon the necessity! Here I could as soon
have taken the cow as such a milkmaid.

Sadd. The wine and the meat's good, and the company.

Jolly. When at a Tuesday meeting the country comes in
to a match at two shillings rubbers, where they conclude at

dinner what shall be done this parliament, railing against the court and Pope after the old Elizabeth way of preaching till they are drunk with zeal; and then the old knight of the shire from the board's end in his coronation breeches vies clinches with a silenced minister, a rogue that railed against the reformation merely to be eased of the trouble of preaching.

Constant. Nay, as I live, now you are to blame and wrong him. The man's a very able man.

Jolly. You'll be able to say so one day upon your wife's report. I would he were gelt, and all that hold his opinion. By this good day, they get more souls than they save.

Sadd. And what think you of the knight's son? I hope he's a fine gentleman when his green suit and his blue stockings are on, and the welcomest thing alive to Mistress Abigail but Tib and Tom in the stock.

Jolly. Who? Master Geoffrey? Hobbinol the second! By this life, 'tis a very veal, and he licks his nose like one of them. By his discourse you'd guess he had eaten nothing but hay. I wonder he doth not go on all four too and hold up his leg when he stales—he talks of nothing but the stable. The cobbler's blackbird at the corner has more discourse. He has not so much as the family jest, which these Corydons use to inherit. I posed him in Booker's Prophecies till he confessed he had not mastered his almanac yet.

Constant. But what was that you whispered to him in the hall?

Jolly. Why, the butler and I by the intercession of March beer had newly reconciled him to his dad's old codpiece corslet in the hall, which when his zeal was up he would needs throw down because it hung upon a cross.

Constant. But what think you of my neighbour? I hope her charity takes you.

Jolly. Yes, and her old waiting-woman's devotion. She sighed in the pew behind me—a Dutch skipper belches not so loud or so sour. My lady's miserable sinner with the white eyes, she does so squeeze out her prayers and so wring out, 'Have mercy upon us', I warrant her she has a waiting-woman's sting in her conscience. She looks like a dirty-souled bawd.

Constant. Who is this? My Lady Freedom's woman that he describes?

Jolly. The same, the independent lady. I have promised to send her a cripple or two by the next carrier. Her subject husband would needs show me his house one morning. I never visited such an hospital! It stunk like Bedlam, and all the servants were carrying poultices, juleps and glisters, and several remedies for all diseases but his. The man sighed to see his estate crumbling away. I counselled him either to give or take an ounce of ratsbane to cure his mind.

Constant. She is my cousin, but he made such a complaint to me I thought he had married the company of Surgeon's Hall, for his directions to me for several things for his wife's use were fitter for an apothecary's shop than a lady's closet.

Jolly. I advised him to settle no jointure but her old stills and a box of instruments upon her. She hates a man with all his limbs. A wooden leg, a crutch, and *fistula in ano* wins her heart. Her gentleman-usher broke his leg last dog-days merely to have the honour to have her set it—a foul, rank rogue, and so full of salt humours that he posed a whole college of old women with a gangrene (which spoiled the jest and his ambling before my lady) by applying a handsaw to his gartering-place. And now the rogue wears booted bed-staves and destroys all the young ashes to make him legs.

Sadd. I never saw such a nasty affection: she would ha' done well in the incurable—a handmaid to have waited on the cripples.

Jolly. She converses with naked men, and handles all their members though never so ill affected and calls the fornication charity. All her discourse to me was flat bawdry, which I could not chide, but spoke as flat as she till she rebuked me, calling mine beastliness and hers natural philosophy. By this day, if I were to marry, I would as soon have chosen a drawn whore out of mine own hospital and cure the sins of her youth as marry a she-chirurgeon, one that for her sins in her first husband's days cures all the crimes of her sex in my time. I would have him call her Chiron the Centaur's own daughter, a chirurgeon by sire and dam,

Apollo's own colt. She's red-haired too, like that bonny beast with the golden mane and flaming tail.

Sadd. You had a long discourse with her, Jolly; what was't about?

Jolly. I was advising her to be divorced and marry the man in the almanac. 'Twould be fine pastime for her to lick him whole.

Sadd. By this day, I never saw such a mule as her husband is to bear with her madness. The house is a good house and well furnished.

Jolly. Yes, but 'tis such a sight to see great French beds full of found children, sons of bachelors, priests' heirs, Bridewell orphans. There they lie by dozens in a bed, like sucking-rabbits in a dish or a row of pins. And then they keep a whole dairy of milch-whores to suckle them.

Sadd. She is successful, and that spoils her and makes her deaf to counsel. I bade him poison two or three to disgrace her, for the vanity and pride of their remedies make those women more diligent than their charity.

Jolly. I asked him why he married her and he confessed if he had been sound he had never had her.

Constant. He confessed she cured him of three claps before he married her.

Jolly. Yes, and I believe some other member (though then ill affected) pleaded more than his tongue. And the rogue is like to find her business still, for he flies at all. My God, I owe thee thanks for many things, but 'tis not the least I am not her husband, nor a country gentleman, whither I believe you cannot easily seduce me again unless you can persuade London to stand in the country. To Hyde Park or so I may venture upon your lady-fair days, when the filly foals of fifteen come kicking in, with their manes and tails tied up in ribands, to see their eyes roll and neigh when the spring makes their blood prick them; so far I am with you by the way of a country gentleman and a beer drinker.

Sadd. For all this dislike, Master Jolly, your greatest acquaintance lies with country gentlemen.

Jolly. Ay, at London; there your country gentlemen are good company, where to be seen with them is a kind of credit. I come to a mercer's shop in your coach: 'Boy, call your master.' He comes bare; I whisper him, 'Do you know the Constants and the Sadds of Norfolk?' 'Yes, yes,' he replies, and strokes his beard. 'They are good men,' cry I. 'Yes, yes.' 'No more, cut me off three suits of satin.' He does it, and in the delivery whispers, 'Will these be bound?' 'Pish! Drive on, coachman. Speak with me tomorrow.'

Constant. And what then?

Jolly. What then? Why, come again next day.

Sadd. And what if the country gentleman will not be bound?

Jolly. Then he must fight.

Sadd. I would I had known that before I had signed your bond: I would have set my sword sooner than my seal to it.

Jolly. Why, if thou repent there's no harm done: fight rather than pay it.

Sadd. Why, do you think I dare not fight?

Jolly. Yes, but I think thou hast more wit than to fight with me; for if I kill thee 'tis a fortune to me, and others will sign in fear; and if thou shouldst kill me, anybody that knows us would swear 'twere very strange and cry, 'There's God's just judgement now upon that lewd youth,' and thou procur'st his hangman's place at the rate of thy estate.

Constant. By this hand, he is in the right, and, for mine, I meant to pay when I signed. Hang it, never put good fellows to say, 'Prithee, give me a hundred pounds.'

Sadd. 'Tis true, 'tis a good ganty way of begging; yet, for being killed if I refuse it—would there were no more danger in the widow's unkindness than in your fighting. I would not mistrust my design.

Jolly. Why, ay, there's a point now: in nicety of honour I should kill you for her, for you know I pretended first; and it may be if I had writ sad lines to her and hid myself in my cloak and haunted her coach, it may be in time she would have sought me. Not I, by this hand, I'll not trouble myself for a wench, and married widows are but customary authorized wenches.

Constant. Being of that opinion, how cam'st thou to think of marrying one?

Jolly. Why, faith, I know not. I thought to rest me, for I was run out of breath with pleasure and grew so acquainted with sin I would have been good for variety. In these thoughts 'twas my fortune to meet with this widow, handsome, and of a clear fame.

Constant. Didst love her?

Jolly. Yes, faith; I had love, but not to the disease that makes men sick; and I could have loved her still but that I was angry to have her refuse me for a fault I told her of myself. So I went no more.

Sadd. Did she forbid you but once?

Jolly. Faith, I think I slipped a fair opportunity: a handsome wench and three thousand pounds per annum in certainty, besides the possibility of being saved.

Constant. Which now you think desperate?

'Widow *and* Pleasant *looking out at a window.*'

Pleasant. That is you. Cross or pile, will you have him yet or no?

Widow. Peace, observe them.

Jolly. Faith, no, I do not despair, but I cannot resolve.

'*Enter* Wild, Careless, *and the* Captain, *going in haste; he comes in at the middle door.*'

Widow. Who are those?

Careless. Captain, whither in such haste? What, defeated? Call you this a retreat or a flight from your friends?
                                                    [*They embrace.*]

Pleasant. Your nephew and his governor and his friend! Here will be a scene. Sit close, and we may know the secret of their hearts.

Widow. They have not met yet since they returned. I shall love this bay window.

Captain. Prithee, let me go. There's mischief a-boiling, and if thou shak'st me once more, thou wilt jumble a lie together I have been hammering this hour.

Careless. A pox upon you! A-studying lies?

Captain. Why then, they are no lies but something in the praise of an old lady's beauty. What do you call that?

'*They spy each other.*'

Jolly. Who are those?

Sadd. Is't not the Captain and my friend?

'*Jolly salutes them; then he goes to the Captain to embrace him. The Captain stands in a French posture and slides from his old way of embracing.*'

Jolly. Ned Wild! Tom Careless! What ail'st thou? Dost thou scorn my embraces?

Captain. I see you have never been abroad, else you would know how to put a value on those whose careful observation brought home the most exquisite garb and courtship that Paris could sell us.

Jolly. A pox on this fooling and leave off ceremony!

Captain. Why then, agreed. Off with our masks and let's embrace like the old knot.   '*They embrace.*'

Jolly. Faith, say where have you spent these three years time? In our neighbour France? Or have you ventured o'er the Alps to see the seat of the Caesars?

Sadd. And can tell us, ignorant, doomed to walk upon our own land, how large a seat the goddess fixed her flying Trojans in?

Constant. Yes, yes, and have seen, and drunk perhaps of Tiber's famous stream.

Jolly. And have been where Aeneas buried his trumpeter and his nurse. Tom looks as if he had sucked the one and had a battle sounded by the other for joy to see our nation, ambitious not to be understood or known when they come home.

Captain. So now I'm welcome home. This is freedom and these are friends, and with these I can be merry, for, gentlemen, you must give me leave to be free too.

Jolly. So you will spare us miserable men, condemned to London and the company of a Michaelmas term, and never travelled those countries that set mountains on fire a purpose to light us to our lodgings.

Wild. Why, this is better than to stay at home and lie by hearsay, wearing out yourselves and fortunes like your clothes, to see her that hates you for being so fine, then appearing at a play dressed like some part of it, while the company admire the mercer's and the tailor's work and swear they have done their parts to make you fine gentlemen.

Careless. Then leap out of your coach and throw your cloak over your shoulder—the casting-nets to catch a widow—while we have seen the world and learned her customs.

Captain. Yes, sir, and returned perfect monsieurs.

Sadd. Yes, even to their diseases. I confess my ignorance: I cannot amble, nor ride like St. George at Waltham.

Jolly. Yet, upon my conscience he may be as welcome with a trot as the other with his pace. ('*The* Captain *has a patch over his nose.*') And faith, Jack (to be a little free), tell me, dost thou not think thou hadst been as well to pass here with that English nose thou carried'st hence as with the French tongue thou hast brought home?

Captain. It is an accident, and to a soldier 'tis but a scar. 'Tis true such a sign upon Master Jolly's face had been as ill as a red cross and *Lord have mercy upon us* at his lodging door to have kept women out of court.

Jolly. For aught you know of the court.

Captain. I know the court, and thee and thy use, and how you serve but as the handsomest moveables, a kind of implement above stairs, and look much like one of the old court servants in the hangings.

Wild. But that they move and look fresher, and your apparel more modern.

Careless. Yet, faith, their office is the same—to adorn the room and be gazed on. Alas, he's sad. Courage, man, these riding clothes will serve thee at the latter day.

Captain. Which is one of their grievances, for nothing troubles them more than to think they must appear in a foul winding-sheet and come undressed.

Jolly. Gentlemen, I am glad to find you know the court; we know a traveller too, especially when he is thus changed and exchanged as your worships, both in purse and person, and have brought home foreign visages and inscriptions.

Constant. Why, that's their perfection, their ambition to have it said, 'There go those that have profitably observed the vices of other countries and made them their own, and the faults of several nations at their return are their parts.'

Jolly. Why, there's Jack Careless—he carried out as good stable manners as any was in Suffolk, and now he is returned with a shrug and a trick to stand crooked, like a scurvy bow unbent, and looks as if he would maintain oil and salads against a chine of beef. I knew a great beast of this kind; it haunted the court much and would scarcely allow us (fully reduced to civility) for serving up mutton in whole joints.

Constant. What, silent?

Sadd. Faith, the Captain is in a study.

Jolly. Do, do, con the rivers and towns perfectly, Captain; thou mayst become intelligencer to the people and lie thy two sheets a week in corantos too.

Constant. And could you not make friends at court to get their pictures cut ugly in the corner of a map, like the old navigators?

Jolly. We'll see, we'll see.

'*Enter* Widow *and* Pleasant *above.*'

Widow. I'll interrupt them. Servant, you're welcome to town. How now, nephew! What, dumb? Where are all our travelled tongues?

Jolly. Servant! who doth she mean? By this hand, I disclaim the title.

Pleasant. Captain, Secret has taken notes and desires you would instruct her in what concerns a waiting-woman and an old lady.

Captain. Very good! Yet this shall not save your dinner.

Widow. Nay, while you are in this humour I'll not sell your companies, and though Master Jolly be incensed I hope he will do me the favour to dine with me.

Jolly. Faith, lady, you mistake me if you think I am afraid of a widow, for I would have the world know I dare meet her anywhere, but at bed. (*Exit* Jolly.)

Wild. No more, aunt, we'll come; and if you will give us good meat, we'll bring good humours and good stomachs.

'Widow *shuts the curtain.*'

Careless. By this day, I'll not dine there; they take a pleasure to raise a spirit that they will not lay. I'll to Banks'.

Captain. A pox forbid it, you shall not break company now you know what we are to do after dinner.

Careless. I will consent, upon condition you forbid the spiritual nonsense the age calls Platonic love.

Captain. I must away too, but I'll be there at dinner. You will join in a plot after dinner?

Wild. Anything, good, bad, or indifferent, for a friend and mirth.   (*Exeunt all but the* Captain.

Captain. I must go and prevent the rogue's mischief with the old lady.   (*Exit* Captain.

ACT II · SCENE I

'*Enter* Jolly *and the old* Lady Love-all.'

Love-all. Away, unworthy, false, ingrateful! With what brow dar'st thou come again into my sight, knowing how unworthy you have been and how false to love?

Jolly. No, 'tis you are unworthy and deserve not those truths of love I have paid here; else you would not believe every report that envy brings, and condemn without hearing me whom you have so often tried and found faithful.

Love-all. Yes, till I, too credulous, had pity on your tears; till I had mercy you durst not be false.

Jolly. Nor am not yet.

Love-all. What dost thou call false? Is there a treachery beyond what thou hast done? When I had given my fame, my fortune, myself, and my husband's honour all in one obligation, a sacrifice to that passion which thou seem'st to labour with despair of, to tell and brag of a conquest o'er a woman fooled by her passion and lost in her love to thee, unworthy—   '*She turns away her head.*'

Jolly. By this day, 'tis as false as he that said it! Hang him, son of a bachelor, a slave that envying my fortune in such a happiness as your love and chaste embraces took this way to ruin it! Come, dry your eyes and let the guilty weep. If I were guilty I durst as soon approach a constable drunk as come here. You know I am your slave.

Love-all. You swore so, and honour made me leave to triumph over your miseries.

Jolly. Do you repent that I am happy? If you do, command my death.

Love-all. Nay, never weep, nor sit sadly. I am friends, so you will only talk and discourse, for 'tis your company I only court.

Jolly. No, you cannot forgive, because you have injured me. 'Tis right woman's justice: accuse first, and harder to reconcile when they are guilty than when they are innocent, or else you would not turn from me thus.

Love-all. You know your youth hath a strong power over me. Turn those bewitching eyes away; I cannot see them with safety of mine honour.

Jolly. Come, you shall not hide your face; there's a charm in it against those that come burnt with unchaste fires; for let but your eyes or nose drop upon his heart, it would burn it up, or quench it straight.

Love-all. No cogging, you have injured me; and now, though my love plead, I must be deaf—my honour bids me—for you will not fear again to prove unworthy when you find I am so easy to forgive. Why, you will not be uncivil?

'*Jolly kisses her and she shoves him away with her mouth.*'

Jolly [*Aside*]. So, the storm is laid. I must have those pearls. She shoved me away with her mouth. I'll to her again.

Love-all. Where are you? What do you take me for? Why, you will not be uncivil?

'*Still as he offers to touch her she starts as if he plucked up her coats.*'

Jolly. Uncivil! By thy chaste self, I cannot, chick. Thou hast such a terror, such a guard in those eyes, I dare not approach thee nor can I gaze upon so much fire. Prithee, sirrah, let me hide thee from their power here.

Love-all. You presume upon the weakness of our sex. What shall I say or do? Tyrant love!

Jolly. There's a charm in those pearls. Pull them off. If they have a frost in them, let me wear them and then we are both safe.

Love-all. I would you had taken them sooner; I had then been innocent and might with whiteness have worn my love which I shall ne'er outlive.

Jolly. Dear, do not too fast pour in my joys lest I too soon reach my heaven.

Love-all. Be gone then, lest we prove (having gained that height) this sad truth in love: 'the first minute after noon is night'.

Jolly. Part now? The Gods forbid! Take from me first

this load of joys you have thrown upon me, for 'tis a burden harder to bear than sadness. I was not born till now, this my first night in which I reap true bliss.

Love-all. No, no, I would it had been your first night; then your falsehood had not given argument for these tears. And I hate myself to think I should be such a foolish fly thus again to approach your dangerous flame.

Jolly. Come, divert these thoughts. I'll go see your closet.

Love-all. No, no, I swear you shall not.

Jolly. You know I am going out of town for two days.

Love-all. When you return I'll show it you; you will forget me else when you are gone and at court.

Jolly. Can your love endure delays? Or shall business thee from hence remove? These were your own arguments. Come, you shall show it me.

Love-all. Nay then, I perceive what unworthy way your love would find. Ye Gods, are all men false?

Jolly. As I live, you shall stay. Come, you ought to make me amends for slandering of me. Hang me if ever I told, and he that reports it is the damn'dst rogue in a country. Come, I say—

> '*He pulls her bodkin that is tied in a piece of black bobbin.*'

Love-all. Ah, as I live, I will not, I have sworn. Do not pull me. I will not be damned, I have sworn—

> '*He pulls her and says this.*'

Jolly. As I live, I'll break your bodkin then. A weeping tyrant! Come, by this good day, you shall be merciful.

Love-all. Why, you will not be uncivil? You will not force me, will you? As I live, I will not.

Jolly. Nay, an you be wilful, I can be stubborn too.

> '*He pulls still.*'

Love-all. Hang me, I'll call aloud. Why, Nan! Nay, you may force me, but, as I live, I will do nothing.

> (*Exeunt ambo.*

SCENE II

'*Enter* Captain.'

Captain. A pox upon you, are you earthed? The rogue
has got her necklace of pearl, but I hope he will leave the rope
to hang me in. How the pox came they so great? I must have
some trick to break his neck, else the young rogue will work
me out. 'Tis an excellent old lady, but I dare not call her so.
Yet, would she were young enough to bear—we might do
some good for our heirs by leaving such a charitable brood
behind. She's a woman after the first kind: 'tis but going
in to her and you may know her. Then she'll oblige so
readily, and gives with greater thanks than others receive,
takes it so kindly to be courted. I am now to oblige her (as
she calls it) by professing young Wild's love and desiring
an assurance she's sensible of his sufferings, which, though
it be false and beyond my commission, yet the hopes of such
a new young thing that has the vogue of the town for handsomest—'twill so tickle her age and so blow up her vanity
to have it said he is in love with her, and so endear her to
me for being the means, that the Parson's malice will be able
to take no root. She comes. I must not be seen.

[*Exit* Captain.]

'*Enter* Love-all *and* Jolly.'

Love-all. Give me that letter; I'll swear you shall not
read it.

Jolly. Take it; I'll away. What time shall I call you? In
the evening? There's a play at court tonight.

Love-all. I would willingly be there, but your ladies are
so censorious and malicious to us young ladies in the town,
especially to me, because the wits are pleased to afford me
a visit or so; I could be content else to be seen at court.
Pray what humour is the queen of? The captain of her
guard I know.

Jolly. The queen? ('*The* Captain *knocks.*') Who's that
knocks at the back door?

Love-all. Smoothe my band. I know not. Go down that
way, and look you be not false. If you should be false, I'll
swear I should spoil myself with weeping.

Jolly. Farewell. In the evening I'll call you. (*Exit* Jolly.
Love-all ('*She takes a book in her hand and sits down.*').
Who's there?

[*Enter* Captain.]

Captain? Where have you been all this while? I might sit
alone, I see, for you, if I could not find conversation in books.

Captain. Faith, madam, friends newly come to town engaged me and my stay was civility rather than desire. What
book's that?

Love-all. I'll swear he was a witch that writ it, for he
speaks my thoughts as if he had been within me. The
original, they say, was French.

Captain. Oh, I know it: 'tis *The Accomplished Woman*—
yourself he means by this, while you are yourself.

Love-all. Indeed, I confess I am a great friend to conversation if we could have it without suspicion. But the
world's so apt to judge that 'tis a prejudice to our honour
now to salute a man.

Captain. Innocence, madam, is above opinion, and your
fame's too great to be shook with whispers.

Love-all. You are ever civil and therefore welcome. Pray,
what news is there now in town, for I am recluse here.
Unless it be yours I receive no visits, and I'll swear I charged
the wench today not to let you in. I wonder she let you come.

Captain. Faith, madam, if it had been my own business I
should not have ventured so boldly. But the necessity that
forces me to come concerns my friend, against whom if your
mercy be now bounded with those strict ties of honour and
cold thoughts which I have ever found guard your heart,
my friend, a young and handsome man, is lost—is lost in his
prime and falls like early blossoms. But methinks you should
not prove the envious frost to destroy this young man, this
delicate young man, that has whole bundles of boys in his
breeches. Yet if you be cruel, he and they die, as useless as
open-arses gathered green.

'*She must be earnest in her looks all the time he speaks,
desirous to know who he speaks of.*'

Love-all. Good Captain, out with the particular. What
way can my charity assist him? You know by experience I

cannot be cruel. Remember how I fetched you out of a swound and laid you in my own bed.

Captain. That act preserved a life that has always been laboured in your service, and, I dare say, your charity here will find as fruitful a gratitude.

Love-all. But I hope he will not be so uncivil as you were. I'll swear I could have hanged you for that rape, if I would have followed the law. But I forgave you upon condition you would do so again. But what's this young man you speak of?

Captain. Such is my love to you and him that I cannot prefer mine own particular before your contents; else I'd have poisoned him ere I'd have brought him to your house.

Love-all. Why, I pray?

Captain. Because he's young, handsome, and [of] sound parts. That, I'm sure, will ruin me here.

Love-all. His love may make all these beauties, else I have an honour will defend me against him were he as handsome as young Wild.

Captain. Why, ay, there it is: that one word has removed all my fears and jealousies with a despair, for that's the man whose love, life, and fortune lies at your feet. And if you were single, by lawful ways he would hope to reach what now he despairs of.

Love-all. Let him not despair. Love is a powerful pleader, and youth and beauty will assist him. And if his love be noble I can meet it, for there's none that sacrifices more to friendship-love than I.

Captain. My friend's interest makes me rejoice at this. Dare you trust me to say this to him, though it be not usual? Pray speak. Nay, you are so long still a-resolving to be kind. Remember, charity is as great a virtue as chastity, and greater, if we will hear nature plead: for the one may make many maids, the other can but preserve one. But I know you will be persuaded; let [it] be my importunity that prevailed. Shall I bring him hither one evening?

Love-all. Why do you plead thus? Pray be silent, and when you see him, tell him he has a seat here, and I—

                              '*She turns away.*'

Captain. Out with it! What is't? Shall he call you mistress, and his Platonic?

Love-all. Away, away! Me?

Captain. No niceness, is't a match?

Love-all. Lord, would I were worthy as willing; pray tell him so. He shall find me one of the humblest mistresses that ever he was pleased to honour with his affections.

Captain. Dare you write this to him and honour me with bearing it? I confess I am such a friend to friendship-love too that I would even bring him on my back to a midnight's meeting.

Love-all. If you will stay here I'll go in and write it.

'She's going out and he calls her.'

Captain. Madam, I forgot to ask your ladyship one question.

Love-all. What was't?

Captain. There happened a business last night betwixt Master Wild and one Jolly, a courtier, that brags extremely of your favour. I swear if it had not been for friends that interposed themselves there had been mischief, for Master Wild was extreme zealous in your cause.

Love-all. Such a rascal I know. Villain, to bring my name upon the stage for a subject of his quarrels! I'll have him cudgelled.

Captain. And I'll swear he deserved it, for the quarrel ended in a bet of a buck hunting-nag that sometime today he would bring a necklace and chain of pearl of yours (not stolen but freely given) to witness his power.

Love-all. Did the vain rascal promise that?

Captain. Yes, but we laughed at it.

Love-all. So you might. And, as I live, if the necklace were come from stringing I'd send them both to Master Wild to wear as a favour, to assure him I am his and to put the vain slave out of countenance.

Captain. Ay, marry, such a timely favour were worth a dozen letters to assure him of your love and remove all the doubts the other's discourse may put into his head. And, faith, I'd send him the chain now and in my letter promise him the necklace; he'll deserve such a favour.

Love-all. I'll go in and fetch it immediately. Will you favour me to deliver it?

Captain. I'll wait upon your ladyship.

Love-all. I'll swear you shall not go in; you know I for-swore being alone with you.

'*She goes and he follows her. She turns and bids him stay.*'

Captain. Hang me, I'll go in. Does my message deserve to wait an answer at the door?

Love-all. Ay, but you'll be naught.

Captain. Oh, ne'er trust me if I break.

Love-all. If you break, some such forfeit you'll lose. Well, come in for once.

Captain. You are so suspicious.

Love-all. I'll swear I have reason for 't: you are such another man. (*Exeunt* Love-all *and* Captain.

SCENE III

'*Enter* Wanton *and* Bawd.'

Wanton. Is he gone?

Bawd. Yes, he's gone to the old lady's, high with mischief.

Wanton. Fare him well, easy fool. How the trout strove to be tickled! ('*She plays with the wedding-ring upon her finger.*') And how does this ring become me? Ha, they are fine kind of things, these wedding-rings.

Bawd. Besides the good custom of putting so much gold in 'em they bring such conveniences along.

Wanton. Why, ay, now I have but one to please, and if I please him, who dares offend me? And that wife's a fool that cannot make her husband one.

Bawd. Nay, I am absolutely of opinion it was fit for you to marry, but whether he be a good husband or no—

Wanton. A pox of a good husband, give me a wise one; they only make the secure cuckolds, the cuckold in grain; for, d'ye a husband that has wit but with an opinion thou art honest and see who dares wash the colour out. Now your fool changes with every drop, dotes with confidence in the morning and at night jealous even to murder, and his love (Lord help us) fades like my gredaline petticoat.

Bawd. This is a new doctrine.

Q

Wanton. 'Tis a truth, wench, I have gained from my own observations; and the paradox will be maintained: take wise men for cuckolds and fools to make them; for your wise man draws eyes and suspicion with his visit and begets jealous thoughts in the husband that his wife may be overcome with his parts, when the fool is welcome to both, pleaseth both, laughs with the one and lies with the other, and all without suspicion. I tell thee, a fool that has money is the man. The wits and the we's—which is a distinct parreal of wit bound by itself and to be sold at Wit-hall or at the sign of the King's Head in the Butchery—these wise things will make twenty jealous ere one man a cuckold, when the family of fools will head a parish ere they are suspected.

Bawd. Well, I see one may live and learn. And if he be but as good at it now you are his own as he was when he was your friend's friend (as they call it), you have got one of the best hiders of such a business in the town. Lord, how he would sister you at a play!

Wanton. Faith, 'tis as he is used at first: if he get the bridle in 's teeth he'll ride to the devil; but if thou beest true, we'll make him amble ere we have done. The plot is here, and if it thrive I'll alter the proverb, *The parson gets the children* to *The parson fathers them.*

Bawd. Anything that may get rule. I love to wear the breeches.

Wanton. So do we all, wench. Empire—'tis all our aim; and I'll put my ranting Roger in a cage but I'll tame him. He loves already, which is an excellent ring in a fool's nose, and thou shalt hear him sing,

> Happy only is that family that shows
> A cock that's silent and a hen that crows.

Bawd. Do this, I'll serve you for nothing. The impetuous slave had wont to taunt me for beating of my husband and would sing that song in mockery of me.

Wanton. In revenge of which thou (if thou wilt be faithful) shalt make him sing,

> Happy is that family that shows
> A cock that's silent and a hen that crows.

(*Exeunt* Wanton *and* Bawd.

SCENE IV

'*Enter* Parson, Love-all, *and* Faithful.'

Love-all. Go, you are a naughty man. Do you come hither to rail against an honest gentleman? I have heard how you fell out. You may be ashamed on 't, a man of your coat.

Parson. What, to speak truth and perform my duty? The world cries out you are a scabbed sheep, and I come to tar you, that is, give you notice how your fame suffers i'th' opinion of the world.

Love-all. My fame, sirrah? 'Tis purer than thy doctrine. Get thee out of my house.

Faithful. You uncivil fellow, do you come hither to tell my lady of her faults as if her own Levite could not discern 'em?

Love-all. My own Levite? I hope he's better bred than to tell me of my faults.

Faithful. He finds work enough to correct his dearly beloved sinners.

Parson. And the right worshipful my lady and yourself— they mend at leisure.

Love-all. You are a saucy fellow, sirrah, to call me sinner in my own house. Get you gone with your '*Madam, I hear,*' and '*Madam, I could advise but I am loth to speak; take heed, the world talks—*' and thus with dark sentences put my innocence into a fright with '*You know what you know, good Mistress Faithful.*' So do I, and the world shall know too, thou hast married a whore.

Parson. Madam, a whore?

Faithful. No sir, 'tis not so well as a madam-whore; 'tis a poor whore, a captain's cast whore.

Love-all. Now bless me, marry a whore! I wonder any man can endure those things. What kind of creatures are they?

Parson. They're like ladies but that they are handsomer. And though you take a privilege to injure me, yet I would advise your woman to tie up her tongue and not abuse my wife.

Love-all. Fie, art thou not ashamed to call a whore wife? Lord bless us, what will not these men do when God leaves them! But for a man of your coat to cast himself away upon a whore! Come, wench, let's go, and leave him. I'll swear 'tis strange the state doth not provide to have all whores hanged or drowned.

Faithful. Ay, and 'tis time they look into it, for they begin to spread so, that a man can scarce find an honest woman in a country. They say they're voted down now; 'twas moved by that charitable member that got an order to have it but five miles to Croydon for ease of the market-women.

Love-all. Ay, ay, 'tis a blessed parliament.

(*Exeunt* Love-all *and* Faithful.

Parson. That I have played the fool is visible. This comes of rashness. Something I must do to set this right or else she'll hate and he'll laugh at me. I must not lose him and my revenge too. Something's that mischief I am resolved to do.

(*Exit* Parson.

SCENE V

'*Enter* Wild *and* Careless.'

Wild. Now, is the Parson's wife so contemptible?

Careless. No, but I'm so full of that resolution to dislike the sex that I will allow none honest, none handsome. I tell thee, we must beat down the price with ourselves, court none of 'em, but let their maidenheads and their faces lie upon their hands till they're weary of the commodity. Then they'll haunt us to find proper chapmen to deal for their ware.

Wild. I like this, but 'twill be long a-doing, and it may be ere they be forced to sell, our bank will be exhausted and we shall not be able to purchase.

Careless. Ay, but we'll keep a credit, and at three six-months thou and the Captain shall be my factors.

Wild. You had best have a partner, else such an under-taking would break a better back than yours.

Careless. No partners in such commodities: your factor that takes up maidenheads, 'tis upon his own account still.

Wild. But what course will you take to purchase this trade with women?

Careless. I am resolved to put on their own silence and modesty, answer *forsooth*, swear nothing but *God's nigs*, and hold arguments of their own cold tenents, as if I believed there were no true love below the line; then sigh when 'tis proper, and with forced studies betray the enemy, who, seeing my eye fixed on her, her vanity thinks I am lost in admiration, calls and shakes me ere I wake out of my design, and being collected, answer out of purpose, 'Love, divinest? Yes, who is it that is mortal and does not? Or which amongst all the senate of the Gods can gaze upon those eyes and carry thence the power he brought?' This will start her.

Wild. Yes, and make her think thee mad.

Careless. Why, that's my design, for then I start too and rub my eyes as if I waked, then sigh and strangle a yawn, till I have wrung it into tears, with which I rise as if o'er-come with grief; then kiss her hands and let fall those witnesses of faith and love, bribed for my design. This takes, for who would suspect such a devil as craft and youth to live together?

Wild. But what kind of women do you think this will take?

Careless. All kind of women: those that think themselves handsome, it being probable, concludes it real; and those that are handsome in their opinion, that small number will believe it because it agrees with their wishes.

Wild. And when you are gone, it may be they sigh and their love breaks out into paper, and what then?

Careless. What then? Why, then I'll laugh, and show thee their letters and teach the world how easy 'tis to win any woman.

Wild. This is the way, and be sure to dislike all but her you design for; be scarce civil to any of the sex besides.

Careless. That's my meaning—but to her that I mean my prey, all her slave. She shall be my deity and her opinion my religion.

Wild. And while you sad it thus to one, I'll talk freer than a privileged fool and swear as unreasonably as losing game-sters and abuse thee for thinking to reclaim a woman by thy love; call them all bowls thrown, that will run where they will run, and lovers like fools run after them crying, 'Rub' and 'Fly for me'. I believe none fair, none handsome, none honest, but the kind.

Careless. We must make the Captain of our plot lest he betray us. This will gain us some revenge upon the lovers, to whom I grudge the wenches—not that I believe they're worth half the cost they pay for them. And we may talk, but 'tis not our opinion can make them happier or [more] miserable.

'*Enter* Jolly.'

Wild. Jolly, Will! where hast thou been? We had such sport with the Parson of our town. He's married this morning to Wanton.

Jolly. Who? The Captain's wench? He's in a good humour then. As you love mirth, let's find him. I have news to blow his rage with, and 'twill be mirth for us to see him divided betwixt the several causes of his anger and lose himself in his rage while he disputes which is the greater. ('*Here he pulls out the pearl.*') Your opinion, gentlemen: is this, or his wench, the greater loss?

Careless. What hast thou there? Pearl! They're false, I hope.

Jolly. Why do you hope so?

Careless. Because I am your friend and would be loth to have thee hanged for stealing.

Jolly. I will not swear they are honestly come by, but I'll be sworn there's neither force nor theft in 't.

Wild. Prithee speak out of riddles; here's none but your friends.

Jolly. Faith, take it. You have heard the Captain brag of an old lady, which he thinks he keeps close in a box—but I know where hangs a key can let a friend in or so. From her, my brace of worthies, whose wits are dulled with plenty, this morning with three good words and four good deeds I earned this toy.

Careless. The mirth yet we will all share. I am in pain

till we find him that we may vex his wit that he presumes so much on.

Wild. Let's go, let's go. I will desire him to let me see his wench. I will not understand him if he says she's gone.

Careless. I'll beg of him for old acquaintance sake to let me see his old lady.

Jolly. Hark, I hear his voice.

Captain [Within]. Which way?

Careless. The game plays itself. Begin with him, Ned, while we talk as if we were busy. We'll take our cue.

Wild. When I put off my hat.

'Enter Captain.'

Captain. 'Sblood, I thought you had been sunk; I have been hunting you these four hours. Death, you might ha' left word where you went and not put me to hunt like Tom Fool. 'Tis well you are at London, where you know the way home.

Wild. Why in choler? We have been all this while searching you. Come, this is put on to divert me from claiming your promise. I must see the wench.

Captain. You cannot, adad. Adad, you cannot.

Wild. I did not think you would have refused such a kindness.

Careless. What's that?

Wild. Nothing, a toy. He refuses to show me his wench.

Careless. The devil he does. What, have we been thus long comrades and had all things in common and must we now come to have common wenches particular? I say thou shalt see her, and lie with her too if thou wilt.

Jolly. What, in thy dumps, brother? Call to thy aid thy two-edged wit. The Captain sad? 'Tis prophetic. I'd as lief have dreamt of pearl or the loss of my teeth. Yet if he be musty, I'll warrant thee, Ned, I'll help thee to a bout. I know his cloak, his long cloak that hides her. I am acquainted with the Parson; he shall befriend thee.

Captain. 'Tis very well, gentlemen, but none of you have seen her yet?

Wild. Yes, but we have, by thyself, by thy anger, which is now bigger than thou. By chance we crossed her coming from church, leading in her hand the Parson, to whom she swore she was this day married.

Jolly. And our friendships were now guiding us to find thee out to comfort thee after the treachery of thy Levite.

Careless. Come, bear it like a man. There are more wenches. ('*He gives no answer but peeps on Jolly's hat.*') What hast thou spied?

Wild. His pearl, I believe.

Captain. Gentlemen, I see you are merry. I'll leave you; I must go a little way to enquire about a business.

Wild. H'as got a sore eye, I think.

Captain. I will only ask one question and return.

Careless. No, faith, stay and be satisfied.

Jolly. Do, good brother, for I believe there is no question that you now would ask but here's an oracle can resolve you.

Captain. Are those pearls true?

Jolly. Yes.

Captain. And did not you steal them?

Jolly. No.

Careless. Nor did he not buy them with ready money, but took them upon mortgage of himself to an old lady.

Jolly. Dwelling at the sign of the Buck, in Broad Street. Are you satisfied, or must I play the oracle still?

Captain. No, no, I am satisfied.

Jolly. Like jealous men that take their wives at it, are you not?

Captain. Well, very well, 'tis visible, I am abused on all hands. But, gentlemen, why all against me?

Careless. To let you see your wit's mortal and not proof against all.

Wild. The Parson hath shot it through with a jest.

Captain. Gentlemen, which of you, faith, had a hand in that?

Jolly. Faith, none, only a general joy to find the Captain over-reached.

Captain. But do you go sharers in the profit as well as in the jest?

Jolly. No, faith, the toy's mine own.

Captain. They are very fine, and you may afford a good pennyworth. Will you sell them?

Jolly. Sell them? Ay; where's a chapman?

Captain. Here, I'll purchase them.

Jolly. Thou? No, no, I have barred thee, by and main, for I am resolved not to fight for them. That excludes thy purchase by the sword; and thy wench has proved such a loss in thy last adventure of wit that I'm afraid it will spoil thy credit that way too.

Captain. Gentlemen, as a friend, let me have the refusal. Set your price.

Wild. He's serious.

Careless. Leave fooling.

Jolly. Why, if thou couldst buy them, what wouldst thou do with them?

Captain. They're very fair ones. Let me see them. Methinks they should match very well with these.

Jolly. These! Which?

Omnes. Which?

Careless. They are true.

Captain. Yes, but not earned with a pair of stolen verses of 'I was not born till now, this my first night,' and so forsooth, nor given as a charm against lust.

Careless. What means all this?

Jolly. What? Why, 'tis truth, and it means to shame the devil. By this good day he repeats the same words with which I gathered these pearls.

Wild. Why then, we have two to laugh at.

Careless. And all friends hereafter. Let's fool all together.

Captain. Gentlemen with the fine wits, and my very good friends, do you, or you, or he, think I'll keep you company to make you laugh but that I draw my honey from you too?

Careless. Come, come, the Captain's in the right.

Captain. Yes, yes, the Captain knows it and dares tell you your wit, your fortune, and his face are but my ploughs; and I would have my fine monsieur know, who in spite of my counsel will be finer than his mistress, and appears before her so curiously built she dares not play with him for fear of spoiling him; and to let him know the truth I speak, to his fair hands I present this letter, but withal give him to understand the contents belong to me.

'*He reads the letter.*'

Wild. The pearl are sent to me.

Captain. I deny that unless you prove you sent me, for the letter begins, 'Sir, this noble gentleman, the bearer, whom you are pleased to make the messenger of your love,' and so forth. And now you should do well to enquire for that noble gentleman and take an account of him how he has laid out your love, and it may be he'll return you pearl for it. And now, gentlemen, I dare propose a peace, at least a cessation of wit (but what is defensive) till such time as the plot which is now in my head be effected, in which you have all your shares.

Wild. So she knows I have not the pearl I am content.

Captain. She'll quickly find that when she sees you come not tonight according to my appointment and hears I have sold the pearl.

Jolly. Here then ceaseth our offensive war.

Captain. I'll give you counsel worth two ropes of pearl.

Careless. But the wench—how came the Parson to get her?

Captain. Faith, 'tis hard to say which laboured most, he or I, to make that match; but the knave did well. There it is (if you assist) I mean to lay the scene of your mirth tonight, for I am not yet fully revenged upon the rogue; for that I know him miserable is nothing till he believe so too. Wanton and I have laid the plot.

Jolly. Do you hold correspondence?

Captain. Correspondence? I tell thee the plots we laid to draw him on would make a comedy.

'*Enter* a Servant.'

Servant. Sir, the ladies stay dinner.

Jolly. And as we go I'll tell you all the story, and after dinner be free from all engagements as we promised thee; and follow but your directions, I'll warrant you mirth and a pretty wench.

Omnes. Agreed; anything that breeds mirth is welcome.

Jolly. Not a word at the Widow's; let them go on quietly and steal their wedding too.

Captain. I heard a bird sing as if it were concluded amongst the couples.

Wild. They have been long about it; my coz is a girl deserves more haste to her bed. He has arrived there by carrier's journeys.

Careless. But that I hate wooing, by this good day, I like your aunt so well and her humour, she should scarce be thrown away upon paleface, that has sighed her into a wedding-ring and will but double her jointure.

Captain. Why, ay, thus it should be. Pray let us make them the seat of the war all dinner and continue united and true among ourselves; then we may defy all foreign danger.

Jolly. And with full bowls let us crown this peace and sing, 'Wit without war no mirth doth bring.'

(*Exeunt omnes.*

SCENE VI

'*Enter* Parson *and* Wanton.'

Wanton. Was she deaf to your report?

Parson. Yes, yes.

'*The* Parson *walks troubled up and down.*'

Wanton. And ugly, her Abigail, she had her say too?

Parson. Yes, yes.

Wanton. And do you walk here biting your nails? Do you think I'll be satisfied with such a way of righting me?

Parson. What wouldst have me do?

Wanton. Have you no gall? Be abused and laughed at by a dull captain that a strict muster would turn fool! You had wit and could rail when I offended you, and none so sudden, none so terrible, none so sure in his revenge when I displease you.

Parson. Something I'll do.

Wanton. Do it then, or I shall curse that e'er I saw you. Death, let the sign of my lady, an out of fashion whore that has paid for sin ever since yellow starch and wheel fardingales were cried down, let her abuse me and say nothing? If this passes—

Parson. As Christ bless me, but I did, sweetheart. And if it were not Church livings are mortal—and they are always hitting me in the teeth with 'a man of your coat'—she should find I am no churchman within nor Master Parson but in my coat. Come to dinner, and after dinner I'll do something.

Wanton. I shall do something shall vex somebody.

'*Enter* Bawd.'

Bawd. Will you please to come to dinner? The company stays.

Parson. Come, let's go in.

Wanton. No, I must walk a little to digest this breakfast; the guests else will wonder to see I am troubled.

Parson. Come, let this day pass in mirth, spite of mischief, for luck's sake. (*Exit* Parson.

Wanton. I'll follow you, and do what I can to be merry.

Bawd. Why, he stands already.

Wanton. Peace, let me alone, I'll make him jostle like the miller's mare and stand like the dun cow till thou mayst milk him.

Bawd. Pray break him of his miserableness—it is one of the chief exceptions I have against him. He reared a puppy once till it was ten days old with three hap'orth of milk, and then with his own dagger slew it and made me dress it; blessed myself to see him eat it, and he bid me beg the litter, and swore it was sweeter and wholesomer than suckingrabbits or London pigs, which he called Bellmen's issue.

Parson (*Within*). Why, sweetheart.

Wanton. Hark, he calls me. We must humour him a little; he'll rebel else. (*Exeunt* Wanton *and* Bawd.

SCENE VII

'*Enter* (*at the windows*) *the* Widow *and* Master Careless, Mistress Pleasant *and* Master Wild, Captain, Jolly, Secret. *A table and knives ready for oysters.*'

Widow. You're welcome all, but especially Master Jolly. No reply with, 'I thank your ladyship.'

Pleasant ('*She speaks to* Master Jolly). I beseech you, sir, let us never be better acquainted.

Jolly. I shall endeavour, lady, and fail in nothing that is in my power to disoblige you, for there is none more ambitious of your ill opinion than I.

Pleasant. I rejoice at it, for the less love the better welcome still.

Widow. And as ever you had an ounce of love for the Widow, be not friends among yourselves.

Wild. Aunt, though we were at strife when we were alone, yet now we unite like a politic state against the common enemy.

Pleasant. The common enemy—what is that?

Wild. Women, and lovers in general.

Widow. Nay then, we have a party, niece. Claim quickly; now is the time, according to the proverb, keep a thing seven years and then if thou hast no use on 't, throw 't away.

Pleasant. Agreed; let's challenge our servants. By the love they have professed they cannot in honour refuse to join with us. And see where they come.

'*Enter* Sadd *and* Constant, *and meet* Secret. *She whispers this to* Sadd.'

Secret. Sir, 'tis done.

Sadd. Be secret and grave, I'll warrant our design will take as we can wish.

Constant. Sweet Mistress Pleasant!

Widow. Servant Sadd.

Sadd. Madam.

Widow. We are threatened to have a war waged against us. Will you not second us?

Sadd. With these youths we'll do enough, madam.

Widow. I'll swear my servant gave hit for hit this morning as if he had been a master in the noble science of wit.

Pleasant. Mine laid about him with spick and span new arguments, not like the same man, his old sayings and precedents laid by.

Widow. Thus armed then, we'll stand and defy them.

Wild. Where's your points? Sure, aunt, this should be your wedding-day, for you have taken the man for better for worse.

Widow. No, nephew, this will not prove the day that we shall either give or take a ring.

Careless. Hang me if I know you can go back again with your honour.

Wild. Or in justice refuse him liberty that has served out his time. Either marry him or provide for him, for he is maimed in your service.

Widow. Why, servant Sadd, you'll arm? My nephew has thrown the first dart at you.

Captain. Has't hit, has't hit?

Wild. No, Captain, 'twas too wide.

Captain. Too wide? Marry, he's an ill marksman that shoots wider than a widow.

Jolly. We are both in one hole, Captain; but I was loth to venture my opinion lest her ladyship should think I was angry, for I have a good mind to fall upon the widow.

Pleasant. You're a constant man, Master Jolly; you have been in that mind this twelvemonths day.

Constant. You are in the right, madam: she has it to show under his hand, but she will not come in the list with him again; she threw him the last year.

Widow. Come, shall we eat oysters? Who's there? Call for some wine. Master Jolly, you are not warm yet. Pray be free; you are at home.

Jolly. Your ladyship is merry.

Widow. You do not take it ill to have me assure you you are at home here?

Wild. Such another invitation (though in jest) will take away Master Sadd's stomach. '*Oysters not brought in yet.*'

Sadd. No, faith, Ned, though she should take him, it will not take away my stomach. My love is so fixed I may wish my wishes but she shall never want them to wait upon hers.

Pleasant. A traitor! Bind him, h'as pulled down a side. Profess your love thus public?

Jolly. Ay, by my faith, continue, Master Sadd; give it out you love and call it a new love, a love never seen before; we'll all come to it as your friends.

Sadd. Gentlemen, still I love, and if she to whom I thus sacrifice will not reward it, yet the worst malice can say is, I was unfortunate, and misfortune not falsehood made me so.

Jolly. In what chapter shall we find this written and what verse? You should preach with a method, Master Sadd.

Widow. Gentlemen, if ever he spoke so much dangerous sense before (either of love or reason), hang me.

Sadd. Madam, my love is no news where you are; know your scorn has made it public, and though it could gain no return from you, yet others have esteemed me for the faith and constancy I have paid here.

Pleasant. Did not I foretell you of his love? I foresaw this danger. Shall I never live to see wit and love dwell together?

Captain. I am but a poor soldier and yet never reached to the honour of being a lover, yet from my own observations, Master Sadd, take a truth: 'tis a folly to believe any woman loves a man for being constant to another; they dissemble their hearts only and hate a man in love worse than a wencher.

Jolly. And they have reason, for if they have the grace to be kind, he that loves the sex may be theirs—

Careless. When your constant lover, if a woman have a mind to him and be blest with so much grace to discover it, he out of the noble mistake of honour hates her for it and tells it perchance, and preaches reason to her passion and cries, 'Miserable beauty to be so unfortunate as to inhabit in so much frailty.'

Captain. This counsel makes her hate him more than she loved before. These are troubles those that love are subject to, while we look on and laugh to see both thus slaved while we are free.

Careless. My prayers still shall be, Lord deliver me from love.

Captain. 'Tis plague, pestilence, famine, sword, and sometimes sudden death.

Sadd. Yet I love, I must love, I will love, and I do love.

Captain. In the present tense.

Widow. No more of this argument, for love's sake.

Captain. By any means, madam, give him leave to love, an you are resolved to walk tied up in your own arms, with your love as visible in your face as your mistress's colours in your hat, that any porter at Charing Cross may take you like a letter at the carrier's, and having read the superscription deliver Master Sadd to the fair hands of Mistress or my Lady Such-a-one, lying at the sign of the hard heart.

Pleasant. And she, if she has wit (as I believe she hath), will scarce pay the post for the packet.

Widow. Treason! How now, niece, join with the enemy?
'*They give the* Captain *wine.*'

Captain. A health, Ned—what shall I call it?

Careless. To Master Sadd! He needs it that avows himself a lover.

Sadd. Gentlemen, you have the advantage, the time, the place, the company, but we may meet when your wits shall not have such advantage as my love.

Pleasant. No more of love, I am so sick on't.

Constant. By your pardon, mistress, I must not leave love thus unguarded; I vow myself his follower.

Jolly. Much good may love do him. Give me a glass of wine here. Will, let them keep company with the blind boy— give us his mother, and let them preach again, hear that will. He has good luck persuades me 'tis an ugly sin to lie with a handsome woman.

Captain. A pox upon my nurse, she frighted me so when I was young with stories of the devil, I was almost fourteen ere I could prevail with reasons to unbind my reason, it was so slaved to faith and conscience. She made me believe wine was an evil spirit and fornication was like the whore of Babylon, a fine face but a dragon under her petticoats; and that made me have a mind to peep under all I met since.

Widow. Fie, fie, for shame, do not talk so! Are you not ashamed to glory in sin, as if variety of women were none?

Jolly. Madam, we do not glory in fornication, and yet I thank God I cannot live without a woman.

Captain. Why, does your ladyship think it a sin to lie with variety of handsome women? If it be, I would I were the wicked'st man in the company.

Pleasant. You have been marked for an indifferent sinner that way, Captain.

Captain. Who, I? No, faith, I was a fool; but an I were to begin again, I would not do as I have done. I kept one, but if ever I keep another, hang me. Nor would I advise any friend of mine to do it.

Jolly. Why, I am sure 'tis a provident and safe way: a man may always be provided and sound.

Pleasant. Fie upon this discourse!

Captain. Those considerations betrayed me. A pox, it is a dull sin to travel like a carrier's horse, always one road.

Widow. Fie, Captain, repent for shame and marry.

Captain. Your ladyship would have said, 'Marry and repent.' No, though it be not the greatest pleasure, yet it is better than marrying; for when I am weary of her, my unconstancy is termed virtue and I shall be said to turn to grace. Beware of women for better for worse; for our wicked nature, when her sport is lawful, cloys straight. Therefore, rather than marry, keep a wench.

Jolly. Faith, he is in the right, for 'tis the same thing in number and kind, and then the sport is quickened and made poynant with sin.

Captain. Yet 'tis a fault, faith, and I'll persuade all my friends from it, especially here, where any innovation is dangerous. 'Twas the newness of the sin that made me suffer in the opinion of my friends, and I was condemned by all sorts of people, not that I sinned, but that I sinned no more.

Careless. Why, ay, hadst thou been wicked in fashion and privily lain with everybody, their guilt would have made them protect thee; so that to be more wicked is to be innocent, at least safe. A wicked world, Lord help us!

Captain. But being particular to her and not in love nor subject to it, taking an antidote every morning before I ventured into those infectious places where love-beauty dwells, this enraged the maiden beauties of the time, who thought it a prejudice to their beauties to see me careless, and securely pass by their conquering eyes, my name being found amongst none of those that decked their triumphs. But from this 'tis easy to be safe, for their pride will not let them love nor my leisure me. Then the old ladies that pay for their pleasures, they upon the news beheld me with their natural frowns, despairing when their money could not prevail, and hated me when they heard that I for my pleasure would pay as large as they.

Jolly. Gentlemen, take warning: a fee from every man, for by this day there's strange counsel in this confession.

Widow. Captain, you forget to pledge Master Careless. Here, will you not drink a cup of wine? Who's there? Bring the oysters.

Captain. Yes, madam, if you please.

Wild. Proceed, Captain.

Pleasant. Fie, Master Wild, are you not ashamed to encourage him to this filthy discourse?

Captain. A glass of wine there, and I'll drink to all the new-married wives that grieve to think at what rate their fathers purchase a little husband. These, when they lie thirsting for the thing they paid so dear for—

'*Enter a servant with oysters.*'

Careless. These, methinks, should be thy friends and point thee out as a man for them.

Captain. Yes, till the faithful nurse cries, 'Alas, madam, he keeps such a one, he has enough at home.' Then she swells with envy and rage against us both, calls my mistress ugly, common, unsafe, and me a weak, secure fool.

Jolly. These are strange truths, madam.

Widow. Ay, ay, but these oysters are a better jest.

Captain. But she's abused that will let such reason tame her desire, and a fool in love's school; else she would not be ignorant that variety is such a friend to love that he which rises a sunk coward from the lady's bed would find new fires at her maid's. Nor ever yet did the man want fire if the women would bring the fuel.

Pleasant. For God's sake leave this discourse.

Widow. The Captain has a mind we should eat no oysters.

Wild. Aunt, we came to be merry and we will be merry, and you shall stay it out. Proceed, Captain.

Widow. Fie, Captain, I'm ashamed to hear you talk thus. Marry—then you will have a better opinion of women.

Captain. Marry! Yes, this knowledge will invite me. It is a good encouragement, is it not, think you? What is your opinion? Were not these marriages made in heaven? By this good day, all the world is mad and makes haste to be fooled but we four. And I hope there's none of us believes there has any marriages been made in heaven since Adam.

Jolly. By my faith, 'tis thought the devil gave the ring there too.

Widow. Nephew, I'll swear I'll be gone.

Captain. Hold her, Ned, she goes not yet. There's a fourth kind of women that concerns her more than all the rest. *Ecce signum* ('*He points to* Sadd'): she is one of those who, clothed in purple, triumph over their dead husbands. These will be caught at first sight and at first sight must be catched. 'Tis a bird that must be shot flying, for they never sit. If a man delay, they cool and fall into considerations of jointure and friends' opinion; in which time, if she hears thou keep'st a wench, thou hadst better be a beggar in her opinion, for then her pride, it may be, would betray her to the vanity of setting up a proper man, as they call it; but for a wencher, no argument prevails with your widow, for she believes they have spent too much that way to be able to pay her due benevolence.

Widow. As I live, I'll be gone if you speak one word more of this uncivil subject.

Jolly. Captain, let me kiss thy cheek for that widow. You understand this, Widow? I say no more. Here, Captain, here's to thee. As it goes down, a pox of care.

Widow. Jesus! Master Jolly, have you no observations of the court that are so affected with this of the town?

Constant. Faith, they say there's good sport there sometimes.

Pleasant. Master Jolly is afraid to let us partake of his knowledge.

Jolly. No, faith, madam.

Captain. By this drink, if he stay till I have eaten a few more, I'll describe it.

Jolly. What should I say? 'Tis certain the court is the bravest place in the kingdom for sport, if it were well looked to and the game preserved fair. But as 'tis, a man may sooner make a set in the Strand, and it will never be better whilst your divine lovers inhabit there.

Careless. Let the king make me Master of the Game.

Captain. And admit us laity-lovers.

Jolly. I would he would; for as 'tis, there's no hopes amongst the ladies. Besides, 'tis such an example to see a king and queen good husband and wife that to be kind will grow out of fashion.

Captain. Nay, that's not all, for the women grow malicious because they are not courted. Nay, they bred all the last mischiefs and called the king's chastity a neglect of them.

Jolly. Thou art in the right: an Edward or a Harry, with seven queens in buckram, that haught among the men and stroked the women, are the monarchs they wish to bow to. They love no tame princes but lions in the forest.

Captain. Why, and those were properly called the fathers of their people that were indeed akin to their nobility. Now they wear out their youth and beauty without hope of a monumental ballad or trophy of a libel that shall hereafter point at such a lord and cry, 'That is the royal son of such-a-one.'

Jolly. And these were the ways that made them powerful at home; for the city is a kind of tame beast: you may lead her by the horns any whither if you but tickle them in the ear sometimes. Queen Bess of famous memory had the trick on 't; and I have heard them say, in eighty-eight, ere I was born, as well I can remember, she rode to Tilbury on that bonny beast, the mayor.

Captain. I would I might counsel him; I'd so reform the court.

Careless. Never too soon; for now, when a stranger comes in and spies a covey of beauties would make a falconer unhood, before he can draw his leash he is warned that's a marked partridge, and that, and every he has by their example a particular she.

Wild. By this light, the six fair maids stand like the working days in the almanac, one with A scored upon her breast, that is as much to say, I belong to such a lord; the next with B, for an elder brother; C, for such a knight; D, possessed with melancholy, and at her breast you may knock an hour ere you get an answer, and then she'll tell you there's no lodging there, she has a constant fellow courtier that has taken up all her heart to his own use. In short, all are disposed of but the good mother, and she comes in like the sabbath, at a week's end; and I warrant her make anyone rest that comes at her.

Careless. Ay, marry, but if she were like the Jews' sabbath, it were somewhat; but this looks like a broken commandment, that has had more work done upon her than all the week besides.

Captain. And what think you—is not this finely carried? You that are about the king counsel him, if he will have his sport fair, he must let the game be free, as it has been in former ages. Then a stranger that has wit, good means and handsome clothes, no sooner enters the privy chamber and beat[s] about with three graceful legs but he spring a mistress that danced as well as he, sung better, as free as fair. Those at first sight could speak, for wit is always acquainted; these fools must be akin ere they can speak. And now the friends make the bargain and they go to bed ere they know why.

Jolly. Faith, he's in the right. You shall have a buzzard now hover and beat after a pretty wench till she is so weary of him she's forced to take her bed for covert and find less danger in being trussed than in flying.

Captain. And what becomes of all this pudder? After he has made them sport for one night, to see him towse the quarry, he carries her into the country and there they two fly at one another till they are weary.

Careless. And all this mischief comes of love and constancy. We shall never see better days till there be an act of parliament against it, enjoining husband[s] not to till their wives but change and lay them fallow.

Jolly. A pox, the women will never consent to it; they'll be tilled to death first.

Widow. Gentlemen, you are very bold with the sex.

Captain. Faith, madam, it is our care of them. Why, you see they are married at fourteen, yield a crop and a half, and then die. 'Tis merely their love that destroys 'em, for if they get a good husbandman, the poor things yield their very hearts.

Pleasant. And do you blame their loves, gentlemen?

Jolly. No, not their love, but their discretion. Let them love, and do, a God's name, but let them do with discretion.

Wild. But how will you amend this?

Jolly. Instead of two beds and a physician, I'd have the state prescribe two wives and a mistress.

Wild. Ho! It will never be granted: the state is made up of old men, and they find work enough with one.

Jolly. We will petition the lower house. There are young men and (if it were but to be factious) would pass it if they thought the upper house would cross it. Besides, they ought to do it. Death, they provide against cutting down old trees and preserving highways and post-horses, and let pretty wenches run to decay!

Careless. Why may it not come within the statute of depopulation? As I live, the state ought to take care of those pretty wenches. Be you judge, madam: is't not a sad sight to see a rich young beauty, with all her innocence and blossoms on, subject to some rough rude fellow that ploughs her, and esteems and uses her as a chattel till she is so lean a man may find as good grass upon the common, where it may be she'll sit coughing, with sunk eyes, so weak that a boy (with a dog) that can but whistle may keep a score of them?

Widow. You are strangely charitable to our sex on a sudden.

Captain. I know not what they are, but for my part I'll be a traitor ere I'll look on and see beauty go thus to wrack. It is enough custom has made us suffer them to be enclosed. I am sure they were created common and for the use of man and not intended to be subject to jealousy and choler, or to be bought or sold or let for term of lives or years as they are now, or else sold at outcries: 'Oh yes, who'll give most take her.'

Widow. Why do not some of you, excellent men, marry and mend all these errors by your good example?

Jolly. Because we want fortunes to buy rich wives or keep poor ones and be loth to get beggars or whores, as well as I love 'em.

Pleasant. Why, are all their children so that have no fortune, think you?

Jolly. No, not all. I have heard of Whittington and his cat, and others that have made fortunes by strange means, but I scarce believe my son would rise from hop, a halfpenny and a lambskin. And the wenches, commonly having more

wit and beauty than money, foreseeing small portions, grow
sad and read romances, till their wit spy some unfortunate
merit like their own, without money too, and they two sigh
after one another till they grow mysterious in colours and
become a proverb for their constancy; and when their love
has worn out the cause, marry in the end a new couple; then,
grown ashamed of the knowledge they so long hunted, at
length part by consent and vanish into Abigail and governor.

Widow. Well, gentlemen, excuse me for this one time,
and if ever I invite you to dinner again, punish me with such
another discourse. In the meantime let's go in and dine;
meat stays for us.

Captain. Faith, madam, we were resolved to be merry.
We have not met these three years till today, and at the Bear
we meant to have dined; and since your ladyship would have
our company, you must pardon our humour. Here, Mistress
Sadd, here's the widow's health to you. (*Exeunt omnes.*

ACT III · SCENE I

'*Enter all* [Widow, Wild, Careless, Jolly, Captain,
Pleasant, Secret, Sadd, Constant] *from dinner.*'

Widow. Nephew, how do you dispose of yourself this
afternoon?

Wild. We have a design we must pursue which will rid
you of all this troublesome company, and we'll make no
excuse, because you peeped into our privacies today.

Careless. Your humble servant, ladies. Gentlemen, we'll
leave you to pursue your fortunes. (*Exit Careless.*

Jolly. Farewell, Widow. Mayst thou live unmarried till
thou run'st away with thyself. (*Exit Jolly.*

Captain. No, no, when that day comes, command the
humblest of your servants. (*Exit Captain.*

Wild. Farewell, aunt. Sweet Mistress Pleasant, I wish
you good fortune. (*Exit Wild.*

Widow. Farewell, farewell, gentlemen. ('*She speaks aside.*')

Niece, now if we could be rid of these troublesome lovers too, we would go see a play.

Pleasant. Rid of them? Why, they are but now in season. As I live, I would do as little to give mine content as any she in town, and yet I do not grudge him the happiness of carrying me to a play.

Widow. Ay, but the world will talk, because they pretend. And then we shall be sure to meet my nephew there and his wild company, and they will laugh to see us together.

Pleasant. Who will you have? Tim the butler, or Formal your gentleman-usher? I would take Philip the foreman of the shop as soon.

Widow. Let's mask ourselves and take Secret and go alone by water.

Pleasant. Yes, and follow her like one of my aunts of the suburbs; it is a good way to know what you may yield in a market, for I'll undertake there are those shall bid for you before the play will be done.

Secret. As I live, madam, Mistress Pleasant is in the right. I had such a kindness offered me once, and I came to a price with him in knavery, and hang me if the rogue was not putting the earnest of his affection into my hand.

Widow. Let's go to the Glasshouse then.

Pleasant. I'll go to a play with my servant and so shall you—hang opinion—and we'll go to the Glasshouse afterwards. It is too hot to sup early.

Secret. Pray, madam, go; they say 'tis a fine play, and a knight writ it.

Pleasant. Pray let Secret prevail. I'll propose it to the lovers. In the meantime go you and bid the coachman make ready the coach.   'Secret *whispers* Sadd, *'Twill take*.'

Secret. Alas, madam, he's sick, poor fellow, and gone to bed; he could not wait at dinner.

Widow. Sick?

Pleasant. Why, see how all things work for the young men: either their coach or afoot. Master Constant, what think you of seeing a play this afternoon? Is it not too hot to venture this infectious time?

Constant. Fie, madam, there's no danger; the bill decreased twenty last week.

Sadd. I swear they say 'tis a very good play today.

Widow. Shall we go, niece?

Pleasant. Faith, 'tis hot, and there's nobody but we.

Sadd. Does that hinder? Pray, madam, grudge us not the favour of venturing yourself in our company.

Widow. Come, leave this ceremony. I'll go in and put on my mask. Secret shall bring you yours.

Pleasant. No, I'll go and put it on within.

(*Exeunt omnes.*

SCENE II

'*Enter* Wild, Careless, Captain, *and* Jolly.'

Careless. By this day, you have nettled the Widow.

Wild. The Captain neglected his dinner for his mirth as if he had forgot to eat.

Jolly. When did he oversee his drinking so?

Captain. Gentlemen, still it is my fortune to make your worships merry.

Wild. As I live, Captain, I subscribe and am content to hold my wit as tenant to thee; and tonight I'll invite you to supper, where it shall not be lawful to speak till thou hast victualled thy man of war.

Captain. Shall's be merry? What shall we have?

Wild. Half a score dishes of meat. Choose them yourself.

Captain. Provide me then the chines fried and the salmon calvered, a carp and black sauce, red deer in the blood, and an assembly of woodcocks, and jack-snipes so fat you would think they had their winding-sheets on. And upon these, as their pages, let me have wait your Sussex wheatear with a feather in his cap; over all which let your countryman, General Chine of Beef command. I hate your French potage, that looks as the cook-maid had more hand in it than the cook.

Wild. I'll promise you all this.

Careless. And let me alone to cook the fish.

Captain. You cook it? No, no, I left an honest fellow in town when I went to Italy, Signor Ricardo Ligones, one of the ancient house of the Armenian ambassador's; if he be alive he shall be our cook.

Wild. Is he so excellent at it?

Captain. Excellent? You shall try, you shall try. Why, I tell you I saw him once dress a shoeing-horn and a joiner's apron that the company left pheasant for it.

Wild. A shoeing-horn?

Captain. Yes, a shoeing-horn. Marry, there was garlic in the sauce.

Wild. Is this all you would have?

Captain. This, and a bird of paradise to entertain the rest of the night—and let me alone to cook her.

Wild. A bird of paradise? What's that?

Captain. A girl of fifteen, smooth as satin, white as her Sunday apron, plump, and of the first down. I'll take her with her guts in her belly and warm her with a country dance or two, then pluck her and lay her dry betwixt a couple of sheets; then pour into her so much oil of wit as will make her turn to a man, and stick into her heart three corns of whole love, to make her taste of what she is doing; then, having strewed a man all over her, shut the door and leave us—we'll work ourselves into such a sauce as you can never surfeit on, so poynant and yet no hogough. Take heed of a hogough; your onion and woman make the worst sauce. This shook together by an English cook (for your French season-ing spoils many a woman), and there's a dish for a king.

Wild. For the first part I'll undertake.

Captain. But this for supper, no more of this now. This afternoon, as you are true to the petticoat, observe your instructions and meet at Ned's house in the evening.

Omnes. We will not fail.

Captain. I must write to Wanton to know how things stand at home and to acquaint her how we have thrived with the old lady today.

Wild. Whither will you go to write?

Captain. To thy house, 'tis hard by; there's the Fleece.

Jolly. Do, and in the meantime I'll go home and dispatch a little business and meet you.

Wild. Make haste then.

Jolly. Where shall I meet you?

Wild. Whither shall we go till it be time to attend the design?

Careless. Let's go to court for an hour.

Jolly. Do, I'll meet you at the queen's side.

Wild. No, prithee; we are the monsieurs new come over, and if we go fine they will laugh at us and think we believe ourselves so; if not, then they will abuse our clothes and swear we went into France only to have our cloaks cut shorter.

Careless. Will you go see a play?

Captain. Do, and thither I'll come to you, if it be none of our gentlemen-poets, that excuse their writings with a prologue that professes they are no scholars.

Jolly. On my word, this is held the best penned of the time, and he has writ a very good play. By this day, it was extremely applauded.

Captain. Does he write plays by the day? Indeed a man would ha' judged him a labouring poet.

Jolly. A labouring poet? By this hand, he's a knight. Upon my recommendation venture to see it. Hang me if you be not extremely well satisfied.

Careless. A knight and write plays? It may be, but it's strange to us. So they say there are other gentlemen poets without land or Latin; this was not ordinary. Prithee, when was he knighted?

Jolly. In the north the last great knighting, when 'twas God's great mercy we were not all knights.

Wild. I'll swear they say there are poets that have more men in liveries than books in their studies.

Captain. And what think you, gentlemen? Are not these things to start a man? I believe 'tis the first time you have found them lie at the sign of the page, footmen and gilded coaches. They were wont to lodge at the thin cloak—they and their muses made up the family—and thence sent scenes to their patrons like boys in at windows, and one would return with a doublet, another with a pair of breeches, a third with a little ready money, which, together with their credit with a company, in three terms you rarely saw a poet repaired.

Jolly. This truth nobody denies.

Wild. Prithee, let us resolve what we shall do, lest we meet with some of them, for it seems they swarm, and I fear nothing like a dedication, though it be but of himself, for I must hear him say more than either I deserve or he believes. I hate that in a poet. They must be dull or all upon all subjects, so that they can oblige none but their muse.

Jolly. I perceive by this you will not see the play. What think you of going to Sim's to bowls till I come?

Careless. Yes, if you will go to see that comedy. But there is no reason we should pay for our coming in and act too like some whose interest in the timber robs them of their reason, and they run as if they had stolen a bias.

Wild. Resolve what you will do; I am contented.

Careless. Let's go walk in the Spring Garden.

Wild. I'll do it for company, but I had as lief be rid in the horse-market as walk in that fools' fair, where neither wit nor money is, nor sure to take up a wench—there's none but honest women.

Captain. A pox on't, what should we do there? Let's go and cross the field to Pike's. Her kitchen is cool, winter and summer.

Careless. I like that motion well, but we have no time, and I hate to do that business by half. After supper, if you will, we'll go and make a night on't.

Captain. Well, I must go write; therefore resolve of somewhat. Shall I propose an indifferent place where 'tis probable we shall all meet?

Omnes. Yes.

Captain. Go you before to the Devil and I'll make haste after.

Careless. Agreed, we shall be sure of good wine there and in fresco, for he is never without patent snow.

Wild. Patent snow—what, doth that project hold?

Jolly. Yes, faith, and now there is a commission appointed for toasts against the next winter.

Wild. Marry, they are wise and foresaw the parliament and were resolved their monopolies should be no grievance to the people.

Captain. Farewell. You will be sure to meet?

Omnes. Yes, yes.   (*Exeunt omnes.*

SCENE III

'*Enter* Wanton *and her* Maid [Bawd], *with her lap full of things.*'

Wanton. Bid them ply him close and flatter him and rail upon the old lady and the Captain. And, do you hear, give him some hints to begin the story of his life. Do it handsomely and you shall see how the sack will clip his tongue.

Bawd. I warrant you I'll fit him.

Wanton. When he is in his discourse, leave him and come down into the parlour and steal away his box with the false rings that stands by his bedside. I have all his little plate here already.

Bawd. Make you haste; I'll warrant you I'll dress him.

(*Exeunt* Wanton *and* Bawd.

SCENE IV

'*Enter* Captain *with a letter in his hand, and his* Boy *to him with a candle, his going to write the superscription.*'

Boy. Sir, the Lady Love-all passed by even now.

Captain. The Lady Love-all? Which way went she?

Boy. To the rich lady, the widow, where your worship dined.

Captain. 'Tis no matter. Here, carry this letter and bring an answer to the Devil quickly, and tell her we'll stay there till the time be fit for the design.

(*Exeunt* Captain *and* Boy.

SCENE V

'*Enter* Careless, Wild *and a* Drawer; *at the* Devil.'

Careless. Jack, how goes the world? Bring us some bottles of the best wine.

Drawer. You shall, sir. Your worship is welcome into England.

Careless. Why, look you, who says a drawer can say nothing but, 'Anon, anon, sir. Score a quart of sack in the Half-moon.'?

Drawer. Your worship is merry, but I'll fetch you that, sir, shall speak Greek and make your worship prophesy. You drank none such in your journey.

Wild. Do it then, and make a hole in this angel thou mayst creep through. ('*Gives him an angel.*') Who is't that peeps? A fiddler? Bring him by the ears.

'*Enter the* Tailor *that peeps.*'

Tailor. A tailor, an't like your worship.

Careless. A tailor? Hast thou a stout faith?

Tailor. I have had, an't like your worship, but now I am in despair.

Careless. Why then thou art damned. Go, go home and throw thyself into thine own hell; it is the next way to the other.

Tailor. I hope your worship is not displeased.

Careless. What dost do here? A tailor without faith, dost come to take measure of ours?

Tailor. No, I come to speak with one Master Jolly, a courtier, a very fine spoken gentleman and a just counter but one of the worst paymasters in the world.

Wild ('*Aside*'). As thou lov'st me, let's keep him here till he comes, and make him valiant with sack that he may urge him till he beats him. We shall have the sport and be revenged upon the rogue for dunning a gentleman in a tavern.

Careless. I'll charge him.—Here, drink poor fellow, and stay in the next room till he comes.

Tailor. I thank your worship, but I am fasting, and if it please your worship to call for a dozen of manchets that I may eat a crust first, then I'll make bold with a glass of your sack.

Wild. Here, here, drink in the meantime. Fetch him some bread.

Tailor. Will your worship have me drink all this vessel of sack?

Careless. Yes, yes, off with 't; 'twill do you no harm.

'*The* Tailor *drinks.*'

Wild. Why do you not take some order with that Jolly to make him pay thee?

Tailor. I have petitioned him often but can do no good.

Careless. A pox upon him! Petition him? His heart is hardened to ill. Threaten to arrest him; nothing but sergeant can touch his conscience.

Tailor. Truly, gentlemen, I have reason to be angry, for he uses me ill when I ask him for my money.

Jolly ('*Speaks within.*'). Where is Master Wild and Master Careless?

Tailor. I hear his voice.

Jolly [*Within*]. Let the coach stay.

'*Enter* Jolly.'

How now, who would he speak with?

Wild. Do you not know?

Jolly. Yes, and be you judge if the rogue does not suffer deservedly. I have bid him any time this twelvemonth but send his wife and I'll pay her, and the rogue replies nobody shall lie with his wife but himself.

Careless. Nay, if you be such a one—

Tailor. No more they shall not. I am but a poor man.

Jolly. By this hand, he's drunk.

Tailor. Nay then, I arrest you in mine own name at his majesty's suit.

Wild. As I live, thou shalt not beat him.

Jolly. Beat him? I'll kiss him, I'll pay him, and carry him about with me and be at the charge of sack to keep him in the humour.

Tailor. Help, rescue! I'll have his body, no bail shall serve. '*He hugs the quart pot.*'

'*Enter* Drawer.'

Drawer. Sir, yonder is a gentleman would speak with you. I do not like his followers.

Jolly. What are they? Bailiffs?

Drawer. Little better.

Jolly. Send him up alone and stand you ready at the stairs feet.

Careless. Who can that be?

Jolly. It is the scrivener at the corner. Pick a quarrel with him for coming into our company. The drawers will be armed behind them and we will so rout the rascals. Take your swords and let him sleep.

Careless. What scrivener?

Jolly. Cropp, the Brownist, he that the ballad was made on.

Careless. What ballad?

Jolly. Have you not heard of the scrivener's wife that brought the blackamoor from the Holy Land and made him a Brownist, and in pure charity lay with him and was delivered of a magpie, a pied prophet; which when the elect saw, they prophesied if it lived 'twould prove a great enemy to their sect, for the midwife cried out 'twas born a bishop, with tippet and white sleeves; at which the zealous mother cried, 'Down with the idol.'? So the midwife and she in pure devotion killed it.

Wild. Killed it! What became of them?

Jolly. Why, they were taken and condemned, and suffered under a Catholic sheriff that afflicted them with the litany all the way from Newgate to the gallows, which in roguery he made to be set up altar-wise too, and hanged them without a psalm.

Wild. But how took they that breach of privilege?

Jolly. I know not. Gregory turned them off, and so they descended and became Brown-martyrs.

Wild. And is the husband at door now?

Jolly. Yes, yes, but he's married again to a rich widow at Wapping, a wench of another temper, one that you cannot please better than by abusing him. I always pick quarrels with him that she may reconcile us—the peace is always worth a dinner at least. Hark, I hear him.

[*Enter* Cropp.]

Save you, Master Cropp, you are come in the nick to pledge a health.

Cropp. No, Sir, I have other business. Shall I be paid my money or no?   '*Jolly drinks.*'

Jolly. Yes.

Cropp. Sir?

Jolly. You asked whether you should be paid your money or no, and I said yes.

Cropp. Pray, sir, be plain.

Careless. And be you so, sir. How durst you come into this room and company without leave?

Cropp. Sir, I have come into good lords' company ere now.

Careless. It may be so, but you shall either fall upon your knees and pledge this health or you come no more into lords' companies, no, by these hilts.

Cropp. 'Tis idolatry. Do, martyr me! I will not kneel nor join in sin with the wicked.

'*They tug him and make him kneel.*'

Jolly. Either kneel or I'll tear thy cloak, which by the age and looks may be that which was writ for in the time of the primitive church.

Cropp. Pay me and I'll wear a better. It would be honestlier done than to abuse this and profane the text, a text that shows your bishops in those days wore no lawn sleeves. And you may be ashamed to protect him that will not pay his debts. The cries of the widow will come against you for it.

Jolly. Remember, sirrah, the dinners and suppers, fat venison and good words I was fain to give you, christening your children still by the way of brokage. Count that charge, and how often I have kept you from fining for Sheriff, and thou art in my debt. Then I am damned for speaking well of thee so often against my conscience, which you never consider.

Cropp. I am an honest man, sir.

Jolly. Then ushering your wife and Mistress Ugly her daughter to plays and masques at court—you think these courtesies deserve nothing in the hundred? 'Tis true they made room for themselves with their dagger elbows, and when Spider your daughter laid about her with her breath, the devil would not have sat near her.

Cropp. You did not borrow my money with this language.

Jolly. No, sirrah; then I was fain to flatter you and endure the familiarity of your family and hear, nay, feign sometimes to join in, the lying praises of the holy sister that expired at Tyburn.

Cropp. Do, abuse her, and be cursed. 'Tis well known she

R

died a martyr, and her blood will be upon some of you. 'Tis
her orphan's money I require and this is the last time I'll
ask it. I'll find a way to get it.

'*He offers to go and* Jolly *stays him.*'

Jolly. Art serious? By that light, I'll consent, and take
it for an intimate obligation if thou wilt teach the rest of my
creditors that trick; 'twill save me a world of labour, for
hang me if I know how to do 't.

Cropp. Well, sir, since I see your resolution, I shall make
it my business.

Careless. Prithee, let's be rid of this fool.

Cropp. Fool? Let him pay the fool his money and he'll be
gone.

Jolly. No, sir, not a farthing. 'Twas my business to borrow it and it shall be yours to get it in again. Nay, by this
hand, I'll be feasted too and have good words. Nay, thou
shalt lend me more ere thou get'st this again.

Cropp. I'll lay my action upon you.

Jolly. Your action, you rogue! Lay two!

Careless. Lay three, for battery.

'*They kick him and thrust him out of the room* [Jolly
follows.] *Enter* Faithful. Wild *and* Careless *return
and meet her.*'

What have we here? A she-creditor too? Who would she
speak with?

Wild. She looks as if she had trusted in her time.

Careless. Would you speak with any here, old gentlewoman?

Faithful. My business is to Master Jolly.

Careless. From yourself, or are you but a messenger?

Faithful. My business, sir, is from a lady.

Careless. From a lady? From what lady, pray? Who so
coy?

Faithful. From a lady in the town.

Careless. Ho, ho, from a lady in the town! Is it possible
I should have guessed you came from a lady in the suburbs,
or some country-madam, by your riding face?

'*Enter* Jolly *again.*'

Jolly. I think we have routed the rascals. Faithful! What makes thy gravity in a tavern?

Faithful. Sport, it seems, for your saucy companions.

Jolly. Ho ho, Mull, ho! No fury, Faithful.

Faithful. 'Tis well, sir. My lady presents her service to you and hath sent you a letter. There's my business.

Careless. Prithee, who is her lady?

Jolly. The Lady Love-all.

Careless. Oh, oh, does she serve that old lady? God help her.

Faithful. God help her! Pray for yourself, sir; my lady scorns your prayers.

Jolly. Faithful, come hither. Prithee, is thy lady drunk?

Faithful. Drunk, sir?

Jolly. Ay, drunk or mad. She'd never writ this else. She requires me, here, to send back by you the pearl she gave me this morning, which sure she'd never do if she were sober, for you know I earned them hard.

Faithful. I know? What do I know? You will not defame my lady, will you?

Careless. By no means. This is by way of counsel. Fie! Give a thing and take a thing? If he did not perform he shall come at night and pay his scores.

Faithful. 'Tis well, sir. Is this your return for my lady's favours? Shall I have the pearl, sir?

Jolly. No; and tell her 'tis the opinion of us all, he that opens her stinking oyster is worthy of the pearl.

Faithful. You are a foul-mouthed fellow, sirrah, and I shall live to see you load a gallows when my lady shall find the way to her own again.

Jolly. If she miss, there are divers can direct her, you know. Adieu, Faithful. Do you hear, steal privately down by the back door lest some knavish boy spy thee and call thine age bawd.   (*Exit* Faithful.

Careless. Prithee, who is this thing?

Jolly. 'Tis my lady's waiting-woman, her bawd, her she-confessor, herself at second-hand. Her beginning was simple and below-stairs, till her lady, finding her to be a likely promising bawd, secret as the key at her girdle, obedient as her thoughts, those virtues raised her from the flat petticoa and kercher to the gorget and bum-roll. And I remember 'twas good sport at first to see the wench perplexed with her metamorphosis. She since has been in love with all the family and now sighs after the Levite; and if he forsake her too, I prophesy a waiting-woman's curse will fall upon her, to die old, despised, poor, and out of fashion.

'*Enter* Captain.'

Captain. Why do you not hang out a painted cloth and take twopence a-piece and let in all the tame fools at door, those sons of wonder that now gape and think you mad?

Careless. 'Tis no matter what they think; madness is proper here. Are not taverns Bacchus his temples, the place of madness? Does not the sign of madness hang out at the door?

Jolly. While we within possess our joys and cups, as full of pleasure as weeping Niobe's afflicted eyes were swelled with grief and tears. Blessing on the cause that made our joys thus complete! For see, Plutus in our pockets, Mars by our sides, Bacchus in our head, self-love in our hearts, and change of virgins in our arms, beauties whose eyes and hearts speak love and welcome, no rigid thinkers, no niggard beauties that maliciously rake up their fire in green-sickness to preserve a spark that shall flame only in some dull day of marriage—let such swear and forswear till (of the whole parish) they love each other least, whilst we wisely set out our cobwebs in the most perspicuous places to catch these foolish flies.

Careless. He's in the right. Dost think we retreated hither to beat a bargain for a score of sheep, or dispute the legality of votes and weigh the power of prerogative and parliament, and club for concluding sack, or read the Fathers here till we grow costive, like those that have worn their suffering elbows bare to find a knowledge to perplex 'em? A pox on such brain-breaking thoughts! Avoid them and take with me into thy hand a glass of eternal sack and prophesy the restoration of senses and the fall of a lover from grace, which our dear friend Master Jolly will prove, to whom the Lady Love-all (by Faithful lately departed) sent for the pearl you wot of.

Captain. But I hope he had the grace to keep them.

Jolly. No, no; I'm a fool, I.

Captain. Was not my boy here?

Jolly. No, we saw him not.

Captain. A pox of the rogue, he's grown so lazy.

Wild. Your boy is come in just now and called for the key of the back door. There's women with him.

Captain. Oh, that's well, 'tis Wanton. I sent for her to laugh over the story of the old lady and her pearl.

'*Enter* Boy.'

Where have you been all this while, sirrah?

Boy. I could overtake the coach, sir, no sooner.

Captain. The coach? What coach?

Boy. The Lady Love-all's.

Captain. The Lady Love-all's? Why, what had you to do with her coach?

Boy. I went to give her the letter your worship sent her.

Captain. The letter? What letter?

Boy. That your worship gave me.

Captain. That I writ at Ned's house to Wanton?

Boy. The letter you gave me, sir, was directed to the Lady Love-all, and she stormed like a madwoman at the reading of it.

Careless. Why, thou wilt not beat the boy for thy own fault? What letter was it?

Captain. 'Twas enough—only a relation of the pearl, wherein she finds herself sufficiently abused to Wanton.

Jolly. Now, gentlemen, you have two to laugh at.

Captain. A pox of fooling, let's resolve what to do. There's no denying, for she has all the particulars under my hand.

Boy. You must resolve of something, for she's coming, and stayed only till the back door was opened.

Captain. How did she know I was here?

Boy. Your worship bade me tell her you would stay here for her.

Careless. How came this mistake?

Captain. Why, the devil ought us a shame, it seems. You know I went home to give Wanton an account how we advanced in our design, and when I was writing the super-scription I remember the boy came in and told me the Lady Love-all passed by.

Jolly. And so it seems you in pure mistake directed your letter to her.

Careless. Well, resolve what you'll do with her when she comes.

Captain. Faith, bear it like men—'tis but an old lady lost. Let's resolve to defy her; we are sure of our pearl. But lest we prolong the war, take the first occasion you can all to avoid the room. When she's alone, I'll try whether she'll listen to a composition.

Jolly. Have you no friends in the close committee?

Captain. Yes, yes, I am an Essex man.

Careless. Then get some of them to move it may be voted no letter.

Jolly. Ay, ay, and after 'tis voted no letter, then vote it false, scandalous, and illegal; and that is in it: they have a precedent for it in the Danish packet which they took from a foolish fellow who, presuming upon the law of nations, came upon an embassy to the king without an order or pass from both houses.

Captain. Hark, I hear her coming.

'*Enter* Love-all *and* Faithful.'

Love-all. Sir, I received a letter, but by what accident I know not, for I believe it was not intended me though the contents concern me.

Captain. Madam, 'tis too late to deny it. Is it peace or war you bring? Without dispute, if war, I hang out my defiance; if peace, I yield my weapon into your hands.

Love-all. Are you all unworthy? Your whole sex false-hood? Is it not possible to oblige a man to be loyal? This is such a treachery no age can match. Apply yourself with youth and wit to gain a lady's love and friendship only to betray it? Was it not enough you commanded my fortune but you must wrack my honour too, and instead of being grateful for that charity which still assisted your wants, strive to pay me with injuries, and attempt to make the world believe I pay to lose my fame and then make me the scorned

subject of your whore's mirth? ('*He smiles.*') Base and unworthy, do you smile, false one? I shall find a time for you
too, and my vengeance shall find you all.

Faithful. Yea, sir, and you that had such a ready wit to
proclaim my lady whore and me bawd, I hope to see you
load a gallows for it.

Captain. Once again, is it peace or war?

Love-all. Peace! I'll have thy blood first. Dog, where's
my pearl? ('*She speaks to* Wild.') You ought to right me,
sir, in this particular: it was to you I sent them.

Wild. Madam, I sent not for them.

Captain. No more words. I have them, I earned them,
and you paid them.

Faithful. You are a foul-mouthed fellow, sirrah.

Love-all. Peace, wench, I scorn their slander. It cannot
shake my honour; 'tis too weighty and too fixed for their
calumny.

Jolly. I'll be sworn for my part on't I think it is a great
honour. I am sure I had as much as I could carry away in
ten nights, and yet there was no miss on't.

Captain. You? I think so. There's no mark of my work,
you see, and yet I came after thee, and brought away loads
would have sunk a sedan-man.

Wild. By this relation she should be a woman of a great
fame.

Careless. Let that consideration, with her condition and
her age, move some reverence, at least to what she was.
Madam, I am sorry I cannot serve you in this particular.

(*Exeunt* Jolly *and* Careless.

Love-all. I see all your mean baseness; pursue your scorn.
Come, let's go, wench. I shall find some to right my fame.
And though I have lost my opinion, I have gained a knowledge how to distinguish of love hereafter, and I shall scorn
you and all your sex, that have not soul enough to value a
noble friendship.

Wild. Pray, madam, let me speak with you.

Captain. We'll have no whispering. I said it and I'll
maintain it with my sword.

'*Enter* Drawer.'

Drawer. Sir, there's one without would speak with you.

Captain. With me?

Drawer. No, sir, with Master Wild.

Wild. Madam, I'll wait upon you presently.

(*Exit* Wild.

Captain. Madam, I know my company is displeasing to you; therefore I'll take my leave. Drawer, show me another room.

'*The* Captain *makes a turn or two; they look at each other; then he goes out.*'

Love-all. O Faithful, Faithful, I am most miserably abused, and can find no way to my revenge.

Faithful. Madam, I'll give them ratsbane, and speedily too, ere they can tell, for the rascal the Captain has a tongue else will proclaim you and undo your fame for ever.

Love-all. Ay, ay, my fame, my fame, Faithful! And if it were not for mine honour (which I have kept unstained to this minute), I would not care.

Faithful. This it is: you will still set your affection upon every young thing. I could but tell you on't.

Love-all. Who could have suspected they would have been so false in their loves to me that have been so faithful to them?

'*Enter* [*two*] Drawer[*s*].'

Honest friend, where is Master Wild?

Drawer. The other gentlemen carried him away with them.

Love-all. Are they all gone then?

Drawer. Yes, by this hand. ('*Aside.*') These gentlemen are quickly satisfied. What an ugly whore they have got. How she states it!

Love-all. Come, let's go, wench.   '*She offers to go.*'

Drawer. Mistress, who pays the reckoning?

Love-all. What says he?

Faithful. He asks me who pays the reckoning.

Love-all. Who pays the reckoning? Why, what have we to do with the reckoning?

Drawer. Shut the door, Dick. We'll have the reckoning before you go.

Faithful. Why, goodman sauce-box, you will not make my lady pay for this reckoning, will you?

Drawer. My lady! A pox of her title, she'd need of something to make her pass.

Faithful. What do you say, sirrah?

Drawer. I say the gentlemen paid well for their sport and I know no reason why we should lose our reckoning.

Love-all. What do you take me for, my friend?

Drawer. In troth I take you for nothing, but I would be loth to take you for that use I think they made shift with you for.

Faithful. Madam, this is that rascally Captain's plot.

Love-all. Patience, patience! Oh for a bite at the slave's heart! Friend, mistake me not, my name is Love-all, a lady. Send one along with me and you shall have your money.

Drawer. You must pardon me, madam, I am but a servant. If you be a lady, pray sit in an inner room and send home your woman for the money. The sum is six pounds, and be pleased to remember the waiters.

Love-all. Go, Faithful; go fetch the money. Oh, revenge, revenge! Shall I lose my honour and have no revenge?

(*Exeunt omnes.*)

ACT IV · SCENE I

'*Enter* Wanton, Captain, Careless, *and* Wild.'

Wanton. By all that a longing bride hopes for, which I am not, I am better pleased with this revenge than mine own plot, which takes as I could wish. I have so anointed my high priest with sack that he would have confuted Baal's priests, and now he does so slumber in his ale, and calls to bed already, swears the sun is set.

Captain. Faith, wench, her abusing of me made me leave her for the reckoning.

Careless. Yes, faith, they have treated her upsey whore, lain with her, told, and then pawned her.

Wanton. Yes, yes, you are fine things; I wonder women can endure you. For me, I expect you worse and am armed for 't.

Wild. Faith, let's send and release her; the jest is gone far enough. As I live, I pity her.

Wanton. Pity her? Hang her and rid the country of her. She is a thing wears out her limbs as fast as her clothes, one that never goes to bed at all nor sleeps in a whole skin, but is taken to pieces like a motion as if she were too long. She should be hanged for offering to be a whore.

Captain. As I live, she is in the right. I peeped once to see what she did before she went to bed. By this light, her maids were dissecting her, and when they had done, they brought some of her to bed and the rest they either pinned or hung up, and so she lay dismembered till morning; in which time her chamber was strewed all over like an anatomy school.

Wanton. And when she travels anywhere she is transported with as great a care and fear of spoiling as a juggler's motion when he removes from fair to fair.

Careless. She is a right broken gamester, who, though she lacks wherewithal to play, yet loves to be looking on.

'Enter [Bawd,] Wanton's *maid.'*

Bawd. He is awake and calls for you impatiently. He would fain be in bed; the company is all gone.

Wanton. Are you instructed?

Bawd. Let me alone, I'll warrant you for my part.

Wanton. Farewell then. You are all ready? Who plays Master Constable?

Captain. I, I, and Ned Jolly the summoner.

Wanton. Farewell, farewell then.

(*Exeunt* Wanton *and* Bawd.

Wild. It is a delicate wench.

Careless. ('*They whisper this.*') She has excellent flesh and a fine face. By this light, we must depose the Captain from his reign here.

Wild. I like her shrewdly. I hate a wench that is all whore and no company; this is a comedy all day and a fair at night.

Careless. I hope to exalt the Parson's horn here.

Captain. And what think you? Is it not a sweet sin, this lying with another man's wife?

'[*Enter*] Wanton *above*.'

Wanton. Is Jolly come?

Captain. No, but he'll be here instantly.

Wild. Is he abed?

Wanton. Yes, yes, and he sleeps as if he had been put to bed by his sexton with *Dust to dust and ashes to ashes*.

Captain. And we'll wake him with that shall be as terrible to him as the latter day.

Wanton. Let him sleep awhile, that he may be fresh; else the jest is spoiled, for it is his sense of his disgrace must work my ends.

Wild. I'll go home then and get supper ready and expect you.

'*Enter* Jolly.'

Captain. Do, our scene is here. Who's there? Jolly?

Jolly. Yes.

Captain. Are you fitted?

Jolly. Yes, I have got the Blackfriar's music. I was fain to stay till the last act and who do you think I saw there?

Wild. I know not.

Jolly. Guess.

Wild. I prithee, I cannot guess.

Jolly. Your aunt and Mistress Pleasant and trusty Secret.

Wild. What man?

Jolly. The lovers only, so close in a box!

Captain. It will be a match and there's an end. Prithee let them go to't; what is't to us? Let's mind our business now and think on them hereafter.

Wanton. A pox upon them for a couple of stalk-hounds. Have they killed at last? Why, this is fools' fortune; it would be long enough ere one that has wit got such a wife.

Captain. No more of this now. Have you borrowed the watchmen's coats?

Jolly. Yes, and bills, beards, and constable's staff and lanthorn; and let me alone to fit him for the summoner. But when this is done I expect my fee—a tithe-night at least.

Wanton, I will lie with thee for thy roguery. What, are you dumb? You will not refuse me, I hope?

Wanton. No, if I thought thou desired'st it, but I hate to have it desired indifferently and but so-so done neither when 'tis done.

Jolly. I hope you will not disgrace my work, will you?

Wanton. Faith, they say thy pleasure lies in thy tongue, and therefore, though I do not give thee leave to lie with me, yet I will give thee as good a thing that will please thee as well.

Jolly. Some roguery I expected.

Wanton. No, faith, I am serious. And because I will please you both, Master Wild shall lie here and you shall have leave to say you do, which will please you as well.

Jolly. Faith, and my part is some pleasure; else *I have loved, enjoyed, and told* is mistook.

Wanton. Ay, but never to love, seldom enjoy, and always tell? Faugh, it stinks, and stains worse than Shoreditch dirt, and women hate and dread men for 't. Why, I that am a whore professed cannot see [youth] digest it, though it be my profit and interest. For to be a private whore in this town starves in the nest like young birds when the old one's killed.

Careless. Excellent girl, 'tis too true! Jolly, your tongue has kept many a woman honest.

Wanton. Faith, 'tis a truth, this I shall say, you may all better your pleasures by, if you will observe it. I dare say the fear of telling keeps more women honest than Bridewell hemp. And were you wise men and true lovers of liberty, now were the time to bring wenching to that perfection no age could ever have hoped. Now you may sow such seed of pleasure you may be prayed for hereafter. Now, in this age of zeal and ignorance, would I have you four, in old clothes and demure looks, present a petition to both houses and say you are men touched in conscience for your share in that wickedness which is known to their worships by the pleasure of adultery, and desire it may be death, and that a law may be passed to that purpose. How the women will pray for you and at their own charges rear statues in memory of their benefactors! The young and kind would then haunt your chambers, pray, and present you, and court the sanguine youth for the sweet sin secured by such a law. None would lose an occasion nor churlishly oppose kind nature nor refuse to listen to her summons when youth and passion calls for those forbidden sweets. When such security as your lives are at stake, who would fear to trust? With this law all oaths and protestations are cancelled; letters and bawds would grow useless too; by instinct the kind will find the kind, and having one nature become one mind. Now we lose an age to observe and know a man's humour ere we dare trust him. But get this law, then 'tis like and enjoy. And whereas now with expense of time and fortune you may glean some one mistress amongst your neighbours' wives, you shall reap women whole armfuls as in the common field. There is one small town, wise only in this law, and I have heard them say that know it well there has been but one execution this hundred years; yet the same party searched seven years and could not find an honest woman in the town.

Careless. An excellent plot, let us about it! Ink and paper, dear Wanton, we will draw the petition presently.

Wanton. Will Master Jolly consent too? You must not then, as soon as a handsome woman is named, smile and stroke your beard, tell him that is next you you have lain with her. Such a lie is as dangerous as a truth, and 'twere but justice to have thee hanged for a sin thou never committed'st, for having defamed so many women.

Jolly. If all those liars were hanged, I believe the scale would weigh down the guilty.

Wanton. One rogue hanged for example would make a thousand kind girls. If it take, it shall be called my law, Wanton's law. Then we may go in petticoats again, for women grew imperious and wore the breeches only to fright the poor cuckolds and make the fools digest their horns. Are you all ready? Shall I open the door?

Captain. Yes.

Wild. I'll expect you at my house.

'*Exit* Wild *one way, and the rest of the company another.*'

Omnes. We'll come, we'll come.

'*They knock within, and the* Parson *discovered in bed and the* Bawd *with him.*'

Captain [*Within*]. So, knock louder.

Parson. Who's there? What would you have?

Captain [*Within*]. Here's his majesty's watch, and Master Constable's worship must come in. We have a warrant from the lords to search for a delinquent.

Parson. You come not here. I'll answer your warrant tomorrow.

Jolly [*Within*]. Break open the door.

Parson. I would you durst.

Bawd. Lord, dear, what shall we do?

Parson. Why, sweet, I'll warrant you. Art thou not my wife, my rib, bone of my bone? I'll suffer anything ere one hair of thee shall be touched.

Bawd. Hark, they break open the door.

Parson. They dare not. Why dost thou tremble so? Alas, sweet innocence, how it shakes.

Captain [*Within*]. Break open the door.

Parson. I'll complain to the bishop of this insolence.

Bawd. They come, they come, lamb.

Parson. No matter, sweet, they dare not touch thee.

'[*Enter* Captain, Jolly *and* Watch.] *He delivers the warrant.*'

What would you have, Master Constable? You are very rude.

Captain. Read our warrant and our business will excuse us. Do you know any such person as you find there?

Parson. Yes, sir, but not by this name. Such a woman is my wife and no Lindabrides. We were married today and I'll justify her my wife the next court day. You have your answer and may be gone.

Jolly. We must take no notice of such excuses now. If she be your wife, make it appear in court and she will be delivered unto you.

Parson. If she be my wife, sir? I have wedded her and bedded her; what other ceremonies would you have?—Be not afraid, sweetheart.

Jolly. Sir, we can do no less than execute our warrant; we are but servants. And, Master Constable, I charge you in the king's name to do your duty. Behold the body of the delinquent.

Parson. Touch her that dares, I'll put my dagger in him. ('*He takes his dagger*') Fear nothing, sweetheart. Master Constable, you'll repent this insolence offered to a man of my coat.   '*Here they strive to take her out.*'

Bawd. Help, my dearest! Will you let me be haled thus?

Parson. Villains, what will you do? Murder! Rape!

Captain. Yes, yes, 'tis likely; I look like a ravisher.

Jolly. Hold him and we'll do well enough with her.

'*As they go to pull her out of bed, they discover the* Bawd. *When they let him go, he turns to her and holds her in his arms.*'

Captain. What have we here, an old woman?

Parson. Let me go, slaves and murderers.

Captain. Let him go.

Jolly. Do any of you know this woman? This is not she we looked for.

Parson. No? Rascal, that mistake shall not excuse you.

Jolly. It is old goodman what-d'ye-call him his wife.

Captain. Hold the candle and let's see her face.

'*When they hold the candle, she lies in his bosom and his arms about her. She must be as nastily dressed as they can dress her. When he sees her, he falls into a maze and shoves her from him.*'

Jolly. What have we here? Adultery? Take them both. Here will be new matter.

Parson. Master Constable, a little argument will persuade you to believe I am grossly abused. Sure, this does not look like a piece that a man would sin to enjoy. Let that then move your pity and care of my reputation. Consider my calling and do not bring me to a public shame for what you're sure I am not guilty of but by plot of some villains.

Bawd. Dear, will you disclaim me now?

Parson. Oh, impudence!

Jolly. Master Constable, do your duty. Take them both away, as you will answer it.

Captain. Give him his cassock to cover him.

'*They put on his cassock and her coat and lead them away.*'

Parson. Why, gentlemen, whither will you carry me?

Captain. To the next justice; I think it is Master Wild.

He is newly come from travel. It will be a good way, neighbours, to express our respects to him.

Parson. No, faith, gentlemen, e'en go the next way to Tyburn and dispatch the business without ceremony, for ye'll utterly disgrace me. This is that damned Captain. My wife is abroad too; I fear she is of the plot.

Jolly. Come, away with 'em.

Bawd. Whither will they lead us, dear?

Parson. Oh, oh, impudence! Gentlemen, do not lead us together, I beseech you.

Captain. Come, come, lead them together. No ceremonies, your faults are both alike. (*Exeunt omnes.*

SCENE II

'*Enter* Wanton *and* Wild.'

Wanton. You had best brag now and use me like my lady what'st-you-call; but if you do I care not.

Wild. Come, you're a fool; I'll be a faithful friend and make good conditions for thee before thy husband be quit.

Wanton. You must do it now or never.

Wild. Hark, hark, I hear them.

'Wild *sits down with* Wanton *in his lap.*'

'*Enter* Captain, Jolly, Watch, Bawd, *and* Parson.'

What's the news?

Captain. We have brought a couple of delinquents before your worship. They have committed a very foul fault.

Jolly. And we have brought the fault along too, that your worship may see it. You will be the better able to judge of the offenders.

Parson. Ha, what do I see? My wife in Master Justice's lap?

Wanton. What has the poor fellow done?

Captain. Why, madam, he has been taken abed with this woman, another man's wife.

Wanton. In bed with her? And do you raise him to punish him? Master Constable, if you would afflict him, command them to lie together again. Is not the man mad?

Parson. This is fine roguery. I find who rules the roost.

Wild. Well, to the business. You say he was taken in bed with another man's wife.

Captain. Yes, an't like your worship.

Wild. Make his *mittimus* to the hole at Newgate.

Wanton. Sure, I have seen this fellow's face. Friend, have I never seen your face before?

Parson. If I mistake not, I have seen one very like your ladyship's too. She was a Captain's cast whore in the town. I shall have a time to be revenged.

Wild. How now, sirrah! Are you threatening? Away with him!

Captain. I'll fetch a stronger watch, sir, and return presently. [*Exit* Captain.]

Wild. Do, Master Constable, and give the poor woman something and set her free, for I daresay 'twas his wickedness. She looks like one that ne'er thought on such a thing.

Bawd. God bless your worship! I am innocent. He never left making love till I consented.

'*Enter* Captain *in his own shape.*'

Parson. Oh, miserable, miserable!

Captain. How now, what's the news here? My honoured friend, and Master Parson, what makes you here at this time of night? Why, I should have thought this a time to have envied you for your fair bride's embraces. ('*Plays with the cord that binds his arms.*') Do you give these favours? Are these your bride-laces? It's a new way.

Parson. Is it new to you?

Wanton. How now, Captain.

Captain. Wanton, is this your plot to endear your husband to you?

Parson. No, 'tis thy plot, poor beaten Captain; but I shall be revenged.

Captain. Yes, faith, it was my plot, and I glory in 't, to undermine my Macchiavel, which so greedily swallowed that sweet bait that had this hook.

Parson. 'Tis well.

Captain. But my anger ends not here. Remember the base language you gave me—son of a thousand fathers, captain of a tame band and one that got my living by the longstaff speeches? For which, and thy former treacheries, I'll ruin thee, slave. I'll have no more mercy on thee than old women on blind puppies. I'll bring you to your commendations in Latin epistles again, nor leave thee anything to live on, no, not bread, but what thou earn'st by raking gentlewomen's names in anagrams. And Master Justice, if ever you oblige me, stand to me now, that I may procure the whipping of him from the reverend bench.

Parson. I am undone.

Wild. I can do nothing but justice; you must excuse me. I shall only make it appear how fit it is to punish this kind of sin in that coat in time, and to crush such serpents in the shells.

Parson. Mercy, oh mercy!

Wild. Officers, away with him!　　　'*They pull him away.*'

Parson. No mercy?

Wanton. Yes, upon conditions there may be some mercy.
　　　　　　　　　　'*The* Parson *looks very dejected.*'

Wild. And these they are—let the watch stay in the tother room. ('*Exit* Watch.') First, your wife shall have her liberty and you yours as she reports of you; and when you bring her with you, you shall be welcome. Then, you shall not be jealous—that's another point.

Captain. That he shall have a cure for.

Wanton. Yes, yes, I'll apply something to his eyes shall cure him of his doubt.

Wild. Then you shall ask the Captain pardon, and your wife. To him you shall allow half your parsonage to maintain her. The deeds are ready within; if you'll sign them and deliver your wife to our use, she shall discharge you.

Parson. I submit, sir; but I hope your worship will desire no witness to the use of my wife. The summoner and the watch, too, I hope your worship will enjoin them silence.

Wanton. You shall not need to fear; I'll have a care of your credit. Call in the watch. ('*She discovers them.*') Do you know these faces?

Parson. Ha! Abused!

Jolly. Nay, no flinching. If you do, I betake me to Master Summoner again.

Captain. And I become severe Master Constable in a trice.

Parson. No, no, I submit, and I hope we are all friends. I'm sure I have the hardest part, to forgive.

Wanton. And I, before all this company, promise to forget and forgive thee, and am content to take thee again for my dear and mortal husband now you are tame. But you must see you do so no more, and give yourself to be blind when it is not fit for you to see, and practise to be deaf and learn to sleep in time and find business to call you away when gentlemen come that would be private.

Captain. Why so, now things are as they should be, and when you will obey, you shall command; but when you would be imperious, then I betake me to my constable's staff till you subscribe, *Cedunt armis togae.* And if it be false Latin, Parson, you must pardon that too.

Jolly. By this hand, I must have my tithe-night with thee, thou art such a wag. Say when. When wilt thou give me leave, ha?

Wanton. Never.

Jolly. Never?

Wanton. No, never.

Jolly. D'ye hear, I am none of them that work for charity. Either resolve to pay or I kick down all my milk again.

Wanton. What would you have?

Jolly. Give me leave to lie with you.

Wanton. No, indeed.

Jolly. No?

Wanton. No; but rather than quarrel, as I said before, I will give you leave to say you have lain with me.

Wild. I am of opinion she owes you nothing now. So, Mistress Wanton, take your husband, and to remove all doubts this night I'll be at the charge of a wedding supper.

Parson. This is better than Newgate hole yet, Bridewell hemp, brown bread and whipcord.　　　(*Exeunt omnes.*

SCENE III

'*Enter the* Widow *and* Mistress Pleasant, Master Sadd
and Master Constant.'

Widow. By my troth, it was a good play.

Pleasant. And I am glad I am come home, for I am e'en as weary with this walking. For God's sake, whereabouts does the pleasure of walking lie? I swear I have often sought it till I was weary and yet I could ne'er find it.

'*A* Watch *at the* Widow's *door.*'

Sadd. What do these halberds at your door?

Widow. Halberds? Where?

Sadd. There, at your lodging.

Constant. Friend, what would those watchmen have?

Watchman. The house is shut up for the sickness this afternoon.

Pleasant. The sickness?

Watchman. Yes, forsooth, there's a coachman dead, full of the tokens.

Sadd. Where is the officer?

Watchman. He is gone to seek the lady of the house and some other company that dined here yesterday, to bring her in or carry her to the pest-house.

Widow. Ha! What shall we do, niece?

Sadd. If you please to command our lodging—

Pleasant. It will be too much trouble.

Widow. Let's go to Love-all's.

Pleasant. Not I, by my faith; it is scarce for our credits to let her come to us.

Widow. Why? Is she naught?

Constant. Faith, madam, her reputation is not good.

Widow. But what shall we do then?

Constant. Dare you adventure to oblige us?

Widow. Thank you, sir, we'll go to my nephew's at Covent Garden. He may shift among his acquaintance.

Pleasant. It was well thought on; the Piazza is hard by too.

Widow. We'll borrow your coach thither and we'll send it you back again straight.

Constant. We'll wait upon you, madam.

Widow. This accident troubles me. I am heartily sorry for the poor fellow.

Pleasant. I am sorry too, but pray, aunt, let us not forget ourselves in our grief. I am not ambitious of a red cross upon the door.

Constant. Mistress Pleasant is in the right, for if you stay the officers will put you in.

Widow. We shall trouble you, sir, for your coach.

(*Exeunt omnes.*

SCENE IV

'*Enter* Parson, Captain, Wild, Wanton, Careless *and* Jolly.'

Parson. I am reconciled and will no longer be an uncharitable churchman. I think this sack is a cooler.

Captain. What, does it make you to see your error?

Parson. Yes, and consider my man of war; nor will I again dispute his letters of mart nor call them passes for pirates. I am free.

Captain. And welcome. Anything but anger is sufferable, and all is jest when you laugh. And I will hug thee for abusing me with thy eyes in their scabbards, but when you rail with drawn eyes, red and naked, threatening a Levite's second revenge to all that touches your concubine, then I betake me to a dark lanthorn and a constable's staff, and, by help of these fathers whom I cite, I prove my text: women that are kind ought to be free.

Parson. But, Captain, is it not lawful for us shepherds to reclaim them?

Captain. A mere mistake; for sin, like the sea, may be turned out but will ne'er grow less. And though you should drain this Mistress Doll, yet the whore will find a place and perhaps overflow some maid till then honest. And so you prove the author of a new sin and the defiler of a pure temple. Therefore, I say, while you live, let the whore alone till she wears out. Nor is it safe to vamp them, as you shall find—read Ball the first and the second.

Wild. No more discourse, strike up the fiddlers.

'[*Enter* Fiddlers.] *A country dance. When they are merry, singing catches and drinking healths, the* Widow, Mistress Pleasant *and the two lovers knock at the door.*'

Captain. See who's that knocks.

[*Enter* Servant.]

Servant. Sir, 'tis Mistress Pleasant and the two gentlemen that dined there today.

Wild. My aunt and Mistress Pleasant!

Jolly. What a pox makes them abroad at this time of night?

Captain. It may be they have been a-wenching.

Servant. Sir, they were upon alighting out of the coach when I came up.

Wild. Quickly, Mistress Wanton, you and your husband to bed. There's the key. Master Parson, you know the way to the old chamber and to it quickly. All is friends now.

Parson. Sweetheart, we'll steal away.

Wanton. The devil on them, they have spoiled our mirth.
                                        (*Exeunt* Parson *and* Wanton.

Wild. Jack, get you and your company down the back way into the kitchen and stay there till we see what this visit means.   (*Exeunt* Fiddlers.

Captain. Means! What should it mean? It is nothing but the mischievous nature all honest women are endued with and naturally given, to spoil sport. I wonder what fart blew them hither tonight.

Wild. Nay, have a little patience, Captain. You and Master Jolly must sit quietly awhile within till we know the cause.

Captain. It is but deferring our mirth for an hour or so.

Servant. Sir, here's my lady.

Wild. Quickly remove those things there. Captain, step in there.   [*Exeunt* Captain *and* Jolly.]

'*Enter* Widow, Pleasant, Sadd, *and* Constant.'

Widow. Nephew, do you not wonder to see me here at this time of night?

Wild. I know it is not ordinary, therefore I believe 'tis

some design. What is it, Mistress Pleasant? Shall I make one?

Pleasant. As I live, sir, pure necessity; neither mirth nor kindness hath begot this visit.

Careless. What, is your coach broke?

Widow. Faith, nephew, the truth is the sickness is in my house and my coachman died since dinner.

Wild. The sickness?

Pleasant. Ay, as I live. We have been walking since the play, and when we came home we found the watch at the door and the house shut up.

Sadd. And a constable gone in search of all those that dined there today with order to furnish us lodgings in the pest-house.

Widow. Are you not afraid to receive us?

Wild. As I live, the accident troubles me, and I am sorry such a misfortune should beget me this favour, and I could wish myself free from the honour if the cause were removed too.

Pleasant. As I live, Master Wild, I must have been forced to have lain with my servant tonight if you had not received me.

Wild. If I thought so, I would carry you out in my arms, I am so much Master Constant's friend.

Pleasant. But are you more his friend than mine, Master Wild?

Wild. No, but I presume by this he has gained so much interest as he would not be very displeasing to you.

Constant. Oh, your humble servant, sir.

Pleasant. If I had had a mind to that lodging, I had ne'er come hither; for when I have a mind to it, I'll marry without dispute, for I fear nobody so much as a husband; and when I can conquer that doubt, I'll marry at a minute's warning.

Widow. No dispute now. Can you furnish us with a couple of beds?

Wild. Yes, yes.

Widow. And have you e'er a woman in the house?

Wild. My sister's maid is here.

Careless. Madam, if you resolve to do us this honour, you shall find clean linen and your beds quickly ready.

Widow. But where will my nephew and you, sir, lie tonight?

Careless. Oh, madam, we have acquaintance enough in the town.

Widow. Well, sir, we'll accept this courtesy; and when you come into Suffolk, you shall command my house.

Wild. Prithee, call Bess and bid her bring sheets to make the bed. I'll go and fetch in a pallet—'tis as good a bed as the other—and if you will stay the removing, we'll set up a bedstead.

Pleasant. No, a pallet, pray. But what shall we do for night-clothes, aunt?

Wild. Why, what are those you bought my sister?

Widow. Is not that linen gone yet?

Careless. No, faith, madam, his man forgot it till the carriers were gone last week.

Wild. Will that serve?

Pleasant. Yes, yes, pray do us the favour to let us have it; 'tis but washing of it again.

Wild. Nay, if it will serve, discourse no more. I'll fetch the bundle, and prithee fetch the combs and looking-glasses I bought the other day. For other necessaries that want a name the wench shall furnish you with.

Widow. Nay, but where is she, nephew?

Wild. I'll call her if she be not gone to bed. It is an ignorant young thing—I am to send her to my sister's in the country—I have had such ado to put her in the fashion.

Pleasant. What country is she? Prithee, Master Wild, let's see her.

Wild. I'll call her down.   (*Exit* Wild.

Sadd. Madam, now we see you're safe, we'll kiss your hands and wait upon you tomorrow.

Widow. It must be early then, sir, for I shall borrow my nephew's coach and be gone betimes into the country to take a little fresh air and prevent the search.

Constant. Pray, madam, be pleased to command ours.

Widow. No, sir, I humbly thank you; my nephew's will hold our company.

Constant. Your humble servant, Mistress Pleasant.

Sadd. Your servant, madam.

Pleasant. Good night, Master Constant.

Widow. Sir, you'll excuse us, we have nobody here to light you down.

Careless. Madam, I am here your servant as much as those that wear your livery, and this house holds no other. We can be civil, madam, as well as extravagant.

Widow. Your humble servant, Master Careless.

Careless. Gentlemen, if you'll wait on my lady to her chamber, then I'll wait upon you down.

Sadd. You oblige us, sir.   (*Exeunt omnes.*

SCENE V

'*Enter* Wild, Captain, Wanton, Parson, *and* Jolly.'

Captain. The plague?

Wild. The plague, as I live, and all my relation is truth, every syllable. But, Mistress Wanton, now must you play your masterpiece. Be sure to blush and appear but simple enough and all is well. Thou wilt pass for as arrant a chambermaid as any is in the parish.

Parson. Hum, new plots?

Captain. Let me put on a petticoat and a muffler and I'll so chambermaid it and be so diligent with the clean smock and the chamber-pot. Now would I give all the shoes in my shop to lie with 'em both.

Wanton. Let me alone to fit them; I can make a scurvy curtsy naturally. Remember, I am an Essex woman if they ask.

Wild. Come, come quickly, take those sweetmeats, bring the great cake and knife and napkins, for they have not supped; and, Captain, make some lemonade and send it by the boy to my chamber. And do you hear, Jolly, you must stay till we come, for we must lie with you tonight.

Jolly. We'll stay, but make haste then.

Captain. And bring our cloaks and swords out with you.

Wild. I will, I will; but be quiet all.

Parson. Master Wild, I hope there is no plot in this.

Captain. There's no jealousy, Master Parson; 'tis all serious, upon my life. Come away with us. (*Exeunt omnes.*

SCENE VI

'The tiring-room, curtains drawn, and they discourse. His chamber; two beds, two tables, looking-glasses, night-clothes, waistcoats, sweet-bags, sweetmeats and wine. Wanton dressed like a chambermaid. All above if the scene can be so ordered. Enter Widow and Mistress Pleasant, Wild and Careless. The Widow and Mistress Pleasant salute Wanton.'

Wild. Faith, aunt, 'tis the first time I have had the honour to see you in my house, and as a stranger I must salute you.

Widow. As I live, nephew, I'm ashamed to put you to this trouble.

Wild. It is an obligation. Mistress Pleasant, I know you have not supped; I pray you, be pleased to taste these sweetmeats—they are of Sall's doing. But I understand not sweetmeats; the wine I'll answer for. And in a word you are welcome. You are Patrona and we your slaves.

Careless. Good rest and a pleasing dream your humble servant wishes you.

Widow. Good night, nephew. Goodnight, Master Careless.

Pleasant. Good night, Master Careless. Your humble servant, Master Wild.   (*Exeunt* Wild *and* Careless.

Widow. Why, ay, here are men have some wit. By this good night, had we lain at my servant's we should have found the laced cap and slippers that have been entailed upon the family these five descents advanced upon the cupboard's head instead of plate.

> *'They sit down to undress them.'*

Pleasant. They are a couple of the readiest youths too. How they run and do all things with a thought! I love him for sending his sister a pretty wench.

Widow. Pray, let's go to bed; I am weary.

Pleasant. You will not go to bed with all those windows open? Sweetheart, prithee shut them and bring me hither— dost understand me? As I live, 'tis a great while since I went to the play.

Widow. It has been one of the longest days; a year of them would be an age.

Pleasant. Oh, do you grow weary? You'll break your covenant ere the year go out.

Widow. Prithee shut the windows and come pin up my hair.   *'The curtains are closed.'*

SCENE VII

'Enter Wild, Jolly, Careless, Captain *and* Parson, *and*
   Fiddlers, *and one with a torch, with their cloaks and
   their swords, putting them on. Enter* Wild's *man.'*

Wild. See you wait diligently and let them want nothing they call for. Come, shall we go? 'Tis very late.

                       [Exit Wild's *man.]*

Captain. But how does Wanton carry it?

Wild. They saluted her, and Mistress Pleasant swore you might see the country simplicity in her face.

Parson. A pox upon her, crafty gypsy.

Captain. Why, art not thou glad to see she can be honest when she will?

Parson. I'll show you all a trick for her within these few days, or I'll miss my aim.

Jolly. Come, let's go.   *'They all offer to go.'*

Captain. I have a mind to stay till Wanton comes.

Wild. Stay a little then, for 'twill not be long ere they be abed.

Captain. I hear Wanton's voice.

           'Enter Wanton.'

Wild. Are they abed?

Wanton. Yes, and have so admired you and Master Careless and abused the lovers. Well, gentlemen, you are the wits of the time. But if I might counsel, well, they might lie alone this night but it should go hard if I lay not with one of them within a month.

Careless. Were they so taken with their lodging?

Wanton. All that can be said they said: you are the friendliest men, the readiest men, the handsom'st men that had wit, and could tell when to be civil and when to be wild;

and Mistress What's-her-name, the younger, asked why Master Wild did not go a-wooing to some rich heir. Upon her conscience, she said, you would speed.

Careless. Well, well, there's a time for all things. Come, let's go.

Wild. Take a light. Goodnight, Wanton.

'*They offer to depart.*'

Captain. D'ye hear, d'ye hear, let me speak with you.

Wild. What's the business? '*They all come back again.*'

Captain. I cannot get hence this night but your good angels hang at my heels, and if I can prevail, you shall stay.

Wild. What to do?

Captain. What to do? Why, I'll be hanged if all this company do not guess.

Jolly. Prithee, what should we stay for?

Captain. For the widow and her niece. Are they worth the watching for a night?

Wild. Yes, certainly.

Captain. Then take my counsel and let me give it out you're married. You have new clothes come home this morning, and there's that you spoke of I'll fetch from the tailor's, and here's a parson shall rather give them his living than stay for a licence. The fiddlers too are ready to salute 'em.

Careless. But if they refuse?

Jolly. Which, upon my conscience, they will.

Captain. As you hope, else you are laughed at for missing the widow. Ned, follow my counsel: appear at her chamber window in thy shirt and salute all that passes by. Let me alone to give it out and invite company and provide dinner. Then, when the business is known and I have presented all your friends at court with ribands, she must consent or her honour is lost, if you have but the grace to swear it and keep your own counsel.

Careless. By this hand, he has reason. And I'll undertake the widow.

Wild. It will incense them and precipitate the business which is in a fair way now; and if they have wit they must hate us for such a treachery.

Captain. If they have wit they will love you. Beside, if it come to that, we two will swear we saw you married and the Parson shall be sworn he did it. Priest, will you not swear?

Parson. Yes, anything. What is't, Captain?

Wild. If this jest could do 't—yet 'tis base to gain a wife so poorly. She came hither too for sanctuary. It would be an uncivil and an unhospitable thing and look as if I had not merit enough to get a wife without stealing her from herself. Then, 'tis in mine own house.

Captain. The better! Nay, now I think on't, why came she hither? How do you know the plague is there? All was well at dinner. I'll be hanged if it be not a plot. The lovers too, whom you abused at dinner, are joined with them. A trick, a mere trick of wit to abuse us! And tomorrow, when the birds are flown, they'll laugh at you and say, 'Two country ladies put themselves naked into the hands of three travelled city wits and they durst not lay hold on them.'

Careless. A pox upon these niceties!

Wanton. If they have not some design upon you, hang me. Why did they talk so freely before me else?

Careless. Let's but try. We are not now to begin to make the world talk, nor is it a new thing to them to hear we are mad fellows.

Captain. If you get them, are they worth having?

Wild. Having? Yes.

Captain. If you miss them, the jest is good. Prithee, Ned, let me prevail. 'Tis but a mad trick.

Wild. If we would, how shall we get into the chamber?

Wanton. Let me alone for that. I'll put on my country simplicity and carry in a chamber-pot; then, under pretence of bolting the back door I'll open it. And yet I grudge them the sport so honestly, for you wenchers make the best husbands: after you are once married, one never sees you.

Captain. I warrant thee, wench.

Wanton. No, faith, I have observed it: they are still the dotingest husbands, and then retreat and become justices of the peace, and none so violent upon the bench as they against us poor sinners. Yet I'll do it; for upon my conscience, the young gentlewoman will fall upon her back and thank me.   (*Exit* Wanton.

Captain. Away! Go then, and leave your fooling, and in the morning, Ned, get in and plead naked with your hands in the bed.

Parson. And if they cry, put your lips in their mouths and stop them.

Captain. Why, look you, you have the authority of the church too.

Wild. Well, I am now resolved. Go you about your part and make the report strong.

Careless. And, d'ye hear, be sure you set the cook at work, that if we miss we may have a good dinner and good wine to drink down our grief.

Captain. Miss? I warrant thee, thrive.   (*Exit* Captain.

Careless. Nay, if I knock not down the Widow, geld me and come out tomorrow complete uncle and salute the company with, 'You are welcome, gentlemen,' and, 'Good morrow, nephew Ned.'

Wild. Uncle Tom, good morrow, uncle Tom.

'*Enter* Wanton.'

Wanton. All's done. The door is open and they're as still as children's thoughts. 'Tis time you made you ready, which is to put off your breeches, for 'tis almost day. And take my counsel, be sure to offer force enough, the less reason will serve: especially you, Master Wild, do not put a maid to the pain of saying ay.

Wild. I warrant thee, wench; let me alone.

Careless. We'll in and undress us and come again, for we must go in at the back door.

Wild. I'll meet you. Is the Captain gone?

(*Exeunt* Wild *and* Careless.

Wanton. Yes, yes, he's gone.

Jolly. Come, Master Parson, let us see the cook in readiness. Where are the fiddlers? What will become of our plot for the coachman? Master Sadd and his friend will stink of their jest if this thrive.

Parson. They have slept all night on purpose to play all day.

Jolly. When the ribands and points come from the Exchange, pray see the fiddlers have some. The rogues will play so out of tune all day else, they will spoil the dancing if the plot do take.

'*Enter* Wild *and* Careless, *in their shirts, with drawers under, night-gowns on, and in slippers.*'

Wanton. Let's see them in the chamber first, and then I shall go with some heart about the business. So, so, creep close and quietly. You know the way. The widow lies in the high bed and the pallet is next the door.

Wild. Must we creep?

Wanton. Yes, yes, down upon your knees always till you get a woman, and then stand up for the cause. Stay, let me shake my smock over you for luck sake.

'*They kneel at the door to go in. She shakes her coats over them.* [*Exeunt* Wild *and* Careless.]'

Jolly. Why, so I warrant you thrive.

Parson. A pox take you, I'll pare your nails when I get you from this place once.

Wanton. Sweetheart, sweetheart, off with your shoe.

Parson. Ay, with all my heart. There's an old shoe after you. Would I gave all in my shop the rest were furnished with wives too.

Jolly. Parson, the sun is rising; go send in the fiddlers and set the cook on work. Let him chop soundly.

Parson. I have a tithe pig at home; I'll e'en sacrifice it to the wedding.   (*Exit* Parson.

Wanton. They will find them in good posture; they may take privy marks if they please, for they said it was so hot they could endure no clothes, and my simplicity was so diligent to lay them naked and with such twists and turns fastened them to the feet I'll answer for 't they find not the way into them in an hour.

'*Enter a* Servant *and* Parson.'

Jolly. Why then, they may pull up their smocks and hide their faces.

Servant. Master Jolly, there was one without would speak with you.

Jolly. Who was it?

Servant. It is the lady that talks so well.

Jolly. They say indeed she has an excellent tongue; I would she had changed it for a face. 'Tis she that has been handsome.

Parson. Who? Not the poetess we met at Master Sadd's?

Jolly. Yes, the same.

Parson. Sure, she's mad.

Jolly. Prithee tell her I am gone to bed.

Servant. I have done as well, sir: I told her Mistress Wanton was here, at which, discreetly, being touched with the guilt of her face, she threw out a curse or two and retreated.

Wanton. Who is this you speak of? I will know who 'tis.

Parson. Why, 'tis she that married the Genoa merchant. They cozened one another.

Wanton. Who? Peg Driver, bugle-eyes?

Jolly. The same, the same.

Wanton. Why, she is ugly now?

Parson. Yes, but I have known her, by this hand, as fine a wench as ever sinned in town or suburbs. When I knew her first, she was the original of all the wainscot chambermaids with brooms and barefoot madams you see sold at Temple Bar and the Exchange.

Wanton. Ah, thou'rt a devil! How couldst thou find in thy heart to abuse her so? Thou lov'st antiquities too; the very memory that she had been handsome should have pleaded something.

Jolly. Was handsome signifies nothing to me.

Wanton. But she's a wit, and a wench of an excellent discourse.

Parson. And as good company as any 's i' th' town.

Jolly. Company? For whom? Leather-ears, his majesty of Newgate watch? There her story will do well while they louse themselves.

Parson. Well, you are curious now, but the time was when you have skipped for a kiss.

Jolly. Prithee, Parson, no more of wit and was handsome, but let us keep to this text ('*He kisses* Wanton'), and with joy think upon thy little Wanton here, that's kind, soft, sweet, and sound. These are epithets for a mistress, nor is there any elegancy in a woman like it. Give me such a naked scene to study night and day; I care not for her tongue so her face be good. A whore dressed in verse and set speeches tempts me no more to that sweet sin than the statute of whipping can keep me from it. This thing we talked on, which retains nothing but the name of what she was, is not only poetical in her discourse, but her tears and her love, her health, nay, her pleasure, were all fictions and had scarce any live flesh about her till I administered.

Parson. Indeed, 'tis time she sat out and gave others leave to play, for a reverend whore is an unseemly sight. Besides, it makes the sin malicious which is but venial else.

Wanton. Sure, he'll make a case of conscience on't. You should do well, sweetheart, to recommend her case to your brethren that attend the committee of affection, that they may order her to be sound and young again for the good of the commonwealth.   [*Exeunt omnes.*]

ACT V · SCENE I

'*Enter* Fiddlers, Jolly, *and* Wanton.'

Jolly. Oh, are you ready, are you ready?

Fiddlers. Yes, an't like your worship.

Jolly. And did you bid the cook chop lustily and make a noise?

Fiddlers. Yes, sir, he's at it.

Wanton. I hear the Captain.

'*Enter* Captain.'

Jolly. Have you brought clothes and ribands?

Captain. Yes, yes, all is ready. Did you hear them squeak yet?

Wanton. No, by this light. I think 'tis an appointment and we have been all abused.

Captain. Give the fiddlers their ribands and carry the rest in. Mistress Wanton, you must play my lady's woman today and mince it to all that come, and hold up your head

S

finely when they kiss you, and take heed of swearing when you are angry, and pledging whole cups when they drink to you.

Wanton. I'll warrant you for my part.

Captain. Go get you in then and let your husband dip the rosemary.

Jolly. Is all ready?

Captain. All, all. Some of the company are below already. I have so blown it about. One porter is gone to the Exchange to invite Master Wild's merchant to his wedding, and by the way to bid two or three fruiterers to send in fruit for such a wedding; another in my lady's name to Sall's, for sweetmeats. I swore at Bradborn in his shop myself that I wondered he would disappoint Master Wild for his points, and having so long warning. He protested 'twas not his fault but they were ready and he would send John with them presently. One of the watermen is gone to the melon garden, the other to Cook's at the Bear for some bottles of his best wine, and thence to Gracious Street to the poulterers, and all with directions to send in provisions for Master Wild's wedding. And who should I meet at door but Apricock Tom and Mary, waiting to speak with her young master. They came to beg that they might serve the feast. I promised them they should if they would cry it up and down the town, to bring company, for Master Wild was resolved to keep open house.

Jolly. Why then, here will be witnesses enough.

Captain. But who should I meet at the corner of the Piazza but Joseph Taylor? He tells me there's a new play at the Friars today and I have bespoke a box for Master Wild and his bride.

Jolly. And did not he wonder to hear he was married?

Captain. Yes, but I told him 'twas a match his aunt made for him when he was abroad.

Jolly. And I have spread it sufficiently at court by sending to borrow plate for such a wedding.

'*Enter a* Servant.'

Servant. There's half a dozen coachfuls of company lighted. They call for the bride-laces and points.

Captain. Let the fiddlers play then, and bid God give them joy, by the name of my Lady Careless and Mistress Wild.

Fiddlers. Where shall we play, sir?

Jolly. Come with us, we'll show you the window.

[*Exeunt omnes.*]

SCENE II

'*The* Fiddlers *play in the tiring room, and the stage curtains are drawn and discover a chamber, as it was, with two beds and the ladies asleep in them,* Master Wild *being at* Mistress Pleasant's *bedside and* Master Careless *at the* Widow's. *The music awakes the* Widow.'

Widow. Niece, niece, niece Pleasant!

'*She opens the curtain and calls her; she is under a canopy.*'

Pleasant. Ha! I hear you, I hear you. What would you have?

Widow. Do you not hear the fiddlers?

Pleasant. Yes, yes, but you have waked me from the finest dream.

Widow. A dream? What was 't? Some knavery.

Pleasant. Why, I know not, but 'twas merry, e'en as pleasing as some sins. Well, I'll lie no more in a man's bed for fear I lose more than I get.

Widow. Hark, that's a new tune.

Pleasant. Yes, and they play it well. This is your jaunty nephew. I would he had less of the father in him; I'd venture to dream out my dream with him. In my conscience he's worth a dozen of my dull servant, that's such a troublesome visitant, without any kind of conveniency.

Widow. Ay, ay, so are all of that kind. Give me your subject lover; those you call servants are but troubles, I confess.

Pleasant. What is the difference, pray, betwixt a subject and a servant lover?

Widow. Why, one I have absolute power over, the other's

at large. Your servant lovers are those take mistresses upon trial, scarce give them a quarter's warning before they are gone.

Pleasant. Why, what do your subject lovers do? I am so sleepy.

Widow. Do? All things for nothing. Then they are the diligent'st and the humblest things a woman can employ. Nay, I ha' seen of them tame and run loose about a house. I had one once, by this light. He would fetch and carry, go back, seek out—he would do anything. I think some falconer bred him.

Pleasant. By my troth I am of your mind.

Widow. He would come over for all my friends, but it was the dogged'st thing to my enemies: he would sit upon his tail and frown like John-a-Napes when the Pope is named. He heard me once praise my little spaniel bitch Smut for waiting, and hang me if I stirred for seven years after but I found him lying at my door.

Pleasant. And what became of him?

Widow. Faith, when I married he forsook me. I was advised since that if I would ha' spit in 's mouth sometimes he would have stayed.

Pleasant. That was cheap, but 'tis no certain way, for 'tis a general opinion that marriage is one of the certain'st cures for love that one can apply to a man that is sick of the sighings. Yet if you were to live about this town still, such a fool would do you a world of service. I'm sure Secret will miss him—and [he] would always take such a care of her; h'as saved her a hundred walks for hoods and masks.

Widow. Yes, and I was certain of the earliest fruits and flowers that the spring afforded.

Pleasant. By my troth 'twas foolishly done to part with him. A few crumbs of your affection would have satisfied him, poor thing.

Widow. Thou art in the right. In this town there's no living without 'em. They do more service in a house for nothing than a pair of those what-d'ye-call-'ems, those he-waiting-women, beasts, that custom impose[s] upon ladies.

Pleasant. Is there none of them to be had now, think you? I'd fain get a tame one to carry down into the country.

Widow. Faith, I know but one breed of them about the town that's right and that's at the court. The lady that has them brings 'em all up by hand. She breeds some of them from very puppies. There's another wit too in the town that has of them, but hers will not do so many tricks. Good, sullen, diligent waiters those are which she breeds, but not half so serviceable.

Pleasant. How does she do't? Is there not a trick in't?

Widow. Only patience; but she has a heavy hand, they say, at first, and many of them miscarry. She governs them with signs and by the eye, as Banks breeds his horse. There are some too that arrive at writing, and those are the right breed, for they commonly betake themselves to poetry; and if you could light on one of them, 'twere worth your money, for 'tis but using of him ill and praising his verses sometimes and you are sure of him for ever.

Pleasant. But do they never grow surly, aunt?

Widow. Not if you keep them from raw flesh, for they are a kind of lion lovers, and if they once taste the sweet of it they'll turn to their kind.

Pleasant. Lord, aunt, there will be no going without one this summer into the country. Pray let's enquire for one, either a he-one to entertain us or a she-one to tell us the story of her love. 'Tis excellent to bed-ward, and makes one as drowsy as prayers.

Widow. Faith, niece, this parliament has so destroyed 'em, and the Platonic humour, that 'tis uncertain whether we shall get one or no. Your leading members in the lower house have so cowed the ladies that they have no leisure to breed any of late. Their whole endeavours are spent now in feasting and winning close committee men, a rugged kind of sullen fellows, with implacable stomachs and hard hearts, that make the gay things court and observe them as much as the foolish lovers use to do. Yet I think I know one she-lover, but she is smitten in years o' th' wrong side of forty. I am certain she is poor too, and in this lean age for courtiers she perhaps would be glad to run this summer in our park.

Pleasant. Dear aunt, let us have her. Has she been famous? Has she good tales, think you, of knights, such as have been false or true to love, no matter which?

Widow. She cannot want cause to curse the sex: handsome, witty, well-born and poor in court cannot want the experience how false young men can be. Her beauty has had the highest fame, and those eyes that weep now unpitied have had their envy and a dazzling power.

Pleasant. And that tongue, I warrant you, which now grows hoarse with flattering the great law-breakers, once gave law to princes. Was it not so, aunt? Lord, shall I die without begetting one story?

Widow. Penthesilea nor all the cloven knights the poets treat of, yclad in mightiest petticoats, did her excel for gallant deeds; and, with her honour, still preserved her freedom. My brother loved her, and I have heard him swear Minerva might have owned her language; an eye like Pallas, Juno's wrists, a Venus for shape, and a mind chaste as Diana but not so rough; never uncivilly cruel nor faulty kind to any; no vanity, that sees more than lovers pay, nor blind to a gallant passion. Her maxim was, he that could love and tell her so handsomely was better company, but not a better lover, than a silent man. Thus, all passions found her civility, and she a value from all her lovers. But alas, niece, this *was* (which is a sad word), *was* handsome, and *was* beloved, are abhorred sounds in women's ears.

'*The* Fiddlers *play again.*'

Pleasant. Hark, the fiddlers are merry still. Will not Secret have the wit to find us this morning, think you?

Fiddlers [*Within*]. God give you joy, Master Careless! God give your ladyship joy, my lady Wild!

Widow. What did the fellow say? God give me joy?

Pleasant. As I live, I think so.

Fiddlers [*Within*]. God give you joy, Mistress Pleasant Wild.

Widow. This is my nephew; I smell him in this knavery.

Pleasant. Why did they give me joy by the name of Mistress Wild? I shall pay dear for a night's lodging if that be so, especially lying alone. By this light, there is some knavery afoot.

'*All the company confused without and bid God give them joy.*'

Jolly [*Within*]. Rise, rise, for shame, the year's afore you.

Captain [*Within*]. Why, Ned Wild, why, Tom, will you not rise and let's in? What, is it not enough to steal your wedding overnight but lock yourselves up in the morning too? All your friends stay for points here and kisses from the brides.

Wild. A little patience! You'll give us leave to dress us?
'*The women squeak when they speak.*'

Careless. Why, what's a-clock, Captain?

Captain [*Within*]. It's late.

Careless. Faith, so it was before we slept.

Widow. Why, nephew, what means this rudeness? As I live, I'll fall out with you. This is no jest.

Wild. No, as I live, aunt, we are in earnest. But my part lies here, and there's a gentleman will do his best to satisfy you. ('*They catch the women in their arms.*') And, sweet Mistress Pleasant, I know you have so much wit as to perceive the business cannot be remedied by denials. Here we are, as you see, naked, and thus have saluted hundreds at the window that passed by and gave us joy this morning.

Pleasant. Joy? Of what? What do you mean?
'*Careless kisses the* Widow.'

Careless. Madam, this is visible; and you may coy it and refuse to call me husband, but I am resolved to call you wife, and such proofs I'll bring as shall not be denied.

Widow. Promise yourself that; see whether your fine wits can make it good. You will not be uncivil?

Careless. Not a hair but what you give, and that was in the contract before we undertook it, for any man may force a woman's body, but we have laid we will force your mind.

Wild. But that needs not, for we know by your discourse last night and this morning we are men you have no aversion to. And, I believe, if we had taken time and wooed hard, this would have come a course; but we had rather win you by wit, because you defied us.

Widow. 'Tis very well, if it succeed.

Careless. And, for my part, but for the jest of winning you, and this way, not ten jointures should have made me marry!

Widow. This is a new way of wooing.

Careless. 'Tis so, madam; but we have not laid our plot

so weakly (though it were sudden) to leave it in any body's power but our own to hinder it.

Pleasant. Do you think so?

Wild. We are secure enough if we can be true to ourselves.

Careless. Yet we submit in the midst of our strength and beg you will not wilfully spoil a good jest by refusing us. By this hand, we are both sound and we'll be strangely honest and never in ill humours, but live as merry as the maids and divide the year between the town and the country. What say you—is 't a match? Your bed is big enough for two, and my meat will not cost you much. I'll promise nothing but one heart, one purse betwixt us, and a whole dozen of boys. Is 't a bargain?

Widow. Not if I can hinder it, as I live.

Wild. Faith, Mistress Pleasant, he hath spoken nothing but reason, and I'll do my best to make it good. Come, faith, teach my aunt what to do and let me strike the bargain upon your lips.

Pleasant. No, sir, not to be half a queen. If we should yield now, your wit would domineer for ever, and still in all disputes (though never so much reason on our side) this shall be urged as an argument of your master-wit to confute us. I am of your aunt's mind, sir, and if I can hinder it, it shall be no match.

Wild. Why then, know it is not in your powers to prevent it.

Widow. Why, we are not married yet.

Careless. No, 'tis true.

Widow. By this good light then, I'll be dumb for ever hereafter lest I light upon the words of marriage by chance.

Pleasant. 'Tis hard when our own acts cannot be in our own power, gentlemen.

Wild. The plot is only known to four, the minister and two that stood for fathers, and a simple country maid that waited upon you last night, which plays your chambermaid's part.

Pleasant. And what will all these do?

Wild. Why, the two friends will swear they gave you, the Parson will swear he married you, and the wench will swear she put us to bed.

Widow. Have you men to swear we are married?

Pleasant. And a parson to swear he did it?

Both. Yes.

Widow. And a wench that will swear she put us to bed?

Both. Yes, by this good light, and witness of reputation.

Pleasant. Dare they or you look us in the face and swear this?

Careless. Yes, faith, and all but those four know no other but really it is so; and you may deny it, but I'll make Master Constable put you to bed with this proof at night.

Widow. Pray let's see these witnesses.

Wild. Call in the four only.   (*Exit* Careless.

Pleasant. Well, this shall be a warning to me. I say nothing, but if ever I lie from home again—

Wild. I'll lie with you.

Pleasant. 'Tis well, I dare say we are the first women (if this take) that ever were stolen against their wills.

Wild. I'll go call the gentlemen.   (*Exit* Wild.

Widow. I that have refused a fellow that loved me these seven years, and would have put off his hat and thanked me to come to bed, to be beaten with watchmen's staves into another's! For by this good light, for aught that I perceive, there's no keeping these out at night.

Pleasant. And unless we consent to be their wives today, Master Justice will make us their whores at night. Oh, oh, what would not I give to come off! Not that I mislike them, but I hate they should get us thus.

'*Enter* Wild, Jolly, Captain, Careless ,Parson, Wanton, *with rosemary in their hands and points in their hats.*'

Careless. Follow. Will not you two swear we were married last night?

Jolly, Captain. Yes, by this light will we.

Wild. Will not you swear you married us?

Parson. Yea, verily.

Careless. And come hither, pretty one; will not you swear you left us all abed last night, and pleased?

Wanton. Yes, forsooth, I'll swear anything your worship shall appoint me.

Widow. But, gentlemen, have you no shame, no conscience? Will you swear false for sport?

Jolly. By this light, I'll swear, if it be but to vex you. Remember you refused me.—('*Speaks these words aside.*') That is contrary to covenants, though, with my brace of lovers. What will they do with their coachman's plot? But 'tis no matter, I have my ends; and so they are cozened I care not who does it.

Captain. And, faith, madam, I have sworn many times false to no purpose, and I should take it ill, if it were mine own case, to have a friend refuse me an oath upon such an occasion.

Pleasant. And are you all of one mind?

Parson. Verily we will all swear.

Pleasant. Will you verily? What shall we do, aunt?

'*Pleasant laughs.*'

Widow. Do you laugh? By this light, I am heartily angry.

Pleasant. Why, as I live, let's marry them, aunt, and be revenged.

Widow. Marry? Where's the parson?

Captain. Here, here, Master Parson, come and do your office.

Pleasant. That fellow? No, by my troth, let's be honestly joined for luck's sake; we know not how soon we may part.

Wild. What shall she do for a parson? Captain, you must run and fetch one.

Captain. Yes, yes, but methinks this might serve turn. By this hand, he's a Marshall and a Case, by sire and dam; pray try him. By this light, he comes of the best preaching kind in Essex.

Widow. Not I, as I live; that were a blessing in the devil's name.

Parson. A pox on your wedding! Give me my wife and let me be gone.

Captain. Nay, nay, no choler, Parson; the ladies do not like the colour of your beard.

Parson. No, no, fetch another, and let them escape with that trick; then they'll jeer your beards blue, i'faith.

Careless. By this hand, he's in the right: either this

Parson or take one another's words. To bed now, and marry when we rise.

Pleasant. As I live, you come not here till you are married. I have been nobody's whore yet and I will not begin with my husband.

Wild. Will you kiss upon the bargain and promise before these witnesses not to spoil our jest but rise and go to church?

Pleasant. And what will Master Constant and Master Sadd say?

Captain. Why, I'll run and invite them to the wedding, and you shall see them expire in their own garters.

Jolly. No, no, ne'er fear 't, their jest is only spoiled.

Captain. Their jest? What jest?

Jolly. Faith, now you shall know it, and the whole plot. In the first place, your coachman is well, whose death we by the help of Secret contrived, thinking by that trick to prevent this danger and carry you out of town.

Captain. But had they this plot?

Jolly. Yes, faith, and see how it thrives. They'll fret like carted bawds when they hear this news.

Pleasant. Why, aunt, would you have thought Master Sadd a plotter? Well, 'tis some comfort we have them to laugh at.

Widow. Nay, faith, then, gentlemen, give us leave to rise and I'll take my venture if it be but for a revenge on them.

Careless. Gentlemen, bear witness.

Captain. Come, come away. I'll get the points. I'm glad the coachman's well; the rogue had like to have spoiled our comedy. (*Exeunt omnes.*

SCENE III

'*Enter the* Lady Love-all, Master Sadd, *and* Constant, *undressed and buttoning themselves as they go.*'

Sadd. Married?

Constant. And to them?

Love-all. Ay, married, if you prevent it not. Catched with a trick, an old stale trick! I have seen a ballad on't.

Sadd. We shall go near to prevent 'em. Boy, my sword.

'*Enter* Captain.'

Captain. Whither so fast?

Sadd. You guess.

Captain. If you mean the wedding, you come too late.

Constant. Why, are they married?

Captain. No, but lustily promised.

Sadd. We may come time enough to be revenged though.

Captain. Upon whom? Yourselves, for you are only guilty. Who carried them thither last night? Who laid the plot for the coachman?

Sadd. Why, do they know it?

Love-all. Why, you'll find the poet a rogue—'tis he that has betrayed you, and if you'll take my counsel, be revenged upon him.

Constant. Nay, we were told he did not love us.

Captain. By my life, you wrong him; upon my knowledge the poet meant you should have them.

Sadd. Why, who had the power to hinder then?

Captain. I know not where the fault lies directly. They say the wits of the town would not consent to't. They claim a right in the ladies, as orphan-wits.

Constant. The wits! Hang 'em in their strong lines!

Captain. Why, ay, such a clinch as that has undone you; and upon my knowledge, 'twere enough to hinder your next match.

Sadd. Why, what have they to do with us?

Captain. I know not what you have done to disoblige them, but they crossed it. There was amongst 'em too a pair of she-wits, something stricken in years. They grew in fury at the mention of it and concluded you both with an authority out of a modern author. Besides, 'tis said you run naturally into the sixpenny room and steal sayings and a discourse more than your pennyworth of jests every term. Why, just now, you spit out one jest stolen from a poor play that has but two more in five acts. What conscience is there in 't, knowing how dear we pay poets for our plays?

Constant. 'Twas madam with the ill face, one of those

whom you refused to salute the other day at Chipps' house.
A cheesecake had saved all this.

Love-all. Why do you not make haste about your business
but lose time with this babbler?

Sadd. Madam, will you give us leave to make use of your
coach?

Love-all. You may command it, sir. When you have done,
send him to the Exchange, where I'll dispatch a little business and be with you immediately.

(*Exeunt all but the* Captain.

Captain. So, this fire's kindled; put it out that can. What
would not I give for a peeper's place at the meeting? I'll
make haste, and it shall go hard but I'll bear my part of the
mirth too. (*Exit* Captain.

SCENE IV

'*Enter* Widow, Pleasant, Careless, Wild, Parson, Jolly,
Wanton, *and* Secret. *The* Fiddlers *play as they come in.*'

Parson. Master Jolly, I find I am naturally inclined to
mirth this day, and methinks my corns ache more than my
horns, and to a man that has read Seneca a cuckold ought
to be no grief, especially in this parish, where I see such
droves of St. Luke's clothing. There's little Secret too, th'
allay of waiting-women, makes me hope she may prove
metal of the Parson's standard. Find a way to rid me of
Wanton and I'll put in to be chaplain to this merry family.
If I did not enveigle formal Secret, you should hang me. I
know the trick on't: 'tis but praying to, and preaching of, the
waiting-woman, then carefully seeing her cushion laid,
with her book and leaf turned down, does it, with a few
anagrams, acrostics, and her name in the register of my
bible. These charm the soft-souled sinner. Then sometimes
to read a piece of my sermon and tell her a Saturday where
my text shall be—spells that work more than philtres.

Jolly. If you can be serious we'll think of this at leisure.
See how they eye Wanton!

Careless. What, consulting, Parson? Let us be judges
betwixt you. D'ye hear, Jack, if he offers ready money, I

counsel as a friend, take it; for by this light, if you refuse it
your wife will not. D'ye see those gay petticoats?

Parson. Yes, if you mean my wife's.

Careless. You know they're his, and she only wears 'em
for his pleasure, and 'tis dangerous to have a wife under
another man's petticoats. What if you should find his
breeches upon hers?

Parson. Are not you married too? Take care that yours
does not wear the breeches—another kind of danger, but as
troublesome as that or sore eyes; and if she get but a trick
of taking as readily as she's persuaded to give, you may find
a horn at home. I have seen a cuckold of your complexion;
if he had had as much hoof as horn, you might have hunted
the beast by his slot.

Pleasant. How fine she is, and by this light, a handsome
wench! Master Jolly, I am easier persuaded to be reconciled
to your fault than any man's. I have seen of this kind. Her
eyes have more arguments in 'em than a thousand of those
that seduce the world. Hang me if those quivers be not full
of darts! I could kiss that mouth myself! Is this she my aunt
quarrelled with you for?

Jolly. The same, self-same; and by this hand, I was barbarous to her for your aunt's sake, and had I not 'scaped
that mischief of matrimony, by this light I had never seen
her again. But I was resolved not to quit her till I was sure
of a wife, for fear of what has followed. Had I been such an
ass to have left her upon the airy hopes of a widow's oaths,
what a case had I been in now! You see, your aunt's provided of a man. Bless him, and send him patience! 'Twould
have been fine to have seen me walking and sighing upon
cold hunting, seeking my whore again, or forced to make use
of some common mercenary thing that sells sin and diseases,
crimes, penance and sad repentance all together. Here's consolation and satisfaction in Wanton, though a man lose his
meal with the Widow. And, faith, be free—how do you like
my girl? Rid thee of her! What does she want now, pray,
but a jointure, to satisfy any honest man? Speak your conscience. Ladies, don't you think a little repentance hereafter
will serve for all the small sins that good nature can act with
such a sinner?

Parson. Pray, sir, remember she's my wife and be so civil to us both as to forget these things.

Jolly. For that, Jack, we'll understand hereafter. 'Tis but a trick of youth, man, and her jest [w]ill make us both merry, I warrant thee.

Parson. Pray, sir, no more of your jests nor your Jack. Remember my coat and calling. This familiarity both with my wife and myself is not decent; your clergy with Christian names are scarce held good Christians.

Widow. I wonder at nothing so much as Master Jolly's mirth today. Where lies his part of the jest, cozened or refused by all, not a fish that stays in's net?

Jolly. No? What's this? ('Jolly *hugs* Wanton.') Show me a fairer in all your streams. Nor is this my single joy, who am pleased to find you may be cozened, rejoice to see you may be brought to lie with a man for a jest. Let me alone to fit you with a trick too.

Careless. Faith, it must be some new trick, for thou art so beaten at the old one 'twill neither please thee nor her. Besides, I mean to teach her that myself.

Pleasant. I shall never be perfectly quiet in my mind till I see somebody as angry as myself, yet I have some consolation when I think on the wise plot that killed the coachman. How the plague, red cross and halberd has cut their fingers that designed it! Their anger will be perfect. Secret says they are coming and that the Lady Love-all has given 'em the alarm.

'*Enter* Sadd *and* Constant.'

Wild. And see where the parties come—storms and tempests in their minds, their looks are daggers.

Pleasant. Servant, what, you're melancholy and full of wonder. I see you have met the news.

Sadd. Yes, madam, we have heard a report that will concern both your judgement and your honour.

Pleasant. Alas, sir, we're innocent; 'tis mere predestination.

Constant. All weddings, Master Sadd, you know, go by chance, like hanging.

Pleasant. And I thank my stars I have 'scaped hanging; to ha' been his bride had been both.

Constant. This is not like the promise you made us yesterday.

Widow. Why truly, servant, I scarce know what I do yet. The fright of the plague had so possessed my mind with fear, that I could think and dream of nothing last night but of a tall black man that came and kissed me in my sleep and slapped his whip in mine ears. 'Twas a saucy ghost (not unlike my coachman that's dead), and accused you of having a hand in his murder and vowed to haunt me till I was married. I told my niece the dream.

Pleasant. Nay, the ghost sighed and accused Secret and Master Sadd of making him away. Confess, faith: had you a hand in that bloody jest?

Widow. Fie, servant, could you be so cruel as to join with my woman against me?

Constant. 'Tis well, ladies. [*To* Sadd.] Why a pox do you look at me? This was your subtle plot. A pox on your clerk's wit! You said the jest would beget a comedy when 'twas known, and so I believe 'twill.

Sadd. Madam, I find you have discovered our design, whose chief end was to prevent this mischief, which I doubt not but you'll both live to repent your share of before you have done travelling to the Epsoms, Bourbonnes, and the Spas to cure those travelled diseases these knights-errant have with curiosity sought out for you. 'Tis true they're mischiefs that dwell in pleasant countries, yet those roses have their thorns, and I doubt not but these gentlemen's wit may sting as well as please sometime, and you may find it harder to satisfy their travelled experience than to have suffered our home-bred ignorance.

Careless. Hark, if he be not fallen into a fit of his cousin! These names of places he has stolen out of her receipt book; amongst all whose diseases, find me any so dangerous, troublesome or incurable as a fool—a lean, pale, sighing, coughing fool, that's rich and poor both, being born to an estate without a mind or heart capable to use it, of a nature so miserable he grudges himself meat—nay, they say he eats his meals twice, a fellow whose breath smells of yesterday's dinner and stinks as if he had eat all our suppers over again. I would advise you, Master Sadd, to sleep with your mouth open, to air it, or get the brewer to tun it. Faugh, an empty Justice, that stinks of the lees and casks and belches Littleton and Ployden's cases! Dost thou think any woman that has wit or honour would kiss that bung-hole? By this light, his head and belly look as blue and lank as French rabbits or stale poultry. Alas, sir, my lady would have a husband to rejoice with, no green-tailed lecturer to stand sentry at his bedside while his nasty soul scours through him, sneaking out at the back door. These, sir, are diseases which neither the Spa or Bath can cure. Your garters and willow are a more certain remedy.

Constant. Well, sir, I find our plot's betrayed and we have patience left. 'Tis that damned Captain has informed.

Sadd. Yet 'tis one comfort, madam, that you have missed that man of war, that knight of Finsbury. His dowager, with ale and switches, would ha' bred a ballad.

Pleasant. Faith, sir, you see what a difficulty it is in this age for a woman to live honest though she have a proper man to her husband; therefore it behoves us to consider who we choose.

Jolly. The lady has reason; for being allowed but one, who would choose such weasels as we see daily married, that are all head and tail, crooked, dirty, sold vermin, predestined for cuckolds, painted snails with houses on their backs and horns as big as Dutch cows'? Would any woman marry such? Nay, can any woman be honest that lets such hod-mandods crawl o'er her virgin breast and belly and suffer 'em to leave their slimy paths upon their bodies only for jointures? Out, 'tis mercenary and base! The generous heart has only the laws of nature and kindness in her view, and when she will oblige, friend is all the ties that nature seeks, who can both bear and excuse those kind crimes. And, I believe, one as poor as the despised captain and neglected courtier may make a woman as happy in a friendship as Master Sadd, who has as many faults as we have debts, one whose father had no more credit with nature than ours had with fortune, whose soul wears rags as well as the captain's body.

Sadd. Nay then, I'll laugh, for I perceive you're angrier than we. Alas, h'as lost both ventures, Wanton and the Widow.

Jolly. Both, and neither so unlucky as to be thy wife. Thy face is hanged with blacks already; we may see the bells toll in thy eyes. A bride and a wedding short? A sexton and a winding-sheet! A scrivener to draw up jointures? A parson to make thy will, man! By this light, he's as chapfallen as if he had lain under the table all night.

Careless. Faith, Master Sadd, he's parlously in the right. Ne'er think of marrying in this dull clime; wedlock's a trade you'll ne'er go through with. Wives draw bills upon sight, and 't will not be for your credit to protest 'em. Rather, follow my counsel and marry [à] *la* Venetiano for a night, and away. A pistole jointure does it. Then 'tis but repenting in the morning and leave your woman and the sin both i'th'bed. But if you play the fool like your friends and marry in serious earnest, you may repent it too as they do. But where's the remedy?

Widow. What was 't you said, sir? Do you repent?

Careless. By this hand, Widow, I don't know, but we have pursued a jest a great way. Parson, are you sure we're married?

Parson. Yes, I warrant you for their escaping.

Careless. Their escaping? Fool, thou mistak'st me; there's no fear of that. But I would fain know if there be no way for me to get out of this noose, no hole to hide a man's head in from this wedlock?

Parson. Not any but what I presume she'll show you anon.

Careless. Hum, now do I feel all my fears flowing in upon me. Wanton and Mistress Pleasant both grow dangerously handsome, a thousand graces in each I never observed before. Now, just now, when I must not taste, I begin to long for some of their plums.

Widow. Is this serious, sir?

Careless. Yes, truly, Widow, sadly serious. Is there no way to get three or four mouthfuls of kisses from the Parson's wife?

Widow. This is sad, sir, upon my wedding day, to despise me for such a common thing.

Sadd. As sad as I could wish. This is a jest makes me laugh. Common? No, madam, that's too bitter; she's forest only, where the royal chase is as free as fair.

Wanton. Were not you a widow today?

Sadd. Yes, faith, girl, and as foolish a one as ever coach jumbled out of joint.

Wanton. Stay then till tomorrow and tell me the difference betwixt us.

Sadd. I hope thou'lt prove a she-prophet. Could I live to see thee turn honest wife and she the wanton widow!

Wanton. I cannot but laugh to see how easy it is to lose or win the opinion of the world. A little custom heals all; or else what's the difference betwixt a married widow and one of us? Can any woman be pure or worth the serious sighing of a generous heart that has had above one hand laid upon her? Is there place to write above one lover's name, with honour, in her heart? 'Tis indeed for one a royal palace, but if it admits of more, an hospital, or an inn at best as well as ours, only off from the road and less frequented.

Pleasant. Shrewdly urged.

Wanton. And though the sins of my family threw me into want and made me subject to the treachery of that broken faith to whose perjury I owe all my crimes, yet still I can distinguish betwixt that folly and this honour, which must tell you, 'He or she that would be thought twice so was never once a lover.'

Constant. Parson, thou art fitted: a whore, and apothegms! What sport will she make us under a tree with a salad and sayings in the summer?

Wild. Come, Wanton, no fury; you see my aunt's angry.

Wanton. So am I, sir, and yet can calmly reason this truth: married widows, though chaste to the law and custom, yet their second hymens make that which was but dying in the first husband's bed a stain in the second sheets, where all their kindness and repeated embraces want their value because they're sullied and have lost their lustre.

Sadd. By this light, I'll go to school to Wanton! She has opened my eyes and I begin to believe I have 'scaped miraculously. By this hand, wench, I was within an inch of being married to this danger; for what can we call these second submissions but a tolerated lawful mercenariness, which, though it be a rude and harsh expression, yet your carriage deserves it.

Pleasant. Fie, Master Sadd, pray leave being witty. I fear 'tis a mortal sin to begin in the fifth act of your days, upon an old subject too, abusing of widows, because they despise you.

Widow. Alas, niece, let him alone; he may come in for his share. The Parson, that has so oft received 'em, will not refuse him tithes there, in charity.

Wanton. That, or conveniency, interest, or importunity, may by your example prevail. But 'tis not fair play, madam, to turn your lover to the common, as you call it, now he's rid lean in your service. Take heed, Master Careless, and warning, Master Sadd: you see how fit for the scavenger's team your lady leaves her lovers!

Careless. Such a lecture before I had married would ha' made me have considered of this matter. Dost thou hear, Wanton, let us forgive one another being married, for that folly has made us guilty alike.

Wanton. And I would fain know the difference betwixt ours and a wedding crime, which is worst: to let love, youth, and good humour betray us to a kindness, or to be gravely seduced by some aunt or uncle, without consideration of the disparity of age, birth, or persons, to lie down upon a jointure? Ladies, you may flatter yourselves, but the ingenuous part of the world cannot deny but such minds, had they been born where our faults are not only tolerated but protected, would have listened to the same things; interest counsels thereto.

Careless. Parson, what boot betwixt our wives? Either come to a price or draw off your doxy.

Parson. Propose, propose! Here will be mirth anon.

Sadd. Yes, yes, propose, while I break it to your lady. Madam, you see here's a proper man to be had and money to boot. What, dumb?

Wanton. No, she's only thinking. Faith, madam, try 'em both tonight and choose tomorrow.

Wild. Come, no more of this. Aunt, take my word for your husband, that have had more experience of him than all these: 'tis true he will long for these girls as children do for plums, and when h'as done, make a meal upon cheese. And you must not wonder nor quarrel at what he says in his humour, but judge him by his actions; and when he is in his fit and raves most, put him into your bed and fold him close in your arms, aunt. If he does not rise as kind and as good a husband as he that sings psalms best, hang me. Why, you're a fool, aunt: a widow, and dislike a longing bride-groom! I thought you had known better. Do you love a spurred horse rather than a duker that neighs and scrapes? I would not say this but that I know him. Let him not go out of your sight, for he's now in season, a ripe, mature husband. No delays! If you let him hang longer upon hope, his fruit will fall alone.

Widow. You are merry, sir, but if I had known this humour—

Wild. You'd ha' kissed him first; but being ignorant, let me make you blush. Come, a kiss, and all's friends. How now, sir! Again, again. Aunt, look to yourself!

'*She kisses Careless and he kisses her twice.*'

Careless. Hum, by this light, sweetheart, and I thank thee. Nay, Widow, there's no jesting with these things.

'*Kisses her again.*'

Nay, I am a lion in my love. Aware, puss, if you flatter me, for I shall deceive you.

Parson. Since all are cozened, why should I be troubled at my fortune? Faith, gentlemen, what will you two give me for a wife, betwixt you?

Constant. Faith, they're mischiefs dear bought though a man get 'em for nothing.

Parson. I'm almost of his mind; and if other people find no more pleasure in a married life than I upon my wedding day, I'd pass my time in the Piazza with the mountebank and let him practise upon my teeth, and draw 'em too, ere he persuades the words of matrimony out of my mouth again. Ay, ay, Master Constant, you may laugh—you ha' missed a wife. Would I were in your case; the world should see how cheerfully I should bear such an affliction.

Constant. Jack, I ha' made my peace at home, and by see-ing others shipwrecked will avoid the danger and here resolve never to sigh again for any woman. They're weeds grow in every hedge, and transplanting of 'em thus to our beds gives certain trouble, seldom pleasure, never profit.

'*Enter* Captain.'

Parson. See where the enemy comes! Now if you be wise, arm and unite against him as a common foe. He's come from his old lady, designing a reconciliation. The rogue's provident and would fain have a nest for his age to rest in. Buff and feathers do well in the youth and heat of thirty, but in the winter of old age captain at threescore, lame and lean, may lie with the almanac, out of date.

Captain. The Parson's grown witty and prophesies upon the strength of bride-cake. If I guess aright, thou'lt be hanged, for 'tis a truth, I have been endeavouring to make it appear, her fears were mistaken in me, but I find the witch more implacable than the devil. The waiting-woman is harder to forgive her part than my lady. Faithful will not be reconciled; the merciless bawd is all fire and sword, no quarter. Bless me from an old waiting-woman's wrath! She'll never forgive me the disappointing her of a promise when I was drunk. Her lady and she are coming, but in such a fury I would not have the storm find you in the street. Therefore I counsel you to avoid the boys and take shelter in the next house.

Wild. No, let's home and with all diligence get our dinner to defend us, and let the porter dispute it at the wicket till she signs articles of peace.

Omnes. Agreed.

'Careless *is kind to the* Widow *as he goes out*; Wild *and* Pleasant *go together*, Jolly *and the* Parson's *wife go together*.'

Wild. See how they pair now! 'Tis not threescore year will part 'em now he has tasted a kiss or two.

Jolly. Parson, I'll be your bridegroom.

Parson. 'Tis well, sir; I shall ha' my time too.

Jolly. Ay, by this hand. Nay, we'll share fairly.

Captain. That's but reason, Wanton; and since he grows tame, use him kindly for my sake.

Parson. Can any of you digest sponge and arsenic?

Captain. Arsenic? What's that?

Parson. An Italian salad, which I'll dress for you, by Jove, ere I'll walk in my canonical coat lined with horn. Death, if I suffer this we shall have that damned courtier pluck on his shoes with the Parson's musons. Fine, i' faith! None but the small Levite's brow to plant your shoeing-horn seed in? ('*As he is going off the* Captain *stays him.*') How now?

Captain. Prithee, Jack, stay and say something to the gentlemen by way of epilogue. Thou art a piece of a scurvy poet thyself; prithee oblige the author and give us a line or two in praise of his play.

Parson. I oblige him? Hang him and all his friends and hurt nobody! Yes, I'm likely to speak for him! You see how I ha' been used today betwixt you. I shall find a time to be revenged. Let go my cloak. I have a province within of my own to govern. Let me go.

Captain. Who? Thy wife? Faith, stay and give them an opportunity; thy pain will be the sooner over. You see 'tis a thing resolved betwixt 'em, and now thou'rt satisfied in the matter be wise and silent. Who knows what good she may do thee another time? I dare say if she had as many souls in her as she had men, she'd bring thee a cure of herself.

Parson. Let me go, or I shall be as troublesome as you are injurious, for all your titles, sir.

Captain. Lend me your cloak then to appear more decent; you'd not ha' me present epilogue in buff, whoreson dunce with a red nose?

Parson. Sir, my business is praying, not epilogues.

Captain. With that face? By this light, 'tis a scandal to see it flaming so near the altar. Thou look'st as if thou'dst cry tope in the face of the congregation instead of amen.

Parson. Thou'rt an ass; 'tis proper there: 'tis zeal and fervour in't and burns before the altar like the primitive lamps.

Captain. I cry thee mercy. By this light, he'll make it sacrilege anon to steal his nose; thou'lt entitle the altar to that coal. Was't not kindled *ex voto*? Nay, I will have your cloak.

Parson. Take it; would 'twere Nessus his shirt, for you and your poet's sake.   (*Exit* Parson.

Captain. What, does the rogue wish 'twere made of nettles?

'Captain *puts on his cloak and addresses himself to speak the epilogue and is interrupted by the* Lady Love-all *and* Faithful *her woman, who in haste and full of anger pull him by the cloak.*'

Love-all. By your favour, sir, did you see any company pass this way? '*The music plays.*'

Captain. None but the three brides, and they are gone before you. Hark, the music will guide you.

Love-all. Is it certain, then, they're married?

Captain. Yes, lady; I saw the church's rites performed.

Faithful. Why does your ladyship lose time in talking with this fellow? Don't you know him, madam? 'Tis the rascally Captain, hid in a black coat. I know you, sirrah.

Love-all. She has reason. Now I mark him better. I should know that false face too. See, Faithful, there are those treacherous eyes still.

Captain. Alas, you mistake me, madam, I am Epilogue now; the Captain's within. And as a friend I counsel you not to incense the gentlemen against the poet, for he knows all your story, and if you anger him he'll put it in a play. But if you'll do friendly offices I'll undertake instead of your pearl you lost to help you to the jewel—the Scotch dictionary will tell you the value of it. Let them go alone and fret not at their loss. Stay and take my counsel; it shall be worth three revenges.

Love-all. Well, what is't, sir?

Captain. They say you have a great power over the Parson. If you can prevail with him to express his anger in some satiric comedy (for the knave has wit and they say his genius lies that way), tell him 'tis expected he should be revenged upon the illiterate courtier that made this play. If you can bring this business about, I may find a way as Epilogue to be thankful, though the Captain abused you today. Think on't: Stephen is as handsome when the play is done as Master Wild was in the scene.

Love-all [*Aside*]. There's something of reason in what he says.—But, my friend, how shall one believe you? You that were such a rascal today in buff, is it to be hoped you can be honest only with putting on a black cloak? Well, I'll venture once again, and if I have any power, he shall sting the malicious rascal; and I think he is fit for such a business. I'm sure he has the worst tongue, and a conscience that neither honour nor truth binds; and therefore 'tis to be believed if he will rail in public he may be even with your poet. I will clothe and feed him and his muse these seven years, but I will plague him. Secret tells me 'twas your poet too that pawned me today in the tavern.

Captain. By my faith did he; nay, 'twas he that told me of your friendship with Jolly.

Love-all. I wonder the Parson has been so long silent, a man of his coat and parts to be beaten with a pen by one that speaks sense by rote, like parrots, one that knows not why sense is sense but by the sound, one that can scarce read, nay, not his own hand. Well, remember your promise.

Captain. Leave it to me, he is yours. And if our plot take, you shall all have your shares in the mirth, but not the profit of the play, and the Parson more than his tithe—a second day.

Love-all. We will discourse of this some other time. And pray dispatch what 'tis you have to say to this noble company that I may be gone, for those gentlemen will be in such fury if I stay, and think because we are alone God knows what.

Captain. 'Tis no matter what they think; 'tis not them we are to study now but these guests, to whom pray address yourself civilly and beg that they would please to become fathers and give those brides within. What say you, gentlemen? Will you lend your hands to join them? The match, you see, is made. If you refuse, Stephen misses the wench and then you cannot justly blame the poet. For, you know, they say that alone is enough to spoil the play.

FINIS

PRINTED IN GREAT BRITAIN
AT THE UNIVERSITY PRESS, OXFORD
BY VIVIAN RIDLER
PRINTER TO THE UNIVERSITY